Baked Omelet, page 36

*New England Blueberry Pie,
page 249*

*Chicken and Dumplings,
page 139*

FIX-IT and ENJOY-IT!

POTLUCK HEAVEN

543 *Stove-Top and Oven Dishes*
That Everyone Loves

FIX-IT and ENJOY-IT!®

POTLUCK HEAVEN

543 *Stove-Top and Oven Dishes That Everyone Loves*

By *The New York Times* bestselling author

PHYLLIS PELLMAN GOOD

Good Books®

Intercourse, PA 17534
800/762-7171
www.GoodBooks.com

Acknowledgments

I am immensely grateful to the generous contributors of recipes for this book and to the discerning testers of those recipes. This has been a community effort—and our own version of a potluck!

My sincere thank you, also, to our diligent and imaginative staff who helped in so many ways to bring this book into being—especially Tony, Esther, Margaret, and Cliff.

—PPG

Cover illustration and illustrations throughout the book by Cheryl Benner
Design by Cliff Snyder

FIX-IT AND ENJOY-IT!® POTLUCK HEAVEN
Copyright © 2011 by Good Books, Intercourse, PA 17534

International Standard Book Number: 978-1-56148-732-5 (paperback edition)
International Standard Book Number: 978-1-56148-734-9 (hardcover gift edition)
International Standard Book Number: 978-1-56148-733-2 (comb-bound paperback edition)
Library of Congress Catalog Card Number: 2011032600

The information in this book has been developed with care and accuracy and is presented in good faith. However, no warranty is given nor are results guaranteed. Neither the author nor the publisher has control over the materials or procedures used, and neither has any liability for any loss or damage related to the use of information contained in the book. Should any corrections be needed, they will be posted at www.GoodBooks.com. If a correction is not posted, please contact custserv@GoodBooks.com.

Library of Congress Cataloging-in-Publication Data
Fix-it and enjoy-it! potluck heaven : 543 stove-top and oven dishes that everyone loves / [compiled by] Phyllis Pellman Good.
     p. cm.
  Includes index.
  ISBN 978-1-56148-732-5 (pbk. : alk. paper) -- ISBN 978-1-56148-733-2 (comb-bound : alk. paper) -- ISBN 978-1-56148-734-9 (hardcover : alk. paper) 1. Cooking, American. 2. Cookbooks. I. Good, Phyllis Pellman, 1948- II. Title: Potluck heaven.
  TX715.F574 2011
  641.5973--dc23   2011032600

Table of Contents

Potluck Heaven's Time is Here!

Eating together has been one of the great human pleasures since forever.

Potlucks Make Eating with Friends Possible

But now more than ever, sharing the job of preparing that food is important, maybe even necessary, if eating together is going to happen. Otherwise, we may not sit down to a meal with friends anymore — except in a restaurant.

Mercifully, most of our good friends and family also live over-full lives. They know we aren't lazy, disloyal, inept, or cheap if our invitation to a meal together comes with a food assignment.

Family Reunions and Fellowship Meals

When I was growing up, we took a hot dish and a cold dish to family reunions and church fellowship meals. That's when I learned that Dorothy's deviled eggs were the best and Luetta's rhubarb pie was unmatched.

Neighborhood Picnics

When our kids were growing up, we lived between two great families. Our kids played together, but we grown-ups seldom had more than two-sentence-long conversations. That's when we instituted three backyard picnics a summer.

Phyllis Pellman Good

3

Each time, one of us made a main dish (usually grilled), another provided salad and veggies, and the other brought dessert. We took turns bringing the different foods. Whoever hosted the event took care of dinnerware. Unless we were running short on plates or silver and asked for a little assistance from the others. It was that kind of easy atmosphere.

Which Potluck Today?

When our kids were in college and growing weary of cafeteria food, they devised a scouting system to find out which nearby churches were having fellowship meals on Sunday noon. When the word came back, a raft of students showed up at those places, probably mystifying the congregants with their sudden interest.

Our Book-Reading Group

Our book-reading group gets together to talk about the books we've all agreed to read, but our half-days in each other's company would dim a little if we did away with that meal in the middle.

Here's how it works. We take turns hosting, which involves making a simple main dish—ahead of time, of course, since we all want to be part of the book discussion. The host also provides bread and beverages. The rest of us are asked to bring either salads or desserts.

We meet at 4:00 in the afternoon and talk about one book until 5:30. We eat from 5:30-6:30. We talk about the other book from 6:30-8:00. It's good for our bodies and our souls—and nobody gets worn out with hosting.

Our Scattered Family

Ever since both of Merle's parents are gone, the sibs and spouses meet for a quarterly potluck. We take turns hosting, which also means making a basic main dish—and asking the rest to bring either a salad or dessert. I know we see more of each other because we share the responsibility of food prep, and we are less tempted to try to outdo each other with this kind of set-up and expectation.

Potluck Benefits

So here are the pleasures of potlucks:

1. Good chance you'll see your friends and family more.
2. You'll likely be less tempted to feel pressured to impress your guests.
3. I believe this is a maxim: The more comforting the food, the more casual the atmosphere, the more fun people have.
4. If you're the host, you'll have company in the kitchen. No more just listening to the fun going on in the family room or on the deck while you sweat and slave.
5. Whether you're a guest or a host, it's okay to use convenience foods if they make it possible for you to participate—rotisserie chicken, store-bought canned or frozen vegetables, boxed chicken broth, frozen whipped topping, canned soups, and baking mixes.*
6. Potlucks can be contagious. Instigate one, and you double your chances of being invited back to one. Give your social circles permission to share food together in this way—in the prepping as well as the eating.
7. Give thanks for good food—and relaxing times together with your friends. And make sure you do your part to make them happen.

But These Are Any-Time Recipes!

Of course, these are great any-time recipes. Don't wait for a potluck to make and enjoy them.

Phyllis Pellman Good

* We do offer from-scratch recipes for creamed soups (page 258-259),
hash browns (page 259), and a cornbread baking mix (page 259),
if you have the time and the will.

Carrying-in-the-Food Tips

1. Choose a dish that you can make almost completely in advance. (Almost completely? Well, so that all you need to do is add the almonds and the dressing to the green salad or the crushed nachos to the top of the casserole.)

2. Make a dish that will travel well. (A 4-layer cake with wobbly decorations on top? Probably not. A frozen dessert? Only if it's a 10-minute drive or less to the destination, with a freezer immediately available when you get there.)

3. Prepare a dish that won't self-destruct if it sits and waits. (Skip a soufflé or a designed dusting of confectioners sugar on a warm volcano cake.)

4. If you have a winner of a dish, double or triple it, depending on the size of the group. But make sure it's a recipe that survives that kind of expansion—and that you have adequately-sized containers to prepare and then transport it.

5. If kids are attending the potluck, keep them in mind when you decide what to make. Finger foods are especially easy for kids to handle.

6. If you made the dish last year and people loved it, make it again this year. Good chance someone's hoping you'll show up with that same amazing Chicken Chili Bake. The idea is not to show your versatility as a cook, but to bring the dish that always gets eaten up after the first pass-through.

7. Label your container and its lid.

8. Take your own serving spoon. (The host probably doesn't have an infinite supply). Label it, too.

9. If you don't have time to cook, put together a cheese board.

   Eight or fewer people eating? Choose two or three cheeses, about one pound of each. You can go mild and creamy, paired with hard and bitey.

   For eight to twelve people, select about 4 different cheeses, again a variety of textures and flavors.

   Add some cut-up fruit that's not too juicy (apples, grapes, dates, dried apricots), breadsticks, or crackers, maybe some mustards for dipping.

   Have a separate knife for each kind of cheese.

Hosting Tips

1. Clear your fridge so people can park the food they've brought in it until it's time to eat.

2. Be prepared to offer serving spoons for anyone who forgets to bring their own.

3. Be prepared with lots of leftover containers so any leftovers can be shared among the guests.

4. Remember any vegetarians in your group, and make sure there's food that they can eat and enjoy.

5. Offer simple tent signs (rectangles of stiff paper folded in half that will stand up straight) and pens for contributors to write the names of the dishes they brought. Place them in front of the dishes so guests know what they're looking at.

6. Plan in advance where you'll line up the dishes of food — and in what order. (Should the Salads go before the Hot Dishes, or after, and so on.)

7. Set up a drink station at a location away from the buffet table to prevent traffic jams.

8. Put out several trash receptacles that are easy for your guests to find. Have a back-up supply of trash bags so you can empty them throughout the event if they get full.

9. You can plan a Potluck for any reason at all, but don't forget these occasions which go better with friends and family: tailgating at a game, a concert in the park, the Super Bowl, 4th of July, extended family get-togethers.

Appetizers, Snacks, and Beverages

FINGER FOOD

Warm Bacon Cheese Dip in a Bread Bowl

Kayla Snyder
North East, PA

Makes 8-10 servings

Prep. Time: 30 minutes
Baking Time: 1 hour

1 lb. round loaf sourdough
  bread
8-oz. pkg. cream cheese
1½ cups sour cream
2 cups shredded cheddar
  cheese
1½ tsp. Worcestershire
  sauce
½-¾ lb. bacon, fried and
  crumbled
½ cup chopped green
  onion

1. Cut off top of bread; set aside.
2. Hollow out the bread bowl; save for bread cubes.
3. Beat cream cheese, sour cream, cheddar cheese, and Worcestershire sauce.
4. Stir in bacon and onions.
5. Pour filling back into bread bowl. Put the top back on bread bowl.
6. Wrap bread bowl in foil and set on baking sheet.
7. Bake at 325° for 1 hour.
8. Serve with cubed bread, crackers, or pretzels.

Variation:
   Bake in a pretty covered casserole dish. Add ½ cup chopped green chilies.

Good Go-Alongs:
   Fresh veggie tray

I always make this for our Christmas celebration with friends.

Pigs in a Blanket

Janie Steele
Moore, OK

Makes 12 servings

Prep. Time: 30 minutes
Cooking Time: 20-25 minutes

2 Tbsp. butter
1 large onion, chopped
sea salt
pepper
1 egg
1 Tbsp. water
2 8-oz. cans refrigerated
 crescent rolls
16-oz. pkg. cocktail
 sausages

dipping sauce:
 spicy Chinese mustard
 or favorite mustard
 ranch dressing

1. Fry onions in the butter
in a frying pan until golden
brown, 10-12 minutes.
2. Salt and pepper to taste.
Set aside to cool.
3. Whisk egg with water.
4. Lay each crescent roll
out flat and brush with egg
mixture.
5. Top each crescent roll
with 2 tsp. onions and 1
sausage.
6. Roll up and put on
baking sheet.
7. Brush each roll with egg
and water mix.
8. Bake 20-25 minutes at
375° until golden brown.
Serve with dipping sauce of
choice.

Reuben Appetizer Squares

Mary Ann Lefever
Lancaster, PA

Makes 2 dozen squares

Prep. Time: 20 minutes
Baking Time: 12-15 minutes

2 cups baking mix
½ cup milk
2 Tbsp. vegetable oil
1 cup sauerkraut, well
 drained
2½-oz. pkg. thinly sliced
 smoked corned beef,
 coarsely chopped
⅔ cup mayonnaise
1 Tbsp. pickle relish
1 Tbsp. ketchup
1½ cups shredded Swiss
 cheese (about 6 oz.)

1. Mix baking mix, milk,
and oil until soft dough
forms.
2. Press into ungreased
9 × 13 baking pan.
3. Top with sauerkraut and
corned beef.
4. Mix mayonnaise, relish,
and ketchup.
5. Spread over corned beef.
Sprinkle with cheese.
6. Bake at 450° until
cheese is bubbly and crust is
golden brown, 12-15 minutes.
7. Cut into 2" squares.

These squares are very
different for a potluck and are
always well received.

Veggie Pizza

Jean Butzer
Batavia, NY
Julette Rush
Harrisonburg, VA

Makes 10-12 servings

Prep. Time: 20-30 minutes
Cooking Time: 9-12 minutes
Cooling Time: 30 minutes

2 8-oz. pkgs. refrigerated
 crescent rolls
8-oz. pkg. cream cheese,
 softened
½-¾ cup salad dressing *or*
 mayonnaise
1 tsp. dill weed
½ tsp. onion salt
¾-1 cup broccoli florets
¾-1 cup green pepper *or*
 mushrooms, chopped
 fine
¾-1 cup tomato,
 membranes and seeds
 removed, chopped fine
½ cup sliced ripe olives
¼ cup sweet onion *or* red
 onion, chopped fine
¾ cup cheddar cheese,
 shredded fine, *optional*

1. Separate dough into 4
rectangles.
2. Press onto bottom and
up sides of 10 × 13 jelly roll
baking pan to form crust.
3. Bake 9-12 minutes at
350° or until golden brown.
Cool at least 30 minutes.
4. Mix cream cheese,
dressing, dill, and onion salt
until well blended.
5. Spread over cooled crust.
6. Top with chopped
vegetables and optional cheese.

7. Press down lightly into cream cheese mixture.

8. Refrigerate. Cut into squares to serve.

Tips:

1. Replace the dill weed and onion salt with 1 packet dry Hidden Valley Ranch Dressing mix.

2. Use vegetable garden flavor cream cheese.

3. Add veggies of your preference and availability

4. Do not put the cream cheese mixture on too thick. There may be ¼ cup left after spreading it on the crescent rolls. This can be saved to use as a dip with any leftover vegetables you have.

Crust from Scratch

1 cup flour
2 tsp. sugar
2 tsp. baking powder
½ tsp. salt
3 Tbsp. butter
½ cup milk *or* buttermilk

1. Mix well.

2. Press dough into 9 × 13 baking pan.

3. Bake at 350° for 10-15 minutes until golden.

4. Allow to cool and proceed with toppings.

Mrs. Anna Gingerich
Apple Creek, OH

FINGER FOOD

Stuffed Mushrooms

Gloria Lehman
Singers Glen, VA

Makes 10 servings

Prep. Time: 25 minutes
Cooking/Baking Time: 20-40 minutes

1 lb. fresh mushrooms
¼ to ⅓ cup margarine *or* butter
2 Tbsp. onion, finely chopped
2 Tbsp. mushroom stems, finely chopped
½ cup Italian seasoned bread crumbs
grated Parmesan cheese
2-4 Tbsp. oil

1. Wash mushrooms; remove stems.

2. Place mushrooms in greased baking pan, stem side up.

3. Sauté onion and mushroom stems in margarine or butter.

4. Turn off heat and stir in crumbs.

5. Fill each mushroom cap with mixture.

6. Sprinkle Parmesan cheese over all. Drizzle with oil.

7. Bake at 350° for 20-30 minutes.

Variation:

To plain cracker crumbs, add 1 Tbsp. dried parsley, ½ tsp. garlic salt, 3 Tbsp. minced onion, 2 Tbsp. melted butter, pepper to taste, and minced mushroom stems. Do not sauté. Stuff mushroom caps and proceed as listed.

Melva Baumer
Mifflintown, PA

This is a simple dish to prepare and shop for. But it is fabulous.

Don't be afraid to try new recipes, but learn some basic ones from cooks you trust.

Colleen Heatwole, Burton, MI

Shrimp Hors d'oeuvres

Barbara A. Hershey
Lititz, PA

Makes 48 pieces

Prep. Time: 20 minutes
Cooking/Baking Time: 20 minutes

1 stick (½ cup) butter
4-oz. jar Old English cheese spread
3 Tbsp. mayonnaise
4½-oz. can shrimp, drained
6 English muffins, opened into 12 halves

1. Melt butter and cheese in heavy saucepan.
2. Add mayonnaise and continue stirring until thick.
3. Add shrimp.
4. Immediately spread on muffin halves. Cut into quarters.
5. Cover with plastic wrap and freeze up to 3 weeks.
6. Bake on cookie sheet at 350° for 10 minutes.

Tip:
Do not freeze assembled muffins. Broil 5-10 minutes until tops are just browned—watch carefully!

Easy Turkey Roll-Ups

Rhoda Atzeff
Lancaster, PA

Makes 12 pieces

Prep. Time: 10 minutes

3 6" flour tortillas
3 Tbsp. chive and onion cream cheese
12 slices deli shaved turkey breast
¾ cup shredded lettuce

1. Spread tortillas with cream cheese.
2. Top with turkey.
3. Place lettuce on bottom halves of tortillas; roll up.
4. Cut each into 4 pieces and lay flat to serve.

Tip:
Use deli shaved ham and vegetable cream cheese—this is very good! You can use light cream cheese.

Good Go-Alongs:
A batch of each (turkey and ham) makes a quick lovely dish for a potluck or fellowship meal. Good just as a snack with a few chips or crackers.

Spinach Roll-ups

Esther Gingerich
Kalona, IA

Makes 8-10 servings

Prep. Time: 30 minutes
Chilling Time: 12 hours

2 10-oz. boxes frozen spinach, thawed and drained
2-oz. bacon bits (half of a small jar)
¼ cup chopped water chestnuts
1 pkg. Ranch dressing mix
1 cup sour cream
6 green onions, chopped
1 cup mayonnaise
7 large tortillas
toothpicks

1. Mix together ingredients except tortillas.
2. Spread the mixture on the tortillas.
3. Roll up and secure with toothpicks.
4. Cover. Refrigerate overnight.
5. Slice into 1" pieces to serve.

Tip:
Arrange on a pretty plate or tray to serve.

Our church often has "finger food" potlucks and this works well for that.

Smoky Barbecue Meatballs

Carla Koslowsky
Hillsboro, KS

Sherry Kreider
Lancaster, PA

Jennie Martin
Richfield, PA

Makes 6-8 servings

Prep. Time: 30 minutes
Baking Time: 1 hour

1½ lbs. hamburger
½ cup quick oats
½ cup evaporated milk *or* milk
1 egg
¼-½ cup finely chopped onion, *optional*
¼ tsp. garlic powder
¼ tsp. pepper
¼ tsp. chili powder
1 tsp. salt

Sauce:
1 cup ketchup
¾ cup brown sugar
¼ cup chopped onion
¼ tsp. liquid smoke

1. Mix hamburger, oatmeal, milk, egg, onion, garlic powder, pepper, chili powder, and salt together.
2. Form balls 2" in diameter.
3. Place in 9 × 13 baking dish.
4. Mix sauce ingredients together. Pour over meatballs.
5. Bake at 350° for 50-60 minutes.

Tips:
I usually bake for about ¾ of the time and then pour off the grease, adding the sauce then. It's easy to double the recipe to share, or freeze. You can also make this as a meat loaf.

Carla Koslowsky
Hillsboro, KS

You can also bake these meatballs for 2 hours at 300°. Cover with foil the first hour, then uncover.

Sherry Kreider
Lancaster, PA

These meatballs can be served as part of a full cooked meal or luncheon, or just as an appetizer.

Jennie Martin
Richfield, PA

Tangy Cocktail Franks

Linda Sluiter
Schererville, PA

Makes 8-10 servings

Prep. Time: 15 minutes
Cooking Time: 15 minutes

12-oz. jar red currant jelly
¼ cup mustard
3 Tbsp. dry sherry
¼ tsp. ground allspice
20-oz. can pineapple chunks, drained
12-oz. pkg. cocktail franks

1. In saucepan, melt jelly. Add mustard, sherry, and allspice.
2. Add pineapple and cocktail franks to the pan.
3. Cook on medium heat about 10 minutes.

Easy peasy! Always gone.

Party Kielbasi

Mary C. Wirth
Lancaster, PA

Makes 8-10 servings

Prep. Time: 15 minutes
Cooking/Baking Time: 2½ hours

3 lbs. kielbasa *or* smoked
  sausage
1 cup ketchup
½ cup chili sauce
½ cup brown sugar, packed
2 Tbsp. Worcestershire
  sauce
1 Tbsp. lemon juice
¼ tsp. prepared mustard

1. Cut kielbasa or smoked
sausage into 6 or 9 large
pieces. Lay it in a large
saucepan of water.
2. Simmer 20 minutes.
Drain.
3. Cool slightly. Cut into
bite-size pieces.
4. Mix all other ingredients
in 9 × 13 baking dish.
5. Add kielbasa. Toss to
coat with sauce.
6. Bake at 325° for 1½-2
hours, stirring occasionally.

Tip:
  You can keep this warm in
a slow cooker or chafing dish.

Good Go-Alongs:
  Pasta salad, macaroni or
potato salad, green salad

*I first tried this at a house
warming party and kept remind-
ing the hostess about the recipe
until she remembered to share it.*

Tasty Treats

Mary Ann Lefever
Lancaster, PA

Makes 8-10 servings

Prep. Time: 20-30 minutes
Baking Time: 20 minutes

20 chicken livers
8-oz. can water chestnuts,
  cut in half
20 slices bacon

1. Place chicken livers on
½ piece of water chestnut
then wrap in bacon.
2. Place on wire rack on
broiler pan so bacon grease
can drain.
3. Bake at 350° for 20
minutes or until bacon is
done.
4. Serve with toothpicks
and optional Dijon mustard
for dipping.

Hot Pizza Dip

Linda Abraham
Kimberly, OR

Beverly High
Bradford, PA

Makes 6-8 servings

Prep. Time: 20 minutes
**Cooking/Baking Time: 5-20
minutes**

8-oz. pkg. cream cheese,
  softened
½ tsp. dried oregano
½ tsp. dried parsley
¼ tsp. dried basil
1 cup shredded mozzarella
  cheese, *divided*
1 cup grated Parmesan *or*
  cheddar cheese, *divided*
½-1 cup pizza sauce
2 Tbsp. chopped green bell
  pepper
2 Tbsp. diced pepperoni
2 Tbsp. sliced black olives,
  optional
¼ cup chopped onions,
  optional

1. In a small bowl, beat
together cream cheese,
oregano, parsley, and basil.
2. Spread mixture in
bottom of greased 9" glass pie
plate.
3. Sprinkle ½ cup moz-
zarella and ½ cup Parmesan

*When a recipe calls for softened cream cheese,
remove the cream cheese from the refrigerator at least
2 hours before starting the prep.*
Mamie Christopherson, Rio Rancho, NM

cheese on top of cream cheese mixture.

4. Spread the pizza sauce over all.

5. Sprinkle with remaining cheese.

6. Top with green pepper, pepperoni, olives, and onions.

7. Cover and microwave 5 minutes or bake at 350° for 20 minutes.

8. Serve hot with sliced French baguette bread, focaccia, tortilla chips, or fresh veggies.

Tips:
Add ½ cup sour cream to the cream cheese and herbs.
Gloria Mumbauer
Singers Glen, VA

Add ½ tsp. garlic powder and ⅛ tsp. cayenne pepper to the cream cheese mixture.
Juanita Mellinger
Abbottstown, PA

This makes a great Sunday supper or snack for company. You get the pizza flavor without the work of making a crust.
Juanita Mellinger
Abbottstown, PA

FINGER FOOD

Jalapeño Popper Dip

Jamie Mowry
Arlington, TX

Makes 6 servings

Prep. Time: 15 minutes
Baking Time: 30 minutes

2 8-oz. pkgs. cream cheese, softened
1 cup mayonnaise
4-oz. can chopped green chilies, drained
2-oz. can diced jalapeño peppers, drained
½ cup grated Parmesan cheese
½ cup panko bread crumbs

1. Mix cream cheese and mayonnaise in large bowl until smooth. Stir in chilies and peppers.

2. Pour pepper mixture in a greased baking dish.

3. Combine Parmesan and panko. Put on top of pepper mixture.

4. Bake at 350° for 30 minutes until golden and bubbly.

Tip:
Serve with pita chips or regular corn chips or whatever "dipper" you like. This is even good using veggies.

My mother-in-law, Marilyn Mowry, sent recipes in to Good Books in 1991 or 1992 for your cookbook, Favorite Recipes from Quilters. *I have followed your books ever since as she continues to send in recipes for each new book you publish. I've always wanted to send my own recipes in and finally did it!*

FINGER FOOD

Hot Hamburger Dip

Marilyn Korver
Ladysmith, WI

Makes 4-6 servings

Prep. Time: 30 minutes
Cooking Time: 20 minutes

2 lbs. hamburger
1 small onion, chopped
10½-oz. tomato soup
10½-oz. mushroom soup
¼ green pepper, chopped
1 tsp. chili powder
½ tsp. garlic salt
1-2 cups salsa
corn chips

1. In a saucepan, fry hamburger and onion. Drain.
2. Add soups, pepper, chili powder, and garlic salt. The salsa gives it the zip, so add 1-2 cups according to taste.
3. Heat gently until hot through.
4. Serve hot with corn chips.

This is a popular item at our house, a recipe I've given out often.

FINGER FOOD

Buffalo Chicken Dip

Deb Martin
Gap, PA

Makes 8 cups

Prep. Time: 15 minutes
Cooking Time: 20-60 minutes

10-oz. cans chunk chicken, drained
2 8-oz. pkgs. cream cheese, softened
1 cup Ranch dressing
¾ cup Frank's Red Hot sauce
1½-3 cups shredded cheddar jack cheese
tortilla chips

1. Heat chicken and hot sauce in a large frying pan over medium heat until heated through.
2. Stir in cream cheese and Ranch dressing. Cook, stirring until well blended and warm.
3. Mix in half of shredded cheese.
4. Transfer the mixture to a small slow cooker. Sprinkle the remaining cheese over the top.
5. Cover and cook on Low setting until hot and bubbly. Serve with tortilla chips.

Variation:
Replace hot sauce with 1 cup buffalo wing sauce. Spread cream cheese in bottom of small shallow baking dish. Layer with shredded chicken, buffalo wing sauce, ranch dressing, and shredded cheese. Bake at 350° for 20 minutes or until cheese is melted.

Donna Treloar
Muncie, IN

FINGER FOOD

Party Starter Bean Dip

Leona M. Slabaugh
Apple Creek, OH

Makes 15-20 servings

Prep. Time: 20-25 minutes
Baking Time: 20 minutes
Standing Time: 5 minutes

16-oz. can Old El Paso refried beans *or* vegetarian refried beans
8-oz. pkg. cream cheese, softened
12-oz. jar salsa, divided
Nachips Tortilla Chips

1. Spread beans into bottom of a 9" pie pan or a decorative pan, spreading up the sides a bit.
2. In a bowl, beat cream cheese, then add ⅔ cup salsa and beat until smooth.
3. Spread cream cheese mixture over beans.
4. Bake 20 minutes at 350°.
5. Spread remaining salsa over dip which has set for 5 minutes. Serve with Nachips.

Good Go-Alongs:
This is nice with a good dish of fruit and assorted snack crackers when eaten as a snack.

FINGER FOOD

Easy Layered Taco Dip

Lindsey Spencer
Morrow, OH
Jenny R. Unternahrer
Wayland, IA

Makes 8-10 servings
Prep. Time: 15 minutes

8-oz. cream cheese,
  softened
8-oz. sour cream
8-oz. taco sauce *or* salsa
shredded lettuce
chopped tomato
chopped green pepper,
  optional
shredded cheese, cheddar
  or Mexi-blend
tortilla chips

1. Blend cream cheese and sour cream until smooth.
2. Spread in bottom of a 9 × 13 dish.
3. Layer taco sauce over sour cream mixture, then lettuce, tomato, and cheese.
4. Serve with tortilla chips.

Tips:
  If you can, add the lettuce, tomato and cheese at the last minute so the lettuce doesn't get soggy.
  Jenny R. Unternahrer
  Wayland, IA

  Instead of salsa, use 1¼-oz. container of taco dip to mix with the cream cheese and sour cream. Add a layer of salsa.
  Virginia Graybill
  Hershey, PA

Omit salsa and lettuce. Add 3 Tbsp. taco seasoning to the sour cream and cream cheese and add a layer of chopped onion.
  Barbara J. Bey
  Hillsboro, OH

FINGER FOOD

Taco Appetizer Platter

Rachel Spicher Hershberger
Sarasota, FL

Makes 10 servings
Prep. Time: 20 minutes
Cooking/Baking Time: 10 minutes

1½ lbs. ground beef
½ cup water
1 envelope taco seasoning
2 8-oz. pkgs. cream cheese,
  softened
4-oz. can chopped green
  chilies, drained
2 medium tomatoes,
  seeded and chopped
1 cup chopped green onions
lettuce, *optional*
½ to ¾ cup honey
  barbecue sauce
1½ cup shredded cheddar
  cheese
large corn chips

1. In a skillet, cook beef over medium heat until no longer pink.
2. Drain. Add water and taco seasoning, simmer for 5 minutes.
3. In a bowl, combine the cream cheese and milk.

4. Spread on 14" serving platter or pizza pan.
5. Top with meat mixture. Sprinkle with chilies, tomatoes and onions. Add lettuce, if desired.
6. Drizzle with barbecue sauce. Sprinkle with cheddar cheese.
7. Serve with corn chips.

Tip:
  I put this on my cake server with a pedestal. It looks great.

FINGER FOOD

Basic Deviled Eggs and Variations

Makes 12 halves

Prep. Time: 30 minutes
Cooking Time: 20 minutes

To hardboil eggs:
1. Place eggs in a single layer in a lidded pan.
2. Fill the pan with cold water to just cover the eggs.
3. Bring to a full boil over high heat, covered.
4. As soon as the water begins the full boil, immediately turn the heat down to low for a simmer. Allow to barely simmer for exactly 18 minutes.
5. Pour off hot water. Run cold water and/or ice over the eggs to quickly cool them.

To make deviled eggs:
1. Cut eggs in half lengthwise. Gently remove yolk sections into a bowl.
2. Mash all yolk sections together with a fork. Stir in remaining ingredients with yolk mixture until smooth.
3. Fill empty egg whites. The filling will make a little mound in the egg white.
4. Garnish, optional. Refrigerate.

VARIATION #1
Traditional Eggs

Jan Mast
Lancaster, PA

6 large eggs, hardboiled and peeled
¼ cup plain yogurt *or* mayonnaise
1 Tbsp. onion, minced
1 tsp. dried parsley
1 tsp. lemon juice
1 tsp. prepared mustard
¼ tsp. salt
¼ tsp. Worcestershire sauce
⅛ tsp. pepper
paprika
olive slices *or* pimento pieces to garnish

VARIATION #2
Basic Deviled Eggs

Joanne Warfel
Lancaster, PA

6 large eggs, hardboiled and peeled
¼ cup mayonnaise
1 tsp. vinegar
1 tsp. prepared mustard
⅛ tsp. salt
sprinkle of pepper
paprika
parsley sprigs for garnish

VARIATION #3
Dill Pickle Eggs

Jan Mast
Lancaster, PA

6 large eggs, hardboiled and peeled
¼ cup plain yogurt *or* mayonnaise
1 Tbsp. pickle relish
1 tsp. dill weed
1 tsp. vinegar
1 tsp. prepared mustard
¼ tsp. salt
¼ tsp. Worcestershire sauce
⅛ tsp. pepper
paprika
pickle slice to garnish

VARIATION #4
Sweet & Spicy Deviled Eggs

Gwendolyn Chapman
Gwinn, MI

12 large eggs, hardboiled and peeled
½ cup light mayonnaise
3 Tbsp. apricot preserves
1 tsp. curry powder
½ tsp. salt
⅛ tsp. cayenne pepper

Let your kids help in the kitchen. They love to crack eggs, add ingredients, and mix. Yes, the mess will be bigger, but the time together is well spent.
Beth Maurer, West Liberty, OH

VARIATION #5
Tex-Mex Eggs

Jan Mast
Lancaster, PA

6 large eggs, hardboiled
  and peeled
¼ cup plain yogurt *or*
  mayonnaise
1 Tbsp. finely diced onion
1 tsp. lemon juice
1 tsp. prepared mustard
1 tsp. taco seasoning
¼ tsp. salt
⅛ tsp. pepper
paprika
black olive slices to garnish

VARIATION #6
Horseradish Eggs

Anna Marie Albany
Broomall, PA

6 large eggs, hardboiled
  and peeled
¼ cup mayonnaise
1-2 Tbsp. horseradish
½ tsp. dill weed
¼ tsp. ground mustard
⅛ tsp. salt
dash pepper
dash paprika

VARIATION #7
Tuna Eggs

Jan Mast
Lancaster, PA

6 large eggs, hardboiled
  and peeled
¼-⅓ cup plain yogurt *or*
  margarine
4½-oz. can tuna, drained
  and flaked
1 tsp. pickle relish
1 tsp. prepared mustard
1 tsp. onion, minced
¼ tsp. salt
⅛ tsp. pepper
paprika, olive slices *or*
  pimento pieces to garnish

VARIATION #8
Frances' Stuffed Eggs

Nanci Keatley
Salem, OR

12 eggs, hardboiled and
  peeled
2 Tbsp. mayonnaise
1 Tbsp. horseradish
1 tsp. sweet pickle relish
1 tsp. fresh Italian parsley,
  chopped fine
½ tsp. kosher salt
¼ tsp. dry mustard

*My Grandma Frances was
an amazing cook. I loved her
take on this classic recipe.*

Tips for all deviled eggs:
  1. When fresh parsley is
in season, it makes a lovely
garnish, both as sprigs on the
serving plate and chopped on
eggs.
  2. Chill the eggs for an
hour to improve the flavor.
  3. The egg yolk filling can
be spooned into a resealable
bag and tip of the bag snipped
off to serve as an icing-style
bag. Pipe egg yolk filling into
the egg whites.

FINGER FOOD

Hot Reuben Dip

Leona Miller
Millersburg, OH

Makes 6 servings

Prep. Time: 10 minutes
Baking Time: 35 minutes

8-oz. cream cheese,
  softened
½ cup sour cream
2 Tbsp. ketchup
½ lb. deli corned beef,
  finely chopped
1 cup sauerkraut, chopped,
  rinsed, and drained
1 cup shredded Swiss
  cheese
2 Tbsp. onion, finely
  chopped
snack rye bread *or* crackers

  1. In a mixing bowl, beat cream cheese, sour cream, and ketchup until smooth.
  2. Stir in corned beef, sauerkraut, Swiss cheese, and onion until blended.
  3. Transfer to a greased 1-quart baking dish.
  4. Cover and bake at 375° for 30 minutes. Uncover and bake 5 minutes longer or until bubbly.
  5. Serve warm with rye bread or crackers.

FINGER FOOD

Shrimp Appetizer Platter

Tammy Smith
Dorchester, WI

Makes 5 cups

Prep. Time: 15 minutes
Chilling Time: 1 hour

8-oz. cream cheese,
  softened
½ cup sour cream
¼ cup salad dressing *or*
  mayonnaise
1-2 4-oz. cans broken
  shrimp, drained and
  rinsed
1 cup cocktail sauce
2 cups shredded cheese
1 pepper, chopped
1 tomato, chopped
3 green onions, chopped

  1. Beat together cream cheese, sour cream and salad dressing.
  2. Put on a 12" platter.
  3. Layer rest of ingredients in order given.
  4. Cover and chill at least 1 hour. Serve with crackers.

FINGER FOOD

Molded Crab Spread

Marsha Sabus
Fallbrook, CA

Makes 10-12 servings

Prep. Time: 10 minutes
Cooking Time: 5-7 minutes
Chilling Time: 4 hours

6-oz. can crab
1 cup celery, chopped
2 green onions, chopped
1 cup mayonnaise
8-oz. cream cheese, softened
10¾-oz. can cream of
  mushroom soup
1-oz. envelope unflavored
  gelatin
3 Tbsp. cold water
assorted crackers *or* bread

  1. In a small microwave safe bowl, sprinkle gelatin over cold water. Let stand 1 minute.
  2. Microwave uncovered on High 20 seconds. Stir. Let stand 1 minute or until gelatin is completely dissolved.
  3. In a large saucepan, combine soup, cream cheese, mayonnaise, and gelatin/water.
  4. Cook and stir over medium heat for 5-7 minutes or until smooth.
  5. Remove from heat and add crab, celery, and onion.
  6. Transfer to a 5 cup ring mold, lightly greased.

To make your own cream of mushroom soup, please turn to pages 258-259.

7. Cover and refrigerate 4 hours or until set.

8. Unmold onto serving platter. Serve with crackers or bread.

Tips:

1. You can also substitute shrimp for crab.

2. You can reduce calories by using light mayonnaise, cream cheese, and soup.

Fiesta Crab Dip

Amy Bauer
New Ulm, MN

Makes 3 cups

Prep. Time: 15 minutes

8-oz. pkg. cream cheese
1 cup picante sauce
8-oz. pkg. imitation crab
1 cup shredded Mexican cheese
⅓ cup sliced green onions
2 Tbsp. sliced ripe olives
2 Tbsp. diced tomatoes
2 Tbsp. minced fresh cilantro
crackers

1. Soften cream cheese and mix with picante sauce.

2. Chop crab and add with cheese and onions. Mix well.

3. Cover and refrigerate.

4. To serve, garnish with olives, tomato and cilantro. Serve with crackers.

Shrimp Dip

Joyce Shackelford
Green Bay, WI

Makes 1½ cups

Prep. Time: 15 minutes
Chilling Time: 1 hour

3-oz. pkg. cream cheese, softened
1 cup sour cream
2 tsp. lemon juice
5-oz. pkg. Italian salad dressing mix
2 Tbsp. green pepper, finely chopped
½ cup finely chopped shrimp

1. Blend all ingredients together.

2. Chill at least 1 hour.

3. Serve with chips or crackers.

Mustard Dip

Mary Kay Nolt
Newmanstown, PA

Jessica Stoner
West Liberty, OH

Makes 3 cups

Prep. Time: 10 minutes

1 cup mayonnaise
1 cup prepared mustard
1 cup sour cream *or* plain yogurt
½ cup sugar
1-oz. pack Hidden Valley Ranch dressing mix
1 Tbsp. horseradish, *optional*
½ cup dried minced onion, *optional*

1. Stir together and store covered in refrigerator.

Good Go-Alongs:

Mustard dip is great with pretzels, crackers, or vegetables. It's even great on your favorite salad.

Once you taste it, look out, you'll keep coming back for more.

BLT Dip

Amy Bauer
New Ulm, MN

Makes 3 cups

Prep. Time: 15 minutes
Chilling Time: 1 hour

6 slices cooked crumbled
   bacon *or* 3-oz. can real
   bacon bits
1 cup sour cream
1 cup mayonnaise
3 plum tomatoes, seeds
   and membranes
   removed, chopped
crackers

1. Combine bacon, sour
cream, mayonnaise, and plum
tomatoes in medium bowl,
stirring until blended.
2. Cover. Refrigerate for
1 hour to blend flavors.
3. Serve with crackers.

Mexican Corn Dip

Janie Steele
Moore, OK

Makes 8 cups

Prep. Time: 10 minutes

8-oz. sour cream
1 cup mayonnaise
2 11-oz. cans Mexican-style
   corn
4 green onions, chopped
1 can chopped green chilies
1¼ cups shredded cheddar
   cheese
1-3 jalapeño peppers, seeds
   removed, chopped
Fritos Scoops chips

1. Mix ingredients together,
except chips.
2. Serve with Fritos.

Pineapple Salsa

Lorraine Stutzman Amstutz
Akron, PA

Makes 2½ cups

Prep. Time: 30 minutes

1½ cups fresh pineapple
1 cup cucumber
¼ cup red onion
2-4 tsp. jalapeño
1 tsp. garlic
2 Tbsp. chopped cilantro
¼ cup lime juice
1 tsp. grated lime peel
1 tsp. sugar
¼ tsp. salt

1. Pulse ingredients
together in food processor
until just chopped.
2. Serve with your favorite
tortilla chips.

Tip:
   If you don't have a food
processor, simply chop the
pineapple, cucumber, onion,
jalapeño, garlic and cilantro.
Combine with lime, sugar,
and salt.

Texas Caviar

Elaine Rineer
Lancaster, PA
Amy Bauer
New Ulm, MN

Makes 7½ cups

Prep. Time: 15 minutes
Cooking Time: 10 minutes
Chilling Time: 12-24 hours

1 15½-oz. can black-eyed peas, rinsed
2 11-oz. cans white shoepeg corn
1 15½-oz. can black beans, rinsed
8-oz. jar, chopped pimento
small green pepper, finely diced
1 cup chopped celery
small red onion, chopped
½-¾ cup sugar
¼ cup oil
salt and pepper, to taste
¾ cup apple cider vinegar
1 Tbsp. water

1. In saucepan, combine sugar, oil, salt, pepper, vinegar and water. Heat until boiling, then cool.
2. Mix together peas, corn, green pepper, beans, pimento and onion.
3. Pour cooked sauce over mixture. Stir. Serve cold.

Tips:
1. Best if refrigerated 24 hours before serving.
2. Serve with a scoop of Fritos or corn chips as a dip, or serve as a salad.

Variations:
Add Rotel, 2 diced Roma tomatoes, and 2 sliced avocados. Omit corn and pimento. As dressing, use 1 cup Zesty Italian dressing with a squeeze of lime juice.
Angie Van Steenvoort
Galloway, OH

Festive Fruit and Nut Spread

Lucille Hollinger
Richland, PA

Makes 1½ cups

Prep. Time: 15 minutes
Chilling Time: 30 minutes

8-oz. cream cheese, softened
¼ cup orange juice
½ cup dried cranberries
½ cup pecans, chopped

1. In a small mixing bowl, beat cream cheese and orange juice until smooth.
2. Fold in cranberries and pecans.
3. Cover and refrigerate 30 minutes.
4. Good with crackers or spread on bagels

Cheese and Olive Spread

Suzanne Yoder
Gap, PA

Makes 2 cups

Prep. Time: 15 minutes
Chilling Time: 1 hour

8-oz. pkg. shredded mild cheddar cheese
8-oz. pkg. cream cheese, softened
½ cup mayonnaise
¼ cup stuffed green olives, chopped
¼ cup chopped green onions
2 Tbsp. lemon juice
¼ tsp. ground red pepper *or* to taste
Ritz crackers

1. Mix ingredients except crackers.
2. Refrigerate at least an hour. Serve with Ritz crackers.

I usually have these ingredients on hand so it's simple to have a little something ready for unexpected guests.

FINGER FOOD

Appetizer Ham Ball

Dot Reise
Westminster, MD

Makes 8-12 servings

Prep. Time: 30 minutes
Chilling Time: 3 hours

8-oz. cream cheese, room
  temperature, *divided*
½ cup mayonnaise, *divided*
2 lbs. canned ham
¼ cup nuts
¼ cup green onions
¼ cup sweet pickle relish
maraschino cherries
parsley sprigs

1. Prepare topping by mixing 2 Tbsp. mayonnaise and 4 oz. cream cheese. Set aside.
2. Chop ham, nuts, and onions in food processor until finely chopped.
3. Stir ham mixture together with the other 4 oz. cream cheese and pickle relish. Form into ball.
4. Spread previously made topping over ball.
5. Coat with more chopped nuts.
6. Add chopped maraschino cherries for color.
7. Chill in refrigerator several hours on pretty platter. Garnish with parsley sprigs. Serve with crackers.

FINGER FOOD

Pineapple Cheese Dip

Mamie Christopherson
Rio Rancho, NM

Makes 10-12 servings

Prep. Time: 10 minutes

2 8-oz. pkgs. cream cheese,
  softened
8-oz. can crushed
  pineapple, drained
2 cups chopped pecans
2 Tbsp. finely chopped
  onions
1 Tbsp. seasoned salt

1. Beat cream cheese with mixer until fluffy.
2. Add pineapple, pecans, onions, and salt. Serve with crackers.

Variation:
  Leave out 1 cup of the pecans. Chill mixture for several hours. Shape into a ball and roll in the reserved pecans.

Joyce Shackelford
Green Bay, WI

FINGER FOOD

Father Todd's Favorite Baked Brie

Nanci Keatley
Salem, OR

Makes 8-12 servings

Prep. Time: 15 minutes
Baking Time: 20-25 minutes

16-oz. round brie
½ cup chopped pecans
¾ cup dried cherries
1 cup brown sugar, packed
¼ cup amaretto
French bread slices for
  serving

1. Place brie in oven-safe round casserole or pie plate.
2. Mix brown sugar and amaretto together; spread on top of cheese.
3. Sprinkle with pecans and cherries.
4. Bake at 375° for 20-25 minutes. Serve with French bread slices.

Tip:
  You can use Grand Marnier or a hazelnut liqueur instead. You can also use macadamia nuts or filberts instead of pecans.

I've made this for many occasions. The best was when we celebrated our renewing of vows and our priest, Father Todd, came to the small party we had. He loved the baked brie so much that I changed the recipe's name to honor him!

Pretty Fruit Kabobs with Dip

Anya Kauffman
Sheldon, WI

Makes 20 servings

Prep. Time: 30 minutes

8-oz. cream cheese,
  softened
8-oz. frozen whipped
  topping, thawed
12-oz. jar marshmallow
  cream
1 tsp. vanilla
1 honeydew, cut in 80
  pieces
1 pineapple, cut in 80
  pieces
2 lbs. strawberries, cut in
  40 pieces
1 lb. red grapes
1 lb. green grapes
40 8" skewers

1. Beat cream cheese until
fluffy.
2. Fold in whipped topping
and marshmallow cream.
Add vanilla.
3. Refrigerate until ready to
serve.
4. For kabobs, thread
green grape, pineapple, red
grape, honeydew, strawberry,
honeydew, red grape,
pineapple, green grape on
skewers. Serve.

Tip:
  Stick the kabobs in a foam
block placed in a low pan and
covered with lettuce, making
a "fruit bouquet."

Fruit Salsa with Cinnamon Chips

Jackie Halladay
Lancaster, PA

Makes 4-6 servings

Prep. Time: 45 minutes
Baking Time: 12 minutes

Cinnamon Chips:
  2 pkgs. flour tortillas
  ½ cup sugar
  1 Tbsp. cinnamon
  butter flavor cooking
    spray

Salsa:
  1 orange, peeled and
    chopped
  1 apple, chopped
  1 kiwi, peeled and
    chopped
  1 cup chopped
    strawberries
  ½ cup blueberries
  2 Tbsp. honey
  2 Tbsp. jam (any flavor)
  ¼ cup orange juice
  ¼-½ tsp. cinnamon
  ¼ tsp. nutmeg
  salt

1. To make cinnamon
chips, cut tortillas into 12
wedges and arrange on a
baking sheet. Lightly mist
with cooking spray.
2. Mix cinnamon and sugar
together.
3. Sprinkle tortilla wedges
with the cinnamon sugar.
4. Bake 10 minutes at 350°,
then broil 2 minutes. Remove
from pan until cool.
5. To make salsa, toss all

prepared fruit together in a
large bowl.
6. In a smaller bowl, mix
honey, orange juice, jam,
cinnamon, nutmeg, and salt.
7. Stir honey mixture
into fruit. Tastes best when
allowed to marinate in the
refrigerator for several hours.

Tips:
1. A food processor helps
with all the chopping.
2. You can really use any
combination of fruit.
3. Whole wheat tortillas
make it even healthier.

Dressed Up Fruit Salad

Michelle D. Hostetler
Indianapolis, IN

Makes 1¼ cups

Prep. Time: 10 minutes

1 cup sour cream
¼ cup brown sugar
½ tsp. cinnamon
¼ tsp. vanilla

1. Mix together.
2. Serve with cut up apples,
grapes and bananas.

Apple Dippers

Christine Lucke
Aumsville, OR

Makes 1 cup
Prep. Time: 15 minutes

8-oz. pkg. cream cheese
2 tsp. milk
½ cup brown sugar
5 apples, sliced

1. Whip cream cheese, milk, and brown sugar to a smooth, fluffy consistency.
2. Serve sliced apples with cream cheese and brown sugar for dipping.

Tips:
1. I like Braeburn or Cameo apples.
2. You can use some lemon juice and water to keep the apples from browning, but I just slice right before serving and the Braeburns don't turn brown before they are eaten.

We make this as a VBS snack and we have adults lingering in the kitchen hoping for handouts. We have others jumping for joy because it is apple dip night.

Strawberry Yogurt Dip

Teresa Koenig
Leola, PA

Makes 5½ cups
Prep. Time: 20 minutes

8-oz. frozen lite whipped topping, thawed
2 6-oz. cartons light strawberry yogurt
1-1½ cups mashed strawberries, fresh *or* thawed frozen
variety of sliced fresh fruit

1. Combine whipped topping, yogurt, and mashed berries.
2. Serve with variety of sliced fresh fruit.

Tip:
Also tastes good with pretzels or as a topping for scones.

Sweet Cheese Ball

Mary Ann Lefever
Lancaster, PA

Makes 8-10 servings
Prep. Time: 10 minutes
Chilling Time: 4 hours

2 8-oz. pkgs. cream cheese, softened
3-oz. French vanilla instant pudding
15-oz. can fruit cocktail, well drained
4 Tbsp. orange juice
1 cup sliced almonds
buttery crackers (like Town House)

1. Mix cream cheese, pudding, fruit, and juice.
2. Refrigerate to set up, approximately 4 hours.
3. Shape into a ball and roll in almonds.
4. Store in refrigerator. Serve with buttery crackers, graham crackers, or apple slices.

A friend always brought this to get-togethers or served at her home and would not "give out" the recipe. Finally she got tired of me asking and gave me the recipe. Always a hit at parties.

8-oz. container frozen whipped topping = 3 cups

S'mores Dip

Jessalyn Wantland
Napoleon, OH
Melissa Wenger
Orrville, OH

Makes 3 cups
Prep. Time: 20 minutes

2 8-oz. pkgs. cream cheese,
  softened
2 sticks (1 cup) butter
1 Tbsp. vanilla
4 Tbsp. brown sugar
1½ cups confectioners
  sugar
12-oz. pkg. miniature
  chocolate chips
chocolate graham crackers
  or graham cracker sticks

1. Beat cheese and butter
together until fluffy.
2. Stir in vanilla, sugars,
and chocolate chips.
3. Refrigerate. Serve with
chocolate graham crackers or
graham cracker sticks.

Tips:
1. Before serving, form in
mound and top with 1½ cup
pecans.
2. Margarine is not a good
substitute for butter in this
recipe!

Orange Pecans

Janice Muller
Derwood, MD

Makes 5½ cups

Prep. Time: 3 minutes
Cooking Time: 10 minutes
Cooling Time: 30 minutes

¼ cup orange juice
1 Tbsp. grated orange rind
½ tsp. cinnamon
¼ tsp. allspice
¼ tsp. ginger
pinch salt
1 cup sugar
1 lb. pecan halves, whole

1. Combine orange juice,
orange rind, cinnamon,
allspice, ginger, salt, and
sugar in a large flat pot so
that it will be easy to coat
pecans with the hot mixture.
2. Cook on medium heat
until mix comes to a full boil.
3. Stir in pecans. Keep
stirring until the pecans are
well coated and the syrup is
absorbed.
4. Remove from heat; stir
until pecans separate. Spread
onto waxed paper to cool.

Good Go-Alongs:
The sugared pecans are
good by themselves, or you
can sprinkle them over
vanilla ice cream, or a green
salad.

I can't keep enough of
these in the house during the
holidays, and they're fun to
take to gatherings. People can
take as few or as many as

they want. I've also packaged
these in pretty bags as gifts for
neighbors during the holidays.

Creamy Caramel Dip

Mary Kay Nolt
Newmanstown, PA

Makes 2½ cups

Prep. Time: 20 minutes
Chilling Time: 1 hour

8-oz. pkg. cream cheese,
  softened
¾ cup brown sugar
1 cup sour cream
2 tsp. vanilla
1 cup milk
3.4-oz. instant vanilla
  pudding

1. Beat cream cheese and
brown sugar.
2. Add sour cream, vanilla,
milk, and pudding and mix.
3. Chill at least 1 hour.
4. Serve as a dip for
pineapples, apples, grapes,
strawberries, etc.

Party Mix

Kayla Snyder
North East, PA

Makes 30 cups

Prep. Time: 30 minutes
Baking Time: 1¼-2 hours

4 cups Cheez-Its *or* cheese
  curls
4 cups Corn Chex
4 cups Rice Chex
4 cups Cheerios
4 cups Kix
10-oz. thin pretzel sticks
1½ lb. salted peanuts
1 lb. assorted nuts
1 lb. (4 sticks) butter, melted
1½ Tbsp. onion salt
1½ Tbsp. seasoned salt
3 Tbsp. Worcestershire
  sauce

1. Mix Cheez-Its, cereals, pretzels, and nuts together.
2. Mix melted butter, onion salt, seasoned salt, and Worcestershire sauce together.
3. Pour over dry ingredients. Mix until all the cereal is totally covered.
4. Spread mix evenly on 2 cookie sheets.
5. Bake at 225° for 1¼-2 hours, stirring every 15 minutes until toasted and crispy.

Crispix Snack Mix

Lorraine Stutzman Amstutz
Akron, PA

Makes 1 gallon

Prep. Time: 20 minutes
Cooking/Baking Time: 70
minutes
Cooling Time: 30 minutes

1½ cups brown sugar
1½ sticks (¾ cup) butter
¾ cup dark corn syrup
12-oz. box Crispix cereal
3 cups cashews

1. Mix brown sugar, butter, and corn syrup in saucepan and bring to boil.
2. Pour over cereal and cashews, stirring quickly to coat evenly.
3. Spread mixture onto cookie sheet.
4. Bake at 250° for 1 hour, stirring every 15 minutes.
5. As it cools, continue stirring every 10 minutes or so to keep from sticking together.
6. When completely cool, store in airtight container.

White Chocolate Party Mix

Joy Reiff
Mt. Joy, PA

Makes 10-15 servings

Prep. Time: 10 minutes
Cooking Time: 5 minutes
Standing Time: 45 minutes

4 cups mini pretzels
5 cups Cheerios cereal
5 cups Corn Chex cereal
2 cups salted peanuts
1 lb. M&Ms
2 12-oz. pkgs. vanilla chips
3 Tbsp. vegetable oil

1. Mix pretzels, cereals, peanuts and M&Ms. Set aside.
2. Melt vanilla chips and oil in microwave, stirring until melted.
3. Pour over cereal mixture and mix well.
4. Spread on cookie sheet lined with waxed paper.
5. Allow to set and then break apart and store in an air-tight container.

Tip:
  Sometimes I use mint or peanut M&Ms.

Keep a notebook of when you have guests over for a meal. List how many people attended, the weather, menus, how much you made, and how much was left over. This is handy to look at when you are planning for new guests.

Jane Geigley, Lancaster, PA

White Chocolate Popcorn Delight

Debbie Hershey
Lancaster, PA

Makes 15-20 servings

Prep. Time: 15-20 minutes
Cooking Time: 5 minutes
Standing Time: 3 hours

2 bags microwave popcorn,
  butter flavored, popped
1 lb. honey-roasted peanuts
  (approximately 3 cups)
1¼ lb. white chocolate
  wafers *or* chips
⅓ cup peanut butter

1. Sort through the popcorn and remove unpopped kernels.
2. In a very large bowl, mix popcorn and peanuts.
3. Melt chocolate and peanut butter in a saucepan over low heat or in microwave.
4. Pour over popcorn and nut mixture. Stir until completely coated.
5. Spread out on waxed paper until set, approximately 3 hours. Or refrigerate for faster setting.
6. Break apart and store in an airtight container.

Puffed Rice Candy

Betty Hostetler
Allensville, PA

Makes 15-20 servings

Prep. Time: 5 minutes
Cooking Time: 25 minutes
Cooling Time: 1 hour

1 cup table syrup
½ cup sugar
½ cup water
3 Tbsp. peanut butter
8 cups puffed rice

1. Combine syrup, water, and table syrup in large skillet or saucepan.
2. Cook over medium heat to softball stage or 235° on a candy thermometer for 20 minutes.
3. Blend in peanut butter and remove from heat.
4. Add the puffed rice and mix together until the puffed rice is thoroughly coated.
5. Spread on buttered 11×17 cooking sheet and press.
6. Cool at least 1 hour.
7. Break into pieces and store in an airtight container with waxed paper between layers.

Mother often made this candy for Christmas and other occasions. She always used the 10" Griswald skillet to boil the syrup and mixed the puffed rice with it. This recipe was "handed down."

These are also known as "Frying Pan Cookies" and can be made with cornflakes.

Crisp Snack Bars

Norma Saltzman
Shickley, NE

Makes 16 servings

Prep. Time: 30 minutes
Cooking Time: 10 minutes

½ cup honey
½ cup chunky peanut
  butter
½ cup non-fat dry milk
½ cup milk, *optional*
4 cups crisp rice cereal

1. In a large saucepan, combine honey, peanut butter, and milk powder.
2. Cook and stir over low heat until peanut butter is melted and mixture is warm.
3. Remove from heat. If the mixture is too thick to stir easily, thin with a little milk.
4. Stir in cereal.
5. Press into an 8" square dish coated with non-stick cooking spray. Let stand until set.
6. Cut into 16 square bars.

Variations:
  Melt chocolate chips along with the peanut butter mixture. Reduce the cereal to 2 cups.

Karen Burkholder
Narvon, PA

Caramel Popcorn Crunch

Jamie Schwankl
Ephrata, PA
Deb Martin
Gap, PA

Makes 8 servings

Prep. Time: 5 minutes
Cooking/Baking Time: 1 hour 40 minutes

2-4 quarts popped corn
1 cup brown sugar
1 stick (½ cup) margarine
   or butter
¼ cup corn syrup *or*
   molasses
½ tsp. salt
½ tsp. baking soda
½ tsp. vanilla, *optional*

1. Pour popped corn into a large roasting pan.
2. Sort through the popcorn to remove kernels that are unpopped.
3. In a medium sauce pan, combine sugar, margarine, corn syrup, and salt over medium heat, stirring frequently. Bring to a boil.
4. Boil for 5 minutes. Remove syrup from heat.
5. Stir in baking soda and optional vanilla until mixture becomes foamy.
6. Pour syrup over popcorn, stirring quickly and thoroughly to coat.
7. Bake at 200° for 1-1½ hours, stirring every 15 minutes.
8. Allow to cool, stirring occasionally to keep kernels from sticking together.
9. Store in an airtight container.

Variation:
   Add 1 cup nuts.
                   Renée Hankins
                   Narvon, PA

Garlic Pretzels

Rachel Spicher Hershberger
Sarasota, FL

Makes 8 servings

Prep. Time: 15 minutes
Standing Time: 2 hours

½ cup oil
¼ tsp. garlic powder
¼ tsp. dill weed
¼ tsp. lemon pepper
¼ tsp. lemon and herb
   seasoning

2 Tbsp. dry ranch dressing mix
9-oz. bag Snyder's Butter Snap pretzels

1. Combine oil, garlic powder, dill weed, lemon pepper, lemon & herb, and dressing mix.
2. Pour over pretzels. Keep stirring occasionally for about 2 hours until oil is absorbed.
3. Store in air-tight container or bag.

Soft Pretzels

Lydia K. Stoltzfus
Gordonville, PA

Makes 24 servings

Prep. Time: 15 minutes
Rising Time: 30 minutes
Cooking/Baking Time: 15 minutes

4 tsp. active dry yeast
3 cups lukewarm water
pinch of salt
⅓ cup brown sugar
7½ cups flour
3 Tbsp. baking soda
2 cups water
pretzel salt

1. Dissolve yeast in water.
2. Add brown sugar and pinch salt.
3. Stir in flour slowly. Knead well.
4. Cover and let rise 30 minutes.
5. Divide dough into small pieces and form into pretzel shapes.
6. Meanwhile mix baking soda and 2 cups water in a saucepan and heat until hot.
7. Dip each twisted pretzel in hot solution and rub back side on paper towels, so it will not stick to pan.
8. Lay dipped pretzels on greased baking sheets.
9. Sprinkle salt on pretzels.
10. Bake at 500° for 7-10 minutes.

Tips:
Dip pretzel in melted butter. You could also serve mustard or cheese sauce.

Grape Cider

Evelyn Page
Gillette, WY

Makes 14-16 servings

Prep. Time: 30 minutes
Cooking Time: 3 hours

5 lbs. Concord grapes
8 cup water, *divided*
1½ cups sugar
8 whole cloves
4 4" cinnamon sticks
dash ground nutmeg

1. In a large saucepan, combine grapes and 2 cups water.
2. Bring to a boil, stirring constantly.
3. Pour grapes and liquid through a strainer. Press on the cooked grapes to get out all the juice. Discard skins and seeds.
4. Pour the juice through a double layer of cheesecloth into a 5-quart slow cooker.
5. Add sugar, cloves, cinnamon sticks, nutmeg, and remaining water.
6. Cover and cook on Low for 3 hours.
7. Discard cloves and cinnamon sticks. Serve hot.

Raspberry Punch

Gloria Martin
Ephrata, PA

Makes 4 quarts

Prep. Time: 20 minutes

3 3-oz. pkgs. raspberry gelatin
4 cups boiling water
¾-1 cup sugar
4 cups cold water
2¼ cups orange juice concentrate
1¼ cups lemonade concentrate
1 quart ginger-ale
10-oz. pkg. frozen raspberries

1. Dissolve gelatin in boiling water.
2. Add sugar and cold water and stir to dissolve.
3. In a punch bowl, mix orange juice concentrate, lemon juice concentrate, ginger-ale, and raspberries.
4. Pour gelatin mixture into punch bowl. Stir. Serve with ice.

Tip:
Float scoops of raspberry sherbet on top of the punch.

Piña Colada Punch

Melissa Raber
Millersburg, OH

Makes 20 cups

Prep. Time:20 minutes
Chilling Time:2-4 hours

½ gallon vanilla ice cream
20-oz. can crushed pineapple
16-oz. can coconut cream
 or coconut milk
46-oz. can pineapple juice
2-liter lemon-lime soda

1. Combine ingredients except soda in bowl.
2. Freeze until slushy, 2-4 hours.
3. Combine with soda and serve in punch bowl.

Tip:
 Put the crushed pineapple in the blender for a smoother texture.

Orange Lemon Drink

Rhonda Freed
Croghan, NY

Makes 1 gallon

Prep. Time: 10 minutes

12-oz. can frozen orange
 juice concentrate
1½ cups sugar
½ cup lemon juice
1 gallon water, *divided*

1. Mix juice concentrate, sugar, lemon juice, and ½ gallon water.
2. Add water to make a full gallon. Serve cold.

When juicing a lemon, let it come to room temperature. You'll get more juice if you do. Then, using some pressure, roll it under your hand on the counter before juicing it so that it releases its juice more easily. Freeze any extra juice in 1 Tbsp. amounts in an ice cube tray.

Becky Frey, Lebanon, PA

Cocoa for a Crowd

Joy Reiff
Mt. Joy, PA

Makes 65 1-cup servings

Prep. Time: 5 minutes
Cooking Time: 20-30 minutes

5 cups unsweetened cocoa
 powder
4-6 cups sugar
2 tsp. salt
5 quarts (20 cups) water,
 divided
10 quarts (2½ gallons) milk
1 quart heavy whipping
 cream
2 Tbsp. vanilla
whipped cream and
 additional baking cocoa
 for garnish, *optional*

1. In each of two large stockpots, combine 2½ cups cocoa, 2 cups sugar and 1 teaspoon salt.
2. Gradually stir 5 cups water into each pot.
3. Bring to a boil, covered. Turn heat to low.
4. Whisk in milk, cream, remaining 10 cups water; heat through, but do not boil.
5. Turn off heat. Stir in vanilla. Taste, and add sugar to your taste.
6. Garnish with whipped topping and additional cocoa.

I like to serve this at my open house in the winter.

Breakfast and Brunch Dishes

California Egg Bake

Leona M. Slabaugh
Apple Creek, OH

Makes 2 servings

Prep. Time: *10-15 minutes*
Baking Time: *25-30 minutes*

3 eggs
¼ cup sour cream
¼ tsp. salt
1 medium tomato, chopped
1 green onion, sliced
¼ cup shredded cheese

1. In a small bowl, beat eggs, sour cream, and salt.
2. Stir in tomato, onion, and cheese.
3. Pour into greased 2-cup baking dish.
4. Bake at 350° for 25-30 minutes, or until a knife inserted in center comes out clean.

Eggs à la Shrimp

Willard E. Roth
Elkhart, IN

Makes 6 servings

Prep. Time: *15 minutes*
Cooking Time: *15 minutes*

2 Tbsp. butter
3 green onions with tops, sliced, *or* 1 small onion, chopped fine
¼ cup finely chopped celery with leaves
4 oz. shrimp, frozen, *or* canned
3 Tbsp., plus ¼ cup white wine, *divided*
8 large eggs
4 oz. frozen peas, *or* fresh
¼ tsp. salt
¼ tsp. pepper
fresh parsley

1. Preheat electric skillet to 375°, or cast iron skillet to medium high.
2. Melt butter in skillet. Sauté onions, until limp.
3. Add celery and sauté until softened.
4. Add shrimp and 3 Tbsp. white wine. Cover and steam over low heat for 3 minutes.
5. In a medium-sized mixing bowl, whisk eggs with ¼ cup white wine. Pour into skillet.
6. Stir in peas and seasonings.
7. Turn skillet to 300°, or medium low. Stir gently as mixture cooks. Cook just until mixture sets according to your liking.
8. Serve on warm platter surrounded with fresh parsley.

Good Go-Alongs:
Freshly baked muffins
Fresh fruit in season

A simple but special brunch—or supper—entrée.

Egg Scramble

Elva Bare
Lancaster, PA

Makes 4 servings

Prep. Time: 30-45 minutes
Cooking Time: 10 minutes

1 medium-large potato,
  enough to make ¾ cup
  grated potatoes
5-6 strips (4 oz.) bacon,
  low-sodium if you can
  find it
¼ cup chopped red bell
  pepper
¼ cup chopped green bell
  pepper
⅓ cup chopped onion
4 oz. bacon (5-6 strips),
  low-sodium
8 eggs
⅓ cup low-fat sour cream
¼ cup low-fat milk
½ tsp. onion salt
¼ tsp. garlic salt
⅛ tsp. pepper
1 cup (4 oz.) shredded
  cheddar, *or* Cooper
  sharp, cheese

1. Place a whole potato
with skin on in a small pan.
Add about ½" water, cover,
and cook over low heat until
fork-tender.
2. Remove and allow to
reach room temperature.
3. Chill thoroughly. Grate.
4. Meanwhile, sauté bacon
in skillet until crispy. Remove
bacon (reserving drippings
in skillet) and drain on paper
towel. Crumble bacon when
cool.

5. Sauté peppers and
onion in bacon drippings 3-5
minutes.
6. In a blender, combine
eggs, sour cream, milk, onion
salt, garlic salt, and pepper.
Cover and process until
smooth.
7. Stir grated potato and
bacon into vegetables in
skillet.
8. Pour egg mixture over
vegetables.
9. Cook and stir over
medium heat until eggs are
set.
10. Sprinkle with cheese.
Cover skillet with lid until
cheese melts.
11. Cut in wedges in skillet
and serve on heated dinner
plates.

Tips:
1. You can do a lot of the
prep for this dish the day or
evening before serving it.
Cook the potato in advance
and chill it. Chop the
vegetables ahead of time and
refrigerate them. You can
even blend the eggs, sour
cream, milk, salts, and pepper the day before and then
refrigerate the mixture. The
morning of your breakfast
you're ready to go.
2. I heat the dinner plates
in my oven, turned on Low,
for 5-10 minutes.

Good Go-Alongs:
Serve toasted bagels and
fresh fruit. Add a broiled
tomato, which you've cut
in half and sprinkled with
Parmesan cheese before
running under the broiler.

Baked Eggs

Esther J. Mast
Lancaster, PA

Make 6-8 servings

Prep. Time: 15 minutes
Baking Time: 40-45 minutes

1 stick (½ cup) butter, *or*
  less
1 cup buttermilk baking
  mix
1½ cups cottage cheese
2 tsp. chopped onion
1 tsp. parsley
½ tsp. salt
½ lb. grated cheddar
  cheese
6 eggs, slightly beaten
1 cup milk

1. Cut butter into chunks
and place in 7 × 11 baking
dish. Turn oven to 350°
and put dish in oven to melt
butter.
2. Meanwhile, mix together
buttermilk baking mix,
cottage cheese, onion, parsley,
salt, cheese, eggs, and milk in
large mixing bowl.
3. Pour mixture over
melted butter. Stir slightly to
distribute butter.
4. Bake 40-45 minutes until
firm but not drying out.
5. Allow to stand 10
minutes. Cut in squares and
serve.

Good Go-Alongs:
Serve with muffins and a
fresh fruit cup.

Artichoke Egg Casserole

Marie Davis
Mineral Ridge, OH

Makes 4-6 servings

Prep. Time: 15 minutes
Baking Time: 35-40 minutes

4- or 6½-oz. jar marinated
  artichoke hearts
½ cup chopped green
  onions
2-3 garlic cloves
1 Tbsp. vegetable oil
8 eggs
4½-oz. can sliced
  mushrooms, drained
3 cups shredded sharp
  cheddar cheese
1 cup butter-flavored
  cracker crumbs (25
  crackers, crushed)

1. Drain artichoke hearts,
reserving ½ cup marinade.
Cut artichokes into small
pieces.
2. In small skillet, sauté
green onions and garlic in oil
until tender.
3. In large bowl, beat eggs.
4. Stir in artichokes, onion
mixture, mushrooms, cheese,
and cracker crumbs.
5. Bake at 350° for 35-40
minutes.

Tip:
  You can use ¼ lb. fresh
mushrooms, sliced, instead
of canned mushrooms in this
dish. If you use fresh ones,
sauté with onion and garlic in
Step 2.

Southwestern Egg Casserole

Eileen Eash
Lafayette, CO

Makes 12 servings

Prep. Time: 20-30 minutes
Baking Time: 35-45 minutes
Standing Time: 5-10 minutes

10 eggs
½ cup flour
1 tsp. baking powder
⅛ tsp. salt
⅛ tsp. pepper
4 cups shredded Monterey
  Jack, *or* cheddar, cheese
2 cups cottage cheese
1 stick (½ cup) butter, melted
2 4-oz. cans chopped green
  chilies

1. Beat eggs in a large
mixing bowl.
2. In a smaller bowl,
combine flour, baking
powder, salt, and pepper.
3. Stir into eggs. Batter will
be lumpy.
4. Add cheeses, butter, and
chilies to batter.
5. Pour into greased 9 × 13
baking dish.
6. Bake at 350° for 35-45
minutes, or until knife
inserted near center comes
out clean.
7. Let stand 5-10 minutes
before cutting.

Tips:
  1. This is a great recipe
for brunch. I usually put it
together the night before and
then refrigerate it.
  2. To take to a potluck after
baking it, I transport it in an
insulated carrier which I wrap
in an old mattress pad. It stays
hot for at least an hour.

Baked Omelet

Eileen M. Landis
Lebanon, PA

Makes 8-10 servings

Prep. Time: 15-20 minutes
Baking Time: 45 minutes
Standing Time: 5-10 minutes

8 eggs, beaten
2 cups cubed cooked ham
2 cups grated or cubed
   American cheese
2 cups milk
1 cup crushed saltine
   crackers
¼ cup chopped onion
¼ cup chopped green bell
   pepper
¼ cup chopped red bell
   pepper
½ tsp. salt

1. In a large bowl, combine beaten eggs, ham, cheese, milk, crackers, onion, green pepper, red pepper, and salt.
2. Pour into greased 9 × 13 baking dish.
3. Bake at 350° for 45 minutes, or until knife inserted in center comes out clean. If it doesn't, allow to bake 5 minutes more. Test again. Continue baking if needed, and test again until done.
4. Let stand 5-10 minutes before serving.

Mushroom Quiche

Janice Muller
Derwood, MD

Makes 6-8 servings

Prep. Time: 20 minutes
Baking Time: 35-40 minutes

half stick (4 Tbsp.) butter
1 onion, chopped
½ lb. fresh mushrooms,
   sliced
1 Tbsp. parsley, chopped
dash of salt
freshly ground black
   pepper
3 eggs
½ cup light cream
1 cup cheddar cheese,
   grated
9" pie shell, unbaked

1. In a large skillet, sauté onions and mushrooms gently in butter for 5 minutes.
2. Remove skillet and drain off cooking liquid. Add parsley, salt and pepper.
3. In a large mixing bowl, beat together eggs and cream.
4. Stir cheese and mushroom mixture into eggs and cream.
5. Pour into pie shell.
6. Bake at 400° for 35-40 minutes. Serve hot or cold.

Mom's Heavenly Quiche

Barbara Forrester Landis
Lititz, PA

Makes 6-8 servings

Prep. Time: 15 minutes
*Cooking/Baking Time: 35-45
   minutes*

6 eggs, *or* equivalent
   amount of Egg Beaters
2 Tbsp. flour
2 cups cottage cheese
1 cup shredded cheddar
   cheese
half stick (4 Tbsp.) butter,
   melted
4-oz. can diced green
   chilies, undrained

1. In a good-sized mixing bowl, beat eggs or pour in Egg Beaters.
2. Stir in flour.
3. When well mixed, stir in cottage cheese, shredded cheese, butter, and chilies.
4. Pour into greased 10" pie plate.
5. Bake 40-45 minutes, or until set in center. Insert blade of knife in center. If it comes out clean, the quiche is finished. If it doesn't, bake for 5 more minutes. Test again, and continue baking if needed.
6. Let stand 10 minutes before cutting to allow cheeses to firm up.

Tips:
1. You can use any kind of flour. I use whole wheat.

2. You can use any kind of cottage cheese. I use low fat.

3. This is delicious eaten cold the next day if there's any left.

4. If you have leftover cooked veggies in your fridge, place them in the bottom of the pan and cover with egg mixture as a variation.

Breakfast Pie

Darlene Bloom
San Antonio, TX

Makes 6 servings

Prep. Time: 20 minutes
Baking Time: 30 minutes

1 lb. meat —your choice of
   sausage, ham, *or* bacon
1 cup chopped onions
1 cup chopped bell pepper,
   red *or* green
½ tsp. salt
1 cup shredded cheddar
   cheese
½ cup buttermilk baking
   mix
1 cup milk
2 eggs

1. Brown meat, onion, and bell pepper in skillet until done. Drain off drippings.

2. Place cooked ingredients in a greased 9" pie plate.

3. Sprinkle with salt.

4. Top with layer of shredded cheese.

5. In a mixing bowl, whisk baking mix, milk, and eggs together. Pour over ingredients in pie plate.

6. Bake at 400° for 30 minutes.

7. Allow to stand 5-10 minutes before cutting and serving.

Tips:

1. Double this recipe and prepare in a 9×13 baking pan. I take this to potlucks all the time, warm out of the oven.

2. You can use ground turkey or beef as your choice of meats and add 1 envelope taco seasoning mix to the skillet as you cook. I call this version Taco Bake and often make it for dinner.

Southwest Brunch Casserole

Janita Mellinger
Abbottstown, PA

Makes 4 servings

Prep. Time: 20-30 minutes
Chilling Time: 3-8 hours
Baking Time: 25 minutes

1-2 Tbsp. butter, softened
2 English muffins, split
½ lb. bulk pork sausage
4 eggs
¼ cup low-fat sour cream
½ cup grated cheddar
   cheese
¼ cup chopped chilies,
   optional

1. Spread butter over cut sides of each muffin half.

2. Place buttered side up in 8" square baking pan coated with non-stick cooking spray.

3. In a small skillet, cook sausage. Drain off drippings.

4. Spoon sausage over muffin halves.

5. In a small mixing bowl, whisk eggs and sour cream together.

6. Pour over sausage.

7. Sprinkle with cheese and chilies if you wish.

8. Cover and refrigerate 3 hours or overnight.

9. Remove from refrigerator 30 minutes before baking.

10. Bake uncovered at 350° for 20-25 minutes, or until knife inserted near center comes out clean.

Tip:

This is great for sleep-in mornings or overnight guests. You can avoid the morning rush.

Potato-Bacon Gratin

Valerie Drobel
Carlisle, PA

Makes 6 servings

Prep. Time: 15 minutes
Baking Time: 1 hour

6-oz. bag fresh spinach
1 clove garlic, minced
1 Tbsp. olive oil
4 large potatoes, peeled or
  unpeeled, *divided*
6-oz. Canadian bacon
  slices, *divided*
6-oz. Swiss cheddar, *or*
  Gruyere, cheese, grated
  and *divided*
1 cup chicken broth

1. In large skillet, sauté spinach and garlic in olive oil just until spinach is wilted.
2. Cut potatoes into thin slices.
3. In 2-quart baking dish, layer ⅓ the potatoes, half the bacon, ⅓ the cheese, and half the wilted spinach.
4. Repeat layers ending with potatoes. Reserve ⅓ cheese for later.
5. Pour chicken broth over all.
6. Cover and bake at 350° for 45 minutes.
7. Uncover and bake 15 more minutes. During last 5 minutes, top with cheese.
8. Allow to stand 10 minutes before serving.

Tips:
  Leftovers are delicious.

Make two of these Bakes at a time and freeze one.

Good Go-Alongs:
  Baked apples or applesauce

Shredded Potato Omelet

Mary H. Nolt
East Earl, PA

Makes 6 servings

Prep. Time: 15 minutes
Cooking Time: 20 minutes

4 slices bacon
2 cups shredded cooked
  potatoes
¼ cup chopped onion
¼ cup chopped green bell
  pepper
4 eggs
¼ cup milk
½ tsp. salt
⅛ tsp. black pepper
1 cup cheese of your
  choice, grated

1. In large skillet, fry bacon until crisp. Remove bacon and crumble. Leave drippings in skillet.
2. Mix potatoes, onion, and green peppers in bowl. Spoon into skillet. Cook over low heat—without stirring—until underside is crisp and brown.
3. Blend eggs, milk, salt, and pepper in mixing bowl.
4. Pour over potato mixture.
5. Top with cheese and bacon.
6. Cover. Cook over low heat approximately 10 minutes, or until set. Loosen omelet and serve.

The first time I remember eating this Omelet was when we were helping to pick raspberries before breakfast at our son's place in New York. We were so hungry when we went to the house, and our daughter-in-law served this omelet. I have made it a lot since, often serving it to overnight guests for breakfast.

Cheesy Eggs and Potato Breakfast

Jean Halloran
Green Bay, WI

Makes 12 servings

Prep. Time: 15-20 minutes
Baking Time: 35 minutes

2 tsp. oil
1 medium onion, chopped
7 large eggs, lightly beaten
4 cups shredded hash browns, thawed
2 cups cheddar cheese, shredded and *divided*
1½ cups Swiss cheese
1½ cups cottage cheese
¼ lb. bacon, browned and crumbled, *divided*

1. Put oil in skillet. Stir in onion and cook until softened.
2. In large bowl, combine eggs, hash browns, 1 cup cheddar cheese, and all of Swiss cheese and cottage cheese.
3. Stir in half of bacon and all of sautéed onion.
4. Spoon into well-greased 9 × 13 baking dish.
5. Sprinkle 1 cup cheddar cheese and remaining bacon pieces over top.
6. Bake at 350° for 35 minutes or until knife inserted comes out clean.
7. Allow to stand 10 minutes before cutting into squares and serving.

Tips:
To make a smaller portion, reduce ingredients by half. The baking time will decrease slightly. Do the knife test after baking for 20 minutes. If knife does not come out clean, bake 5 minutes longer. Test again. Continue baking until done.

Brunch Delight

Jean Butzer
Batavia, NY

Makes 12 servings

Prep. Time: 15 minutes
Baking Time: 35-45 minutes

½ cup chopped onion
½ cup chopped green bell pepper
12 eggs
1 cup milk
½ lb. cooked ham, cut into small cubes
16 oz. frozen shredded hash brown potatoes, thawed
4 oz. shredded *or* cubed cheddar cheese
¾ tsp. salt
½ tsp. pepper
½ tsp. dill weed

1. Sauté onion and green pepper in small nonstick skillet. Or cook just until soft in microwave.
2. In large bowl whisk together eggs and milk.
3. Stir in cooked vegetables, ham, potatoes, cheese, salt, pepper, and dill weed.

4. Spoon into well-greased 9 × 13 baking pan.
5. Bake at 350° for 35-45 minutes, or until knife blade inserted in center comes out clean.
6. Allow to stand 10 minutes before cutting into squares to serve.

Variation:
Add ½ cup diced green chilies to Step 3.
Mamie Christopherson
Rio Rancho, NM

Tips:
1. This is a flexible recipe, so vary the ingredients as you wish. For example, you can use ½ lb. cooked bacon or sausage, turkey ham, or no meat.
2. Frozen cubed potatoes work well, too. Or you can make your own from-scratch potatoes, cooking, cooling, and cubing them.
3. When we make this for a breakfast at church, we prepare all the pans the afternoon before, and then cover and refrigerate them until the morning of the event. We remove the pans from the refrigerator and let them stand at room temperature for 30 minutes before baking, or we bake the dish 15-20 minutes longer than called for.

Gold Rush Brunch

Trish Dick
Ladysmith, WI

Makes 12 servings

Prep. Time: 2 hours
Baking Time: 40 minutes

4 large potatoes, peeled or
   unpeeled
half stick (4 Tbsp.) butter,
   divided
2 Tbsp. onion
2 Tbsp. parsley
1 lb. sausage, ham, *or*
   bacon
8 eggs, beaten
1 lb. shredded cheddar
   cheese, *divided*

White Sauce:
   half stick (4 Tbsp.) butter
   ¼ tsp. salt
   1¾ cups milk
   ¼ cup cornstarch
   1 cup sour cream,
      optional

1. Cook potatoes until just
soft. Cool to room temperature.
Then refrigerate until chilled
through.
2. When potatoes are cold,
grate.
3. Melt 2 Tbsp. butter in
large skillet. Stir potatoes and
onion into skillet. Cook until
lightly browned.
4. Spread in well-greased
9 × 13 baking pan.
5. Brown sausage or bacon
or ham in same skillet. Drain
off drippings.
6. Crumble over potato
layer in baking pan.

7. Melt 2 Tbsp. butter in
skillet. Pour eggs into skillet. Cook, stirring up from
the bottom until eggs are
scrambled and just set.
8. Layer eggs over meat.
9. Sprinkle with half of
shredded cheese.
10. Make white sauce by
melting butter in saucepan.
11. Stir in salt, milk, and
cornstarch. Stir continually
with a wooden spoon until
bubbly and thickened.
12. Remove from heat. Stir
in sour cream if you wish.
13. Pour white sauce over
egg layer in pan.
14. Sprinkle with remain-
ing shredded cheese.
15. Bake at 350° for 40
minutes. Insert knife blade
in center. If it comes out
clean, the dish is finished. If
it doesn't, continue baking
another 5 minutes. Test again
with knife blade. Continue
cooking—and testing—as
needed.
16. Allow to stand 10
minutes before cutting and
serving.

*Fair Warning: This is
delicious, but time-consuming!*

To make your own
frozen hash browns,
please turn to page
259.

Hearty Breakfast Casserole

Lucille Amos
Greensboro, NC

Makes 8 servings

Prep. Time: 20 minutes
Baking Time: 40 minutes

1 lb. bulk pork sausage
3 cups frozen shredded
   hash browns
2 cups grated cheddar
   cheese
8 eggs
10¾-oz. can cream of
   mushroom soup
1 cup evaporated milk

1. Crumble sausage in skillet. Cook, stirring frequently,
until no pink remains. Drain
off drippings.
2. Transfer meat to a well-
greased 9 × 13 baking dish.
3. Sprinkle with hash
browns and cheese.
4. In a bowl, whisk eggs,
soup, and milk together.
5. Pour over top of pan
ingredients.
6. Bake at 350° for 40
minutes, or until set and
knife inserted in center comes
out clean.

Tip:
   If you have leftover milk in
the can, measure it, and then
pour it into a small container
with a tight-fitting lid. Mark
the amount on the lid of the
container, and freeze the milk
until you need it.

Brunch Enchiladas

Ann Good
Perry, NY

Makes 10 servings

Prep. Time: 20-35 minutes
Chilling Time: 8-12 hours
Baking Time: 45-60 minutes

¾ cup chopped onion
¾ cup chopped bell peppers
half stick (4 Tbsp.) butter
2 cups chopped cooked ham
2 cups cooked bulk sausage
16-oz. container sour cream

16 eggs
1½ cups milk
2 Tbsp. flour
½ tsp. salt
½ tsp. pepper
16 8" flour tortillas
4 cups shredded cheese,
   divided
16-oz. container sour cream

1. In saucepan, sauté peppers and onion in butter until soft.
2. Stir in meat and cook until heated through.
3. Spread a strip of sour cream through the center of each tortilla.
4. Spoon ⅓ cup meat mixture on top of sour cream on each tortilla.
5. Top with ¼ cup cheese on each tortilla, using a total of 3 cups cheese.
6. Roll up and place seams down in two well-greased 9 × 13 baking pans.
7. In a large mixing bowl, beat together eggs, milk, flour, salt, and pepper.
8. Pour over tortillas. Cover. Refrigerate overnight.
9. Remove from refrigerator for 30 minutes before baking.
10. Bake uncovered at 350° for 45-60 minutes, or until heated through.
11. Remove from oven. Sprinkle with remaining 1 cup cheese.
12. Let stand 5-10 minutes before serving.

Tips:
1. Serve with salsa and sour cream.
2. Top the just-baked enchiladas with thin slices of fresh tomatoes in Step 11 before sprinkling with cheese.
3. This dish freezes well.

Chili Rellenos

Rachel Spicher Hershberger
Sarasota, FL

Makes 10 servings

Prep. Time: 20 minutes
Baking Time: 45 minutes

2 4-oz. cans green chopped
   chilies
1 lb. Monterey Jack, *or*
   Colby, cheese, grated
1 lb. cheddar cheese,
   grated
6 egg whites
6 egg yolks
½ cup evaporated milk
1 Tbsp. flour
1 tsp. salt
2 tomatoes, chopped,
   optional

1. In a large mixing bowl, mix chilies with both cheeses. Place in well-greased 9 × 13 baking dish.
2. In a separate mixing bowl, beat egg whites until stiff. Set aside.
3. In original mixing bowl, beat egg yolks with milk, flour, and salt.
4. Fold egg whites into egg-yolk mixture.
5. Pour over cheese and chilies. Using a spoon, gently push egg mixture down so it settles onto cheese-chili mixture.
6. If you wish, spoon tomatoes evenly over dish.
7. Bake at 325° for 45 minutes, or until knife blade inserted in center comes out clean. If it doesn't, continue baking 5 more minutes. Test again. Repeat until finished baking.

Brunch Pizza

Rachel King
Castile, NY

Makes 8 servings

Prep. Time: 1 hour
Baking Time: 15-18 minutes

8-oz. pkg. crescent rolls
½ lb. bacon, chopped
½ lb. bulk pork sausage
½ lb. fresh mushrooms, sliced
1 small onion, finely chopped
1 small green bell pepper, finely chopped
1 Tbsp. butter
8 eggs, slightly beaten
3-oz. pkg. cream cheese, softened to room temperature
⅓ cup low-fat sour cream
1 garlic clove, minced
¼ tsp. Italian seasoning
2 plum tomatoes, sliced thin
1½ cups shredded cheese of your choice
salsa and additional sour cream, *optional*

1. Open crescent dough tube and unroll. Press crescent dough over bottom and partway up sides of 9 × 13 baking pan.
2. Bake at 375° for 6-8 minutes.
3. Meanwhile, cook bacon in large skillet until crispy. Remove bacon (reserve drippings in pan) and allow to drain on a paper towel.
4. Brown sausage in same skillet. Remove sausage and set aside.
5. Pour off all but 2 Tbsp. drippings. Sauté mushrooms, onions, and peppers in drippings until just tender.
6. Remove vegetables from pan and set aside.
7. Melt butter in skillet. Add eggs and cook, stirring until almost set.
8. In a mixing bowl, beat together cream cheese, sour cream, garlic, and Italian seasoning. Spread over crescent-dough crust in baking pan.
9. Top with eggs, and then meat, and then sautéed vegetables.
10. Top with tomato slices and then cheese.
11. Bake at 375° for 15-18 minutes, or until cheese is melted.
12. Serve with salsa and additional sour cream for each person to add as they wish.

Country Breakfast Pizza

Zoë Rohrer
Lancaster, PA

Makes 8-10 servings

Prep. Time: 25-30 minutes
Baking Time: 27 minutes

2 Tbsp. butter
1 cup whole wheat pastry flour
⅔ cup, plus 2 Tbsp., all-purpose flour
1 Tbsp. flax meal, *optional*
2 tsp. baking powder
½ tsp. salt
¼ cup real maple syrup
scant ½ cup milk

half a green pepper, diced
⅔ lb. bulk pork sausage
9 large eggs
1⅓ cups grated cheddar cheese, *divided*

maple syrup, *or* ketchup, for serving

1. Place butter in a 9 × 13 baking dish. Place dish in oven set at 425°. Keep an eye on butter, and when it's melted (about 5 minutes), take dish out of oven.
2. Meanwhile, in a good-sized bowl, mix together

Experiment with a recipe. If you and others like it, make it your "signature recipe."
Mary S. Kauffman, Harrisonburg, VA

flours, flax if you wish, baking powder, and salt.

3. Add maple syrup and milk. Stir to combine.

4. Knead a few minutes in bowl, or on countertop, to make a ball.

5. Press dough into buttered baking dish.

6. Bake 12 minutes at 425°. Remove from the oven.

7. While crust is baking, brown sausage and peppers in skillet until pink is gone from meat and peppers are just tender. Stir frequently to break up meat. Place cooked meat and peppers on platter (reserve drippings in skillet) and keep warm.

8. Beat eggs in mixing bowl. Pour into drippings in skillet. Stir frequently.

9. Add ⅔ cup cheese while eggs are cooking.

10. When crust is done, top with sausage, then eggs, and then remaining cheese.

11. Bake 10 more minutes or until cheese is melted.

12. Serve immediately with maple syrup or ketchup.

Sausage and Eggs Baked in Mugs

Peggy C. Forsythe
Memphis, TN

Makes 10 servings

Prep. Time: 30 minutes
Baking Time: 25-30 minutes for mugs & ramekins; 1 hour for 9 × 13 baking dish

12 oz. sourdough bread, sliced and cut into ½" cubes
12-oz. pkg. pork sausage patties, *or* ¾ lb. bulk pork sausage
2½ cups milk
4 large eggs
1 Tbsp. Dijon mustard
½ cup buttermilk
10¾-oz. can cream of mushroom soup
1 cup shredded sharp cheddar cheese

1. Spray insides of 10 oven-proof coffee mugs with non-stick cooking spray.

2. Divide bread cubes evenly among mugs.

3. Brown sausage patties on both sides in large skillet. Cut into small pieces. Or brown bulk sausage in skillet, breaking up with wooden spoon and stirring until all pink is gone. Drain off drippings.

4. Top bread cubes in each mug with crumbled sausage.

5. In a mixing bowl, whisk together milk, eggs, and Dijon mustard. Pour evenly over bread and sausage.

6. In same bowl, whisk together buttermilk and cream of mushroom soup. Spoon over bread mixture.

7. Sprinkle each mug with cheddar cheese.

8. Place coffee mugs on baking sheet.

9. Bake at 350° for 25-30 minutes, or until individual casseroles are set and puffed. Serve immediately.

Tips:

1. You can prepare the mugs through Step 7 in advance of serving. Cover mugs with plastic wrap and then foil. Freeze up to one month. When ready to use, thaw overnight in refrigerator. Bake as directed.

2. You may omit the mugs and use ramekins. Or use a 9 × 13 baking dish instead, and then increase baking time to 1 hour, or until casserole is set. Insert a knife blade in center of baking dish. If blade comes out clean, the dish is done. If it doesn't, continue baking another 5 minutes. Test again. Repeat if needed.

3. To make the dish spicier, add Tabasco to milk/egg/mustard mixture in Step 5. Or use hot sausage.

4. If you don't have buttermilk, make your own substitute. Mix 1 Tbsp. white vinegar and ⅞ cup milk. Let sit 15 minutes; do not stir.

To make your own cream of mushroom or celery soup, please turn to pages 258-259.

Bacon Cheese Squares

Katie Ebersol
Ronks, PA

Makes 12 servings

Prep. Time: 30 minutes
Baking Time: 18-20 minutes

2 cups buttermilk baking mix
½ cup cold water
8 oz. cheese, sliced
1 lb. bacon, sliced, cooked crisp, and crumbled
6 eggs
½ cup milk
½ tsp. onion powder

1. In a bowl, combine the baking mix and water. Stir 20 strokes.
2. Turn onto a floured surface. Knead 10 times.
3. Roll into a 10 × 14 rectangle. Place on the bottom and half-way up the sides of a greased 9 × 13 baking dish.
4. Lay cheese evenly over dough. Sprinkle with bacon.
5. In the mixing bowl, beat together eggs, milk, and onion powder.
6. Pour egg-milk mixture over bacon.
7. Bake at 425° for 18-20 minutes, or until a knife blade inserted in center comes out clean. If it doesn't, continue baking another 4 minutes. Test again. Continue baking if needed, or remove from oven.
8. Allow to stand 10 minutes before cutting into squares and serving.

Variation:
Reduce the richness of the dish by reducing the bacon to ½ lb. You can also use turkey bacon (½ lb. or more), browning it in a skillet or under the broiler until crisp.

Breakfast Bake

Judy Buller
Bluffton, OH

Makes 12 servings

Prep. Time: 30-35 minutes
Chilling Time: 24 hours
Baking Time: 1¼ hours

7 cups cubed bread, mixture of French and whole-grain
3 cups finely diced ham
3 cups shredded Colby Jack cheese
3 heaping Tbsp. flour
1 tsp. dry mustard
3½ cups milk
7 large eggs
3 Tbsp. melted butter

1. In a large mixing bowl, toss bread, ham, and cheese together.
2. Spoon into a deep, well-greased 9 × 13 baking dish.
3. In the same bowl, combine flour, mustard, milk, and eggs. Mix well.
4. Drizzle melted butter over bread/ham/cheese mixture.
5. Pour milk mixture over everything.
6. Cover and refrigerate 24 hours.
7. Bake at 350° for 1¼ hours.

Tip:
This is good for a breakfast potluck. It's especially convenient that you can mix it up the day before.

Baked French Toast with Cream Cheese

Blanche Nyce
Hatfield, PA

Makes 6-8 servings

Prep. Time: 15-20 minutes
Soaking Time: 8 hours, or overnight
Baking Time: 40-45 minutes

1-lb. loaf firm bread, *divided*
8-oz. pkg. cream cheese
10 eggs
½ cup half-and-half
¼ cup maple syrup, *or* pancake syrup
1 stick (½ cup) butter, melted
2 cup berries of your choice—strawberries, blueberries, *or* raspberries

1. Cube bread and layer half in well-greased 9 × 13 baking pan.
2. Cut cream cheese into small pieces and scatter across bread.
3. Sprinkle with berries.
4. Cover berries with remaining half of bread.

5. In mixing bowl, beat together eggs, half-and-half, syrup, and melted butter.

6. Pour over bread contents of baking pan.

7. Press down until bread is submerged as much as possible.

8. Cover and refrigerate for 8 hours, or overnight.

9. Bake uncovered at 375° for 40-45 minutes, or until lightly browned and puffy.

Tip:

Day-old bread works best for this toast.

Blueberry French Toast

Stacie Skelly
Millersville, PA

Makes 12 servings

Prep. Time: 30 minutes
Chilling Time: 6-12 hours
Baking Time: 1 hour

12-15 slices day-old bread
8-oz. pkg. cream cheese
1 cup frozen blueberries
12 eggs
2 cups milk
⅓ cup honey

Sauce:
1 cup sugar
2 Tbsp. cornstarch
1 cup water
1 cup blueberries

1. Grease 9 × 13 baking pan.

2. Cube bread and spread in pan.

3. Cube cream cheese. Distribute evenly over bread.

4. Sprinkle blueberries on top.

5. In a mixing bowl, blend eggs, milk, and honey.

6. Pour over baking-pan contents.

7. Cover. Refrigerate 6-8 hours, or overnight.

8. Remove from refrigerator 30 minutes before baking.

9. Bake, covered, at 350° for 30 minutes.

10. Uncover. Bake 30 more minutes. Serve with sauce.

To make sauce:

1. Mix sugar, cornstarch, and water in a saucepan. Bring to a boil.

2. Stir in blueberries.

3. Reduce heat, cooking until blueberries burst.

4. Serve warm over French Toast.

Every summer 5 good friends and I have "Breakfast Club" each Wednesday morning. When it's my turn to host, this is always at the top of the request list.

Fast, Friendly French Toast

Donna Barnitz
Rio Rancho, NM

Makes 4 servings

Prep. Time: 15 minutes
Soaking Time: 1-24 hours
Baking Time: 15 minutes

1 loaf French bread, cut 1" thick slices
1½ cups milk
4 eggs
½ cup orange juice
¼ cup sugar
1 Tbsp. vanilla
cinnamon, *optional*
confectioners sugar

1. Arrange bread slices in a 9 × 13 baking pan.

2. In a mixing bowl, beat milk, eggs, orange juice, sugar, and vanilla together until well blended.

3. Pour over bread.

4. Cover and refrigerate 1-24 hours, according to your schedule.

5. Transfer bread to greased 10 × 15 pan, making sure slices don't touch. Dust with cinnamon, if you wish.

6. Bake 15 minutes at 400°, or until puffy and lightly browned.

7. Dust with confectioners sugar just before serving.

Baked French Toast with Pecans

Judith Houser
Hershey, PA

Makes 8-10 servings

Prep. Time: 15 minutes
Soaking Time: 8 hours, or
*   overnight*
Baking Time: 40 minutes

16-oz. loaf French bread
8 large eggs
3 cups milk
2 Tbsp. sugar
1 tsp. vanilla
¼ tsp. cinnamon
¼ tsp. nutmeg
¼ tsp. salt

Topping:
    1 cup chopped pecans
    1 stick (½ cup) butter,
        softened
    2 Tbsp. light corn syrup
    ½ tsp. cinnamon
    ½ tsp. nutmeg
    1 cup brown sugar

1. Slice bread in 20 slices and arrange in two rows in greased 9 × 13 baking dish, overlapping slices.
2. In a good-sized mixing bowl, combine eggs, milk, sugar, vanilla, cinnamon, nutmeg, and salt.
3. Pour over bread.
4. Cover and refrigerate overnight.
5. In the morning, prepare topping. In a good-sized mixing bowl, combine pecans, butter, corn syrup, cinnamon, nutmeg, and brown sugar. Crumble over top of bread.
6. Bake uncovered at 350° for 40 minutes, or until puffy and browned.

Variations:
    Use 20 slices cinnamon swirl bread instead of French bread.
Deb Martin
Gap, PA

Since we're not fond of cinnamon, I substitute 1 tsp. dried orange peel in the soaking mixture for the bread slices, and 1 tsp. dried orange peel in the topping.
Jeanette Oberholtzer
Lititz, PA

Overnight Apple French Toast

Eileen Eash
Lafayette, CO
Peggy C. Forsythe
Memphis, TN

Makes 9 servings

Prep. Time: 40-45 minutes
Soaking Time: 8 hours, or
*   overnight*
Baking Time: 35-40 minutes

¾ cup packed brown sugar
¾ stick (6 Tbsp.) butter
3-4 large tart apples, peeled
    and sliced ¼" thick
3 eggs
1 cup milk
1 tsp. vanilla
9 slices day old French
    bread, ¾" thick

Syrup:
    ½ cup applesauce
    ¼ tsp. cinnamon
    5-oz. jar apple *or*
        crabapple jelly
    pinch of ground cloves
    sprinkle of nutmeg,
        optional

maple syrup for serving,
    optional
whipped cream, *optional*

1. In a small saucepan, melt sugar and butter together about 3-4 minutes, stirring constantly, until slightly thick.
2. Pour into ungreased 9 × 13 baking pan.
3. Top with apple slices.
4. In a medium-sized mixing bowl, beat together eggs, milk, and vanilla.
5. Dip bread slices in egg mixture, one by one, and then lay over top of apples.
6. Cover and refrigerate overnight.
7. Remove from refrigerator 30 minutes before baking. Sprinkle with nutmeg if you wish.
8. Bake uncovered at 350° for 35-40 minutes.
9. Meanwhile, prepare syrup by cooking applesauce, cinnamon, apple jelly, and ground cloves in small saucepan until hot.
10. Serve over toast.
11. Offer maple syrup and whipped cream as toppings, too.

Waffles with Cinnamon Apple Syrup

Betty L. Moore
Plano, IL

Makes 12 5" waffles and 1¾ cups syrup

Prep. Time: 15 minutes
Cooking Time: about 3 minutes per waffle

Waffles:
2 cups flour
2 Tbsp. sugar
3 tsp. baking powder
½ tsp. salt
2 eggs
1½ cups milk
4 Tbsp. oil

Cinnamon Apple Syrup:
2 Tbsp. cornstarch
½ tsp. cinnamon
⅛ tsp. salt
1 cup water
¾ cup unsweetened apple juice concentrate
½ tsp. vanilla

1. To make waffles, mix flour, sugar, baking powder, and salt together in large bowl.

2. In a separate bowl, beat eggs, milk, and oil together.

3. Add wet ingredients to dry ingredients. Beat just until mixed.

4. Pour scant ½ cup batter onto hot waffle iron. Cook according to your waffle iron's instructions.

5. To make syrup, combine cornstarch, cinnamon, and salt in saucepan.

6. Gradually stir in water and apple juice concentrate until smooth.

7. Over medium heat, and stirring continually, bring to boil.

8. Cook, stirring continually, for 2 minutes, or until thickened.

9. Remove from heat. Stir in vanilla.

10. Serve warm over waffles.

Tips:

1. You can refrigerate any leftover syrup, covered, until the next time you make waffles.

2. We have friends over quite frequently for waffles for breakfast. I serve them with sausage, strawberries, assorted syrups, and orange juice. This recipe works in both my regular waffle iron and my Belgian waffle-maker. We sometimes have waffles for supper if we have leftover batter.

Oatmeal Pancakes

Barbara J. Bey
Hillsboro, OH

Makes 6 pancakes

Prep. Time: 5 minutes
Cooking Time: 10 minutes

½ cup flour
½ cup dry oats, rolled *or* quick-cooking
1 Tbsp. sugar, *or* Splenda
1 tsp. baking powder
½ tsp. baking soda
¾ cup buttermilk
¼ cup milk
2 Tbsp. vegetable oil
1 egg, beaten

1. Stir together flour, oats, sugar, baking powder, and baking soda in a large mixing bowl.

2. In a separate bowl, blend buttermilk, milk, oil, and egg until smooth.

3. Stir wet ingredients into dry ingredients, just until moistened.

4. Drop by scant half-cupfuls into skillet or onto griddle.

5. Cook until small bubbles form on top.

6. Flip and cook until lightly browned.

Baked Oatmeal

Esther Porter
Minneapolis, MN

Makes 12 servings

Prep. Time: 10 minutes
Cooking/Baking Time: 20-25 minutes

¾ cup brown sugar
1 stick (½ cup) margarine, melted
2 eggs, slightly beaten
3 cups quick oats
2 tsp. baking powder
1 cup milk
1 tsp. salt
½ cup raisins *or* dried cranberries

1. Combine brown sugar, margarine, and eggs.
2. Mix and add oatmeal, baking powder, milk, and salt.
3. Stir in raisins or cranberries.
4. Pour into 9 × 13 baking pan.
5. Bake at 350° for 20-25 minutes.

Tips:
Serve with hot milk, cinnamon, baked apple slices, etc. You may cut leftover baked oatmeal in pieces to freeze and microwave for later. Great for brunch.

B&B Blueberry Coffee Cake

Kim Rapp
Longmont, CO

Makes 18 servings

Prep. Time: 15-20 minutes
Baking Time: 55-65 minutes

4 cups flour
1½ cups sugar
5 tsp. baking powder
1 tsp. salt
1 stick (½ cup) butter
1½ cups milk
2 eggs
4 cups fresh, *or* frozen, blueberries

Topping:
¼ cup sugar
⅔ cup flour
1 tsp. cinnamon
½ tsp. nutmeg
1 stick (½ cup) butter, softened

1. In mixing bowl, mix together flour, sugar, baking powder, salt, butter, milk, and eggs. Using mixer, beat vigorously for 30 seconds.
2. If using frozen blueberries, place in large bowl and stir in 3 Tbsp. flour until each blueberry is well coated. (If using fresh berries, no need to add flour.)
3. Carefully fold blueberries into batter.
4. Pour into greased 9 × 13 baking pan.
5. For topping, combine sugar, flour, cinnamon, and nutmeg in a bowl.

6. Using a pastry cutter, or two knives, cut in butter until small crumbs form.
7. Sprinkle crumbs evenly over batter.
8. Bake 55-65 minutes, or until toothpick inserted in center of cake comes out clean.

Overnight Sour Cream Coffee Cake

Debra Herr
Mountaintop, PA
Frances Schrag
Newton, KS

Makes 15 servings

Prep. Time: 20-30 minutes
Chilling Time: 8 hours or overnight
Baking Time: 35-45 minutes

1½ sticks (¾ cup) butter, softened
1 cup sugar
2 eggs
8 oz. sour cream, *or* 1 cup buttermilk
2 cups flour
1 tsp. baking powder
1 tsp. baking soda
½ tsp. salt
¼-1 tsp. nutmeg, according to your taste preference
¾ cup brown sugar, packed
1 tsp. cinnamon
½ cup chopped pecans, *or* walnuts

1. Cream butter and sugar

together with mixer until light and fluffy.

2. Add eggs and sour cream until well mixed.

3. In a separate bowl, combine flour, baking powder, baking soda, salt, and nutmeg.

4. Add to batter and mix well.

5. Pour into greased and floured 9 × 13 baking pan.

6. In a separate bowl, mix brown sugar, cinnamon, and pecans together.

7. Sprinkle evenly over batter.

8. Cover and refrigerate overnight.

9. Uncover and bake at 350° for 35-45 minutes, or until toothpick inserted in center comes out clean.

Variation:
Add 1 cup chocolate chips to the brown sugar, cinnamon, and nuts topping in Step 6, if you wish.

Deb Kepiro
Strasburg, PA

Tip:
I make this for our church breakfasts and either bake it while I'm getting ready for church, or bake it at church.

Debra Herr
Mountaintop, PA

Finnish Coffee Cake

Sharon Shank
Bridgewater, VA
Martha Ann Auker
Landisburg, PA

Makes 24 servings
Prep. Time: 10-20 minutes
Baking Time: 30-35 minutes

1¼ cups sugar
1 cup oil
2 eggs, beaten
1 cup buttermilk
1 tsp. vanilla
2 cups flour
¾ tsp. baking powder
½ tsp. salt
½ tsp. baking soda
4 Tbsp. brown sugar
1-3 tsp. cinnamon, according to your taste preference

Glaze:
2 cups confectioners sugar
1-2 tsp. vanilla, according to your taste preference
1-2 Tbsp. hot water, or a bit more

1. In good-sized mixing bowl, beat together sugar, oil, eggs, buttermilk, and 1 tsp. vanilla.

2. In a separate bowl, sift together flour, baking powder, salt, and baking soda.

3. Stir dry ingredients into buttermilk mixture.

4. Pour half of batter into greased 9 × 13 baking dish.

5. Mix together brown sugar and cinnamon in bowl. Sprinkle half of mixture over batter.

6. Repeat layers.

7. Bake at 350° for 30-35 minutes, or until toothpick inserted in center comes out clean.

8. Poke holes in cake with fork while cake is still warm.

9. In a medium-sized bowl, mix together confectioners sugar, vanilla, and just enough water to make a thin glaze.

10. Drizzle glaze over warm cake.

Variation:
Add ¾ cup chopped walnuts to brown sugar-cinnamon mixture in Step 5.

Carrie Darby
Moreno Valley, CA

Try a recipe first the way it is written. After that, experiment with changes to suit your taste.
Jenny R. Unternahrer, Wayland, IA

Crispy Cookie Coffee Cake

Eileen Eash
Lafayette, CO

Makes 20 servings

Prep. Time: 45 minutes
Chilling Time: 8 hours or
overnight
Baking Time: 12-15 minutes

1 Tbsp. active dry yeast
¼ cup warm water
4 cups flour
1 tsp. salt
¼ cup sugar
2 sticks (1 cup) butter
2 eggs, beaten
1 cup lukewarm milk
1 cup sugar
1-2 Tbsp. cinnamon,
  according to your taste
  preference

1. In a small bowl, dissolve yeast in water.
2. In a good-sized mixing bowl, combine flour, salt, and ¼ cup sugar.
3. Cut in butter with pastry cutter or two knives until mixture resembles small peas.
4. In another bowl, combine eggs, milk, and yeast water.
5. Add wet ingredients to flour mixture. Combine lightly.
6. Cover tightly. Refrigerate overnight.
7. In a small bowl, mix 1 cup sugar and cinnamon. Set aside.
8. Divide chilled dough in half. Roll each half on floured board into 12 × 18 rectangle.
9. Sprinkle each with half of sugar/cinnamon mixture.
10. Roll each up tightly, beginning with the long side.
11. Cut each into 1"-thick slices.
12. Place slices cut-side up on greased baking sheet. Flatten each slice with palm of hand.
13. Bake at 400° for about 12 minutes.

Fruit Swirl Coffee Cake

Jenny R. Unternahrer
Wayland, IA
Sheila Ann Plock
Boalsburg, PA

Makes 20-32 servings

Prep. Time: 15-25 minutes
Baking Time: 35-45 minutes

1½ cups sugar
1 stick (½ cup) butter,
  softened
½ cup shortening
1½ tsp. baking powder
1½ tsp. vanilla, *or* 1 tsp.
  vanilla and ½ tsp.
  almond extract
4 eggs
3 cups flour
1, *or* 2, 21-oz. can(s) fruit
  pie filling, your choice of
  flavor
1 cup confectioners sugar
1-2 Tbsp. milk

1. Place sugar, butter, shortening, baking powder, vanilla, and eggs in an electric-mixer bowl. Beat on Low until blended, and then 3 minutes on High.
2. Stir in flour just until blended.
3. Spread ⅔ of batter in greased 10 × 15 jelly-roll pan.
4. Spoon pie filling over batter. (Use 1 or 2 cans, depending upon how fruity you'd like the finished cake to be.) Spread as evenly as you can without disturbing batter layer.
5. Drop remaining batter by tablespoons over top of filling, as evenly as you can.
6. Bake at 350° for 35-45 minutes, or until light brown and toothpick inserted in center of cake comes out clean.
7. Mix confectioners sugar and milk in small bowl until smooth.
8. Drizzle over coffee cake while still warm.

Easy Coffee Cake

Eleanor Larson
Glen Lyon, PA

Makes 20-24 servings

Prep. Time: 5-10 minutes
Baking Time: 40 minutes

18-oz. box yellow cake mix
1 cup vegetable oil
4 eggs
1 cup sour cream
¾ cup sugar
1½ tsp. cinnamon
1¾ cups chopped walnuts,
    or pecans

1. Combine cake mix oil, eggs, and sour cream in large electric-mixer bowl. Beat 2 minutes on Low.
2. In separate bowl, mix together sugar, cinnamon, and walnuts.
3. Spread half batter in well-greased 9 × 13 baking pan.
4. Sprinkle half of nut mixture over top.
5. Spoon remaining batter on top of nut mixture.
6. Sprinkle evenly with remaining nut mixture.
7. Bake at 350° for 40 minutes, or until a wooden toothpick inserted in center comes out clean.

Tip:
   If you like a back-up dessert on hand, or you need to make a cake in advance of serving it, you can prepare this cake whenever it suits you and freeze it until you need it.

FINGER
FOOD

Morning Maple Muffins

Connie Lynn Miller
Shipshewana, IN

Makes 15-18 muffins

Prep. Time: 15 minutes
Baking Time: 15-20 minutes

Muffins:
   2 cups flour
   ½ cup brown sugar, packed
   2 tsp. baking powder
   ½ tsp. salt
   ¾ cup milk
   1 stick (½ cup) butter, melted
   ½ cup maple syrup
   ¼ cup sour cream
   1 egg
   ½ tsp. vanilla

Topping:
   3 Tbsp. flour
   3 Tbsp. sugar
   2 Tbsp. chopped pecans
   ½ tsp. cinnamon
   2 Tbsp. cold butter

1. To make muffins, combine flour, brown sugar, baking powder, and salt in a large bowl.
2. In another bowl, combine milk, butter, maple syrup, sour cream, egg, and vanilla.
3. Stir wet ingredients into dry ingredients just until moistened.
4. Fill greased or paper-lined muffin cups ⅔ full.
5. For topping, combine flour, sugar, nuts, and cinnamon.
6. Cut in butter, using a pastry cutter or two knives, until crumbly.
7. Sprinkle over batter in muffin cups.
8. Bake at 400° for 15-20 minutes, or until a toothpick inserted near the center comes out clean.
9. Cool 5 minutes before removing from pans to wire racks. Serve warm.

The maple syrup gives these muffins the hint of a hearty pancake breakfast.

Cranberry Buttermilk Scones

Edwina Stoltzfus
Narvon, PA

Makes 12-16 servings

Prep. Time: 20 minutes
Baking Time: 15-20 minutes

3 cups flour
⅓ cup plus 2 Tbsp. sugar,
    divided
2½ tsp. baking powder
¾ tsp. salt
½ tsp. baking soda
1½ sticks (¾ cup) cold
    butter
1 cup buttermilk
1 cup dried cranberries
1 tsp. grated orange peel
1 Tbsp. milk
¼ tsp. ground cinnamon

1. In a bowl, combine flour, ⅓ cup sugar, baking powder, salt, and baking soda.
2. Cut in butter, using a pastry cutter or two knives, until mixture resembles small peas.
3. Stir in buttermilk, just until combined.
4. Fold in cranberries and orange peel.
5. Turn dough onto floured surface. Divide dough in half.
6. Shape each portion into a ball. Pat each into a 6" circle.
7. Cut each circle into 6-8 wedges. Place on lightly greased baking sheet.
8. Brush tops with milk.
9. In a small bowl, combine 2 Tbsp. sugar with cinnamon.

Sprinkle on top of wedges.
10. Bake at 400° for 15-20 minutes, or until golden brown. Serve warm.

Tips:
1. These freeze well after baking.
2. I make my own orange peel by grating the peel of 1 whole orange and then freezing it. It's handy for whenever I need it.

Spiced Apple Twists

Janessa Hochstedler
East Earl, PA

Makes 16 pieces

Prep. Time: 10-20 minutes
Baking Time: 30-35 minutes

¼ cup orange juice, *or*
    water
8-oz. tube crescent rolls
2 large tart, firm apples,
    peeled and cored
2 Tbsp. butter, melted
½ tsp. cinnamon
¼ cup sugar

1. Pour juice into bottom of greased 9 × 9 baking dish.
2. Unroll crescent dough. Separate into 8 triangles. Cut each in half to make 16 triangles.
3. Cut each apple into 8 slices.
4. Place an apple slice at wide end of each triangle.

Roll up.
5. Arrange filled pastries in pan.
6. Drizzle butter over tops.
7. In a small bowl, mix cinnamon and sugar together.
8. Sprinkle cinnamon-sugar mixture over pastries.
9. Bake at 400° for 30-35 minutes.

Variations:
1. If you wish, sprinkle a few raisins or currants over each apple slice before rolling up in Step 4.
2. If you wish, use a sprinkling of nutmeg and/or allspice with cinnamon in Step 7.

Glazed Cinnamon Biscuits

Virginia Graybill
Hershey, PA

Makes 12 servings

Prep. Time: 30 minutes
Baking Time: 18-20 minutes

2 cups flour
4 tsp. baking powder
½ tsp. salt
¼ cup sugar
1 tsp. cinnamon
¾ stick (6 Tbsp.) butter, divided
¾ cup milk

Glaze:
1 cup confectioners sugar
1 Tbsp. butter, melted
¼ tsp. vanilla

1. In a large bowl, combine flour, baking powder, salt, sugar, and cinnamon.
2. Using a pastry cutter or two knives, cut in 4 Tbsp. butter until mixture resembles coarse crumbs.
3. Stir in milk just until moistened.
4. Turn onto a lightly floured surface. Rub a bit of vegetable oil on your hands to keep dough from sticking to your fingers while kneading.
5. Knead gently 8-10 times.
6. Roll dough into an 8 × 11 rectangle, ½" thick.
7. Melt remaining 2 Tbsp. butter and brush 1 Tbsp. over dough.
8. Roll up jelly-roll style, starting with long end.

9. Cut roll into 12 equal slices.
10. Place slices cut-side down in greased 7 × 11 baking pan. Make 3 rows with 4 slices in each row.
11. Brush slices with remaining butter.
12. Bake at 375° for 18-20 minutes, or until golden brown.
13. While biscuits bake, mix glaze ingredients together in a small bowl until smooth.
14. When biscuits finish baking, allow them to cool 5 minutes.
15. Spread with glaze. Serve immediately.

Sticky Buns

Dorothy Schrock
Arthur, IL

Makes 12-15 buns

Prep. Time: 35 minutes
Rising Time: 30 minutes
Baking Time: 15 minutes

Dough:
½ cup warm water
1 Tbsp. yeast
¾ cup milk
half stick (4 Tbsp.) butter
1 tsp. salt
¼ cup sugar
1 egg, beaten
3 cups flour

Sauce:
1 stick (½ cup) butter
1 tsp. cinnamon
1 cup brown sugar

1 Tbsp. water
⅓ cup pecans

1. In a small bowl, stir yeast into warm water until dissolved. Set aside.
2. Heat milk and butter in medium-sized saucepan over low heat until butter melts. Remove pan from heat.
3. Stir salt and sugar into milk mixture until dissolved.
4. Stir yeast water, egg, and flour into other ingredients.
5. Cover and set in warm place and let rise for 30 minutes.
6. Meanwhile, prepare sauce. In a medium-sized saucepan, heat butter, cinnamon, brown sugar, and water together. Make good and hot, but do not allow to boil. If it does, it will harden.
7. Stir in pecans.
8. Pour sauce into well-greased 9 × 13 baking pan. Spread over bottom of pan.
9. Stir down batter. Drop by tablespoons over sauce. You should be able to make 12-15 batter "buns."
10. Bake at 350° for 15 minutes.
11. Cool for 1 minute.
12. Cover baking pan with cookie sheet. Turn upside down carefully to release sticky buns onto cookie sheet.

FINGER
FOOD

Cinnamon Rolls—
Easy Method

Betty L. Moore
Plano, IL

Makes 10 rolls

Thawing Time: 8 hours or
  overnight
Prep. Time: 15-20 minutes
Rising Time: 4-5 hours, or
  overnight
Baking Time: 20-25 minutes

1 loaf frozen bread dough
1 stick (½ cup) butter,
  melted
2 tsp. cinnamon
½ cup sugar
1 cup confectioners sugar
1½ Tbsp. milk

1. Thaw dough at room
temperature.
2. In a long, flat dish, mix
together cinnamon and sugar.
3. Cut thawed bread dough
diagonally into 10 pieces.
4. Roll each piece of dough
between your hands until it
forms a rope.
5. Brush each piece of
dough with melted butter, and
then dip in cinnamon-sugar.
Use a spoon to cover rope
well with mixture.
6. Tie each buttered-
sugared piece in a loose knot.
Lay in greased 9 × 13 baking
pan, keeping as much space
as possible between knots to
allow for rising.
7. Cover loosely and let set
until knots double in size, or
refrigerate overnight.
8. Set out in morning and

allow to rise until doubled, if
knots haven't risen fully.
9. Bake at 350° for 20-25
minutes.
10. Meanwhile, prepare
glaze by mixing confectioners
sugar and milk together in a
bowl until smooth.
11. Drizzle glaze over
cooled buns.

These are messy to make, but
they taste wonderful. We make
these at camp to serve 300-400
people.

FINGER
FOOD

Cinnamon Rolls—
from Scratch

Sarah Miller
Harrisonburg, VA

Makes 24 servings

Prep. Time: 35-40 minutes
Rising Time: 30 minutes
Baking Time: 20 minutes

2 medium potatoes, peeled
2 cups water
2 pkgs. yeast
1 Tbsp. sugar
1 cup warm water
¾ cup sugar
1 stick (½ cup), plus 3 Tbsp.
  butter, softened
3 tsp. salt
2 eggs
9-10 cups flour, *divided*
half stick (4 Tbsp.) butter,
  melted
1¾ cups brown sugar
1 Tbsp. cinnamon

1. Cook potatoes in 2 cups
water until very soft. Drain
off cooking water and reserve.
(You'll need 2 cups cooking
water, so add water if needed
to make 2 cups.)
2. While potatoes are
cooking, dissolve yeast and
1 Tbsp. sugar in 1 cup warm
water in small bowl. Set
aside.
3. Mash potatoes.
4. In large bowl, mix
together ¾ cup sugar, 1 cup
plus 3 Tbsp. butter, salt, eggs,
mashed potatoes, and reserved
2 cups cooking water.
5. Stir in 2 cups flour.
6. Stir in yeast-sugar-water
mixture. Mix thoroughly.
7. Gradually stir in remaining flour, mixing well after
each addition. Knead in flour
when dough becomes too stiff
to stir.
8. When no longer sticky,
place dough in large greased
bowl. Cover. Set aside in
warm place and allow to rise
until doubled.
9. Turn out dough onto
lightly floured surface. Roll
out into rectangular shape
with a rolling pin, about ½"
thick.
10. Spread dough with 4
Tbsp. melted butter.
11. Crumble brown sugar
over top. Sprinkle with
cinnamon.
12. Roll up jelly-roll style,
beginning with one long side.
13. Cut roll into 24 slices.
14. Lay slices cut-side up in
2 greased cake pans.
15. Bake at 375° for 20
minutes, or until lightly
browned.

Breads

FINGER
FOOD

Oatmeal Herb Bread

Stacy Stoltzfus
Grantham, PA

Makes 1 loaf

Prep. Time: 20 minutes
Rising Time: 65-85 minutes
Cooking/Baking Time: 30-35 minutes
Standing Time: 30-45 minutes

1 cup warm water (110-115°)
2 Tbsp. brown sugar
1 Tbsp. yeast
1 egg, lightly beaten
3 Tbsp. olive oil
1 tsp. salt
½ cup quick oats
1 tsp. dried parsley
1 tsp. dried sage
1 tsp. dried oregano
1 tsp. dried basil
1 tsp. dried thyme
3½-4 cups *bread* flour

1. Dissolve sugar in warm water in a large mixing bowl.

2. Sprinkle yeast over top.

3. Let stand 5-10 minutes until yeast begins to foam.

4. Stir in egg, olive oil, salt, oats, and herbs.

5. Gradually add in flour, one cup at a time, mixing until a ball forms that is not too dense. Dough should be soft but not sticky.

6. Knead about 5 minutes on floured surface.

7. Grease a large bowl. Place dough in bowl and cover with a tea towel.

8. Place in warm spot. Let rise until doubled, about 30-45 minutes.

9. Punch down. Form into a loaf.

10. Place in greased loaf pan. Let rise until dough comes to top of pan, about 35-40 minutes.

11. Bake approximately 30-35 minutes at 350°. Loaf should be golden brown and should sound hollow when tapped.

12. Cool 10 minutes before removing from pan.

13. Let cool until lukewarm before slicing to keep moisture in the loaf. Slice the loaf just before serving.

Tips:

1. I always use an instant-read thermometer to ensure the bread is completely baked through. It should register 190-200 when done.

2. This is my favorite herb blend; feel free to substitute other herbs. This bread also makes wonderful croutons!

3. You can use dried herbs instead of fresh herbs. The formula? 1 tsp. dried herbs for 3 tsp. fresh herbs.

FINGER FOOD

French Bread– No knead

Naomi Ressler
Harrisonburg, VA

Makes 2 loaves

Prep. Time: 1½ hours
Baking Time: 20 minutes

2 Tbsp. shortening
2 Tbsp. sugar
2 tsp. salt
1 cup boiling water
1 cup cold water
2¼-oz. pkgs. yeast
1 scant Tbsp. sugar
½ cup warm water
6 cups flour

1. Dissolve shortening, sugar and salt in boiling water.
2. Add cold water to shortening mixture.
3. Dissolve yeast and sugar in warm water. Add to the shortening mixture.
4. Add flour. Do *not* beat. Stir with big spoon every 10 minutes, 4 or 5 times, for approximately an hour.
5. Divide dough in half. Flour dough board or counter and hands and pat each section into rectangle shape about ½" thick.
6. Roll lengthwise in jelly roll fashion and tuck in ends.
7. Cut slits diagonally 2-3 inches apart (shallow) on top of loaves.
8. Put on lightly greased baking sheet. Let rise until double, about 20-30 minutes depending on temperature of room.
9. Bake at 375-400° for approximately 20 minutes.

Tips:
1. You may wish to brush butter or margarine on top of loaf after baking.
2. Delicious with any meal but especially with pasta.
3. Dough will be stiff/thick and difficult to stir, but do the best you can!

Good friends shared this bread with us. I've made many loaves to donate to our Mennonite Relief Sale. It's so quick and easy, as well as delicious, and makes large loaves.

 FINGER FOOD

Icebox Butterhorns

Jolyn Nolt
Leola, PA

Makes 36 rolls

Prep. Time: 15 minutes
Chilling Time: 8 hours or overnight
Rising Time: 1 hour
Baking Time: 15-20 minutes

2 cups milk
1 Tbsp. yeast
2 Tbsp. warm water (110-115°)
½ cup sugar
1 egg
1 tsp. salt
6 cups flour
1½ sticks (¾ cup) butter, melted
additional melted butter

1. Heat milk in small saucepan just until skin forms on top.
2. Remove from heat and allow to cool to 110-115° (check with an instant-read thermometer).
3. Meanwhile, in a large mixing bowl, dissolve yeast in warm water.
4. When milk has cooled (as directed in Step 2), add it, plus sugar, egg, salt, and 3 cups flour to yeast mixture.
5. Beat until smooth.

Always check what you are baking a little earlier than stated in the recipe. Ovens do vary.

Mary Jones, Marengo, OH

6. Beat in 1½ sticks melted butter and remaining flour. The dough will be sticky.

7. Cover bowl. Refrigerate 8 hours or overnight.

8. Then divide dough into three balls.

9. Roll each piece into a 12" circle on lightly floured surface.

10. Cut each circle into 12 wedges each.

11. Roll up each wedge crescent-style, starting with the wide end. Place rolls point-side down, 2 inches apart on waxed paper-lined baking sheets. Curve ends, if you wish, to shape into crescents.

12. Cover and set in warm place. Let rise 1 hour.

13. Bake at 350° for 15-20 minutes.

14. Brush with melted butter after baking.

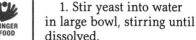

FINGER FOOD

Garlic Breadsticks

Sadie Mae Stoltzfus
Gordonville, PA

Makes 16 servings

Prep. Time: 10 minutes
Rising Time: 20 minutes
Baking Time: 20 minutes

1½ cups warm water, 110-115°
1 Tbsp. yeast
1 Tbsp. oil
1 Tbsp. sugar
1¼ tsp. salt
4 cups *bread* flour

Butter mixture:
3 Tbsp. olive oil, *divided*
1 stick (½ cup) butter, melted
3 Tbsp. olive oil, *divided*
1 tsp. coarsely ground salt
3 Tbsp. Parmesan cheese
1½ tsp. garlic powder
3 Tbsp. dried parsley flakes

1. Stir yeast into water in large bowl, stirring until dissolved.

2. Add 1 Tbsp. oil, sugar, salt and flour. Knead a little in the bowl to make sure ingredients are fully incorporated.

3. Cover with tea towel. Let rise 5-8 minutes in warm spot.

4. Place 1 tsp. olive oil in each of two 9×13 baking pans.

5. Divide dough between baking pans. Spread to cover bottom of each pan. Set aside.

6. Prepare butter mixture by placing melted butter in bowl.

7. Stir in remaining ingredients.

8. Pour butter mixture evenly over 2 pans of dough.

9. Bake at 350° for 20 minutes, or until golden brown.

10. Allow to cool slightly. Then using a pizza cutter, cut dough into sticks, each about ½" wide.

Tips:
1. For lighter breadsticks let dough, topped with butter mixture, rise 15-20 minutes.

2. You can use half whole wheat flour and half white bread flour.

3. Sometimes I serve these with salsa as an appetizer.

FINGER FOOD   FINGER FOOD   FINGER FOOD

Herbed Biscuit Knots

Melissa Wenger
Orrville, OH

Makes 20 servings

Prep. Time: 10 minutes
Baking Time: 9-12 minutes

12-oz. tube refrigerated
  buttermilk biscuits
¼ cup vegetable oil
½ tsp. salt
½ tsp. garlic powder
½ tsp. Italian seasoning

1. Cut each biscuit in half.
2. Roll each portion into a
6"-long rope.
3. Tie each in a loose knot.
Place on greased baking
sheet.
4. Bake at 400 for 9-12
minutes, or until golden
brown.
5. While knots bake,
combine oil, salt, garlic
powder, and Italian seasoning
in small bowl.
6. Brush over warm knots
immediately after baking.
7. Brush knots again with
seasoned butter.

French Onion Pan Rolls

Sherry Mayer
Menomonee Falls, WI

Makes 20 servings

Prep. Time: 15-20 minutes
Rising Time: 45 minutes
Baking Time: 30-35 minutes

2 1-lb. loaves frozen bread
  dough, thawed
1 cup grated Parmesan
  cheese
1 envelope onion soup mix
1 stick (½ cup) butter,
  melted

1. Divide bread dough into
20 portions. Shape each into
a ball.
2. In a bowl, combine
Parmesan cheese and dry
soup mix.
3. Roll each ball in butter,
and then in cheese mixture.
4. Arrange in 9 × 13 baking
dish, making 2 layers if
necessary.
5. Cover and let rise in a
warm place until doubled,
about 45 minutes.
6. Bake at 350° for 30-35
minutes, or until golden
brown.
7. Serve warm.

Irish Freckle Bread

Martha G. Zimmerman
Lititz, PA

Makes 2 loaves

Prep. Time: 30 minutes
Rising Time: 2½ hours
Baking Time: 30-45 minutes

2 envelopes (2 Tbsp.) yeast
1 cup warm potato water
  (left from cooking
  potatoes) *or* warm water
¼ cup lukewarm mashed
  potatoes, made from
  scratch, *or* instant
8 Tbsp. sugar, *divided*
5¼ cups unsifted flour,
  approximately, *divided*
1 tsp. salt
2 eggs, beaten
1 stick (½ cup) butter,
  melted and cooled
1 cup raisins

1. Dissolve yeast in warm
potato water in large mixing
bowl.
2. Stir in mashed potatoes,
2 Tbsp. sugar, and 1 cup
flour. Beat until smooth.
3. Cover and let rise in
warm place until bubbly,
about 30 minutes.
4. Stir down.
5. Add rest of sugar, salt,
and 1 cup flour. Beat until
smooth.
6. Stir in eggs and butter.
7. Add raisins.
8. Stir in enough additional
flour to make soft dough.
9. Turn out onto lightly
floured board. Knead until
smooth and elastic, about 5
minutes.

10. Place in greased bowl, turning to grease top. Cover and let rise in warm place until doubled, about 1 hour.

11. Punch down. Divide into four equal parts. Let rise 50 minutes.

12. Shape each part into slender loaf, about 9 inches long.

13. Put loaves in 9 × 5 baking pans.

14. Cover and let rise again until double, about 40 minutes.

15. Bake at 350° for 30-45 minutes.

This was a recipe I made when my children were young and we only had one car. So for a little income I made this bread and sold it to my neighbors. They loved it.

FINGER FOOD

Cheddar Biscuits

Jean Halloran
Green Bay, WI
Jessalyn Wantland
Napoleon, OH

Makes 12 servings

Prep. Time: 10-20 minutes
Baking Time: 15-17 minutes

2½ cups buttermilk baking mix
half stick (4 Tbsp.) cold butter
1 heaping cup shredded cheddar cheese
¾ cup milk
½ tsp. garlic powder, *divided*
2 Tbsp. butter, melted
¼ tsp. dried parsley flakes

1. In good-sized mixing bowl, cut butter into baking mix using pastry cutter or 2 knives until mixture resembles small peas.

2. Stir in cheese, milk and ¼ tsp. garlic powder until just combined. Do not over-mix.

3. Drop batter by ¼ cupfuls onto greased baking sheet. (An ice cream scoop works well.)

4. Bake 15-17 minutes at 400°, or until tops are lightly browned.

5. Remove from oven. Brush tops with melted butter. Sprinkle with ¼ tsp. garlic powder and parsley flakes. Serve warm.

Variations:
1. Add ¼ tsp. dill to Step 2, and sprinkle another ¼ tsp. dill over tops of baked biscuits in Step 5. I would serve these with seafood, especially salmon.

2. Use pepper Jack cheese instead of cheddar. Add ¼ tsp. chili powder to Step 5 and sprinkle another ¼ tsp. chili powder over tops of baked biscuits in Step 5.

These are dangerously good!

Biscuits Supreme

Lavina Ebersol
Ronks, PA

Makes 6 biscuits

Prep. Time: 30 minutes
Baking Time: 12-15 minutes

2 cups flour
3 Tbsp. sugar
¼ tsp. cream of tartar
¼ tsp. salt
4 tsp. baking powder
½ cup shortening
⅔ cup milk

1. In good-sized mixing bowl, combine flour, sugar, cream of tartar, salt, and baking powder.
2. Using a pastry cutter, or 2 knives, cut in shortening until mixture resembles small peas.
3. Stir in milk until ball of dough forms.
4. Roll dough out on flat surface until about ¾" thick.
5. Using a 3" biscuit cutter, cut out 6 biscuits. Place on ungreased baking sheet.
6. Bake at 450° for 12-15 minutes so that biscuits brown lightly. Do not over-bake!
7. Serve warm.

Good Go-Alongs:
Split these biscuits and serve them topped with sausage gravy.

Cornbread

Rebecca B. Stoltzfus
Lititz, PA

Makes 16 servings

Prep. Time: 10 minutes
Baking Time: 35 minutes

¾ cup sugar
⅓ cup (5⅓ Tbsp.) butter, softened
2 eggs, beaten
½ cup sour cream, *or* buttermilk
1 cup flour
1 cup cornmeal
½ tsp. salt
1 tsp. baking soda
½ tsp. baking powder

1. Cream sugar and butter together well.
2. Mix in sour cream and sour milk, or buttermilk, and eggs well.
3. In a separate bowl, combine flour, cornmeal, salt, baking soda, and baking powder.
4. Add dry ingredients to creamed mixture.
5. Pour batter into greased 8 × 8 baking dish.
6. Bake at 350° for 35 minutes, or until toothpick inserted in center comes out clean.

Sweet Cornbread

Blanche Nyce
Hatfield, PA

Makes 16 servings

Prep. Time: 15 minutes
Baking Time: 30 minutes

1 cup flour
1 cup cornmeal
⅔ cup sugar
1 tsp. salt
3½ tsp. baking powder
1 egg
⅓ cup milk
8 oz. (1 cup) crushed canned corn
⅓ cup vegetable oil

1. In large bowl, combine flour, cornmeal, sugar, salt, and baking powder.
2. Stir in egg, milk, corn, and oil until well combined. Batter will be slightly lumpy.
3. Pour batter in greased 9 × 13 baking pan.
4. Bake at 350° for 30 minutes, or until toothpick inserted in middle comes out clean.

Beside each dish of food on the buffet, place a stack of cards with its recipe written on them. Then guests can take the recipe if they wish.

Anita Troyer, Fairview, MI

Maple Cornbread

Kitty Hilliard
Punxsutawney, PA

Makes 9 servings

Prep. Time: 10 minutes
Baking Time: 20-22 minutes

1¼ cups flour
¼ cup cornmeal
1½ tsp. baking powder
½ tsp. salt
1 egg
¾ cup milk
½ cup maple syrup
3 Tbsp. vegetable oil

1. In a bowl, combine flour, cornmeal, baking powder, and salt.
2. In another bowl, beat egg. Add milk, syrup, and oil.
3. Stir wet ingredients into dry ingredients just until moistened.
4. Pour into a greased 9 × 9 baking pan.
5. Bake at 400° for 20-22 minutes, or until a toothpick inserted in center come out clean.
6. Cool on wire rack for 10 minutes. Cut into squares. Serve warm.

Tip:
I've also made this recipe with ordinary pancake syrup, and it tastes great.

FINGER FOOD

Cocoa Zucchini Bread

Kathy Hertzler
Lancaster, PA
Katie Ebersol
Ronks, PA

Makes 2 or 3 loaves

Prep. Time: 15 minutes
Standing Time: 45-50 minutes
Baking Time: 1 hour

2 cups sugar
3 eggs
1 cup corn, *or vegetable, oil, or* 2 sticks butter, softened
2 cups grated zucchini
½ cup milk
1 tsp. vanilla
3 cups flour
1 tsp. cinnamon
1 tsp. baking soda
1 tsp. baking powder
½ tsp. salt
¼ cup cocoa powder, *optional*
½ cup mini-chocolate chips
½ cup chopped walnuts, *or* pecans

1. Blend sugar, eggs, and oil in large mixing bowl.
2. Stir in zucchini.
3. Add milk and vanilla and stir well.
4. Mix flour, cinnamon, baking soda, baking powder, salt, and optional cocoa powder together in medium-sized mixing bowl.
5. Add dry ingredients to zucchini mixture. Stir thoroughly.
6. Add in chocolate chips and nuts. Stir.
7. Pour into 2 or 3 greased 8 × 4, or 2 9 × 5, loaf pans. Bake at 350° for 1 hour. Test that bread is finished by inserting toothpick into center of each loaf. If pick comes out clean, bread is done. If it doesn't, continue baking 3-5 minutes. Test again.
8. Let cool in pans 15-20 minutes.
9. Remove from pans. Let stand 30 minutes or more before slicing and serving.

Tip:
This is a wonderful bread to serve with whipped cream cheese and hot tea.

My sister first made this for me during a visit. I'm in PA and she's in South Dakota, so it was special to share with her.
Kathy Hertzler
Lancaster, PA

John's Zucchini Bread

Esther Yoder
Hartville, OH

*Makes 2 large loaves,
or 7 small loaves*

Prep. Time: 20-30 minutes
Baking Time: 20-45 minutes

3 eggs
1 cup brown sugar
⅔ cup oil
1 tsp. vanilla
8-oz. pkg. cream cheese,
  softened and cut into
  chunks
1½ cups flour
½ cup quick, or old-
  fashioned, oats
1 tsp. baking powder
1 tsp. baking soda
1½ tsp. cinnamon
½ tsp. nutmeg
1 tsp. salt
1½ cups shredded zucchini
2 cups finely chopped
  walnuts

1. With an electric mixer, beat eggs, sugar, oil, and vanilla 3 minutes.
2. Add cream cheese and beat 1 minute.
3. Mix flour, oats, baking powder, baking soda, cinnamon, nutmeg, and salt in another bowl.
4. Fold gently into egg mixture.
5. Fold in zucchini and nuts.
6. Pour into 2 9×5 greased loaf pans. Bake at 350° for 45 minutes. Or divide among 7 small loaf pans, and then bake at 350° for 20 minutes. Test that loaves are finished by inserting toothpick into center of loaves. If pick comes out clean, baking is complete. If not, bake another 3-5 minutes and test again with toothpick.

Pumpkin Bread

Joanne Warfel
Lancaster, PA

*Makes 2 or 3 larger loaves,
or 8 small loaves*

Prep. Time: 15-20 minutes
**Baking Time: 25-70 minutes,
  depending on size of loaves**

⅔ cup cooking oil
2⅔ cups sugar
4 eggs
16-oz. can (2 cups) pumpkin
⅔ cup water
3⅓ cups flour
2 tsp. baking soda
1 tsp. salt
½ tsp. baking powder
1 tsp. cinnamon
½ tsp. cloves
½ tsp. nutmeg
1 cup raisins
⅔ cup chopped nuts

1. In large bowl, cream oil and sugar until fluffy.
2. Blend in eggs, and then pumpkin and water.
3. In a separate bowl, sift together flour, baking soda, salt, baking powder, cinnamon, cloves, and nutmeg.
4. Stir sifted dry ingredients into pumpkin mixture.
5. Stir in raisins and nuts.
6. Pour into two greased 5 × 9 loaf pans or three 4½ × 8½ loaf pans, or eight 3 × 6 loaf pans. Bake at 350° for 60-70 minutes for larger loaves; 25-30 minutes for small loaves. Test that bread is done by inserting toothpick into center of loaves. If pick comes out clean, bread is finished baking. If it doesn't, continue baking 3-5 minutes more. Test again.
7. Allow to cool in pans 10 minutes. Remove from pan and allow to cool another 30 minutes or so before slicing and serving.

Tips:
1. I like to use garden-grown butternut squash for this recipe. I use 2 cups cooked and mashed squash instead of the 16-oz. can pumpkin. I like the texture of butternut squash better than cooked pumpkin from the traditional neck pumpkins.
2. I make the small loaves so I have them for gifts. They freeze well, and I've been told it's the best pumpkin bread they've ever had.

Healthy Blueberry Muffins

Gloria Lehman
Singers Glen, VA

Makes 18 servings

Prep. Time: 20 minutes
Baking Time: 20 minutes

1 cup flour
½ cup whole wheat flour
¾ cup sugar
¼ cup oat bran
¼ cup wheat germ
¼ cup quick, *or* old-fashioned, oats
1 tsp. baking powder
1 tsp. baking soda
½ tsp. cinnamon
¼ tsp. nutmeg
¼ tsp. allspice
¼ tsp. salt
1 cup blueberries, fresh *or* frozen and partially thawed
½ cup chopped walnuts
1 banana, mashed
1 cup buttermilk
1 egg
1 Tbsp. vegetable oil
1 tsp. vanilla

1. In large bowl, stir together all dry ingredients (through salt) until well blended.
2. Gently stir in blueberries and walnuts. (Adding the blueberries to dry ingredients first helps to prevent turning the batter blue from any juice.)
3. In a separate container, mix together mashed banana, buttermilk, egg, oil, and vanilla.
4. Make a well in dry ingredients. Pour wet ingredients into well. Mix just until blended.
5. Fill greased muffin cups almost to the top.
6. Bake at 350° for approximately 20 minutes, or until toothpick inserted in centers of muffins comes out clean.

Tip:
This moist muffin is made better and healthier by using a banana instead of more oil.

Banana Chocolate Chip Muffins

Jen Hoover
Akron, PA

Jane Steiner
Orrville, OH

Makes 18-24 servings

Prep. Time: 15 minutes
Baking Time: 12-20 minutes

3-4 large ripe bananas, mashed
¾ cup sugar
1 egg
1½ cups flour
1 tsp. baking soda
1 tsp. baking powder
⅓ cup (5⅓ Tbsp.) butter, softened
½ cup chocolate chips

1. In a good-sized mixing bowl, blend together bananas, sugar, egg, and flour
2. Mix in baking soda, baking powder, and melted butter.
3. Stir in chocolate chips.
4. Bake in lined muffin tins at 375° for 12-20 minutes, or until toothpick inserted in center comes out clean. Check after 12 minutes to prevent muffins from over-baking.

Tips:
1. I freeze overly ripe bananas with these muffins in mind. Microwave frozen bananas until soft; then follow recipe.
2. You can use ¾ cup whole wheat flour and ¾ cup white flour for these. You can also add 1 Tbsp. wheat germ or flax seed to Step 1.
3. Before baking these, place a pecan half on top of each muffin.

My boys love these! I make them to take along every time we go on a trip.

With a busy life, it is nice to have potluck dishes that can be made a day or two ahead of time.

Sue Hamilton, Benson, AZ

Strawberry Muffins

Janessa Hochstedler
East Earl, PA

Makes 12-14 muffins

Prep. Time: 10-15 minutes
Standing Time: 30 minutes
Baking Time: 10-12 minutes

1½ cups mashed
    strawberries
¾ cup sugar, *divided*
1¾ cups flour
¼ tsp. nutmeg
¼ tsp. salt
½ tsp. baking soda
2 eggs, beaten
half stick (4 Tbsp.) butter,
    melted
1 tsp. vanilla

1. In a small mixing bowl, combine strawberries and ¼ cup sugar. Set aside for 30 minutes. Drain strawberries, reserving liquid.
2. In a large mixing bowl, combine flour, nutmeg, salt, and baking soda. Set aside.
3. In yet another bowl, mix together eggs, melted butter, vanilla, ½ cup sugar, and juice from berries.
4. Add to flour mixture, stirring just until combined.
5. Fold in berries.
6. Spoon batter into greased muffin tins.
7. Bake at 425° for 10-12 minutes, or until toothpick inserted in centers of muffins comes out clean.

Zucchini Oatmeal Muffins

Donna Lantgen
Arvada, CO

Makes 30 muffins

Prep. Time: 15 minutes
Baking Time: 20-25 minutes

2½ cups flour
1½ cups sugar
½ cup oats, quick *or* old-
    fashioned
1 Tbsp. baking powder
1 tsp. salt
1 tsp. cinnamon
1 cup chopped walnuts
4 eggs
10 oz. zucchini (1¼ cups
    shredded), peeled *or*
    unpeeled
¾ cup oil

1. Mix flour, sugar, dry oatmeal, baking powder, salt, cinnamon, and walnuts together in large mixing bowl.
2. In a separate bowl, combine eggs, zucchini, and oil.
3. Stir wet ingredients into dry ingredients, until just mixed. Do not over-stir.
4. Fill greased baking tins half-full. (Or use paper liners instead of greasing tins.)
5. Bake at 400° for 25 minutes, or until toothpick inserted in centers of muffins comes out clean.

Tip:
    Shredding zucchini in your food processor makes things easier.

Pecan Pie Mini-Muffins

Orpha Herr
Andover, NY

Makes 28-30 mini-muffins

Prep. Time: 10-15 minutes
Baking Time: 20-22 minutes

1 cup packed brown sugar
½ cup flour
1 cup chopped pecans
⅔ cup (10⅔ Tbsp.) butter,
    melted
2 eggs, beaten

1. In a bowl, combine brown sugar, flour, and pecans. Set aside.
2. In another bowl, combine melted butter and eggs. Mix well.
3. Stir butter-eggs mixture into flour mixture.
4. Fill *well-greased and floured* miniature muffin cups two-thirds full. Or use paper liners.
5. Bake at 350° for 20-22 minutes, or until toothpick inserted in centers of muffins comes out clean.
6. Remove immediately and cool on wire racks.

Tips:
    1. If not all of the cups in your tins are filled with batter, fill those empty cups about half full with water. It will help your muffin tins not to warp.
    2. You can double or triple this recipe and bake them in regular-sized muffin tins.

3. You can make muffins a week or more ahead of when you need them and freeze them in an air-tight container. Remember to take them out at least 3-4 hours before serving time.

Ham French Bread

Sharon Timpe
Jackson, WI

Makes 12-15 servings
Prep. Time: 20 minutes
Baking Time: 25-30 minutes

1 loaf crusty French bread
1 stick (½ cup) butter *or*
  margarine, at room
  temperature
½ cup grated Parmesan
  cheese
½-¾ cup finely chopped
  boiled ham
¼ cup chopped fresh basil
¼ cup chopped fresh
  parsley

Topping:
  olive oil
  ¼ cup Parmesan cheese,
    grated
  freshly ground black
    pepper, *optional*

1. Slice bread into 1½-2" slices on the diagonal in one direction, not cutting all the way through. Repeat the other direction, crossing the original cuts, to create diamonds.

2. In a bowl, mix together butter, ½ cup Parmesan, ham, basil, and parsley.
3. Spread between each cut slice of bread.
4. Put bread on a large piece of aluminum foil and drizzle olive oil over the top.
5. Sprinkle on ¼ cup Parmesan and black pepper if using.
6. Wrap foil up and around bread, leaving the top open.
7. Bake at 350° for 25 minutes.

Variations:
  For **Bacon Provolone Bread**, mix ⅔ cup butter with ⅓ chopped green onions. Spread between cut bread diamonds. Put 8oz. sliced provolone between cut bread diamonds also. Add 8oz. chopped bacon to the top. Bake at 400° for 25-30 minutes.
  Charity Brubaker
  Dayton, VA

  For **Bacon Swiss Bread**, use 1 stick butter, ⅓ cup chopped onions, 4 tsp. prepared mustard, and 8 oz. sliced Swiss. Lay 5 bacon slices over top. Bake a directed above.
  Monica Leaman Kehr
  Portland, MI

Tip:
  Guests may tear off a chunk of the bread or you may want to finish cutting through the slices to make it easier. Serve from the foil or put on a platter.

Cheese and Onion French Bread

R. Wright
Stonyford, CA

Makes 16 servings
Prep. Time: 20 minutes
Baking Time: 12-15 minutes
Standing Time: 15-30 minutes

2 cups shredded Italian
  cheese blend
⅔ cup mayonnaise
¼ cup grated Parmesan
  cheese
1 loaf French bread

1. In a good-sized bowl, mix together cheese blend, mayonnaise, and Parmesan cheese.
2. Cut loaf in half lengthwise.
3. Spread mixture on each half of bread. Gently press loaf back together.
4. Wrap gently in tin foil.
5. Bake at 375° for 12-15 minutes.
6. Allow bread to cool 15-30 minutes. Unwrap, slice, and serve warm.

Bacon Cream Cheese Crescents

Chrissy Baldwin
Mechanicsburg, PA

Makes 16 servings

Prep. Time: 10-15 minutes
Baking Time: 12-15 minutes

8-oz. pkg. chive and onion
   cream cheese
1½-oz. jar bacon bits
2 8-oz. cans refrigerated
   crescent dinner rolls

1. Mix cream cheese and bacon bits until blended.
2. Separate each can of dough into 8 triangles each.
3. Cut each triangle in half to create 2 equal triangles.
4. Spread the cream cheese mixture onto each triangle.
5. Roll up each triangle starting at smallest point.
6. Place point sides down on ungreased baking sheet.
7. Bake 12-15 minutes at 375° or until golden brown.

Honey Butter

Donna Lantgen
Arvada, CO

Makes 10-20 servings

Prep. Time: 5 minutes

½ cup honey
1 stick (½ cup) butter,
   softened

1. In good-sized mixing bowl, blend honey and butter together.
2. Spread on corn bread, banana bread, or other bread of your choice.
3. Store in air-tight container.

Soups, Chowders, and Chilis

Mexican Beef and Barley Soup

Rebecca B. Stoltzfus
Lititz, PA

Makes 4-6 servings

Prep. Time: 10 minutes
Cooking Time: 35 minutes

1 lb. lean ground beef
1 small onion, chopped
1 Tbsp. olive oil
3 cups low-sodium beef
　broth
2 cups chunky salsa
½ cup quick cooking
　barley
2 15-oz. cans red kidney
　beans, rinsed and
　drained
4 Tbsp. sour cream
paprika

1. In 12" skillet, brown beef and onion in oil, breaking up with a fork until no longer pink. Drain.

2. Add broth, salsa, and barley. Bring to a boil.

3. Reduce heat to medium and cook uncovered for 15 minutes.

4. Add beans and heat through.

5. Ladle into bowls. Garnish with dollops of sour cream dusted with paprika.

Tips:

1. To use pearl barley, add extra 1½ cups broth or water and cook an additional 40 minutes.

2. To increase Mexican flavor to your taste, add some cumin, chili powder, or cayenne.

So many times we end up with little bits of noodles, veggies, etc. I put them in a container and freeze them. When the container is full, I make a veggie soup by adding browned hamburger and broth. Great way to use leftovers!

Jane Geigley, Lancaster, PA

Broccoli Rabe & Sausage Soup

Carlene Horne
Bedford, NH

Makes 4 servings

Prep. Time: 15 minutes
Cooking Time: 15 minutes

2 Tbsp. olive oil
1 onion, chopped
1 bunch broccoli rabe, approximately 5 cups chopped
1 lb. sweet *or* spicy sausage, casing removed, sliced
32 oz. carton chicken broth
1 cup water
8-oz. frozen tortellini

1. Heat olive oil in a soup pot.
2. Add onions and sausage and sauté until tender.
3. Add broccoli rabe and sauté a few more minutes.
4. Pour broth and water into pan; bring to simmer.
5. Add tortellini and cook a few minutes until tender.

Tips:
1. Substitute any green such as Swiss chard, kale, or spinach for the broccoli rabe.
2. Serve with grated cheese and crusty bread.

Tortellini Soup

Kim Rapp
Longmont, CO

Makes 6-8 servings

Prep. Time: 20 minutes
Cooking Time: 1 hour

1 lb. beef sausage, chopped *or* broken up
1 cup chopped onions
2 cloves garlic, chopped
2 cups chopped peeled tomatoes
1 cup sliced carrots
8-oz. tomato sauce
5 cups beef broth
½ cup water
½ cup dry red wine
1 tsp. basil
1 tsp. oregano
1½ cups sliced zucchini
8-oz. cheese tortellini
1 medium green pepper, chopped
3 Tbsp. chopped parsley

1. Combine sausage, onions, garlic, tomatoes, carrots, tomato sauce, broth, water, wine, basil and oregano in a pot.
2. Bring to a boil, then turn down to a simmer.
3. Simmer uncovered, 30 minutes. Skim fat with a spoon or skimmer.
4. Stir in zucchini, tortellini, and pepper.
5. Simmer 30 minutes. Stir in chopped parsley.

Good Go-Alongs:
Nice crusty bread and green salad. I like to shred

Parmesan cheese over the top.

My friend, Nancy, had this simmering on the stove when I walked into her home for an all-ages Christmas party. It was a fun celebration making ornaments and decorating cookies.

Italian Sausage Soup

Mary Puskar
Forest Hill, MI

Makes 6-8 servings

Prep. Time: 30 minutes
Cooking Time: 1 hour

1½ lbs. sweet Italian sausage
2 large onions, chopped
2 cloves garlic, minced
2 8-oz. cans Italian tomatoes and liquid
42-oz. beef broth
1½ cups dry red wine
½ tsp. dry basil leaves
2 medium zucchini, cut in ¼" slices
2 cups shell pasta
1 medium green pepper, chopped
3 Tbsp. fresh parsley
grated Parmesan cheese

1. Sauté sausage in large soup pot, stirring frequently and breaking up clumps. Drain.
2. Add onions and garlic; sauté until softened.

3. Stir in tomatoes, breaking them up.

4. Add broth, wine and basil. Simmer 30 minutes, covered.

5. Add zucchini, pasta, pepper and parsley. Simmer 15 minutes.

6. Top with lots of grated Parmesan cheese.

Tomato Basil Soup

Barbara Kuhns
Millersburg, OH

Makes 4-6 servings

Prep. Time: 15 minutes
Cooking Time: 25 minutes

¼ cup finely chopped
    onion
1 stick (½ cup) butter
2 10½-oz. cans condensed
    tomato soup
2 cups tomato sauce
6-oz. can tomato paste
2 14½-oz. cans chicken
    broth
garlic cloves, minced,
    optional
¼ cup brown sugar
3 tsp. basil
1 cup heavy whipping
    cream
⅓ cup flour

1. Melt butter in soup pot.
2. Add and sauté onion until softened.
3. Add condensed soup, sauce, paste, broth, basil, brown sugar, and garlic.
4. Cook, covered, until hot.

5. Whisk together flour and cream.

6. Add and heat gently, stirring, until soup is steaming and thick. Do not boil.

Cheeseburger Soup

Rebecca B. Stoltzfus
Lititz, PA

Makes 4-6 servings

Prep. Time: 35 minutes
Cooking Time: 1 hour

½ lb. ground beef
1 cup chopped onion
¾ cup grated carrots
¾ cup chopped celery
1 tsp. dried basil
1 tsp. parsley flakes
3 cups chicken broth
4 cups diced potatoes

4 Tbsp. butter
¼ cup flour
1½ cups milk
8-oz. American cheese,
    sliced or cubed
¼ cup sour cream
½ tsp. salt
¼ tsp. pepper

1. In a soup pot, fry the beef until almost browned. Stir frequently to break up clumps.

2. Add onion, celery, carrots, basil, and parsley. Sauté for a few minutes.

3. Add broth and potatoes.

4. Simmer until tender, 20 minutes.

5. In another pot, melt butter, add flour. Whisk vigorously.

6. Add milk, whisking constantly. Cook and stir over low heat until thickened.

7. Add cheese, sour cream, salt, and pepper.

8. Pour the cheese sauce into the beef soup. Stir gently to combine.

Tip:
Put the recipe in the slow cooker on Low 5 hours.

Instant potatoes are a good stew thickener.
Deb Kepiro, Strasburg, PA

Healthy Hamburger Soup

Chris Peterson
Green Bay, WI

Makes 8 servings

Prep. Time: 20 minutes
Cooking Time: 1-2 hours

2 lbs. ground chuck
14½-oz. can stewed
  tomatoes
1 cup sliced mushrooms
2 cups sliced cabbage
1 cup sliced carrots
2 cups chopped celery
2 cups green beans
6 cups tomato juice
2 tsp. basil
2 tsp. oregano
1 Tbsp. Worcestershire
  sauce
salt and pepper to taste

1. In a soup pot, fry beef until brown, stirring often to break up clumps. Drain off the drippings.
2. Add rest of ingredients.
3. Simmer 1-2 hours.

Tips:
1. Use canned mushrooms (pieces and stems) and a 14½-oz. can green or wax beans; no need to drain. I also sometimes add ¾ cup uncooked barley, quinoa, or broken spaghetti.
2. This is a great recipe for cleaning out your refrigerator. Whatever leftover veggies you have in there—throw them in the soup. I've added broccoli or rice and it's great.

Adirondack Three-Alarm Chili

Joanne Kennedy
Plattsburgh, NY

Makes 6-8 servings

Prep. Time: 25 minutes
Cooking Time: 3 hours

2 lbs. ground beef
3 medium onions, diced
4 garlic cloves, crushed
1 green pepper, chopped
28-oz. can crushed
  tomatoes
2 15½-oz. cans kidney
  beans, drained
16-oz. can tomato sauce
1 Tbsp. brown sugar
1 tsp. oregano
¼-1 tsp. crushed red
  pepper
3 Tbsp. chili powder
1 tsp. salt, *optional*

1. Brown ground beef in large soup pot, stirring often to break up clumps.
2. Add and sauté onion, garlic, and green pepper until softened.
3. Add the rest of ingredients. Simmer covered on low heat for 3 hours.

Tips:
1. Add a can of corn, or replace some of the meat with more beans.
2. Simmer the chili in a slow cooker instead of on the stovetop.

Three Bean Chili

Deb Kepiro
Strasburg, PA

Makes 6 servings

Prep. Time: 15 minutes
Cooking Time: 1 hour

1 large onion, chopped
2 Tbsp. oil
2 cups diced cooked
  chicken
15½-oz. can kidney beans,
  rinsed and drained
15½-oz. can pinto beans,
  rinsed and drained
15½-oz. can black beans,
  rinsed and drained
2 14½-oz. cans diced
  tomatoes
1 cup chicken broth
¾ cup salsa
1 tsp. cumin
¼ tsp. salt
shredded cheese
green onions
sour cream

1. In a soup pot, sauté onion in oil until tender.
2. Add chicken, beans, tomatoes, broth, salsa, cumin, and salt.
3. Bring to a boil. Cover. Reduce heat and let simmer for 30-60 minutes.
4. If desired, garnish with shredded cheese, green onions and sour cream.

Variation:
Add 1 cup corn, 1 Tbsp. chili powder, and 15½-oz. can undrained chili beans.

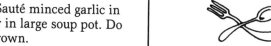

Use ½ lb. ground beef, browned, instead of chicken.

Moreen Weaver
Bath, NY

Good Go-Alongs:
Great with warm corn bread.

Chicken Tortilla Soup

Joanna Harrison
Lafayette, CO

Makes 8 servings
Prep. Time: 30 minutes
Cooking Time: 1 hour

2-4 chicken breast halves, chopped fine
1 Tbsp. butter
1 clove garlic
2 15-oz. cans black beans, undrained
2 15-oz. cans Mexican stewed tomatoes
1 cup salsa
4-oz. can green chilies *or* 4-oz. roasted chopped chilies
14½-oz. can tomato sauce
2 14-oz. cans chicken broth
1 Tbsp. cumin
½ cup chopped fresh cilantro
8-oz. Monterey Jack cheese, shredded
tortilla chips
sour cream

1. Sauté minced garlic in butter in large soup pot. Do not brown.
2. Add beans, tomatoes, salsa, chilies, tomato sauce, broth, and cumin.
3. Cook over medium heat, covered for 1 hour. Turn off heat.
4. Add cilantro and cheese and stir gently until melted.
5. Serve with tortilla chips and sour cream.

Tip:
Use cooked chicken breasts and shred them first. Add them with the beans.

Black Bean Pumpkin Soup

Bev Beiler
Gap, PA

Makes 4-6 servings
Prep. Time: 30 minutes
Cooking Time: 45 minutes

2 medium onions, chopped
½ cup minced shallots
4 cloves garlic, minced
4-5 tsp. ground cumin
1 stick (½ cup) butter
1 tsp. salt
½ tsp. ground pepper
3 15½-oz. cans black beans, drained
1 cup chopped tomatoes
4 cups beef broth
1½ cups cooked pumpkin
½ lb. cooked ham, diced
3 Tbsp. vinegar

1. In a large soup pot, sauté onion, shallot, garlic, cumin, salt, and pepper in butter until vegetables are tender.
2. Stir in beans, tomatoes, broth and pumpkin.
3. Simmer 25 minutes, uncovered, stirring occasionally.
4. Add ham and vinegar. Simmer until heated through.

Good Go-Alongs:
Warm, homemade, buttered bread

Don't apologize if your house is not spotless: your guests will feel more relaxed when they invite you.
Karen Sauder, Adamstown, PA

Basic Chowder Recipe

Janie Steele
Moore, OK

Makes 6-8 servings

Prep. Time: 20 minutes
Cooking Time: 45 minutes

1 Tbsp. olive oil *or* butter
1-2 cups chopped onion
2 carrots, sliced
2 ribs celery, sliced
3-4 large potatoes, cubed
2 cups chicken broth
13-oz. can evaporated
  milk
½ tsp. garlic salt
2 cups milk
pepper to taste

1. Sauté onion, carrots, and celery until they begin to soften.
2. Add potatoes and broth.
3. Bring to a boil, lower heat, and cover. Cook until potatoes soften.
4. Mash some of potatoes against side of pan.
5. Stir in evaporated milk, garlic salt, and pepper.
6. Add additional milk.
7. Continue to cook and mash more potatoes until desired consistency.

Variations:
1. New England Clam— add 2 cans clams to completed chowder.
2. Corn—add 2 cups frozen corn or 1 can corn.
3. Ham—add 1 cup chopped ham.

4. Bacon—add 2 chopped or crumbled pieces of cooked bacon.
5. Add a bay leaf, minced garlic, and dried thyme to taste.

Good Go-Alongs:
Serve with warm bread on a cold day—yum!

Beef and Bacon Chowder

Joan Dietrich
Kutztown, PA

Makes 8-10 servings

Prep. Time: 45 minutes
Cooking Time: 1 hour

12 bacon strips, cut in 1"
  pieces
1 lb. ground beef
2-3 cups diced celery
½ cup diced onion
2 10-¾-oz. cans condensed
  cream of mushroom
  soup
4 cups milk
3-4 cups diced, cooked
  potatoes
2 cups shredded carrots
2 tsp. salt
1 tsp. pepper

1. In a large soup pot, cook bacon until crisp; pour off drippings and remove bacon to paper towel to drain.
2. In the same pot, sauté ground beef with celery and onion until the beef is browned and the vegetables are tender. Drain off the grease.
3. Add soup, milk, potatoes, carrots, salt and pepper.
4. Bring to a boil; reduce heat and simmer until heated through.
5. Add bacon.

There is never a drop of this soup left when I take it to a potluck.

Harvest Corn Chowder

Flossie Sultzaberger
Mechanicsburg, PA

Makes 6-8 servings

Prep. Time: 20 minutes
Cooking Time: 40 minutes

1 medium onion, chopped
1 Tbsp. butter
2 14½-oz. cans cream-style corn
4 cups whole kernel corn
4 cups diced peeled potatoes
6-oz. jar sliced mushrooms, drained
½ medium green pepper, chopped
½-1 medium sweet red pepper, chopped
10¾-oz. can mushroom soup
3 cups milk
ground pepper, to taste
½ lb. bacon, cooked and crumbled

1. In a large saucepan, sauté onion in butter until tender.
2. Add cream-style corn, kernel corn, potatoes, mushrooms, peppers, and milk. Cover.
3. Simmer 30 minutes or until vegetables are tender.
4. To serve, garnish with bacon.

Mom's Soup

Chrissy Baldwin
Mechanicsburg, PA

Makes 8-10 servings

Prep. Time: 20 minutes
Cooking Time: 35 minutes

3 cups diced potatoes
16-oz. frozen broccoli and cauliflower
1 cup chopped carrots
1 cup chopped onions
3 celery ribs, chopped
12-oz. ham cubes
4 chicken bouillon cubes
3 cups water
1 tsp. salt
¼ tsp. pepper
½ cup butter
½ cup flour
2 cups milk
1 cup shredded cheese

1. In soup pot, combine potatoes, broccoli, cauliflower, carrots, onions, celery, ham, bouillon, water, salt, and pepper. Simmer for 20 minutes or until vegetables are tender.
2. In separate saucepan, make a white sauce. Melt butter over low heat and stir in flour to make a thick paste. Whisk in milk. Bring to a boil and stir for 2-3 minutes.
3. Add white sauce to soup pot and simmer for 10 minutes.
4. Add shredded cheese and stir until melted.

Tip:
Simply keep this on the stove on warm or place in slow cooker to keep warm.

Good Go-Alongs:
Best served with a loaf of homemade bread

My mom would make this on cold snowy days.

If you don't have fresh vegetables, frozen ones work well in soups and stews.

Chrissy Baldwin, Mechanicsburg, PA

Potato Soup

Dale Peterson
Rapid City, SD

Makes 4-6 servings

Prep. Time: 20 minutes
Cooking Time: 30 minutes

half stick (4 Tbsp.) butter
¼ cup diced onions
4 cups diced potatoes
1-2 carrots, grated
2 cups water
1 tsp. salt
½ tsp. pepper
1 tsp. dried dill weed
3 cups milk
2 Tbsp. chopped fresh
  parsley

1. In a soup pot, sauté onions in butter until golden and tender.
2. Bring potatoes, carrots, water, salt, pepper, and dill weed to boil.
3. Reduce heat to low and simmer with lid cocked until potatoes are tender.
4. Stir in milk and parsley and heat until hot. Do not boil.

Tip:
If you like thicker soup, add some instant potatoes in Step 4.

Tater Soup

Suellen Fletcher
Noblesville, IN

Makes 4-6 servings

Prep. Time: 15 minutes
Cooking Time: 1 hour

2 14-oz. cans chicken broth
10¾-oz. can cream of
  celery soup
½ cup chopped celery
4 cups diced potatoes
1 Tbsp. onion powder
1 cup skim milk
1 Tbsp. flour

1. In a soup pot, bring to boil broth, soup, celery, potatoes and onion powder.
2. Cook until potatoes are soft. Turn heat down to medium.
3. Whisk together milk and flour.
4. Pour into soup pot. Cook and stir frequently until thickened.

Good Go-Alongs:
Grilled ham and cheese sandwich.

To peel cooked potatoes, use a butter knife and gently scrape across the surface.
Dawn Landowski, Eau Claire, WI

Beef Main Dishes

Barbecued Roast

Meredith Miller
Dover, DE

Makes 8-10 servings

Prep. Time: 10 minutes
Baking Time: 6 hours

3-4 lb. beef roast
1 medium onion, diced
10¾-oz. can cream of
  mushroom soup
½ cup water
¼ cup brown sugar
¼ cup apple cider vinegar
1 tsp. salt
1 tsp. dry mustard
1 tsp. Worcestershire sauce

1. Place roast in roaster. Cover and bake at 350° for 2 hours.

2. Meanwhile, combine onion, soup, water, brown sugar, vinegar, salt, mustard, and Worcestershire sauce in large bowl. Whisk until smooth.

3. Remove roast from oven. Pour sauce over roast.

4. Cover. Bake at 250° for 4 hours longer. (That's not a mistake!)

5. Cut into serving pieces. Mix gravy through meat and serve.

To make your own cream of mushroom or celery soup, please turn to pages 258-259.

Aunt Iris's Barbecue Brisket

Carolyn Spohn
Shawnee, KS

Makes 8-10 servings

Prep. Time: 20-30 minutes
Marinating Time: 8 hours, or
overnight
Baking Time: 3-4 hours
Standing Time: 30 minutes

2-3 lbs. beef brisket
garlic powder
onion powder
celery salt
4 Tbsp. liquid smoke
2 tsp. Worcestershire sauce

Barbecue sauce:
 ½ cup honey
 ⅔ cup soy sauce
 ⅔ cup ketchup
 ½ tsp. Tabasco
 1 tsp. dry mustard
 1 tsp. paprika
 1 cup vinegar
 1 cup orange juice
 1 tsp. salt

1. Sprinkle both sides of brisket with garlic powder, onion powder, and celery salt. Sprinkle liquid smoke on both sides.
2. Place in large bowl or roaster. Refrigerate overnight, tightly covered.
3. In morning, drain meat. Return meat to pan.
4. Sprinkle with Worcestershire sauce.
5. Bake covered at 225° for 3-4 hours, or until meat thermometer registers 175°.
6. Turn off oven, but keep meat in oven for 30 more minutes.
7. Slice and serve with barbecue sauce.
8. While brisket is roasting, prepare barbecue sauce by combining all ingredients in saucepan.
9. Cook uncovered, stirring occasionally, until sauce comes to a boil.
10. Continue simmering for 30 minutes, or until sauce thickens and reduces down.
11. Serve alongside, or spooned over, sliced brisket.

This was one of Aunt Iris's special dishes.

Southern-Style Steak

Jeanette Oberholtzer
Lititz, PA

Makes 6 servings

Prep. Time: 20 minutes
Baking Time: 1 hour

2 lbs. round steak, ½" thick
3 Tbsp. shortening
¼ cup flour
1 tsp. salt
¼ tsp. pepper
1 cup ketchup
½ cup water
1 onion, thinly sliced
1 unpeeled orange, thinly
 sliced
1 unpeeled lemon, thinly
 sliced
6 whole cloves

1. Cut steak in serving-size pieces.
2. Melt shortening in skillet.
3. Mix flour, salt, and pepper in a shallow bowl. Dredge steak pieces in mixture, pressing onto all sides of meat.
4. Place several pieces in skillet, over high heat, being careful not to crowd skillet so they brown rather than steam in each other's juices.
5. Remove pieces when browned on top and bottom and place in single layer in roaster.
6. Continue browning remaining pieces of meat and placing in roaster.
7. Combine ketchup and water in a small bowl. Pour over meat.

8. Arrange onion, orange, and lemon slices over meat. Dot with cloves.

9. Cover and bake at 350° for 1 hour, or just until tender.

Variation:

1. Add 1 tsp. dry mustard to flour, salt, and pepper in Step 3.

2. Instead of topping steak with orange and lemon slices and with whole cloves, top instead with a mixture of:

**14½-oz. can diced
   tomatoes with liquid
1 carrot diced
1 tsp. brown sugar
2 tsp. Worcestershire
   sauce**

Jean Butzer
Batavia, NY

Hearty Pot Roast

Colleen Heatwole
Burton, MI

Makes 6-8 servings

Prep. Time: 30 minutes
Baking Time: 2-2½ hours

**½ cup flour
6-oz. can tomato paste
¼ cup water
1 tsp. instant beef
   bouillon, *or* 1 beef
   bouillon cube
¼ tsp. pepper
4 lb. beef roast, preferably
   rump roast
4 medium red potatoes,
   halved
3 medium carrots,**

**quartered
2 ribs celery, chopped
2 medium onions, sliced**

1. Place roast in 9 × 13 baking pan or roaster.

2. Arrange vegetables around roast.

3. Combine flour, tomato paste, water, bouillon, and pepper in small bowl.

4. Pour over meat and vegetables.

5. Cover. Bake at 325° for 2-2½ hours, or until meat thermometer registers 170°.

6. Allow meat to stand for 10 minutes.

7. Then slice and place on platter surrounded by vegetables.

8. Pour gravy over top. Place additional gravy in bowl and serve along with platter.

Variation:

You can make this in a large oven cooking bag. Combine flour, tomato paste, water, bouillon, and pepper in a bowl. Pour into cooking bag.

Place in 9 × 13 baking pan. Add roast to bag in pan.

Add vegetables around roast in bag.

Close bag with its tie. Make six ½" slits on top of bag.

Bake according to instructions in Step 5 and following.

Oven Beef Stew

Blanche Nyce
Hatfield, PA

Makes 6-8 servings

Prep. Time: 25 minutes
Baking Time: 3½ hours

**1½ lbs. beef cubes
6 carrots
6 ribs celery
6 small potatoes
6 onions
10¾ oz.-can golden
   mushroom soup
½ cup water
salt and pepper, to taste**

1. Cut vegetables into large chunks.

2. Mix ingredients together. Pour into a baking dish.

3. Cover and bake at 300-325° for approximately 3 hours. Longer is better!

Good Go-Alongs:

Tossed salad, coleslaw, gelatin salad. Also peas or corn served on side or on top of stew.

Beef Burgundy

Rosemarie Fitzgerald
Gibsonia, PA

Makes 6 servings

Prep. Time: 20 minutes
Cooking Time: 2¾-3 hours

2 lbs. stewing meat or
  good-sized beef cubes
1 cup chopped green onion
2 cloves garlic
2 cups burgundy
¼-½ tsp. marjoram,
  according to your taste
  preference
½ lb. fresh mushrooms,
  sliced, *or* canned and
  drained
6-oz. can tomato paste
dash of sugar

1. Brown beef in non-stick
Dutch oven with chopped
green onions and garlic.

2. Pour in burgundy. Cover
and simmer 2 hours, or until
tender but not dry.

3. Stir in marjoram and
sliced mushrooms.

4. Cover and simmer
½ hour longer.

5. Add tomato paste and
dash of sugar.

6. Simmer uncovered until
slightly thickened.

7. This is good served over
noodles or potatoes.

Quesadilla Casserole

Lorraine Stutzman Amstutz
Akron, PA

Makes 8 servings

Prep. Time: 20 minutes
Baking Time: 15 minutes

1 lb. hamburger
½ cup chopped onion
15-oz. can tomato sauce
15-oz. can black beans,
  drained
15-oz. can whole-kernel
  corn, undrained
4½-oz. can chopped green
  chilies
2 tsp. chili powder
1 tsp. cumin
1 tsp. minced garlic
½ tsp. oregano
½ tsp. crushed red pepper
8 corn tortillas, *divided*
2 cups shredded cheddar
  cheese

1. Brown beef and onion
in skillet. Drain off any
drippings.

2. Add tomato sauce,
beans, corn, and chilies.

3. Stir in chili powder,
cumin, garlic, oregano, and
red pepper.

4. Bring to boil; simmer
5 minutes.

5. Spread half of beef
mixture in greased 9 × 13 pan.

6. Top with 4 corn tortillas,
overlapping as needed.

7. Top with half remaining
beef mixture and half of
cheese.

8. Top with remaining
tortillas, beef mixture, and
cheese.

9. Bake at 350° for 15
minutes.

Good Go-Alongs:
  I serve this with chopped
lettuce, fresh tomatoes, and
avocado, as well as sour
cream and salsa as toppings,
for each person to add as they
wish.

Learn how to use spices. I'm still learning and it's amazing how the right spice can make a good dish great!

Ann Good, Perry, NY

Whole Enchilada Pie

Cova Rexroad
Baltimore, MD

Makes 10 servings

Prep. Time: 20-25 minutes
Baking Time: 30-40 minutes

1 lb. ground beef
1 medium onion, chopped
2 cloves garlic, minced fine
½ cup picante sauce
16-oz. can refried beans
10- *or* 12-oz. can enchilada
    sauce
1 cup sliced black olives
½ tsp. salt
6 cups crushed corn chips,
    divided
3 cups grated cheddar
    cheese
Garnishes: chopped fresh
    tomatoes, green peppers,
    chopped lettuce, sliced
    green onions

1. Brown ground beef and onion with garlic in large nonstick skillet until beef is no longer pink and onion is soft. Stir frequently to break up chunks of meat.
2. Lower heat and stir in picante sauce, beans, enchilada sauce, olives, and salt. Cook until bubbly. Remove from heat.
3. Line bottom of well-greased 9 × 13 glass pan with ⅓ of corn chips.
4. Layer half of beef mixture on top.
5. Top with layer of half the remaining chips.
6. Top with remaining meat mixture.
7. Top with remaining chips.
8. Top with cheese.
9. Bake 30-40 minutes, or until bubbly and heated through.
10. Serve hot with serving bowls of garnishes.

Tips:
1. Sometimes I add one 8-oz. can whole white beans, drained, to Step 2. They add good texture and nutrition.
2. I try to find less salty corn chips.
3. Add a 4¼-oz. can chopped chilies, drained, to Step 2.
4. Add a 15-oz. can Mexican-flavored diced tomatoes, or Rotel tomatoes, to Step 2.
5. Instead of corn chips, use torn corn tortillas.

Favorite Enchilada Casserole

Janice Muller
Derwood, MD

Makes 6-8 servings

Prep. Time: 20 minutes
Baking Time: 30 minutes

1 lb. ground beef, *or*
    ground turkey
2 onions, chopped
1 red, *or* green, bell
    pepper, chopped
10½-oz. can beef gravy
10½-oz. can beef
    consommé
10½-oz. can mild
    enchilada sauce
7-oz. can pitted black
    olives, *divided*
12 corn tortillas, *divided*
1¾ lbs. longhorn cheddar
    cheese, shredded, *divided*

1. In large nonstick skillet, brown ground meat with onions and bell pepper, until meat is no longer pink and vegetables are just-tender. Drain off any drippings.
2. In saucepan, heat gravy, consommé, and enchilada sauce together.
3. Into a well-greased 9 × 13 baking pan layer half the tortillas, half the beef mixture, half the olives, half the sauce, and half the cheese.
4. Repeat layers.
5. Bake at 350° for 30 minutes.

Easy Taco Casserole

Orpha Herr
Andover, NY

Lori Lehman
Ephrata, PA

Makes 8 servings

Prep. Time: 20 minutes
Baking Time: 20-25 minutes

1 lb. ground beef
1 cup salsa, your choice of
  heat
½ cup light mayonnaise
2 tsp. chili powder
2 cups crushed tortilla
  chips, *divided*
1 cup shredded Colby
  cheese, *divided*
1 cup shredded Monterey
  Jack cheese, *divided*
2 medium tomatoes,
  chopped
3 cups shredded lettuce

1. Brown beef in non-stick skillet, stirring often with wooden spoon to break up clumps. Keep stirring and cooking until pink disappears. Drain off any drippings.
2. Add salsa, mayonnaise, and chili powder to skillet. Mix well.
3. In greased 2-quart baking dish, layer in half of meat mixture, topped by half of chips.
4. Repeat layers of meat mixture, followed by remaining chips.
5. Bake uncovered at 350° for 20-25 minutes or until heated through.
6. Five minutes before end of baking time, top with remaining cheese.
7. Just before serving, top with tomato and lettuce.

Variations:
1. Add 15-oz. can red beans, drained, to Step 2.
Gretchen Maust
Keezletown, VA

2. Reduce ground beef to 1 cup. Add 15-oz. can black pinto beans, drained, or 2 cups cooked rice, to Step 2.
Juanita Weaver
Johnsonville, IL

Impossible Taco Pie

Esther J. Mast
Lancaster, PA

Makes 6-8 servings

Prep. Time: 15-20 minutes
Baking Time: 43-45 minutes

1 lb. ground beef
½ cup chopped onion
1 envelope taco seasoning
  mix
4 eggs
2 cups milk
1⅓ cups baking mix
2 fresh tomatoes, sliced *or*
  chopped
4 oz. shredded cheddar
  cheese
2 cups chopped lettuce
2 cups fresh, chopped
  tomatoes
½ cup sour cream

1. Brown beef and onion together in non-stick skillet. Drain off drippings.
2. Stir in taco seasoning.
3. Spread mixture in greased 10" pie plate.
4. In mixing bowl, beat eggs. Add milk and baking mix and beat until smooth.
5. Pour into plate over top of meat.

6. Bake at 400° for 35 minutes.

7. Arrange 2 sliced or chopped tomatoes on top. Sprinkle cheese on top.

8. Bake 8-10 minutes more until cheese melts.

9. Serve with lettuce, chopped tomatoes, and sour cream for those at your table to add as they wish.

Variation:

If you wish, add 15-oz. can kidney beans, drained, to Step 2.

Fran Sauder
Mount Joy, PA

Beef Taco Bake

Lavina Hochstedler
Grand Blanc, MI
Sarah Miller
Harrisonburg, VA

Makes 4 servings

Prep. Time: 12 minutes
Baking Time: 30 minutes

1 lb. lean ground beef
½ of 1-oz. pkg. taco
  seasoning
10¾-oz. can tomato soup
1 cup thick salsa
½ cup milk, *or* water
6 flour tortillas, cut up
  into 1" pieces
2 cups shredded cheddar
  cheese, *divided*

1. Brown meat in non-stick skillet. Drain off any drippings.

2. Add seasoning, soup, salsa, and milk or water to meat. Stir well.

3. Fold in cut tortillas.

4. Stir in 1 cup cheese.

5. Spoon mixture into greased 2-quart shallow baking dish.

6. Bake at 400° for 30 minutes or until hot.

7. Sprinkle remaining cheese on top and put back in oven a few minutes with oven turned off.

Tips:

1. When I double this recipe, I bake it in a 9 × 13 baking pan.

2. If you don't want to heat up your oven, you can cook this in a heavy skillet. After completing Step 4, spoon mixture into skillet, cover, and cook over low heat for about 20 minutes. Check occasionally to make sure it isn't sticking.

Nacho Pie

Melissa Wenger
Orrville, OH

Makes 8 servings

Prep. Time: 20 minutes
Baking Time: 20-25 minutes

1 lb. ground beef
½ cup chopped onion
8-oz. can tomato sauce
1 envelope dry taco
  seasoning
8-oz. tube refrigerated
  crescent rolls
1½ cups crushed nacho
  tortilla chips, *divided*
1 cup sour cream
1 cup shredded Mexican
  cheese

1. In a nonstick skillet, cook beef and onion until meat is no longer pink, stirring frequently to break up clumps.

2. Stir in tomato sauce and taco seasoning. Bring to boil.

3. Reduce heat. Simmer uncovered 5 minutes.

4. Separate crescent dough into 8 triangles. Place in greased 9" pie plate with points toward center of plate.

5. Press onto bottom and up sides to form crust. Seal perforations with a few drops of water.

6. Sprinkle 1 cup chips over crust.

7. Top with meat mixture.

8. Sprinkle with cheese and remaining chips.

9. Bake at 350° for 20-25 minutes, or until bubbly and heated through.

A Good Mexican Dish

Jane Geigley
Lancaster, PA

Makes 4 servings

Prep. Time: 30-45 minutes
Baking Time: 45 minutes

1 lb. hamburger
1 Tbsp. onion, chopped
6-oz. corn chips, plus 1
    cup crushed corn chips,
    divided
2 cups cheddar cheese,
    divided
4-oz. can taco sauce
8-oz. can tomato sauce
15-oz. can chili with beans
1 cup sour cream

1. Brown hamburger and onion in non-stick skillet, turning frequently to break up clumps, until meat is no longer pink. Drain off any drippings.
2. In mixing bowl, combine browned hamburger and onions, 6 oz. corn chips, 1½ cups cheddar cheese, taco sauce, tomato sauce, and chili with beans.
3. Pour into greased 9 × 13 baking dish.
4. Bake at 325° for 30 minutes.
5. Then spread sour cream over top.
6. Sprinkle with remaining ½ cup cheddar cheese.
7. Crumble remaining 1 cup crushed corn chips on top.

8. Return to oven, but with oven turned off, for 10 minutes.

Burritos

Betty L. Moore
Plano, IL

Makes 10 servings

Prep. Time: 15-20 minutes
Baking Time: 30-40 minutes

1 lb. ground beef
1 small green pepper,
    diced
1 small onion, diced
4-oz. small can sliced
    mushrooms, drained
2 tsp., or 1 envelope, taco
    seasoning
15-oz. can refried beans
10¾-oz. can cream of
    mushroom soup
1 pint sour cream
10 flour tortillas
8-oz. shredded cheddar
    cheese

1. In non-stick skillet, brown ground beef, pepper, and onion. Stir frequently to break up clumps. Drain, if needed.
2. Add mushrooms, taco seasoning, and refried beans. Mix well.
3. Combine soup and sour cream in a bowl.
4. Spoon half of soup-sour cream blend in greased 9 × 13 baking pan.
5. Divide meat mixture evenly between tortillas. Roll up. Place rolled burritos in baking pan.
6. Cover with remaining sauce. Sprinkle with cheese.
7. Bake at 350° for 30-40 minutes, or until bubbly and lightly browned.

Tamale Pie

Joyce Bond
Stonyford, CA

Makes 8 servings

Prep. Time: 25 minutes
Baking Time: 1 hour
Standing Time: 5-10 minutes

1 Tbsp. olive oil
1 medium onion, chopped
2 lbs. hamburger
1 clove garlic, minced
1 tsp. salt
½ tsp. pepper
3 Tbsp. chili powder
2 8-oz. cans tomato sauce
½ cup water
15-oz. can creamed corn
6-oz. can whole pitted
    olives, drained
1 cup evaporated milk
2 eggs, beaten
½ cup yellow cornmeal

1. Place olive oil and onion in 8-quart Dutch oven over medium heat. Cook, stirring frequently, until tender.
2. Add hamburger to onion in Dutch oven. Stir, breaking up clumps of meat, and cook until no longer pink. Drain off any drippings.
3. Off the stove, stir in garlic, salt, pepper, and chili powder.
4. Stir in tomato sauce and water.
5. Add creamed corn, olives, milk, eggs, and cornmeal. Mix together well.
6. Place Dutch oven, uncovered, in oven at 375°. Bake 1 hour until set.
7. Let stand 5-10 minutes before serving.

Tex-Mex Casserole

Ruth E. Miller
Wooster, OH

Makes 6-8 servings

Prep. Time: 35 minutes
Baking Time: 35 minutes

1 lb. hamburger
1 red bell pepper, chopped
1 onion, chopped
1 envelope dry taco
    seasoning
½ cup water
4 cups frozen, cubed hash
    brown potatoes, *or* your
    own cooked and cubed
    potatoes
10-oz. pkg. frozen corn
2½ cups cheese of your
    choice, cubed, *divided*
Garnishes: salsa, sour
    cream, shredded lettuce,
    nacho cheese chips

1. In a non-stick skillet, brown meat with peppers and onions. Stir frequently to break up clumps, until meat is no longer pink.
2. Stir in taco seasoning and water.
3. Add potatoes, corn, and 2 cups cheese. Mix together well.
4. Pour into greased 9 × 13 baking dish.
5. Bake at 350° for 20 minutes, covered.
6. Stir. Sprinkle with remaining cheese.
7. Bake 15 minutes uncovered.
8. Serve with bowls of garnishes for individuals to add as they wish to their servings.

Plan ahead when preparing food for home-entertaining or potlucks. Do as much preparation ahead of time as possible to avoid a last-minute rush. I like to sit down and relax just prior to the event.

Naomi Ressler, Harrisonburg, VA

Grandma's Best Meat Loaf

Nanci Keatley
Salem, OR

Makes 8-10 servings

Prep. Time: 15-25 minutes
Baking Time: 1 hour and 5 minutes

2 lbs. ground beef
2 Tbsp. fresh Italian parsley, chopped
1 tsp. dried oregano
1 small onion, chopped fine
4 cloves garlic, minced
¼ cup, plus 2 Tbsp., Romano cheese
½ cup dried bread crumbs
½ cup ketchup
2 eggs
1 tsp. black pepper
1½ tsp. kosher salt

1. In a large mixing bowl, mix together ground beef, parsley, oregano, onion, garlic, cheese, bread crumbs, ketchup, eggs, pepper, and salt.
2. Roll mixture into a large ball.
3. Place in well-greased 9 × 13 baking dish or roaster. Flattening slightly.
4. Bake at 375° for 1 hour. Keep in oven 5 more minutes.
5. Let stand 10 minutes before slicing to allow meat loaf to gather its juices and firm up.

Tip:
This is great for meat loaf sandwiches the next day—if you have any left!

Succulent Meat Loaf

Lizzie Ann Yoder
Hartville, OH

Makes 4-6 servings

Prep. Time: 20 minutes
Baking Time: 1-1½ hours

1 lb. lean ground beef
⅔ cup quick oats
½ cup milk
1 egg
⅓ cup chopped onions
1 Tbsp. prepared mustard
1 Tbsp. Worcestershire sauce
½ tsp. black pepper
¼ cup ketchup

1. In a large bowl, mix together beef, oats, milk, egg, onions, mustard, Worcestershire sauce, pepper, and ketchup. Blend well.
2. Shape into a loaf and place in well-greased loaf pan.
3. Bake at 350° for 1-1½ hours. Check with meat thermometer after 1 hour of baking to see if loaf is finished. Place thermometer in center of loaf. If temperature registers 160°, it's done baking. Continue baking if it hasn't reached that temperature.
4. Allow to stand 10 minutes before slicing.

Variations:
1. Mix 1 cup shredded cheddar cheese into loaf in Step 1.
2. Shape mixture into 8 small loaves, instead of 1 large loaf, and place in well-greased 9 × 13 baking dish. Bake at 350° for 45 minutes, or until meat thermometer registers 160° in center of mini-loaves.
3. Top single large loaf, or mini-loaves with this glaze before baking: ⅔ cup ketchup, ½ cup brown sugar, 1½ tsp. prepared mustard, mixed together.

Marlene Zimmerman
Bradford, PA

Be sure to always ask for family recipes whenever you get the chance. Don't wait until your loved ones are gone — and their recipes with them.

Nancy Keatley, Salem, OR

Applesauce Meat Loaf

Dale Peterson
Rapid City, SD

Makes 4 servings

Prep. Time: 15 minutes
Baking Time: 40-60 minutes

2 lbs. hamburger
¾ cup quick oats
1 egg
½ cup applesauce
¼ cup chopped onion
1 tsp. salt
dash of pepper
1½ Tbsp. chili powder

1. Combine hamburger, oats, egg, applesauce, onions, salt, pepper, and chili powder in a good-sized mixing bowl.
2. Shape into a loaf. Place in 5 × 9 greased loaf pan.
3. Bake at 350° for 40-60 minutes, or until meat thermometer registers 160° in center of loaf.
4. Allow to stand 10 minutes before slicing to allow meat to gather its juices and firm up.

Tips:
1. You can use bread crumbs instead of oatmeal in this recipe.
2. You can make meatballs with this mixture.

Taco Meat Loaf

Tammy Smith
Dorchester, WI

Makes 8 servings

Prep. Time: 20 minutes
Baking Time: 1-1¼ hours
Standing Time: 10 minutes

3 eggs, lightly beaten
½ cup crushed tomatoes
¾ cup crushed tortilla chips
1 medium onion finely chopped
2 cloves garlic, minced
3 tsp. taco seasoning
2 tsp. chili powder
1 lb. ground beef
1 lb. ground pork
½ tsp. salt
¾ tsp. black pepper

1. In a large bowl, combine all ingredients well.
2. Shape into loaf.
3. Place in a well-greased shallow baking dish.
4. Bake at 350° for 1-1¼ hours, or until meat thermometer registers 160° in center of loaf.
5. Allow to stand 10 minutes before slicing.

Beef and Potato Loaf

Deb Martin
Gap, PA

Makes 4-5 servings

Prep. Time: 15 minutes
Baking Time: 1 hour

4 cups raw, thinly sliced potatoes, peeled or unpeeled
½ cup grated cheese
½ tsp. salt
¼ tsp. pepper
1 lb. ground beef
¾ cup evaporated milk, *or* tomato juice
½ cup quick oats
½ cup chopped onion
dash of pepper
1 tsp. seasoning salt
¼-½ cup ketchup

1. Arrange potatoes evenly over bottom of greased 9 × 13 baking pan.
2. Layer cheese across potatoes.
3. Sprinkle with ½ tsp. salt and ¼ tsp. pepper.
4. In a mixing bowl, mix together ground beef, evaporated milk or tomato juice, oats, onion, ketchup, pepper, and seasoning salt.
5. When well blended, crumble meat mixture evenly over potatoes and cheese.
6. Drizzle with ketchup.
7. Bake at 350° for 1 hour, or until potatoes are tender. Check after 45 minutes of baking. If loaf is getting too dark, cover with foil for remainder of baking time.

Easy Meatballs

Cindy Krestynick
Glen Lyon, PA

Makes 6 servings

Prep. Time: 15 minutes
Cooking Time: 7-15 minutes

1 lb. ground beef
3 slices white bread, torn
    or cubed
1 small onion, chopped
4 sprigs fresh parsley,
    finely chopped
3 Tbsp. grated Parmesan
    cheese
1 egg
1 tsp. salt
¼ tsp. pepper
¾ cup water
vegetable oil

1. Combine beef, bread
pieces, onions, parsley,
cheese, egg, salt, pepper, and
water in a large mixing bowl
until well mixed.
2. Form into 6 or 8 meat-
balls.
3. Brown in oil in skillet
until golden brown on each
side.

Tip:
    Serve with spaghetti sauce
in hoagie rolls, or over cooked
spaghetti.

Oven Porcupines

Clara Byler
Hartville, OH

Makes 4-5 servings

Prep. Time: 45-60 minutes
Baking Time: 50-60 minutes

1 lb. lean ground beef
½-¾ cup uncooked long-
    grain rice, enough to
    help meatballs hold
    together
1½ cups water, *divided*
½ cup chopped onion
½-1 tsp. celery, *or*
    seasoning, salt
⅛ tsp. garlic powder
⅛-1 tsp. pepper, according
    to your taste preference
15-oz. can low-sodium
    tomato sauce
1 Tbsp. Worcestershire
    sauce

1. In bowl, mix beef,
rice, ½ cup water, onion,
celery salt, garlic powder, and
pepper.
2. When well mixed, shape
mixture into 10 balls.
3. Cook in nonstick skillet
until brown on all sides.
Drain.
4. Place meatballs in
greased 8 × 8 baking dish.

5. In a mixing bowl, blend
together 1 cup water, tomato
sauce, and Worcestershire
sauce. Pour over meatballs.
6. Cover and bake at 350°
for 45-50 minutes.
7. Remove cover and
continue baking 10 more
minutes.

Use no-salt-added canned vegetables, soups, and stocks, so that you can control the amount of sodium in your cooking.

Andrea Zuercher, Lawrence, KS

Shaggy Tigers

Shelley Burns
Elverson, PA

Makes 4-5 servings

Prep. Time: 20 minutes
Baking Time: 25 minutes

1 lb. ground beef
1 egg, beaten
½ cup grated raw potatoes
½ cup grated raw carrots
¼ cup chopped onion
1 tsp. salt
¼ tsp. pepper
¼ cup milk, *or* tomato
  juice

1. In a good-sized mixing bowl, mix ingredients very well.
2. When well blended, shape into 4 or 5 thick, oval burgers.
3. Place in greased baking dish.
4. Bake at 425° for 25 minutes, or until thermometer inserted in center of burgers registers 160°.
5. Serve with ketchup, barbecue sauce, and/or mustard.

Texas Cottage Pie

Kathy Hertzler
Lancaster, PA

Makes 6 servings

Prep. Time: 25-30 minutes
Baking Time: 30-35 minutes

1 Tbsp. oil
1 medium onion, diced
1 lb. lean ground beef
½ tsp. salt
½ tsp. cumin
½ tsp. paprika
1 tsp. chili powder
¼ tsp black pepper
¼ tsp. cinnamon
1 tsp. chopped garlic
15-oz. can black beans,
  drained and rinsed
1 cup frozen corn
14½-oz. can diced tomatoes
  with green chilies
3 cups leftover mashed
  potatoes
½ cup milk
1 cup shredded pepper
  jack cheese, *divided*

1. In large skillet, sauté diced onion and ground beef in 1 Tbsp. oil until beef is almost cooked through. Stir frequently to break up clumps of meat. Drain off any drippings.
2. Add salt, spices, seasonings, and garlic to skillet.
3. Cook 2 minutes more on medium heat.
4. Add black beans, corn, and tomatoes with chilies. Stir well.
5. Cover. Cook on low heat 15 minutes.
6. Meanwhile, warm mashed potatoes mixed with ½ cup milk in microwaveable bowl in microwave (2 minutes, covered, on Power 8), or in saucepan on stove top (covered and over very low heat for 5-10 minutes, stirring frequently to prevent sticking).
7. Stir ½ cup cheese into warmed mashed potatoes.
8. Transfer meat mixture to greased 7 × 10 baking dish.
9. Top with mashed potatoes, spreading in an even layer to edges of baking dish.
10. Sprinkle with the remaining ½ cup cheese.
11. Bake at 350° for 30-35 minutes.

Tips:
  The amounts I give here are flexible. For example, the original recipe called for only 1 cup of black beans and 1 cup of tomatoes. You can also use more cheese and more mashed potatoes. It's a very forgiving recipe. Adjust it to accommodate whatever you have on hand, and the people you'll be feeding.

Good Go-Alongs:
  I serve this with a tossed green salad and cornbread.

The first time I made this, I got about 1 cup—my husband, and our 2 sons (13 and 16 years), got the rest. It disappeared in 15 minutes.

Zucchini Beef Lasagna

Dorothy VanDeest
Memphis, TN

Makes 6-8 servings

Prep. Time: 40 minutes
Baking Time: 40 minutes
Standing Time: 10 minutes

1 lb. lean ground beef
¼ cup chopped onion
15-oz. can tomato sauce, *or*
 chopped tomatoes
½ tsp. dried oregano
¼ tsp. ground pepper
½ tsp. salt
½ tsp. dried basil
4 medium zucchini (1¼
 lbs.), peeled or unpeeled,
 divided
1 cup creamed cottage
 cheese
1 egg, beaten
3 Tbsp. flour, *divided*
1½ cups (6 oz.) shredded
 mozzarella cheese,
 divided

1. In large skillet, brown
beef and onion over medium
heat. Drain off drippings.

2. Add tomato sauce,
or chopped tomatoes, and
seasonings to meat in skillet.

3. Bring to boil. Simmer 5
minutes.

4. Meanwhile, slice
zucchini lengthwise into ¼"
slices.

5. In a small bowl, combine
cottage cheese and egg.

6. In a greased 8 × 12
baking pan, place half the
zucchini. Sprinkle with half
the flour.

7. Top with cottage-cheese
mixture and half the meat
mixture.

8. Repeat layer of zucchini
and flour.

9. Sprinkle with half
the mozzarella cheese and
remaining meat mixture.

10. Bake at 375° for about
40 minutes, or until heated
through.

11. Remove from oven.
Sprinkle with remaining
mozzarella cheese.

12. Let stand 10 minutes
before cutting and serving to
allow cheeses to firm up.

Tip:
 Substitute equivalent
amount of sliced eggplant
(peeled or unpeeled) for
zucchini.

Beef and Spinach Hot Dish

Vera Schmucker
Goshen, IN

Makes 6 servings

Prep. Time: 15-20 minutes
Baking Time: 35 minutes

1 lb. ground beef
1 medium onion, chopped
2 garlic cloves, minced
4-oz. can mushroom stems
 and pieces, drained
1 tsp. salt
1 tsp. oregano
¼ tsp. pepper
2 10-oz. pkgs. frozen
 chopped spinach,
 thawed
10¾-oz. can cream of
 celery soup
1 cup sour cream
2 cups shredded mozzarella
 cheese, *divided*

1. In nonstick skillet, cook ground beef, onion, and garlic, until no pink remains in meat. Drain off any drippings.

2. Add mushrooms, salt, oregano, and pepper to skillet.

3. Squeeze thawed spinach by small fistfuls until as dry as possible. Add spinach to skillet.

4. Stir soup, sour cream, and half of cheese to skillet. Stir skillet contents together well.

5. Put in greased 2-quart baking dish.

6. Bake at 350° for 20 minutes.

7. Sprinkle with remaining cheese. Bake 10-15 minutes more, until bubbly and browned.

To make your own cream of mushroom or celery soup, please turn to pages 258-259.

Beef and Cabbage Casserole

Lizzie Ann Yoder
Hartville, OH

Makes 6-8 servings

Prep. Time: 30-45 minutes
Baking Time: 1-1¼ hours

1 lb. ground beef
⅓ cup diced onions
¼ tsp. garlic powder
3 cups shredded cabbage
1 cup sliced carrots
½ cup low-sodium beef broth
¼ tsp. pepper
½ tsp. caraway seeds

1. Cook beef, onions, and garlic powder in non-stick skillet until meat is no longer pink. Stir to break up clumps. Drain off any drippings.

2. Stir cabbage, carrots, broth, pepper, and caraway seeds into skillet. Blend well.

3. Place in greased 2-quart baking dish.

4. Cover. Bake at 350° for 60-75 minutes, until vegetables are as tender as you like them.

Good Go-Alongs:

Slice of your favorite fresh bread or a small dinner roll, baked apples, glass of milk.

German Casserole

Lizzie Ann Yoder
Hartville, OH

Makes 6 servings

Prep. Time: 40-45 minutes
Baking Time: 1½ hours

1 lb. lean ground beef
¾ cup chopped onion
15-oz. can sauerkraut, undrained
½ cup water
½ cup long-grain rice, uncooked
¼ cup finely diced green bell pepper
¼ cup low-sodium beef broth
8-oz. can low-sodium tomato sauce
¼ tsp. black pepper

1. Cook ground beef in non-stick skillet until no longer pink. Stir frequently to break up clumps. Drain off any drippings.

2. In a mixing bowl, combine sauerkraut and its juices, water, uncooked rice, green pepper, and meat and onion.

3. Stir in broth.

4. Spoon into greased 2-quart baking dish.

5. Pour tomato sauce over top. Sprinkle with black pepper.

6. Bake covered at 350° for 1 hour.

7. Cover baking dish. Continue baking 30 more minutes, or until rice is tender.

Shepherd's Pie

Judi Manos
West Islip, NY

Makes 6 servings

Prep. Time: 15 minutes
Cooking/Baking Time: 50 minutes

1¼ lb. red potatoes, unpeeled and cut in chunks
3 garlic cloves
1 lb. extra-lean ground beef
2 Tbsp. flour
4 cups fresh vegetables of your choice (for example, carrots, corn, green beans, peas)
¾ cup beef broth, canned, *or* boxed, *or* your own homemade
2 Tbsp. ketchup
¾ cup sour cream
½ cup shredded sharp cheddar cheese, *divided*

1. In saucepan, cook potatoes and garlic in 1½ inches boiling water for 20 minutes, or until potatoes are tender.
2. Meanwhile, brown beef in large nonstick skillet.
3. Stir in flour. Cook 1 minute.
4. Stir in vegetables, broth, and ketchup. Cover. Cook 10 minutes, stirring frequently.
5. Drain cooked potatoes and garlic. Return to their pan.
6. Stir in sour cream. Mash until potatoes are smooth and mixture is well blended.

7. Stir ¼ cup cheddar cheese into mashed potatoes.
8. Spoon meat mixture into well-greased 8 × 8 baking dish.
9. Cover with mashed potatoes.
10. Bake at 375° for 18 minutes.
11. Top with remaining cheddar cheese. Bake 2 minutes more, or until cheese is melted.

Tips:
1. If you don't have fresh vegetables, use leftovers from your fridge or frozen ones.
2. This is a salt-free dish as stated. Add seasonings if you wish.

Homespun Meat Pie

Suzanne Yoder
Gap, PA

Makes 6 servings

Prep. Time: 20 minutes
Baking Time: 25-30 minutes

1 lb. ground beef
4-oz. can sliced mushrooms, drained
1 egg
⅓ cup chopped onion
¼ cup dry bread crumbs
½ tsp. salt
dash of peper
2 cups cubed cooked potatoes
3 Tbsp. milk

2 cups. cubed cheese of your choice
1 Tbsp. parsley, chopped
¼ tsp. salt
1 pkg. brown gravy, prepared to package directions *or* 1 cup homemade gravy

1. In a mixing bowl, combine meat, mushrooms, egg, onion, bread crumbs, ½ tsp. salt and pepper. Mix lightly.
2. Press mixture onto bottom and up sides of 9" pie plate.
3. Bake at 400° for 15 minutes.
4. Meanwhile, mash potatoes and milk together.
5. Stir cheese, parsley and ¼ tsp. salt into mashed potatoes.
6. Remove meat shell from oven. Spoon or drain off any fat.
7. Reduce oven heat to 350°.
8. Fill meat shell with potato mixture.
9. Return to oven. Continue baking 10-15 minutes, or until heated through.
10. Serve with brown gravy.

Tips:
1. I keep a box of instant mashed potatoes on hand if I'm in a time squeeze, and then within 45 minutes or so I can have this meat and potato meal ready. Okay, it's not my practice to use pre-made foods—but every now and then they have their place.
2. I usually prepare green beans to go with this. The

meat shell shrinks somewhat, so I spoon the cooked beans around the outside edge of the pie. It creates a nice presentation.

Connecticut Supper

Virginia Graybill
Hershey, PA

Makes 8 servings

Prep. Time: 3040 minutes
Baking Time: 1½ hours

2 lbs. hamburger
½ cup onions, chopped
5 or 6 medium-sized
 potatoes
¼ tsp. pepper
10¾-oz. can cream of
 mushroom soup
1 cup sour cream
1¼ cups milk
1½ cups shredded cheddar
 cheese
1 tsp. salt

1. Cook hamburger and onions in non-stick skillet,
stirring frequently to break up clumps of meat. Continue cooking until no pink remains in meat. Drain off any drippings.

2. Place browned meat and onions in bottom of greased 9 × 13 baking dish.

3. Peel and thinly slice potatoes. Distribute over top of meat.

4. In a good-sized mixing bowl, blend together soup, sour cream, and milk until smooth.

5. Stir cheese, salt, and pepper into creamy sauce.

6. Pour over potatoes.

7. Bake at 350° for 1½ hours, or until potatoes are completely tender when poked with a fork.

Kodiak Casserole

Bev Beiler
Gap, PA

Makes 10 servings

Prep. Time: 15-25 minutes
Baking Time: 60 minutes

1 lb. hamburger
1-2 cups diced onions,
 depending on your taste
 preference
½ tsp. minced garlic
3 medium bell peppers,
 chopped
1 cup barbecue sauce
10¾-oz. can cream of
 tomato soup, undiluted
½ cup salsa
15-oz. can black beans,
 drained
4-oz. can mushroom stems
 and pieces, undrained
1 Tbsp. Worcestershire
 sauce
1 cup shredded cheddar
 cheese

1. In a Dutch oven, brown beef with onions and garlic. Stir frequently to break up meat, cooking until no pink remains. Drain off any drippings.

2. Stir peppers, barbecue sauce, soup, salsa, beans, mushrooms, and Worcestershire sauce into Dutch oven. Mix well.

3. Cover and bake at 350° for 45 minutes.

4. Remove cover. Sprinkle with cheese. Continue baking 15 minutes, or until bubbly and heated through.

In the fall when peppers are plentiful, chop them and freeze them in a single layer on cookie sheets. After they're frozen, store in freezer bags. We eat lots of this healthy vegetable when they are so handy for soups and casseroles.

Ann Good, Dayton, VA

Dried Beef Casserole

Mabel Eshleman
Lancaster, PA
Virginia Graybill
Hershey, PA

Makes 4-6 servings

Prep. Time: 20-25 minutes
Chilling Time: 4-6 hours, or
overnight
Baking Time: 1 hour

10¾-oz. can cream of
  mushroom soup
2 cups milk
1 cup finely cut or grated
  cheddar cheese
1 cup uncooked elbow
  macaroni
3 Tbsp. finely chopped
  onion
¼ lb. dried beef, cut in
  bite-size pieces
2 hardboiled eggs, sliced

1. In good-sized mixing
bowl stir soup and milk
together until creamy.
2. Stir in cheese, macaroni,
onion, and beef.
3. Fold in sliced eggs.
4. Put in well-greased 1½-
or 2-quart baking dish.
5. Cover. Refrigerate at
least 4-6 hours, or overnight.
6. Bake, uncovered, at 350°
for 1 hour.

*This is one of my favorite
dishes to make when our whole
family is together for our annual
summer vacation. The real treat
is when my granddaughters,
and sometimes my grandsons,
help me make this simple meal.
It's a special kitchen time for
me and my grandchildren.*

Reuben Casserole

Lois Ostrander
Lebanon, PA
Anne Townsend
Albuquerque, NM

Makes 6 servings

Prep. Time: 20-25 minutes
Baking Time: 35-40 minutes

16-oz. can sauerkraut,
  drained
12-oz. can corned beef,
  broken into small pieces
3 cups shredded Swiss
  cheese
¼ cup mayonnaise
¼ cup Thousand Island
  dressing
2 medium tomatoes, sliced
4-5 cups rye, or Italian,
  bread, cubed
half stick (4 Tbsp.) butter,
  melted

1. Spread sauerkraut over
bottom of greased 9 × 9
baking dish.
2. Top with corned beef.
3. Sprinkle with shredded
cheese.
4. In a small bowl, combine
mayonnaise and Thousand
Island dressing. Spoon over
cheese and spread to cover.
5. Lay tomato slices over
top of dressing.
6. Spread bread cubes over
top of tomato slices.

7. Drizzle with melted
butter.
8. Cover baking dish with
foil. Bake at 350° for 30
minutes.
9. Remove foil. Continue
baking 15 more minutes.

Tip:
  If you cannot find pumper-
nickel melba toast, try rye.

Rice and Beans Bake

Jane Meiser
Harrisonburg, VA

Makes 6 servings
Prep. Time: 20 minutes
Baking Time: 20-25 minutes

1 lb. ground beef
¾ cup onion, chopped
½ cup green pepper, chopped
2 cups salsa, your choice of heat, *divided*
15-oz. can refried beans
1 Tbsp. ground cumin
2 cups cooked rice
2 cups grated sharp cheddar cheese
tortilla chips

1. Brown ground beef with onion and green pepper in large nonstick skillet. Stir frequently to break up clumps and until meat is no longer pink.
2. Stir in 1 cup salsa, beans, and cumin.
3. In a mixing bowl, combine rice and remaining cup salsa.
4. Place rice-salsa mixture in well-greased 2½-quart baking dish.
5. Layer all of ground beef mixture over rice.
6. Top with cheese.
7. Bake at 350° for 20-25 minutes, or until cheese melts.
8. Serve with tortilla chips.

Hearty Meat and Veggies Pilaf

Linda Yoder
Fresno, OH

Makes 6 servings
Prep. Time: 15 minutes
Cooking Time: 20 minutes

½ lb. ground beef, *or* venison
2 Tbsp. olive oil
1 cup sliced onions
1 clove garlic, minced
2 cups water
1 cup long-grain rice, uncooked
¼ lb. fresh mushrooms, sliced, *or* 4-oz. can sliced or cut-up mushrooms, drained
1 beef bouillon cube
1 tsp. salt
1 pint fresh green beans, *or* 1 lb. frozen green beans, thawed
½ tsp. basil
½ tsp. sage
½ tsp. oregano
½ tsp. marjoram
½ tsp. rosemary
½ tsp. thyme
¼ tsp. black pepper

1. In large nonstick skillet brown ground beef in oil. Stir frequently to break up clumps, until no longer pink. Drain off any drippings.
2. Stir in onions and garlic, sautéing until tender.
3. Add water, cover, and bring to boil.
4. Stir in rice, mushrooms, bouillon, salt, green beans, basil, sage, oregano, marjoram, rosemary, thyme and pepper.
5. Bring mixture again to boil, stirring once or twice.
6. Reduce heat, cover, and simmer 20 minutes, or until rice and green beans are tender.
7. Taste and correct seasoning if needed.

Tip:
If you prefer your green beans to have some crunch, add them to the skillet 10 minutes before the end of the cooking time.

When pan-frying and sautéing, always heat your pan first, and then add butter or oil. Meat and even eggs won't stick if you use this method. But watch that you don't get hit with sizzling — spitting — hot oil when it hits the pan.

Marlene Weaver, Lititz, PA

Baked Rice Dinner

Kay Magruder
Seminole, OK

Makes 4 servings

Prep. Time: 15 minutes
Baking Time: 1-1½ hours

¾ stick (6 Tbsp.) butter
10¾-oz. can French onion
  soup
10¾-oz. can beef
  consommé
1 cup long-grain rice,
  uncooked
2-3 cups bite-size pieces
  of left-over roast beef,
  or pork, *or* chicken, *or*
  cooked ground beef,
  optional

1. Use stick of butter to
butter 1-1½-quart baking
dish. Cut remaining butter
into chunks. Place in baking
dish.
2. Add soup, consommé,
rice, and meat if you wish.
3. Cover. Bake at 350° for
1-1½ hours, or until liquid is
absorbed.

Tip:
  When I cook a roast, I use
a large enough piece so that
I'm sure to have leftovers
to make this recipe. It's an
efficient way to make two
wonderfully flavorful meals.

J's Special Rice Dish

Joyce Bond
Stonyford, CA

Makes 6 servings

Prep. Time: 10-15 minutes
Cooking Time: 30 minutes

half stick (4 Tbsp.) butter
1 cup long-grain rice,
  uncooked
3 cups water
3 chicken bouillon cubes
½ tsp. salt
1 Tbsp. parsley flakes
1 Tbsp. chopped onion
1 tsp. minced garlic
¼ lb. fresh mushrooms,
  sliced, *or* 4-oz. can
  mushrooms, drained
1 cup leftover cooked meat
  (lamb, beef, chicken *or*
  pork)

1. Melt butter in saucepan.
2. Stir in rice.
3. Stir in water, bouillon,
salt, parsley flakes, onion,
garlic, and mushrooms.
4. Cover and simmer over
low to medium heat for 20-30
minutes, or until liquid is
absorbed and rice is tender.
5. Stir in cooked meat.
Cover and cook over low heat,
just until meat is hot.

Bounty Rice

Melissa Raber
Millersburg, OH

Makes 6 servings

Prep. Time: 30 minutes
Cooking/Baking Time: 30-60
  minutes

½-1 lb. ground beef
1 cup chopped green bell
  pepper
1 cup chopped onion,
  chopped
1¼ cups long-grain rice,
  uncooked
3 cups water
4 cups diced canned
  tomatoes
4 cups shredded cabbage,
  shredded
1 tsp. salt
½ tsp. dried oregano
½ tsp. dried basil
½ tsp. garlic powder
¼-½ tsp. red, *or* black,
  pepper
1 cup shredded mozzarella
  cheese

1. In large skillet, sauté
beef, peppers, and onion
until meat is browned and
vegetables are soft. Stir often
to break up clumps of meat.
2. Meanwhile, place 3 cups
water in good-sized saucepan.
Cover. Cook over high heat
until water boils.
3. Stir in rice. Cover.
Reduce heat to low or
medium so that rice simmers.
4. Check rice after 20
minutes. If water is absorbed,
turn off heat. If not, continue
cooking another 5-10 minutes.

5. While rice cooks, stir tomatoes, cabbage, salt, oregano, basil, garlic powder, and red pepper into skillet with beef and vegetables.

6. When rice is cooked, stir into skillet, too.

7. Spoon mixture into greased 2-quart casserole.

8. Bake at 325° for 350° for 30-60 minutes, or until cabbage is as tender as you like it and casserole is bubbly.

9. Top with cheese and let melt before serving.

Chili Rice Bake

Lucy Stpierre
Peru, NY

Makes 6-8 servings

Prep. Time: 20-25 minutes
Baking Time: 50-60 minutes

1 lb. lean ground beef
1 small onion, diced
2 celery ribs, diced
14½-oz. can diced tomatoes with juice
1 cup water
15-oz. can chili with beans
1 cup long-grain rice, uncooked

1. Sauté beef, onions, and celery in nonstick medium skillet until meat is no longer pink. Stir frequently to break up clumps of meat.

2. In well-greased 3-quart casserole dish, mix together tomatoes, water, chili, and uncooked rice.

3. Stir in beef mixture.

4. Cover. Bake at 350° for 1 hour, or until rice is tender.

Variations:

1. For more kick, add 1-2 tsp. chili powder to Step 2.

2. Top fully baked casserole with ½ cup grated cheddar cheese. Allow to stand 10 minutes before serving, until cheese melts.

Barb Carper
Lancaster, PA

Upside-Down Pizza

Julia Rohrer
Aaronsburg, PA
Janet L. Roggie
Lowville, NY

Makes 8-10 servings
Prep. Time: 20-30 minutes
Baking Time: 25-30 minutes

2 lbs. hamburger, *or* bulk
  sausage
1 chopped onion
1 medium red, *or* green,
  bell pepper, chopped
1 tsp. dried basil
1 tsp. dried oregano
2 cups pizza, *or* spaghetti,
  sauce
¼ lb. fresh mushrooms,
  chopped, *or* 4-oz. can
  chopped mushrooms,
  drained
2 cups grated mozzarella
  cheese
sprinkling of dried
  oregano
sprinkling of grated
  Parmesan cheese

Batter:
  3 eggs
  1½ cups milk
  1½ Tbsp. oil
  ½ tsp. salt
  1 tsp. baking soda
  1¾ cups flour

1. Brown meat with onion
and pepper in large nonstick
skillet.
2. Stir in seasonings, sauce,
and mushrooms. Simmer 5-8
minutes.

3. Place in well-greased
9 × 13 baking pan.
4. Cover with grated
cheese.
5. Prepare batter by
beating eggs, milk, and oil
together in good-sized mixing
bowl.
6. Add salt, baking soda,
and flour. Stir just until
mixed.
7. Pour over cheese-meat
mixture. Do not stir.
8. Sprinkle with oregano
and Parmesan cheese.
9. Bake at 400° for 25
minutes or until toothpick
inserted in center of dough
comes out clean.

Variation:
  Add a layer of sliced pepperoni, plus a layer of sliced
black olives, immediately
after Step 4—on top of the
cheese layer and under the
dough.

              Joyce Cox
          Port Angeles, WA

Pizza Cups

Alice Miller
Stuarts Draft, VA

Makes 6 servings
Prep. Time: 20-25 minutes
Baking Time: 10-12 minutes

¾-1 lb. ground beef
6-oz. can tomato paste
1 Tbsp. instant minced
  onion
½ tsp. dried oregano
½ tsp. dried basil
½ tsp. salt

Biscuits:
  2 cups flour
  3 tsp. baking powder
  ½ tsp. salt
  ¼ cup shortening
  ¾ cup milk
  ½-¾ cup shredded
    mozzarella cheese,
    divided

1. Cook ground beef in
large skillet, stirring frequently to break up clumps,
until no pink remains. Drain
off drippings.
2. Stir in tomato paste,
onion, and seasonings.
3. Cook over medium heat
an additional 5 minutes,
stirring frequently.
4. Prepare biscuits by sift-
ing flour, baking powder, and
salt together in large bowl.

*I often write on my recipe what size dish I used
for each step.*   *Krista Hershberger, Elverson, PA*

96

5. Cut in shortening using pastry cutter or 2 forks.

6. Add milk and stir with fork until a ball forms.

7. Roll ball onto lightly floured counter. Knead lightly, about 20 turns.

8. Divide ball into 6 pieces.

9. Place a ball in each of 6 muffin cups, pressing to cover bottom and sides as evenly as you can.

10. Spoon meat mixture into cups, distributing evenly.

11. Sprinkle each with cheese.

12. Bake at 400° for 10-12 minutes.

Homemade Hamburgers

Janet Derstine
Telford, PA

Makes 6 servings

Prep. Time: 30-35 minutes
Baking Time: 60 minutes

1 cup bread crumbs
½ cup milk
1 lb. ground beef
¼ cup chopped onion
1 tsp. salt
¼ tsp. pepper

Sauce:
   3 Tbsp. brown sugar
   1 Tbsp. vinegar
   ¼ cup ketchup
   1 Tbsp. Worcestershire
    sauce
   ¼ cup barbecue sauce
   ½ cup water

1. In good-sized mixing bowl, moisten bread crumbs with milk.

2. Add ground beef, onion, salt, and pepper. Mix well. Set aside.

3. In a mixing bowl, mix sauce ingredients together.

4. Shape hamburger mixture into 6 patties.

5. Place in single layer in baking dish.

6. Pour barbecue sauce over patties.

7. Cover and bake at 375° for 30 minutes.

8. Remove cover and bake another 30 minutes, basting occasionally with sauce.

Tips:
You can double or triple the patties and freeze them for a later meal. (I make the sauce when I bake them.)

Baked Barbecued Burgers

Mary H. Nolt
East Earl, PA

Makes 12 servings

Prep. Time: 20 minutes
Baking Time: 30-60 minutes

2 lbs. extra-lean ground
  beef
4 slices bread, torn into
  fine pieces
2 eggs, beaten
½ cup milk
2 tsp. salt
1 Tbsp. minced onion
2 tsp. dried celery flakes
½ tsp. chili powder
18-oz. bottle smoke-
  flavored barbecue sauce,
  divided
12 slices uncooked bacon

1. In a good-sized mixing
bowl, combine ground beef,
bread pieces, eggs, milk, salt,
onion, celery flakes, chili
powder, and 2 Tbsp. barbecue
sauce.
2. When well blended,
form into 12 thick burgers.
3. Wrap a piece of bacon
slice around the middle of each
patty. Secure with a toothpick.
4. Place a rack in a roaster
or baking pan. Place burgers
on rack.
5. Bake at 350° until a
thermometer inserted in
center of burgers registers
160°.
6. Baste frequently while
baking with remaining
barbecue sauce.

Barbecue Sloppy Joes

Winifred Paul
Scottdale, PA

Makes 5 sandwiches

Prep. Time: 10 minutes
Cooking Time: 15 minutes

¾ lb. ground beef
1 Tbsp. oil
1 tsp. lemon juice
1 Tbsp. vinegar
2 Tbsp. water
½ cup ketchup
1 tsp. brown sugar
1 tsp. onion chopped fine
⅓ cup chopped celery
1 tsp. dry mustard
buns

1. Brown beef in oil in
skillet. Stir frequently to
break up clumps and to make
sure meat browns completely.
Drain off drippings.
2. Make sauce by combin-
ing lemon juice, vinegar,
water, ketchup, brown sugar,
onion, celery, and dry mustard in saucepan.
3. Heat thoroughly, but do
not cook enough to soften
vegetables.
4. When beginning to
simmer, combine with meat.
Serve on buns.

So-Good Sloppy Joes

Judy Diller
Bluffton, OH

Makes 18 servings

Prep. Time: 15-20 minutes
Cooking/Baking Time: 1-2 hours

3 lbs. ground beef
1 medium onion, chopped
1 green bell pepper, diced
10¾-oz. can tomato soup
1 cup ketchup
2 Tbsp. prepared mustard
2 Tbsp. vinegar
1 Tbsp. brown sugar
2 Tbsp. Worcestershire
  sauce
18 rolls

1. Brown ground beef in
large skillet or saucepan. Stir
frequently to break up clumps
and to brown thoroughly.
Drain off drippings.
2. Stir onion, pepper, soup,
ketchup, mustard, vinegar,
brown sugar, and Worcestershire sauce into beef.
3. Simmer slowly on
stove-top for 2 hours, or spoon
into a baking dish and bake at
325° for 1 hour.
4. Serve in rolls.

*Don't be afraid to try new recipes, but learn some
basic ones from cooks you trust.*

Colleen Heatwole, Burton, MI

Sloppy Joes

Shelley Burns
Elverson, PA

Makes 5 servings

Prep. Time: 10 minutes
Cooking Time: 20-25 minutes

1 lb. hamburger
1 medium onion, chopped
⅓ cup chopped celery
¾ cup ketchup
1 Tbsp. Worcestershire
  sauce
1 tsp. salt
5 hamburger buns, split
  and toasted

1. Brown hamburger in large skillet, stirring frequently to break up clumps and turn over so it browns completely. Drain off drippings.

2. Stir in onion, celery, ketchup, Worcestershire sauce, and salt. Cover and cook over low heat just until vegetables are tender, 10-15 minutes.

3. Fill toasted buns with meat mixture.

Delicious Sub Casserole

Janice Nolt
Ephrata, PA

Makes 6 servings

Prep. Time: 25 minutes
Baking Time: 30 minutes

1 lb. ground beef
1 cup pizza sauce
12 slices multi-grain bread,
  cubed
1 cup Ranch salad dressing
½ cup mayonnaise
2 cups grated mozzarella
  cheese

1. Brown ground beef in non-stick skillet. Stir frequently to break up clumps, cooking until no pink remains. Drain off any drippings.

2. Stir pizza sauce into beef.

3. Layer bread cubes into greased 9 × 13 baking pan.

4. Mix salad dressing and mayonnaise together in mixing bowl.

5. Spoon over bread.

6. Spoon beef-pizza sauce mixture over top.

7. Sprinkle with grated cheese.

8. Bake at 350° for 30 minutes, or until bubbly and heated through.

FINGER
FOOD

Sandwich for a Crowd

Julie Horst
Lancaster, PA

Makes 12 servings

Prep. Time: 45 minutes
Chilling Time: 8 hours

2 loaves Italian bread
8-oz. pkg. cream cheese,
　softened
1 cup shredded cheddar
　cheese
¾ cup green onions
¼-⅓ cup mayonnaise
1 Tbsp. Worcestershire
　sauce
1 lb. sliced cooked ham
1 lb. thin sliced cooked
　roast beef
12-14 thinly sliced dill
　pickles

1. Cut bread in half lengthwise.
2. Hollow out top and bottom slightly by pulling out crumbs. (Save for your next meat loaf.)
3. In a large mixing bowl, combine cheeses, onions, mayonnaise, and Worcestershire sauce.
4. Spread over cut sides of bread, both tops and bottoms.
5. Layer ham and roast beef over both bottom and top halves of loaves.
6. Place pickles side by side over bottom half of each loaf.
7. Carefully place top half of loaves over bottom halves. Press together and then wrap tightly in plastic wrap.
8. Place in refrigerator for at least 8 hours.
9. When ready to serve, remove plastic wrap. Slice each large loaf in 1½"-thick slices.

Tips:
1. Diagonal slices are attractive.
2. This is a giant sub and is great for packed lunches. Each morning slice another serving for each lunch. It will keep in the fridge for several days.
3. Choose your favorite breads. Use different meats and cheeses than those in the recipe above.

Good Go-Alongs:
　potato chips, coleslaw

I like to make this the day before a ski trip or before going camping. The morning of the event, I slice off a chunk for everyone and wrap them individually. Everyone loves it!

Pork Main Dishes

Saucy Spare Ribs

Joanne Kennedy
Plattsburgh, NY

Makes 4 servings

Prep. Time: 15 minutes
Baking Time: 2 hours

2 lbs. pork spareribs
1 large onion, sliced
2 Tbsp. flour
2 Tbsp. brown sugar
⅓ cup soy sauce
1½ cups water

1. Place ribs in a well-greased 9 × 13 baking pan.
2. Top with sliced onions.
3. In a mixing bowl, combine flour, brown sugar, soy sauce, and water until smooth.
4. Pour over ribs and onions.
5. Cover. Bake at 350° for 1 hour.
6. Uncover. Bake 1 more hour.

Tip:
The sauce makes a great gravy for mashed potatoes, rice, or pasta.

Barbecued Spareribs

Jane Geigley
Lancaster, PA

Makes 3-4 servings

Prep. Time: 15 minutes
Baking Time: 3-4 hours
Grilling or Roasting Time: 30 minutes

3 lbs. spareribs

Sauce:
  ½ cup chopped onions
  2 Tbsp. butter
  2 10½-oz. cans tomato soup
  1 tsp. hot sauce
  1 Tbsp. vinegar
  1 cup brown sugar
  ⅓ cup Worcestershire sauce
  ¼ tsp. ground cloves

1. Lay ribs in a single layer in a roaster or on a baking sheet with sides. Cover.
2. Bake at 300° 3-3½ hours, or until meat is fall-off-the-bones tender.
3. Meanwhile, in medium-sized saucepan, cook onion in butter until tender.
4. Stir in soup, hot sauce, vinegar, brown sugar, Worcestershire sauce, and cloves.
5. Simmer, uncovered, 5 minutes, stirring often.
6. Either continue roasting ribs, uncovered, in oven. Or move to grill.
7. Brush with sauce and roast or grill 5 minutes.
8. Turn ribs over and brush with sauce. Roast or grill 5 more minutes.
9. Turn and brush with sauce for a total of 20 more minutes.

Pork Chops with Apple Stuffing

Arlene Yoder
Hartville, OH

Makes 6 servings

Prep. Time: 20 minutes
Cooking Time: 45-60 minutes

6 pork chops, at least 1" thick
2-4 slices bacon, diced
¼ cup chopped celery
¼ cup chopped onion
3 apples, peeled, cored and diced
¼ cup sugar
½ cup bread crumbs, *or* cracker crumbs
¼ tsp. salt
¼ tsp. pepper
2 tsp. chopped parsley
additional salt and pepper

1. Cut a pocket about 1½" deep into the side of each chop for stuffing.
2. In large nonstick skillet, fry bacon until crisp. Remove bacon slices to paper towel-lined plate to drain, reserving drippings in pan.
3. Stir celery and onion into drippings in skillet. Cook over medium until tender, stirring frequently.
4. Stir in diced apples. Sprinkle with sugar.
5. Cover skillet. Cook apples over low heat until tender and glazed.
6. Stir in bread crumbs.
7. Stir in salt, pepper, and parsley.
8. Spreading open the pocket in each chop with your fingers, stuff with mixture.
9. Return half of stuffed chops to skillet.
10. Sprinkle chops with salt and pepper. Brown on both sides over medium to high heat.
11. Remove browned chops to platter. Cover to keep warm.
12. Repeat Step 10 with remaining chops.
13. Return other chops to skillet.
14. Reduce heat. Add a few tablespoons of water.
15. Cover. Cook slowly over low heat until done, about 20-25 minutes.

French Onion Pork Chop Skillet

Nadine Martinitz
Salina, KS

Makes 6 servings

Prep. Time: 10 minutes
Cooking Time: 20-25 minutes

6 boneless pork chops
  (1½ lbs.), ½" thick
2 onions, thinly sliced
2 Tbsp. Worcestershire
  sauce
6-oz. pkg. Stove Top
  stuffing mix
1½ cups hot water
1 cup shredded mozzarella
  cheese

1. Place half the chops in large nonstick skillet. Over medium to high heat, cook 10 minutes or until done, turning chops after 5 minutes.
2. Remove to platter and cover with foil to keep warm.
3. Repeat Steps 1 and 2 with remaining chops.
4. While chops are cooking, mix stuffing mix and hot water in bowl. Set aside.
5. Place onions in skillet. Cook over high heat, stirring frequently. Cook for 5 minutes, or until golden brown.
6. Stir in Worcestershire sauce.
7. Remove onions from skillet.
8. Return chops to skillet. Top with onion mixture.
9. Spoon stuffing around edge of skillet.
10. Top skillet contents with cheese.
11. Cover and cook 5 minutes, or until cheese is melted.

Pork Chop Casserole

Betty L. Moore
Plano, IL

Makes 4-5 servings

Prep. Time: 15-20 minutes
Baking Time: 1 hour

1-2 Tbsp. vegetable oil
4-5 pork chops, totaling
  about 2 lbs.
3-4 Tbsp. flour
1-2 Tbsp. vegetable oil
5 cups thinly sliced
  potatoes (about 3-4
  potatoes)
3 cups sliced onions (about
  2-3 onions)
10¾-oz. can cream of
  mushroom soup
½ cup water

1. Pour vegetable oil into skillet.
2. Place flour in shallow dish. Dredge chops in flour.
3. Two at a time, place chops in oil in skillet over medium-high heat. Do not crowd pan or chops will steam in their juices rather than browning.
4. Brown 2-3 minutes on each side, just until crust forms. Move browned chops to foil-covered dish and keep warm while browning rest of chops.
5. Place sliced potatoes and onions into well-greased 9 × 13 baking dish.
6. In a bowl, mix soup and water together until smooth.
7. Pour sauce over potatoes.
8. Place browned pork chops on top.
9. Bake, covered, at 350° for 45 minutes.
10. Remove cover from baking dish. Continue baking 15 minutes, or until lightly browned.

To make your own cream of mushroom or celery soup, please turn to pages 258-259.

Gourmet Pork Chops

Elsie R. Russett
Fairbank, IA

Makes 6 servings

Prep. Time: 15-20 minutes
Baking Time: 60-75 minutes

2 Tbsp. vegetable oil
2 Tbsp. flour
1 tsp. salt
dash of pepper
6 loin pork chops, ½" thick
10½-oz. can cream of
    chicken soup
¾ cup water
1 tsp. ground ginger
1 tsp. dried rosemary,
    crushed
3½-oz. can French fried
    onions

1. Place oil in good-sized skillet.
2. Combine flour, salt, and pepper in shallow but wide dish.
3. Dredge chops in mixture one at a time.
4. Place 2 or 3 chops in oil in skillet at a time, being careful not to crowd skillet. Brown chops over medium to high heat, 3-4 minutes on each side, until a browned crust forms.
5. As chops brown, place in well-greased 7 × 11 baking dish.
6. In bowl, combine soup, water, ginger, and rosemary.
7. Pour over chops.
8. Sprinkle with half the onions.
9. Cover. Bake at 350° for 50-60 minutes, or until chops are tender but not dry.
10. Uncover. Sprinkle with remaining onions.
11. Bake uncovered 10-15 minutes. Remove from oven and serve.

Try adding your favorite herbs and spices to your "tried and true" recipes, and you might come up with something even better.

Jeanne Heyerly, Shipshewana, IN

Mexican Barbecue Sauce for Ham Steaks

Annie Boshart
Lebanon, PA

Makes 4 servings

Prep. Time: 15 minutes
Cooking Time: 15 minutes

2 Tbsp. butter
1 small onion, chopped
7-oz. bottle soda 7-Up,
    Sprite, *or* ginger ale
¼ cup ketchup
1 tsp. dry mustard
1 tsp. salt
⅛ tsp. chili powder
⅛ tsp. pepper
4 whole cloves
2 lbs. ham steaks

1. In saucepan, sauté onion in butter until onion browns. Stir frequently to prevent burning.
2. Stir in soda, ketchup, mustard, salt, chili powder, pepper, and cloves.
3. Heat to boiling. Then reduce heat and simmer 10 minutes.
4. Fish out cloves and discard.
5. Brush sauce over both sides of ham steaks as they grill.

Tip:
    Place barbecue sauce in a nonbreakable pouring flask or measuring cup for easy handling while grilling ham.

Pork Cutlets

Audrey Romonosky
Austin, TX

Makes 6-8 servings

Prep. Time: 10 minutes
Cooking Time: 20-25 minutes

3 Tbsp. vegetable oil
2 eggs
½ cup milk
6-8 pork cutlets
salt and pepper
1½ cups seasoned bread
   crumbs
25-oz. jar marinara sauce

1. Heat oil in large skillet.
2. Beat eggs and milk together in shallow dish.
3. Dip cutlets in egg mixture one by one.
4. Place bread crumbs in another shallow dish.
5. Dredge cutlets in bread crumbs.
6. Place cutlets in hot oil in skillet, one by one, being careful not to splash yourself.
7. Do not crowd skillet. Cook cutlets in 2 or 3 batches so that they brown and don't just steam in their own juices.
8. Cook each cutlet 3-3½ minutes per side, until browned.
9. Season each side of each cutlet with salt and pepper.
10. Place browned cutlets on a platter. Cover with foil while you cook the next batch.
11. Heat marinara sauce. Spoon over cooked cutlets.
12. Pass any additional sauce to ladle over individual servings.

Tip:
   You can make this recipe using chicken cutlets instead.

Whipped Potatoes and Ham

June S. Groff
Denver, PA

Makes 6-8 servings

Prep. Time: 20 minutes
Baking Time: 45 minutes

6-8 cups mashed potatoes
½ tsp. garlic salt
3-4 cups cooked ham, chopped
half-pint (8 oz.) heavy
   whipping cream
2 cups shredded cheese

1. In a mixing bowl, stir garlic salt into mashed potatoes.
2. Place potatoes in well-greased 9 × 13 baking pan.
3. Scatter ham pieces over top.
4. Whip heavy cream until soft peaks form.
5. Gently fold cheese into whipped cream.
6. Spread over top of ham.
7. Cover. Bake at 350° for 40 minutes.
8. Uncover. Bake 5 more minutes.

Tips:
   You can make these through Step 6 the day before you serve them. If you put them in the oven cold, increase baking time by 10-15 minutes, or until they're hot in the middle.

Ham-Potatoes-Green Bean Casserole

Sarah Miller
Harrisonburg, VA

Makes 12 servings

Prep. Time: 45 minutes
Baking Time: 30 minutes

half stick (4 Tbsp.) butter
½ cup flour
3 cups milk
1½-2 cups grated cheese of
your choice
5 medium-sized potatoes,
cooked and sliced thin
2 lbs. fresh green beans
with ends nipped off,
or **2 16-oz. pkgs. frozen**
green beans, steamed or
microwaved until just-
tender
3 cups cooked, diced ham
3 Tbsp. butter
2 cups bread crumbs

1. Melt half stick butter in saucepan.
2. Stir in flour.
3. Gradually stir in milk. Stir continually while cooking over low heat until mixture thickens.
4. Add cheese and stir until it melts.
5. Arrange potatoes in well-greased 9 × 13 baking dish.
6. Drain any liquid off green beans. Spread beans over potatoes.
7. Pour half of cheese sauce over beans.
8. Spread ham over sauce.
9. Pour remaining sauce over all.
10. In saucepan melt 3 Tbsp. butter.
11. Stir in bread crumbs. Over low heat, brown lightly.
12. Scatter crumbs over casserole.
13. Bake at 350° for 30 minutes, or until heated through.

Tips:

1. Instead of cooking potatoes, you can use frozen shredded potatoes, thawed.
2. To save more time, you can use 2 15½-oz. cans green beans, drained, instead of fresh or frozen beans.

Ham Loaf *or* Ham Balls

Joette Droz
Kalona, IA

Makes 15-20 servings

Prep. Time: 30 minutes
Baking Time: 1½ hours for Ham
Loaf; 1 hour for Ham Balls

1½ lbs. hamburger
1½ lbs. bulk pork sausage
2 lbs. ground ham
3 eggs, beaten
1 cup graham cracker
crumbs
1 cup soda cracker crumbs
1½ cups milk

Glaze:
10¾-oz. can tomato
soup, undiluted
½-¾ cup vinegar
1½ cups brown sugar
½-1 tsp. dry mustard

1. In a large bowl, combine hamburger, sausage, ground ham, eggs, cracker crumbs, and milk. Mix well. This is a lot of bulk, so mix either with well-washed hands, or with a hefty wooden spoon.
2. Divide mixture in half. Shape each into a loaf, or form into 44 balls, about ¼ cup each.
3. If you're making loaves, place each in a well-greased bread or loaf pan. If you're making balls, arrange in well-greased 9 × 13 baking pan.
4. Bake loaves at 350° for 1½ hours. Bake balls at 350° for 1 hour.
5. Meanwhile, prepare glaze by mixing together soup, vinegar, brown sugar, and mustard in a mixing bowl.
6. For loaves, spread glaze over top after loaves have baked 1 hour. For balls, spread glaze over top after balls have baked 30 minutes.

Glazed Ham Balls

Teresa Koenig
Leola, PA
Dorothy Schrock
Arthur, IL

Makes 6-8 servings
Prep. Time: 20 minutes
Baking Time: 50 minutes

9-oz. can (1 cup) crushed
   pineapple, undrained
⅓ cup brown sugar
1 Tbsp. vinegar
2-3 Tbsp. prepared
   mustard
1½ lbs. ham loaf
¾ cup bread crumbs, *or*
   crushed saltine crackers
2 slightly beaten eggs
½ cup ketchup, *or* milk
⅛ cup chopped onion
¼ tsp. pepper, *optional*

1. In a mixing bowl, mix
together pineapple, sugar,
vinegar, and mustard. Set
aside.
2. In a large mixing bowl,
thoroughly combine ham loaf,
bread crumbs, eggs, ketchup,
and onion.
3. Shape into 1½" balls
(about 18-21 balls). Place in
well-greased shallow baking
dish.
4. Spoon pineapple mixture
over ham balls.
5. Cover. Bake at 350° for
25 minutes.
6. Uncover. Continue
baking 25 more minutes.

Tip:
   You can freeze the balls,
and then reheat them in the
microwave. They're an easy
meal after a long work day.

Variation:
   If you can't find ham loaf,
you can use 1 lb. fresh bulk
sausage and 1½ cups cooked
ground ham, mixed together
well.

Dorothy Schrock
Arthur, IL

Papa's Kielbasa Bake

Elaine Patton
West Middletown, PA

Makes 12 servings
Prep. Time: 20 minutes
Baking Time: 60 minutes

3 lbs. Kielbasa, *or* Polish
   sausage
12-oz. bottle chili sauce
20-oz. can crushed
   pineapple, including
   juice
½ cup brown sugar

1. Cut kielbasa or sausage
into ¾"-thick slices. Place in
roasting pan.
2. Mix in sauce, pineapple
and juice, and brown sugar
until well blended.
3. Cover. Bake at 350° for
40 minutes.
4. Stir. Continue baking,
uncovered, for another 20
minutes.

Tip:
   Any leftovers make great
sandwiches.

*Beside each dish of food on the buffet, place a
stack of cards with its recipe written on them. Then
guests can take the recipe if they wish.*

Anita Troyer, Fairview, MI

Sweet and Sour Sausage Stir-Fry

Colleen Heatwole
Burton, WI

Makes 4-6 servings

Prep. Time: 20 minutes
Cooking Time: 15 minutes

1 lb. reduced-fat Kielbasa, cut into ½"-thick slices
½-¾ cup chopped onion
1 cup shredded carrots
8-oz. can unsweetened pineapple chunks, *or* tidbits
1 Tbsp. cornstarch
½-1 tsp. ground ginger
6 Tbsp. water
2 Tbsp. reduced-sodium soy sauce
hot cooked rice

1. In large nonstick skillet, stir-fry sausage 3-4 minutes, or until lightly browned.
2. Add onions and carrots. Stir-fry until crisp-tender.
3. Drain pineapple, reserving juice. Add pineapple to sausage-vegetable mixture.
4. In small bowl, combine cornstarch and ginger. Stir in water, soy sauce, and reserved pineapple juice until smooth.
5. Add sauce to skillet.
6. Bring to boil. Cook, stirring continually 1-2 minutes, or until sauce is thickened.
7. Serve over rice.

Tip:
You can double everything in the recipe except the meat, and it is still excellent.

Smoked Sausage and Sauerkraut

Joan Terwilliger
Lebanon, PA

Makes 6-8 servings

Prep. Time: 20 minutes
Baking Time: 1¾-2 hours

2 Tbsp. butter
3 apples, peeled, halved, sliced thickly
1 large sweet onion, halved, sliced thickly
4 Yukon Gold potatoes, peeled, cut in ½" cubes
½ cup light brown sugar, packed
¼ cup Dijon mustard
½-1 lb. Kielbasa, sliced ½" thick, depending on amount of meat you like
1 cup apple cider, *or* Riesling
2 lbs. sauerkraut, rinsed and drained

1. Melt butter in large oven-proof Dutch oven over medium-high heat.
2. Sauté apples and onions 10 minutes in butter, stirring occasionally.
3. Add potatoes.
4. In small bowl, mix together sugar and mustard. Add to onion-potato mixture.
5. Place sausage slices on top of onion-potato mixture.
6. Pour in cider or wine.
7. Place sauerkraut on top of sausage.
8. Bake, covered, at 350° for 1¾-2 hours, or until potatoes are tender.

Bubble and Squeak

Mrs. Anna Gingerich
Apple Creek, OH

Makes 6 servings

Prep. Time: 15-20 minutes
Cooking Time: 45 minutes

1 lb. bulk sausage
1 onion, diced
4-6 medium potatoes, sliced thin
½ to 1 head cabbage, sliced thin
⅓ cup vinegar, *optional*
cheese of your choice, sliced or grated, *optional*

1. Sauté onions and sausage together in a deep iron skillet until no pink remains in meat. Stir frequently to break up clumps of meat.
2. Stir in potatoes. Continue cooking over low heat until potatoes begin to become tender. Stir often to prevent sticking and burning, but let potatoes brown.
3. Stir in cut cabbage. Continue cooking until cabbage wilts and potatoes are tender.
4. Stir in vinegar if you wish. Cook a few minutes to blend flavors.
5. Cover contents of skillet with cheese if you wish. Let stand a few minutes until cheese melts.

Good Go-Alongs:
Applesauce, coleslaw or salad

Polish Reuben Casserole

Jean Heyerly
Shipshewana, IN

Makes 10-12 servings

Prep. Time: 25-30 minutes
Baking Time: 1 hour

2 10¾-oz. cans cream of
  mushroom soup
1⅓ cups milk
1 Tbsp. prepared mustard
½ cup chopped onion
2 16-oz. cans sauerkraut,
  rinsed and drained
8-oz. pkg. uncooked
  medium-width noodles
1½ lbs. Polish sausage, cut
  in ½"-thick slices
2 cups (8-oz.) shredded
  Swiss cheese
¾ cup whole wheat bread
  crumbs
2 Tbsp. butter, melted

1. Mix soup, milk, mustard,
and onion in a bowl. Set
aside.
2. Spread sauerkraut in
well-greased 9×13 baking
dish.
3. Top with uncooked
noodles.
4. Spoon soup mixture
evenly over noodles.
5. Top with sliced sausage.
6. Sprinkle with shredded
cheese.
7. In a small bowl, combine
bread crumbs and melted
butter.
8. Sprinkle on top of
cheese.

9. Cover with foil and bake
at 350° for 1 hour, or until
noodles are tender.

Sausage Scalloped Potatoes

Karen Waggoner
Joplin, MO

Makes 4-6 servings

Prep. Time: 20 minutes
Cooking Time: 30-35 minutes
Standing Time: 5 minutes

1 lb. Polish sausage,
  or Kielbasa, cut into
  ¼"-thick slices
2 Tbsp. butter
2 Tbsp. flour
1 tsp. salt
¼ tsp. pepper
2 cups milk
4 medium red potatoes,
  halved and thinly sliced,
  enough to make 3½-4
  cups
¼ cup onions, chopped
2 Tbsp. minced fresh
  parsley, *optional*

1. Place sausage in
microwave-safe dish. Microwave uncovered on High for
3 minutes. Set aside.
2. Place butter in 2½-quart
microwave-safe dish. Microwave on High 45-60 seconds,
or until melted.
3. Whisk flour, salt, and
pepper into butter until
smooth.
4. Gradually whisk in milk.

5. Microwave on High
8-10 minutes until thickened,
stirring every 2 minutes.
6. Stir potatoes and onions
into creamy sauce.
7. Cover. Microwave on
High 4 minutes. Stir.
8. Microwave on High
4 minutes longer.
9. Stir in sausage. Cover.
10. Microwave 8-10
minutes on High, stirring
every 4 minutes. Continue
until potatoes are tender and
sausage is heated through.
Stir.
11. Let stand, covered,
5 minutes.
12. Sprinkle with parsley
and serve.

Hearty Farm Special

Emily Fox
Bethel, PA

Makes 6 servings

Prep. Time: 30 minutes
Baking Time: 70 minutes

1-1½ lbs. bulk sausage,
  depending on how much
  you like meat
2 cups chopped celery
1 medium onion, chopped
8-oz. can tomato sauce
½ cup water
2 Tbsp. prepared mustard
16-oz. can pork & beans
4 medium potatoes, peeled
  or unpeeled, sliced quite
  thin
½ cup grated cheddar
  cheese

1. In large nonstick skillet cook sausage until no longer pink. Stir frequently to break up clumps of meat. Drain off drippings.
2. Add celery and onion. Sauté until crisp-tender.
3. Stir in tomato sauce, water, mustard, and pork and beans, and mustard. Cover. Bring to boil.
4. Stir in potato slices.
5. Spoon into greased 3-quart casserole.
6. Cover. Bake at 350° for 1 hour, or until potatoes are tender.
7. Sprinkle with cheese. Return to oven and bake, uncovered, 10 minutes longer.

Penny Saver

Jane Geigley
Lancaster, PA

Makes 4 servings

Prep. Time: 30 minutes
Baking Time: 45 minutes

6 wieners, *or* ¾ lb. sausage
  of your choice, cut into
  1"-thick chunks
4 medium potatoes, peeled
  or not, diced and cooked
1 tsp. chives
half stick (4 Tbsp) butter,
  melted
1 Tbsp. prepared mustard
10¾-oz. can cream of
  mushroom soup
¼ tsp. salt
¼ tsp. pepper
1 cup frozen peas

1. Combine wieners or sausage, potatoes, chives, and butter in well-greased 2-quart casserole.
2. In a bowl, blend together mustard, soup, salt, and pepper.
3. Stir creamy sauce into casserole.
4. Cover. Bake at 350° for 35 minutes.
5. Stir in peas.
6. Cover. Continue baking 10 more minutes.

Wild Rice Supper

Mamie Christopherson
Rio Rancho, NM

Makes 6-8 servings

Soaking Time: 8 hours, or
  overnight
Prep. Time: 20-30 minutes
Baking Time: 25 minutes

3 cups water
1 cup wild rice
½ lb. bulk sausage
1 finely chopped onion
½ lb. fresh mushrooms,
  sliced, *or* 8-oz. can sliced
  mushrooms, drained
¼ cup flour
¼ cup cream
2½ cups chicken broth
dash of Tabasco sauce
½ tsp. oregano
½ tsp. thyme
½ tsp. marjoram

1. In good-sized bowl, soak rice in water 8 hours, or overnight.
2. Pour rice and soaking water into saucepan. Cover.
3. Over medium heat, bring to boil. Simmer, covered, 12-15 minutes, or until tender.
4. Meanwhile, sauté sausage in large nonstick skillet until no longer pink. Stir often to break up clumps.
5. Remove meat and keep warm.
6. Sauté onions and mushrooms in sausage drippings.
7. Add sausage and rice to skillet.
8. In saucepan, combine flour, cream, and chicken broth. Cook over medium heat, stir-

ring continually until mixture begins to boil and thicken.

9. Add Tabasco sauce, oregano, thyme, and marjoram to saucepan.

10. Add to sausage-rice mixture and combine well.

11. Spoon into well-greased 3-quart casserole dish.

12. Cover. Bake at 375° for 25 minutes, or until bubbly and heated through.

Ham Roll-Ups

Glenda Weaver
Manheim, PA

Makes 25-30 servings

Prep. Time: 30 minutes
Baking Time: 30 minutes

1 stick (½ cup) butter
pinch of saffron, *optional*
¾ cup chopped celery
1 small onion, chopped
1 tsp. salt
¼ tsp. pepper
6-8 slices bread, cubed
4 eggs, beaten
2 cups milk
25-30 slices turkey ham *or* boiled ham
25-30 slices American *or* Swiss cheese
1-2 10-oz. can(s) turkey gravy

1. In a saucepan, simmer together butter, saffron if you wish, celery, onion, salt, and pepper until vegetables are soft. Set aside.

2. In a good-sized mixing bowl, mix together cubed bread, eggs, and milk.

3. Add to celery mixture. Mix well.

4. Let filling mixture stand 10 minutes to firm up.

5. Meanwhile, put 1 slice cheese on top of 1 slice turkey ham or boiled ham

6. Top with 1 Tbsp. filling mixture.

7. Roll up. Lay in well-greased 9 × 13 baking pan.

8. Repeat with each slice of ham and cheese.

9. When finished, pour gravy over top.

10. Bake at 350° for 30 minutes, or until heated through.

Zucchini-Sausage Pie

Julia Horst
Lancaster, PA

Makes 8 servings

Prep. Time: 45 minutes
Baking Time: 30 minutes

8-oz. tube refrigerated crescent rolls
1 lb. bulk sausage
half stick (4 Tbsp.) butter
4 cups thinly sliced zucchini
2 cups chopped onion
2 large eggs
2 Tbsp. freshly chopped parsley
2 tsp. dry mustard
1 tsp. oregano
1 tsp. basil
½ tsp. salt
½ tsp. pepper
¼ tsp. garlic powder
1 cup shredded cheddar cheese
1 cup shredded mozzarella cheese

1. Lightly grease 9 × 13 baking dish. Separate crescent rolls, and then line bottom of baking dish with them.

2. Bake at 375° for 10 minutes. Remove from oven.

3. Meanwhile, brown sausage in good-sized nonstick skillet. Drain off drippings. Set sausage aside.

4. Melt butter in same skillet over medium heat. Add zucchini and onion.

5. Cook vegetables over medium-high 10-12 minutes, stirring frequently, until most of liquid has evaporated.

6. In large bowl, whisk together eggs, parsley, mustard, oregano, basil, salt, pepper, and garlic powder.

7. Stir in sausage, zucchini mixture, and cheeses.

8. Pour over crescent rolls.

9. Bake at 375° for 30 minutes, or until golden brown.

10. Let stand 10 minutes before serving.

Shop at local markets and "invent" with what's in season and usually less expensive.

Barbara Forrester Landis, Lititz, PA

FINGER FOOD

Sandwich for 12

Kinita Martin
East Earl, PA

Makes 12 servings

Prep. Time: 40 minutes
Rising Time: 45 minutes
Baking Time: 25-30 minutes

Bread:
½ cup quick oats
½ cup boiling water
¼ cup oil
16-oz. pkg. hot-roll mix
1 tsp. additional yeast
¾ cup warm water
1 egg, beaten
1 Tbsp. dried minced
   onion

Topping:
1 egg
1 tsp. garlic salt
1 Tbsp. minced onion
1 Tbsp. sesame seeds

Filling:
½ cup mayonnaise
5 tsp. brown grainy
   mustard
lettuce leaves
8 oz. thinly sliced ham
8 oz. thinly sliced turkey
   breast
1 medium green bell
   pepper, sliced
1 medium onion, sliced
6 oz. thinly sliced Swiss
   cheese
2 large tomatoes, sliced

1. To make bread, combine oats, boiling water, and oil in large bowl. Let stand 5 minutes.

2. In separate bowl, dissolve yeast from hot-roll mix, plus additional 1 tsp. yeast, in warm water.

3. Add yeast water to oatmeal mixture.

4. Stir in egg and onion.

5. Add flour mixture from hot roll mix, stirring well. Do not knead.

6. Spread dough into 10" circle on well-greased pizza pan. Cover with plastic wrap coated with nonstick cooking spray.

7. Let rise in warm place until doubled, about 45 minutes.

8. While dough rises, prepare topping. In small bowl, beat egg and garlic salt together.

9. After dough has risen, uncover it and brush egg wash gently over dough.

10. Sprinkle with minced onion and sesame seeds.

11. Bake at 350° for 25-30 minutes, until golden brown.

12. Remove bread from pan to cool on wire rack.

13. When cool, cut through middle of bread to create a top and a bottom.

14. Prepare filling by combining mayonnaise and mustard in small bowl.

15. Spread over cut sides of bread.

16. Layer bottom half of bread with lettuce, ham, turkey, green pepper, onion, cheese, and tomatoes.

17. Put on top half. Cut into wedges and serve.

Poultry Main Dishes

Main Dishes
Chicken

Oven Barbecued Chicken

Carol Eberly
Harrisonburg, VA

Makes 8-12 servings

Prep. Time: 10 minutes
Baking Time: 1¼ hours

3 Tbsp. ketchup
2 Tbsp. Worcestershire sauce
2 Tbsp. vinegar
2 Tbsp. soy sauce
3 Tbsp. brown sugar
1 tsp. spicy brown mustard
1 tsp. salt
1 tsp. pepper
8-12 boneless, skinless
  chicken thighs

1. In a mixing bowl, combine ketchup, Worcestershire sauce, vinegar, soy sauce, brown sugar, mustard, salt, and pepper. Blend well.
2. Lay chicken pieces in one layer in well-greased baking dish.
3. Pour sauce over top.
4. Bake at 350° for 40 minutes.
5. Turn pieces over. Bake 35 more minutes.

Tip:
   You can use chicken legs or chicken breasts, too. Check the legs after they've baked for a total of 50 minutes to be sure they're not drying out. Check breasts after they've baked for a total of 30 minutes to be sure they're not becoming dry.

To tell if chicken is done, pierce the thickest piece with a fork. If the juice runs clear, it's done.
Carolyn Spohn, Shawnee, KS

BBQ Chicken

Alice Miller
Stuarts Draft, VA

Makes 6 servings

Prep. Time: 20-30 minutes
Baking Time: 1-1½ hours

2½-3 lbs. skinned chicken
  legs and/or thighs
1-2 cups water
1 tsp. salt
¼ tsp. pepper
1½ tsp. paprika, *or* chili
  powder
1 tsp. brown sugar
2 Tbsp. Worcestershire
  sauce
1 medium onion, chopped
1 cup ketchup, *or* barbecue
  sauce
1 Tbsp. butter
½ cup chicken broth, saved
  from cooking chicken
⅓ cup lemon juice

1. Place chicken pieces in
stockpot. Add water.
2. Cover. Cook chicken
over medium heat until
tender, about 35-45 minutes.
3. Remove chicken from
broth. Allow to cool.
4. Pour broth into container
and set aside.
5. When chicken is cool
enough to handle, debone.
6. Shred meat using two
forks.
7. Return meat to stockpot.
Stir in salt, pepper, paprika or
chili powder, sugar, Worcestershire sauce, onion, ketchup
or barbecue sauce, butter,
broth, and lemon juice.
8. Cook until onions are
soft.
9. Serve on hamburger
buns.

Encore Dijon Chicken

Dorothy VanDeest
Memphis, TN

Makes 4-6 servings

Prep. Time: 5-10 minutes
Baking Time: 20 minutes

½ tsp. **Italian seasoning**
4 Tbsp. **Dijon mustard**
2 Tbsp. **vegetable oil**
1 tsp. **garlic powder,** *or*
  refrigerated minced
  garlic
4-6 **boneless chicken breast**
  halves, about 6-oz. each
  in weight

1. Grease a 7 × 11 or 9 × 13
baking dish.
2. Mix Italian seasoning,
mustard, oil, and garlic in
either a large bowl or plastic
bag.
3. Add chicken pieces, one
at a time. Dredge or shake to
coat each piece.
4. Lay in baking dish.
5. Bake at 375° for 20
minutes, or until thermometer
inserted in center of each
piece registers 165°.

Golden Chicken Breasts

Lorna Rodes
Port Republic, VA

Makes 8 servings

Prep. Time: 15 minutes
Baking Time: 45-55 minutes

1 cup grated Parmesan cheese
½ cup grated cheddar cheese
1 cup snack cracker crumbs
½ tsp. thyme
2 tsp. basil, crushed
1 tsp. salt
¼ tsp. pepper
1 stick (½ cup) butter, melted
8 boneless, skinless chicken breast halves

1. Grease a 9 × 13 baking dish.
2. In a shallow bowl, combine Parmesan cheese, cheddar cheese, cracker crumbs, thyme, basil, salt, and pepper.
3. Pour butter into another shallow bowl.
4. Roll each piece of chicken in butter and then in crumbs.
5. Place in baking dish.
6. Sprinkle any remaining crumbs over chicken pieces.
7. Drizzle with any remaining butter.
8. Bake at 350° for 45 minutes, or until thermometer inserted into center of chicken registers 165°.

Crispy Chicken

Kitty Hilliard
Punxsutawney, PA

Makes 4 servings

Prep. Time: 10 minutes
Baking Time: 20-25 minutes

2 Tbsp. flour
1½ cups crisp rice cereal, coarsely crushed
½ tsp. salt
¼ tsp. dried thyme
¼ tsp. poultry seasoning
half stick (4 Tbsp.) butter, melted
4 boneless, skinless chicken breast halves, each about 4-6 oz.

1. Grease a 7 × 11 baking dish.
2. In a shallow bowl, combine flour, cereal, salt, thyme, and poultry seasoning.
3. Place butter in another shallow bowl.
4. Dip chicken in butter, then into cereal mixture.
5. Place in greased 7 × 11 baking pan.
6. Drizzle with remaining butter.
7. Bake at 400° for 20-25 minutes, or until thermometer inserted in center registers 165°.

Tip:
You can also put the dry ingredients in an empty cereal bag, then drop chicken pieces in and shake to coat.

Soft Chicken Tenders

LuAnna Hochstedler
East Earl, PA

Makes 4-6 servings

Prep. Time: 20-25 minutes
Baking Time: 10-15 minutes

1 Tbsp. vegetable oil
24 oz. chicken tenders
¼ tsp. salt
¼ tsp. lemon pepper seasoning
4 bacon strips, cooked crisp
1 onion, sliced
¼ cup brown sugar, packed
½ cup shredded cheese
½ cup water

1. Place oil in large skillet.
2. Sprinkle chicken with salt and lemon pepper seasoning.
3. Stir-fry chicken in oil for 13-15 minutes, or until lightly browned and no longer pink.
4. Remove chicken (reserve drippings in skillet) and place in well-greased 7 × 11 baking dish.
5. Sauté onion in drippings in skillet.
6. Stir in brown sugar and continue sautéing until onion is limp and sugar has melted.
7. Layer onions, skillet drippings, bacon, and cheese over chicken.
8. Pour in water around edges.
9. Bake at 350° for 10-15 minutes, or until cheese melts.

Cola Chicken

Esther S. Martin
Ephrata, PA

Makes 4 servings

Prep. Time: 5 minutes
Cooking Time: 1 hour

12-oz. can cola
1 cup ketchup, *or* your
favorite barbecue sauce
4 boneless, skinless,
chicken breast halves,
6-8 oz. each in weight

1. In a large skillet, mix cola and ketchup until smooth.
2. Bring to a boil.
3. Add chicken breasts and submerge in sauce.
4. Cover skillet. Reduce heat, simmering for about 45 minutes, or until chicken is almost tender.
5. Remove cover. Increase heat until liquid boils.
6. Continue cooking until sauce thickens and chicken is cooked but not dried out. (Thermometer inserted into center of pieces should register 165°.)

Good Go-Alongs:
We like the sauce from this dish better than gravy on mashed potatoes.

Cranberry Chicken

Judi Manos
West Islip, NY

Makes 8 servings

Prep. Time: 10 minutes
Baking Time: 50 minutes

4 lbs. skinless, bone-in
chicken pieces; your
choice of breast halves
or thighs
16-oz. can whole cranberry
sauce
8-oz. bottle Catalina
Dressing
1 envelope onion soup mix

1. Place chicken in single layer in two well-greased 9 × 13 baking dishes.
2. In mixing bowl, blend together cranberry sauce, Catalina dressing, and onion soup mix.
3. Pour over chicken pieces.
4. Bake 50 minutes, or until chicken is done. Thermometer inserted in center of meat should register 165°.

Super Easy Chicken

Lauren Eberhard
Seneca, IL

Prep. Time: 10 minutes
Cooking Time: 5-6 minutes each

1 4-oz. chicken breast
for each person you're
serving
**Mrs. Dash Garlic and Herb
flavoring**, *or* any flavor
you like
olive oil
cooking spray

1. Pound each chicken breast to ½" thickness.
2. Use the following instructions for each breast.
3. Heat 2 Tbsp. oil in skillet over medium-high heat.
4. Sprinkle breast with Mrs. Dash on 1 side.
5. Spray seasoned side with a little cooking spray.
6. Place seasoned side of chicken down. Sauté until golden, about 3-4 minutes.
7. While this side is cooking, season the up side as you did previously.
8. Turn chicken over. Continue sautéeing until done, about 2 more minutes. This happens fast, so be careful not to overcook the pieces!
9. As each piece finishes, place on oven-proof platter, covered with foil. Keep covered platter in oven set at 250° until ready to serve.

Tip:
I make extra breasts when I'm in the swing so I have them on hand to cut up for salads and soups.

Lemony Chicken

Cynthia Morris
Grottoes, VA

Makes 4-6 servings

Prep. Time: 20 minutes
Baking Time: 45-60 minutes

1 cup sour cream
10¾-oz. can cream soup,
    your choice of flavor
2 Tbsp. lemon juice
4-6 large chicken breasts
    halves, uncooked and
    cubed
4- *or* 8-oz. can mushrooms,
    drained
1 cup shredded cheese

sleeve of snack crackers,
    crushed, *divided*
half stick (4 Tbsp.) butter,
    melted

1. In large mixing bowl, blend together sour cream, soup, and lemon juice.
2. When smooth, stir in cubed chicken breasts, mushrooms, cheese, and half of crushed crackers.
3. Pour into well-greased 9 × 13 baking pan.
4. Sprinkle with remaining crackers.
5. Drizzle with melted butter.
6. Bake at 350° for 45-60 minutes, or until chicken is cooked through and no pink remains in meat.

Tip:
You can also use already-cooked chicken in this dish. When doing so, reduce baking time to 30-40 minutes, or until heated through.

Creamy Baked Chicken Breasts

Naomi Ressler
Harrisonburg, VA

Jan Rankin
Millersville, PA

Joyce Kaut
Rochester, NY

Anna Musser
Manheim, PA

Makes 8 servings

Prep. Time: 15-20 minutes
Baking Time: 45-55 minutes

8 boneless, skinless
    chicken breast halves,
    each 6-8 oz. in weight
8 slices Swiss cheese
10¾-oz. can cream of
    chicken soup
¼ cup dry white wine, *or*
    water — *or* ¾ cup sour
    cream
2 cups herb-seasoned
    stuffing mix
half stick (4 Tbsp.) butter,
    melted

1. Arrange chicken in lightly greased 9 × 13 baking dish.
2. Top with cheese slices.
3. In a mixing bowl, combine soup and wine until smooth.
4. Spoon evenly over chicken and cheese.
5. Sprinkle with stuffing mix.
6. Drizzle butter over crumbs.
7. Bake at 350° for 45-55 minutes, or until chicken is tender in the middle.

Chicken Cacciatore

Donna Lantgen
Arvada, CO

Makes 6 servings

Prep. Time: 10 minutes
Cooking/Baking Time: 65-
90 minutes, depending on
thickness of chicken

6 boneless skinless chicken
  breast halves, each
  about 6 oz. in weight
1 medium green bell
  pepper, chopped
1 medium onion, chopped
15½-oz. can tomatoes,
  chopped, *or* 2 cups fresh
  tomatoes, diced and
  peeled
1 Tbsp. Italian seasoning
mozzarella, *or* Parmesan
  cheese, shredded

1. Place chicken in well
greased 9 × 13 baking pan.
2. In mixing bowl, stir
together green pepper, onion,
tomatoes, and seasoning.
3. Spoon vegetables evenly
over chicken.
4. Cover. Bake at 350° for
45 minutes.

5. With a sharp knife
make 2-3 vertical slashes in
thickest part of each chicken
breast. (Do not cut the whole
way through.) Baste with pan
juices.
6. Cover. Return to oven
and continue baking 15 more
minutes, or until thermometer
inserted in center of chicken
registers 165°.
7. Top chicken with cheese.
8. Return to oven for 5-10
minutes, or until cheese
melts.

Good Go-Alongs:
  Serve with pasta, vegetables,
and garlic bread.

In the fall when peppers are plentiful, chop them and freeze them in a single layer on cookie sheets. After they're frozen, store in freezer bags. We eat lots of this healthy vegetable when they are so handy for soups and casseroles.

Ann Good, Dayton, VA

Chicken Parmesan

Jessalyn Wantland
Napoleon, OH

Makes 4 servings

Prep. Time: 10 minutes
Baking Time: 45 minutes

4 boneless, skinless
  chicken breast halves,
  about 6 oz. each
1 egg, beaten
¾ cup Italian-seasoned
  bread crumbs
25-oz. jar pasta sauce
1 cup shredded Parmesan
  cheese

1. Grease 7 × 11 baking
dish.
2. Place egg in shallow
bowl.
3. Place bread crumbs in
another shallow bowl.
4. Dip each piece of
chicken in egg, and then in
bread crumbs.
5. Place coated chicken in
baking dish.
6. Bake at 400° for 30
minutes.
7. Spoon pasta sauce over
chicken.
8. Top evenly with cheese.
9. Bake another 15 min-
utes, or until heated through
and cheese is melted.

Easy Chicken Cordon Bleu

Sharon Miller
Holmesville, OH

Makes 4 servings

Prep. Time: 15 minutes
Cooking Time: 45-60 minutes

4 large boneless, skinless chicken breast halves, each about 8 oz. in weight
½-1 cup Italian-seasoned dry bread crumbs
4 large slices Swiss cheese
4 slices deli ham
8 sturdy toothpicks

1. Grease a 9 × 13 baking dish.
2. Pound each chicken breast to about ¼-½" thickness.
3. Place bread crumbs in shallow bowl.
4. Dredge each chicken piece in bread crumbs, coating each side.
5. Lay slice of Swiss cheese and slice of ham on each chicken breast.
6. Tightly roll up each layered breast.
7. Holding roll firmly, re-roll in crumbs.
8. Stick 2 toothpicks through each roll to maintain its shape.
9. Place in baking dish. Cover with foil.
10. Bake at 350° for 30 minutes.
11. Remove foil. Bake an additional 15 minutes.

Tips:
1. The size of chicken breasts varies widely. If you're using extra-large breasts, 2 slices of ham and cheese per breast makes the dish even tastier. Match up chicken size with cheese and ham sizes as well as you can.
2. If the cheese is too "exposed" instead of being enclosed in the bundle, it melts outside the bundle.

Oven-Fried Chicken

Eleanor Larson
Glen Lyon, PA

Makes 8 servings

Prep. Time: 5-10 minutes
Baking Time: 1 hour

8 boneless, skinless chicken thighs, each about 6-oz. in weight
½ cup flour
¼ tsp. paprika
½ tsp. salt
1 stick (½ cup) butter, melted, *divided*

1. Grease a 9 × 13 baking dish well.
2. Combine flour, paprika and salt in plastic bag.
3. Drop chicken into bag, one piece at a time. Shake to coat well.
4. Place coated pieces of chicken in baking dish.
5. Pour half of melted butter evenly over chicken.
6. Bake at 375° for 30 minutes.
7. Turn each piece over.
8. Pour remaining butter evenly over chicken.
9. Return to oven. Bake an additional 30 minutes.

Tips:
You can double this for a larger group.

Crunchy Chicken

Joette Droz
Kalona, IA

Makes 4 servings

Prep. Time: 15-20 minutes
Baking Time: 30-45 minutes

8 boneless skinless chicken
  thighs, about 1 lb.
¼ cup Miracle Whip light
  dressing
6-oz. pkg. stuffing mix for
  chicken, crushed fine
¼ cup grated Parmesan
  cheese

1. Cover baking sheet with
foil.
2. Spread chicken thighs
with Miracle Whip. Place on
foil-covered baking sheet,
3. Empty stuffing mix into
a pie plate. Add cheese and
stir to combine.
4. Roll each piece of
chicken in dry stuffing
mixture. Return to baking
sheet.
5. Bake at 375° for 30-45
minutes.

Herbed Chicken

Dale Peterson
Rapid City, SD

Makes 4-5 servings

Prep. Time: 20 minutes
Baking Time: 50-55 minutes

half stick (4 Tbsp.) butter,
  melted
1 Tbsp. vegetable oil
½ cup flour
½ cup fine dry bread
  crumbs
1 tsp. paprika
1 tsp. salt
¼ tsp. pepper
¼ tsp. ground thyme
3-4 lbs. chicken, cut up

1. Put butter and oil in
9 × 13 baking dish.
2. Mix flour, bread crumbs,
paprika, salt, pepper, and
thyme in plastic bag.
3. Put chicken pieces in
bag, one at a time, and shake.
Place chicken in baking dish.
4. Bake at 375° for 30
minutes.
5. Reduce heat to 350°.
6. Turn each piece of
chicken over.
7. Bake 20-25 minutes
more, or until thermometer
inserted in center of chicken
registers 165°.

Japanese Chicken

Marjorie Nolt
Denver, PA
Erma Martin
East Earl, PA
Mary Jane Musser
Manheim, PA

Makes 6 servings

Prep. Time: 20 minutes
Baking Time: 45 minutes

2 lbs. chicken, skinless
  and boneless breasts *or*
  thighs cut in half
flour
garlic salt
seasoned salt
paprika
1 cup sugar
½ cup vinegar
3 Tbsp. soy sauce
½ cup water
½ tsp. salt

1. Roll chicken in flour.
Sprinkle with garlic salt,
seasoned salt, and paprika.
2. Brown on both sides in
a skillet. Put in 9 × 13 baking
pan.
3. Boil together sugar,
vinegar, soy sauce, water, and
salt until sugar melts.
4. Pour sauce over chicken.
5. Bake uncovered at 350°
for 45 minutes. Serve with
rice if desired.

Chicken Recuerdos de Tucson

Joanna Harrison
Lafayette, CO

Makes 6 servings

Prep. Time: 15 minutes
Cooking Time: 30-40 minutes

---

1 whole chicken, cut up,
   or 6 chicken legs and
   thighs
1 Tbsp. olive oil
1 medium onion, chopped
   coarsely
3 cloves garlic, minced
1 tsp. ground cumin
2-3 green chilies, chopped,
   according to your taste
   preference
1 green bell pepper,
   chopped
1-2 zucchini, sliced
1 cup chopped tomatoes
2 cups corn
2 tsp. oregano
1 tsp. basil
2 cups chicken broth
cilantro for garnish

1. Brown chicken in olive oil in Dutch oven or large stockpot. Remove chicken to platter. Reserve pan drippings.
2. Gently sauté onion and garlic in drippings until wilted.
3. Stir in cumin, green chilies, green pepper, and zucchini. Sauté until peppers wilt.
4. Add tomatoes, corn, oregano, basil, and broth.
5. Return chicken to pot.

6. Cover. Simmer 30-40 minutes, or until chicken is tender to the bone.
7. Garnish with cilantro and serve.

Magra's Chicken & Rice

Carolyn Spohn
Shawnee, KS

Makes 8 servings

Prep. Time: 20 minutes
Baking Time: 40-60 minutes

1-2 tsp. olive oil
2-3 medium carrots,
   chopped
1 medium onion, chopped
1 rib celery, chopped
2 cloves garlic, chopped
¼ tsp. rosemary, crumbled
1½ cups uncooked long-
   grain rice
3 cups chicken broth
8 chicken legs, thighs, *or*
   breasts (if using breast
   meat, cut to size of
   thighs)

1. Sauté carrots, onion, and celery in in olive oil in skillet until softened and lightly browned.
2. Add garlic and sauté 1 minute. Do not brown garlic.
3. Add rosemary and mix well with vegetables.
4. Add uncooked rice to pan with vegetables and stir well to coat rice and evenly mix it with the vegetables.
5. Pour mixture into large, well-greased roaster.
6. Pour chicken broth over rice until it just covers rice.
7. Add chicken pieces on top of rice, pushing down into rice-vegetable mix.
8. Cover. Bake at 350° for approximately 40-60 minutes, or until rice and chicken are nearly cooked but not dry.
9. Remove cover and bake a few more minutes, or until chicken browns slightly.

Tip:
   You may need to use more or less broth to cover rice.

Check your local library for cookbooks with unusual recipes. Make copies of something new that sounds good, and try it ... but not for company, just in case it doesn't work.

John and Carol Ambrose, McMinnville, OR

Lemon-Chicken Oven Bake

Judi Manos
West Islip, NY

Makes 4 servings
Prep. Time: 10-15 minutes
Baking Time: 50 minutes

¼ cup Zesty Italian
　Dressing
½ cup chicken broth
1 Tbsp. honey
1½ lbs. bone-in chicken
　legs and thighs
1 lb. new potatoes,
　quartered
5 cloves garlic, peeled
1 lemon, cut in 8 wedges
1 tsp. dried rosemary,
　optional

1. In a mixing bowl, blend
together dressing, broth, and
honey.
2. Arrange chicken,
potatoes, and garlic in well-
greased 9 × 13 baking dish.
3. Drizzle with dressing
mixture.
4. Situate lemons among
the chicken and potatoes.
5. Bake at 400° for 45-50
minutes, or until chicken is
done and potatoes are tender.
(Temperature probe inserted
into center of chicken should
register 165°.)
6. Serve lemons as garnish
if you wish.

Chicken Baked with Red Onions, Potatoes, and Rosemary

Kristine Stalter
Iowa City, IA

Makes 4 servings
Prep. Time: 10-15 minutes
Baking Time: 45-60 minutes

2 red onions, each cut into
　10 wedges
1¼ lbs. new potatoes,
　unpeeled and cut into
　chunks
2 garlic bulbs, separated
　into cloves, unpeeled
salt
pepper
4 Tbsp. extra-virgin olive
　oil
2 Tbsp. balsamic vinegar
approximately 5 sprigs
　rosemary
4-lb. chicken cut into
　8 pieces, *or* 8 chicken
　thighs

1. Spread onions, potatoes,
and garlic cloves in single
layer over bottom of large
roasting pan so that they will
crisp and brown.
2. Season with salt and
pepper.
3. Pour over the oil and
balsamic vinegar and add
rosemary, leaving some sprigs
whole and stripping the
leaves off the rest.
4. Toss vegetables and
seasonings together.

5. Tuck chicken pieces
among vegetables.
6. Bake at 400° for 45-60
minutes, or until chicken
and vegetables are cooked
through.
7. Transfer to a big platter,
or take to the table in the
roasting pan.

*A neighbor and friend shared
this simple recipe with me
when my family and I were on
sabbatical in the UK.*

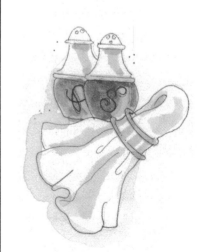

One-Dish Chicken and Gravy

Martha Ann Auker
Landisburg, PA

Makes 6 servings

Prep. Time: 10 minutes
Baking Time: 50 minutes

1 frying chicken, cut up
¼ cup flour
half stick (4 Tbsp.) butter, melted
1 tsp. onion, chopped
1 cup light cream
10¾-oz. can cream of mushroom soup
1 cup mild cheddar cheese, grated
¼-½ tsp. salt, according to your taste preference
¼ tsp. pepper
paprika

1. Pour melted butter in 9 × 13 baking pan. Swirl butter to cover bottom of pan.
2. Roll chicken in flour, one piece at a time. Place in melted butter in baking pan.
3. Bake uncovered at 425° for 30 minutes.
4. While chicken is baking, mix cream, soup, cheese, salt, and pepper together in mixing bowl.
5. Pour over chicken.
6. Sprinkle with paprika.
7. Cover with foil. Reduce heat to 325° and bake 20 more minutes.

Good Go-Alongs:
This is good served with rice.

Quick and Easy Chicken Enchiladas

Ellyn Nolt
Lancaster, PA

Makes 6-8 servings

Prep. Time: 20 minutes
Baking Time: 20 minutes

2 chicken breast halves (about 6-8 oz. each), cooked
15-oz. jar salsa
½ cup (half an 8-oz. pkg.) cream cheese, softened
12 flour tortillas
16-oz. jar taco sauce
2 cups shredded cheddar cheese

1. In large mixing bowl, use 2 forks to shred chicken.
2. Mix salsa and cream cheese into chicken.
3. Grease 9 × 13 baking dish.
4. Put about ¼ cup chicken mixture onto each tortilla and roll up.
5. Place side by side in baking dish, seam side down.
6. Pour taco sauce evenly over top of rolls.
7. Sprinkle rolls evenly with cheese.
8. Bake at 350° for about 20 minutes, or until filling is heated through and cheese is melted.

Tip:
You can customize this to suit your personal taste and those you're serving: the heat of salsa and taco sauces, the addition of onions, canned chilies, etc.

Variations:
1. Add 2¼-oz. can sliced black olives, drained, to Step 7, sprinkling olives over rolls along with cheese.
2. Serve with shredded lettuce and chopped tomatoes as toppings.
3. Instead of cream cheese, use 1 cup sour cream.

Lavonda Hoover
Coatesville PA

Easy Chicken Enchiladas

Lois Peterson
Huron, SD

Makes 4 servings

Prep. Time: 35-45 minutes
Baking Time: 40 minutes

10¾-oz. can cream of
 chicken soup
½ cup sour cream
1 cup picante sauce
2 tsp. chili powder
2 cups cooked chicken,
 chopped
1 cup grated pepper Jack
 cheese
6 6" flour tortillas
1 medium tomato, chopped
1 green onion, sliced

1. Stir soup, sour cream,
picante sauce, and chili
powder in a medium bowl.

2. In a large bowl, combine
1 cup sauce mixture, chicken,
and cheese.

3. Grease 9 × 13 baking
dish.

4. Divide mixture among
tortillas.

5. Roll up each tortilla.
Place in baking dish, seam
side down.

6. Pour remaining sauce
mixture over filled tortillas.

7. Cover. Bake at 350° for
40 minutes or until enchiladas are hot and bubbling.

8. Top with chopped
tomato and onion and serve.

Creamy Chicken Enchilada

Cheryl Martin
Turin, NY

Makes 10 servings

Prep. Time: 30 minutes
Baking Time: 30-40 minutes

2 10¾-oz. cans cream of
 chicken soup
8 oz. sour cream
¼ tsp. cumin
¼ tsp. oregano
3 cups diced, cooked
 chicken
4-oz. can chopped green
 chilies
1 tsp. chili powder
2 cups shredded cheddar
 cheese, *divided*
10 flour tortillas

1. In large mixing bowl,
combine soup with sour
cream, cumin, and oregano to
make sauce.

2. In another bowl combine
1 cup sauce with chicken,
green chilies, chili powder,
and 1 cup shredded cheese.

3. Fill each soft tortilla
with equal portion of chicken
mixture.

4. Grease 9 × 13 glass
baking dish.

5. Roll up tortillas. Arrange
in baking dish.

6. Spoon remaining sauce
over tortillas.

7. Sprinkle with remaining
cheese.

8. Bake at 350° for 30-40
minutes, or until enchiladas
are heated through and sauce
is bubbly.

Tips:

1. You can make this
ahead, and then refrigerate or
freeze it until ready to bake.
If frozen, thaw before baking.

2. Barbecued chicken adds
a tasty, bacon-like flavor to
the dish.

3. I like to use an ice cream
scoop to divide the filling
mixture equally between the
tortillas.

Tex-Mex Chicken Casserole

Ruth C. Hancock
Earlsboro, OK

Makes 6 servings

Prep. Time: 45 minutes
Baking Time: 35 minutes

2 cups shredded cooked
  chicken
2 cups crushed tortilla
  chips
15-oz. can beans, rinsed
  and drained
1 cup corn kernels
⅔ cup sour cream
½-1 tsp. chili powder,
  according to your taste
  preference
2 cups salsa, *divided*
1 cup shredded cheese,
  divided

1. Combine chicken, chips,
beans, corn, sour cream, and
chili powder in mixing bowl.
2. Grease 2-quart baking
dish.
3. Layer half of chicken
mixture into baking dish.
4. Top with half of salsa.
5. Top with half of cheese.
6. Repeat Steps 3-5.
7. Cover with foil.
8. Bake at 350° for 25
minutes.
9. Uncover and bake 10
minutes more.

Mexican Chicken Stack

Diann Dunham
State College, PA

Makes 6 servings

Prep. Time: 30 minutes
Baking Time: 25 minutes

1½-2 cups shredded cooked
  chicken
1 green bell pepper,
  chopped
¼ cup chopped onion
1 tsp. ground cumin
1½ cups chunky salsa
3-oz. pkg. cream cheese,
  softened
11-oz. can Southwestern
  corn (mixture of corn,
  peppers, black beans),
  drained
3 10'-12"flour tortillas,
  divided
1 cup shredded Mexican
  cheese, *divided*

1. Warm chicken, peppers,
and onions in a nonstick
skillet over low heat.
2. Stir in cumin and salsa.
3. Cook 2 minutes.
4. Add cream cheese, stirring and cooking 2 minutes
until melted.
5. Stir in corn.
6. Spray an 8 × 8 baking
dish with non-stick cooking
spray.
7. Put 1 tortilla in dish.
Stack in ⅓ of chicken mixture, and then 1 tortilla, ½ of
remaining chicken mixture,
and ¼ cup shredded cheese.
8. Add last tortilla, and

remaining chicken mixture.
9. Cover with foil. Bake 20
minutes.
10. Uncover. Add remain-
ing cheese.
11. Bake uncovered until
cheese melts, about 5 minutes.
Allow stack to rest 10 minutes
before serving. Cut in squares.

Tips:
1. Pass extra salsa so diners
can add to their individual
servings if they wish.
2. Sprinkle chopped cilantro
on top before serving.

Cheesy Mexican Chicken

Lori Newswanger
Lancaster, PA

Makes 6 servings

Prep. Time: 15 minutes
Baking Time: 35-45 minutes

2 lbs. boneless, skinless
    chicken breasts
10¾-oz. can cream of
    chicken soup
2 cups (8 oz.) shredded
    cheddar cheese, *divided*
½ cup milk
1 envelope taco seasoning
    mix
3 cups corn chips, *or*
    tortilla chips, crushed

1. Grease 9 × 13 baking dish.
2. Slice chicken in 1"-wide strips. Spread chicken in baking dish.
3. Combine soup, 1½ cups cheese, milk, and taco seasoning in mixing bowl. Spoon over chicken.
4. Top with chips.
5. Cover dish.
6. Bake at 375° for 30-40 minutes, or until chicken is cooked through and no pink remains. (Fish out a piece from middle of dish and check.)
7. Remove cover. Top with remaining ½ cup cheese.
8. Bake uncovered until cheese is melted, about 5 minutes.

Good Go-Alongs:
    Serve over rice.

Mexican Egg Rolls

Brittany Miller
Millersburg, OH

Makes 18 egg rolls

Prep. Time: 35-40 minutes
*Cooking Time: 5 minutes/batch;
    about 20 minutes total*

2½ cups shredded chicken,
    cooked
1½ cups (6-oz.) shredded
    Mexican cheese blend
1 cup frozen corn, thawed
1 cup canned black beans,
    rinsed and drained
5 green onions, chopped
¼ cup minced fresh
    cilantro
1 tsp. salt
1 tsp. ground cumin
1 tsp. grated lime peel
¼ tsp. cayenne pepper
16-oz. pkg. egg roll
    wrappers
oil for deep-fat frying

1. In large bowl, combine chicken, cheese, corn, beans, onions, cilantro, salt, cumin, lime peel, and pepper.
2. Place ¼ cup of mixture in center of one egg roll wrapper. (Keep remaining wrappers covered with damp paper towel until ready to use.)
3. Fold bottom corner over filling. Fold sides toward the center over filling. Moisten remaining corner with water. Roll up tightly to seal. Repeat with each wrapper.
4. In electric skillet or deep-fat fryer, heat oil to 375°. Fry egg rolls, a few at a time, for 2 minutes on each side or until golden brown.
5. Drain on paper towels.

Tips:
1. Keep finished egg rolls warm in a covered dish until ready to serve.
2. Serve with salsa and/or sour cream as dipping sauces.
    Carna Reitz
    Remington, VA

An electric skillet of quality is a smart investment. It is a versatile and easy to use cooking vessel for almost any occasion. — *Willard Roth, Elkhart, IN*

White Chicken Chili Casserole

Zoë Rohrer
Lancaster, PA

Makes 8 servings

Prep. Time: 15 minutes
Baking Time: 35 minutes
Standing Time: 10 minutes

1 small onion, diced
1 clove garlic, minced
2 ribs celery, diced
1 green bell pepper, diced
1-2 tsp. oil
4 cups cooked white beans
1 cup chicken broth
1 cup sour cream, *or* ricotta cheese
½ tsp. salt
1 tsp. cumin
½ tsp. black pepper
10¾-oz. can cream of chicken, *or* cream of celery soup
2 cups cooked chopped chicken
4 whole large whole wheat tortillas, *divided*
2 cups shredded cheddar cheese, *divided*

1. In a large skillet, sauté onions, garlic, celery, and green pepper in a bit of oil until soft.
2. Add beans, broth, sour cream, salt, cumin, pepper, and soup. Bring to a boil while stirring.
3. Remove from heat. Stir in chicken.
4. Spread ⅓ of chicken mixture in bottom of well-greased 9 × 13 baking dish.
5. Top with 2 tortillas, cutting them to fit the pan.
6. Spread on half of remaining chicken mixture.
7. Top with half the cheese.
8. Follow with remaining 2 tortillas, a layer of remaining chicken, and a layer of remaining cheese.
9. Bake for 30-35 minutes, or until bubbly.
10. Let stand 10 minutes before serving.

Good Go-Alongs:
    Great served with salsa

Chicken Spinach Casserole

Laverne Nafziger
Goshen, IN

Makes 6 servings

Prep. Time: 15-20 minutes
Baking Time: 35-40 minutes

¾ cup fat-free mayonnaise
¾ cup fat-free yogurt
½ cup low-fat sour cream
1 cup grated cheddar cheese
1 tsp. minced garlic
1½ cups cooked and diced chicken
10-oz. pkg. frozen chopped spinach, thawed and squeezed dry
¾ cup crushed cracker crumbs
⅔ cup grated Parmesan cheese

1. In a good-sized mixing bowl, blend together mayonnaise, yogurt, sour cream, cheddar cheese, and garlic.
2. Stir in chicken and spinach.
3. Spoon into buttered 6½ × 8½ baking dish.
4. In mixing bowl, stir together cracker crumbs and Parmesan cheese.
5. Sprinkle over top.
6. Bake at 350° for 35-40 minutes, or until topping is lightly browned and mixture is bubbly.

Broccoli Chicken Casserole

Joette Droz
Kalona, IA

Makes 6 servings

Prep. Time: 35 minutes
Baking Time: 1 hour

2 10¾-oz. cans cream of
chicken soup
½ cup mayonnaise
2 cups garlic croutons,
slightly crushed
2 cups cooked chopped
chicken
10-oz. pkg. frozen chopped
broccoli, thawed and
drained
8-oz. can sliced water
chestnuts, drained
4-oz. can sliced
mushrooms, drained

1. Mix soup and mayon-
naise together in large mixing
bowl until smooth.
2. Stir in croutons, chicken,
broccoli, water chestnuts, and
mushrooms. Mix well.
3. Spread in well greased
7 × 11 baking pan.
4. Cover with foil.
5. Bake at 350° for 45
minutes.
6. Uncover. Continue
baking for 15 minutes.

Chicken and Broccoli Bake

Jan Rankin
Millersville, PA

Makes 12-16 servings

Prep. Time: 15 minutes
Baking Time: 30 minutes

2 10¾-oz. cans cream of
chicken soup
2½ cups milk, *divided*
16-oz. bag frozen chopped
broccoli, thawed and
drained
3 cups cooked, chopped
chicken breast
2 cups buttermilk baking
mix

1. Mix soup, and 1 cup
milk together in large mixing
bowl until smooth.
2. Stir in broccoli and
chicken.
3. Pour into well-greased
9 × 13 baking dish.
4. Mix together 1½ cups
milk and baking mix in
mixing bowl.
5. Spoon evenly over top of
chicken-broccoli mixture.
6. Bake at 450° for 30
minutes.

Chicken Corn Casserole

Lois Niebauer
Pedricktown, NJ

Makes 4-6 servings

Prep. Time: 30 minutes
Baking Time: 45 minutes

2 cups diced cooked
chicken
1½ cups frozen corn
½ cup shredded cheddar
cheese
3 Tbsp. chopped pimentos
2.8-oz. can fried onions,
divided
2 Tbsp. butter
¼ cup flour
10¾-oz. can chicken broth
¼-½ tsp. salt
¼ tsp. pepper

1. Combine chicken, corn,
cheese, pimentos, and ¾ can
fried onions in mixing bowl.
2. Combine butter, flour,
chicken broth, and seasonings
in small saucepan.
3. Cook over low to
medium heat, stirring until
thickened.
4. Add thickened sauce to
other ingredients and mix
thoroughly.
5. Place in well-greased
7 × 11 baking dish.

*Keep canned or frozen cooked chicken on hand —
you can make a casserole in a short time.*

Elena Yoder, Albuquerque, NM

6. Sprinkle reserved onion over top.

7. Bake at 325° for 45 minutes.

Tips:

You can make this ahead through Step 6 and freeze until you need it. You can put it in the oven frozen; just bake longer until bubbly, about 1-1¼ hours.

Yogurt Chicken Curry

Laverne Nafziger
Goshen, IN

Makes 12 servings

Prep. Time: 20 minutes
Marinating Time: 8 hours, or overnight
Cooking Time: 2 hours

2½ lbs. boneless, skinless chicken breasts, cut into 1" cubes
2 lbs. plain nonfat yogurt
4 heaping tsp. curry powder
2 heaping tsp. turmeric
1 heaping tsp. ground coriander
2 Tbsp. vegetable oil
1 large onion, chopped
5 garlic cloves, chopped
1" ginger grated *or* finely chopped
½ tsp. salt
1 cup sour cream
1 medium potato, grated
1 cup chopped cilantro, *optional*

1. Mix chicken, yogurt, curry powder, turmeric, and coriander in large nonmetallic bowl. Marinate in refrigerator 8 hours or overnight.

2. Sauté onions, garlic, and ginger in oil in large stockpot 2-5 minutes until lightly brown.

3. Add chicken-yogurt mixture, salt, sour cream, and grated raw potato.

4. Cover. Simmer gently for 2 hours.

5. Just before serving, stir in cilantro if you wish.

6. Serve over cooked rice.

Curried Chicken Casserole

Marilyn Mowry
Irving, TX
Penelope Blosser
Beavercreek, OH

Makes 4-6 servings

Prep. Time: 5 minutes
Cooking Time: 20 minutes

1 cup long-grain rice, uncooked
1 Tbsp. butter
1 low-sodium chicken bouillon cube
2½ cups water
2 5-oz. cans chunk white chicken, drained, or 1½ cups cooked chicken breast
⅓ cup raisins
1 tsp. curry powder

1. In a saucepan, sauté rice in butter,
2. Stir in bouillon cube and water.
3. Cover. Bring to boil.
4. Reduce heat and simmer, covered, 15 minutes, or until water is absorbed and rice is soft.
5. Stir in chicken, raisins and curry powder, mixing well.
6. Cover saucepan. Remove from heat and let stand 10 minutes.
7. Fluff mixture with fork. Serve.

Tip:
You can also serve this chilled.

Chicken Curry

Tina Hartman
Lancaster, PA

Makes 8 servings

Prep. Time: 20 minutes
Cooking Time: 10-15 minutes

3 Tbsp. butter
¼ cup minced onion
1½ tsp. curry powder
3 Tbsp. flour
¾ tsp. salt
¾ tsp. sugar
⅛ tsp. ginger
1 cup chicken broth
1 cup milk
2 cups diced, cooked chicken
½ tsp. lemon juice

Toppings to use or choose:
mandarin oranges
cashews
grated coconut
chopped peaches
sliced bananas
sliced black olives
chopped celery
chopped tomatoes
chopped onions
grated cheese of your choice

1. In good-sized skillet, melt butter over low heat.
2. Sauté onions and curry in butter for a few minutes.
3. Blend in flour and seasonings.
4. Cook over low heat until mixture is smooth and bubbly. (This removes the raw flour taste.)
5. Remove from heat.
6. Stir in chicken broth and milk.
7. Return to heat. Bring to a boil, stirring constantly.
8. Boil one more minute, continuing to stir.
9. Remove from heat. Stir in chicken and lemon juice.
10. Serve over cooked rice, and with toppings for individuals to choose.

This is a wonderful family or large gathering meal because of the toppings. You can use any toppings you can imagine. We once had 22 different topping options! We almost always serve this at our extended family gatherings.

Hot Chicken Casserole

Betty L. Moore
Plano, IL

Makes 4 servings

Prep. Time: 20 minutes
Baking Time: 25 minutes

½ cup mayonnaise
1 Tbsp. lemon juice
10¾-oz. can cream of
   chicken soup
2 cups cooked, diced
   chicken
1 cup diced celery
3 hardboiled eggs, diced
1 can water chestnuts,
   drained, *or* ⅓ cup
   slivered almonds, *or*
   both
¼-½ tsp. salt, according to
   your taste preference
¼ tsp. pepper
potato chips, crushed

1. In large mixing bowl,
stir together mayonnaise,
lemon juice, and soup until
smooth.
2. Stir in chicken, celery,
eggs, water chestnuts and
seasonings. Mix gently and
well.
3. Spoon into greased 9 × 13
baking dish.
4. Top with crushed chips.
5. Bake at 350° for 25
minutes, or until bubbly and
heated through.

Chopstick Chicken

Mary Ann Lefever
Lancaster, PA

Makes 4 servings

Prep. Time: 20 minutes
Baking Time: 40 minutes

10¾-oz. can cream of
   mushroom soup
10¾-oz. can cream of
   chicken soup
5-oz. can chow mein
   noodles, *divided*
2 cups chopped celery
1 cup chopped onions
3 cups cooked chicken, cut
   into bite-size pieces
1 small can mandarin
   oranges, drained
1 cup cashews, salted *or*
   unsalted
1 Tbsp. parsley

1. Mix together soups, half
the noodles, celery, onion,
and chicken in a large mixing
bowl.

2. Place in greased cas-
serole dish.
3. Bake at 350° for 20
minutes.
4. Stir in cashews.
5. Return to oven. Bake 20
more minutes, or until bubbly
and heated through.
6. Remove from oven. Top
with oranges and sprinkle
with parsley just before
serving.

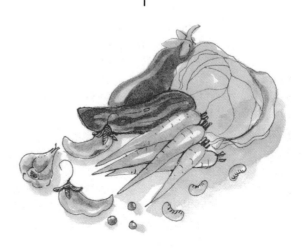

Chicken Spectacular

Rebecca Meyerkorth
Wamego, KS

Melissa Wenger
Orrville, OH

Makes 12 servings

Prep. Time: 30 minutes
Baking Time: 30 minutes
Standing Time: 5 minutes

1 pkg. Uncle Ben's Wild
   Rice with Herbs
3 cups cooked chicken,
   diced
10¾-oz. can cream of
   celery soup
1 medium jar chopped
   pimentos, drained
1 medium onion, chopped
15-oz. can green beans,
   French-cut style, drained
1 cup mayonnaise
½-1 tsp. Worcestershire
   sauce, according to your
   taste preference
¼ tsp. pepper
8-oz. can sliced water
   chestnuts, drained
1 cup grated cheddar cheese

1. Prepare rice according to package directions.
2. Put prepared rice in large bowl. Add chicken, soup, pimentos, onion, beans, mayonnaise, Worcestershire sauce, pepper, and water chestnuts. Mix.
3. Pour into greased 9 × 13 baking dish.
4. Bake at 350° for 30 minutes, or until bubbly and heated through.

5. Sprinkle with cheese. Let stand 5 minutes for cheese to melt

Tip:
   You can prepare through Step 3 and then freeze until needed.

Simmering Chicken Dinner

Trish Dick
Ladysmith, WI

Makes 4 servings

Prep. Time: 10 minutes
Cooking Time: 40 minutes

2½ cups chicken broth
½ cup apple juice
1 bay leaf
½ tsp. garlic powder
½ tsp. paprika
¼ tsp. salt
1½ lbs. boneless, skinless
   chicken breasts, *or*
   thighs, cut into chunks
1 cup uncooked whole-
   grain rice
3 cups fresh, *or* frozen,
   vegetables—your choice
   of one, *or* a mix

½ tsp. paprika, *optional*
parsley as garnish,
   optional

1. Heat chicken broth, apple juice, bay leaf, garlic powder, paprika, and salt in large skillet until boiling, stirring occasionally.
2. Add chicken. Cover. Reduce heat and simmer 10 minutes on low.
3. Turn chicken.
4. Add 1 cup rice around chicken.
5. Top with the vegetables.
6. Cover. Simmer 25 minutes, or until rice is cooked, vegetables are as soft as you like, and chicken is done.
7. Remove bay leaf.
8. Sprinkle with paprika and parsley before serving if you wish.

Tip:
   If you like a bit of zip, add curry powder in place of paprika.

Plan ahead when preparing food for home-entertaining or potlucks. Do as much preparation ahead of time as possible to avoid a last-minute rush. I like to sit down and relax just prior to the event.
   Naomi Ressler, Harrisonburg, VA

Wild-Rice Chicken-Sausage Bake

Carla Elliott
Phoenix, AZ

Makes 8-10 servings

Prep. Time: 1 hour
Baking Time: 1½ hrs

1 lb. bulk sausage
¾ cup uncooked wild rice, cooked according to package directions
¾ cup uncooked long-grain rice, cooked according to package directions
1 medium onion, chopped
1 cup celery, diced
10¾-oz. cream of mushroom soup
½ tsp. salt
¼ tsp. pepper
14½-oz. can chicken broth
4-oz. can sliced mushrooms, drained, *optional*
4 boneless, skinless chicken breast halves, cut into large bite-size pieces

1. Brown sausage in skillet, stirring frequently to break up clumps, until no longer pink.
2. Drain off drippings.
3. In large bowl, mix together sausage, both cooked rices, onion, celery, soup, salt, pepper, broth, and mushrooms if you wish.
4. Spoon into greased 9 × 13 baking pan.
5. Push chicken pieces down into rice mixture.
6. Cover. Bake at 350° for 1 hour.
7. Remove cover and check if mixture is soupy. If so, remove cover. If not, put cover back on.
8. Continue baking 30 more minutes.

Chicken Rice Casserole

Alma Yoder
Baltic, OH

Makes 8 servings

Prep. Time: 20 minutes
Baking Time: 45 minutes

2 cups uncooked long-grain rice
4 cups chicken broth
2 cups diced celery
2 Tbsp. butter
10¾-oz. can mushroom soup
1½ cups mayonnaise
2 Tbsp. chopped onion
2 cups cooked, cubed chicken
2 cups crushed cornflakes
2 Tbsp. butter, melted

1. In large saucepan, cook rice in chicken broth, covered, for about 20 minutes over low heat.
2. While rice is cooking, sauté celery in butter in skillet.
3. When rice is tender, add celery, soup, mayonnaise, onion, and chicken to rice. Mix gently.
4. Spoon mixture into greased casserole dish.
5. Mix crushed cornflakes and melted butter together in small bowl.
6. Scatter cornflake mixture on top.
7. Bake, covered, at 350° for 30 minutes.
8. Uncover. Bake 15 more minutes, or until bubbly and heated through.

Company Casserole

Mary B. Sensenig
New Holland, PA

Makes 8 servings

Prep. Time: 40 minutes
Standing Time: 5 minutes
Baking Time: 45 minutes

¾ cup long-grain rice,
  uncooked
1¾ cups water
1½ Tbsp. butter
10-oz. pkg. broccoli,
  thawed and drained
1½ cups cubed cooked
  chicken
1 cup cubed cooked ham
1 cup (4-oz.) shredded
  cheddar cheese
10¾-oz. can cream of
  mushroom soup
¾ cup mayonnaise
1 tsp. prepared mustard
¼ cup grated Parmesan
  cheese

1. Combine rice, water,
and butter in microwave-safe
container.
2. Cover tightly. Cook on
High 5 minutes.
3. Cook 10 minutes on
Power 5.
4. Let stand 5 minutes,
covered, until water is
absorbed.
5. In greased 2½- or
3-quart casserole layer cooked
rice, broccoli, chicken, ham,
and cheddar cheese.
6. In mixing bowl, combine
soup, mayonnaise, and
mustard.
7. Spread sauce over
casserole.

8. Sprinkle with Parmesan
cheese.
9. Bake at 350° for 45-50
minutes, or until lightly
browned.

Good Go-Alongs:
  Lettuce Salad with Hot
Bacon Dressing (see page 201)

Esther's Hot Chicken Salad

Janice Muller
Derwood, MD

Makes 8-10 servings

Prep. Time: 15 minutes
Baking Time: 40 minutes

4 whole chicken breasts,
  cooked and diced
1½ cups chopped celery
5-oz. can water chestnuts,
  drained and chopped
1 cup mayonnaise
10¾-oz. can cream of
  chicken soup
6-oz. pkg. cornbread
  stuffing mix
1 stick (½ cup) butter

1. In a large mixing bowl,
mix chicken, celery, water
chestnuts, mayonnaise, and
soup together.
2. Place in greased 9 × 13
baking pan.
3. Melt butter in large
stockpot.
4. Brown bread stuffing
in butter, stirring up from
the bottom frequently until

evenly browned.
5. Distribute evenly over
top of chicken mix.
6. Bake at 350° for 40
minutes or until heated
through.

*I'm lucky to have a great
mother-in-law who not only
invites me to potluck gatherings,
but also shares her favorite
recipes with me. She gave me
this recipe after I attended a
party in my parents-in-law's
home where she served this.*

Chicken Cordon Bleu Casserole

Marcia S. Myer
Manheim, PA

Rachel King
Castile, NY

Makes 20-24 servings

Prep. Time: 30 minutes
Baking Time: 1 hour

1 lb. chipped ham
½ lb. grated Swiss cheese
3 cups cooked, diced chicken
10¾-oz. can cream of chicken soup
½ cup milk

Filling:
   8 cups cubed bread
   3 Tbsp. butter
   1½ cups diced celery
   1 small onion, chopped
   2 eggs
   1¾ cups milk
   ½ tsp. salt
   ¼ tsp. pepper

1. Prepare filling by sautéing celery and onion in butter in saucepan until soft.
2. Place cubed bread in large mixing bowl.
3. Pour sautéed vegetables, eggs, 1¾ cups milk, salt, and pepper over bread.
4. Grease 2 9 × 13 baking pans.
5. Layer half of ham, cheese, and filling into each pan.
6. Layer half of chicken into each pan, distributing evenly over top of filling mixture.
7. In mixing bowl, blend soup and ½ cup milk together.
8. Pour soup mixture over top of chicken.
9. Bake at 350° for 60 minutes.

Tip:
   This makes a lot. It's great for big groups.

Overnight Chicken Casserole

Lori Berezovsky
Salina, KS

Makes 4-6 servings

Prep. Time: 20 minutes
Chilling Time: 8 hours or
   overnight
Baking Time: 40-50 minutes

14-oz. pkg. Pepperidge Farm herb stuffing
1 stick (½ cup) butter, cut into pieces
1⅔ cups hot water, *or* chicken broth
4-5 cups diced chicken
½ cup chopped green onions
½ cup mayonnaise
4-oz. can sliced mushrooms, drained, *or* ¼ lb. fresh mushrooms, sliced, *optional*
2 eggs, beaten
2½ cups milk, *divided*
10¾-oz. can cream of mushroom soup
1 cup grated cheddar cheese

1. In large mixing bowl, lightly mix together stuffing, butter, and hot water.
2. Grease 9 × 13 baking pan.
3. Put half of stuffing mixture into baking pan.
4. In another bowl, mix together chicken, onions, mayonnaise, and mushrooms if you wish.
5. Spread chicken layer over stuffing layer.
6. Top with remaining stuffing.
7. In mixing bowl, combine eggs and 2 cups milk.
8. Pour over casserole.
9. Cover and refrigerate 8 hours or overnight.
10. Remove casserole from refrigerator 1 hour before baking.
11. In mixing bowl, blend soup and ½ cup milk until smooth.
12. Spread soup over casserole.
13. Bake at 325° for 30-40 minutes.
14. Sprinkle with grated cheese.
15. Bake 10 minutes more, until cheese is melted.

To make your own cream of mushroom or celery soup, please turn to pages 258-259.

Make-Your-Own-Stuffing Chicken Bake

Mary Jane Musser
Manheim, PA

Makes 5 servings

Prep. Time: 10 minutes
Cooking Time: 75 minutes

1½ lbs. boneless, skinless chicken breast, uncooked, cut into cubes
sprinkling of salt
sprinkling of paprika
5 slices cheese of your choice
10¾-oz. can cream of chicken soup
½ cup water
8 slices bread, cubed
1 egg
¾ cup milk
¼ cup diced celery
2 Tbsp. diced onion

1. Place chicken in greased 7×11 glass casserole dish.
2. Sprinkle with salt and paprika.
3. Lay cheese on top of chicken.
4. Mix soup and water until smooth in mixing bowl.
5. Spread soup over cheese.
6. Mix bread cubes, egg, milk, celery, and onion together in mixing bowl.
7. Pat filling mixture over top of chicken.
8. Cover. Bake at 350° for 1 hour.
9. Uncover. Bake 15 minutes more.

Easy Chicken Stuffing Bake

Leona M. Slabaugh
Apple Creek, OH

Makes 3-4 servings

Prep. Time: 20 minutes
Baking Time: 45 minutes

6-oz. pkg. stuffing mix for chicken
1½ lbs. boneless, skinless chicken breasts, uncooked, cut in 1" pieces
10¾-oz. cream of chicken soup
⅓ cup sour cream
16-oz. pkg. frozen mixed vegetables, thawed and drained

1. Prepare stuffing mix as directed on package. Set aside.
2. In large mixing bowl, mix chicken, soup, sour cream, and vegetables.
3. Arrange in well-greased 9×13 baking pan.
4. Top with stuffing mix.
5. Bake uncovered 45 minutes, or until chicken is tender.

Really Great Chicken 'n Chips

Jean Harris Robinson
Pemberton, NJ

Makes 4 servings

Prep. Time: 30 minutes
Baking Time: 30 minutes

3 Tbsp. butter
1 Tbsp. olive oil
3 Tbsp. chopped green bell pepper
1 small onion, minced
¼ cup flour
1 cup chicken broth
1 cup light cream
½ tsp. salt

½ tsp. pepper
¼ tsp. thyme
2 cups coarsely crushed
   baked potato chips
2 cups cubed cooked
   chicken, *divided*
¼ cup grated Parmesan
   cheese

1. Place butter and oil in saucepan.
2. Stir in green pepper and onion. Cook until soft.
3. Blend in flour. Slowly add chicken broth and cream.
4. Cook until mixture boils and thickens, stirring constantly.
5. Stir in salt, pepper, and thyme.
6. Grease a 2½-3-quart casserole.
7. Arrange potato chips in bottom of casserole.
8. Spread 1 cup chicken over chips.
9. Top with half of sauce.
10. Top with remaining chicken.
11. Top with rest of sauce.
12. Sprinkle top with cheese.
13. Bake at 350° for about 30 minutes, or until casserole is browned, bubbly, and heated through.

Chicken Divan

Linda Sluiter
Schererville, PA

Makes 4 servings

Prep. Time: 20 minutes
Baking Time: 1 hour

2 cups cooked and cubed
   chicken
2 10¾-oz. cans cream of
   chicken soup
1 lb. frozen broccoli,
   thawed and drained
1 cup Minute Rice
2 Tbsp. butter, melted
1 cup milk
8-oz. shredded cheddar
   cheese

1. In large mixing bowl, stir together chicken, soup, broccoli, rice, butter, milk, and cheese.
2. Pour into greased 9 × 13 baking pan.
3. Bake, covered, at 350° for 30 minutes.
4. Remove cover. Bake 30 more minutes.

Chicken Au Gratin

Joy Martin
Myerstown, PA

Makes 3-4 servings

Prep. Time: 10 minutes
Cooking/Baking Time: 35 minutes

2 cups cooked green beans,
   or peas
2 cups diced cooked
   chicken
10¾-oz. can cream of
   chicken soup
¼ cup water
¼ tsp. salt
dash of pepper
⅓ cup (5⅓ Tbsp.) butter
2 cups soft bread cubes
½ cup grated cheese

1. Put beans and chicken in buttered shallow casserole dish.
2. In a mixing bowl, blend soup, water, and seasonings until smooth. Pour over chicken.
3. Melt butter in saucepan. Remove from heat.
4. Mix cheese and bread cubes into butter. Sprinkle on top of chicken and beans.
5. Bake at 350° for 30 minutes, or until browned, bubbly, and heated throughout.

Chicken Pie

Lavina Ebersol
Ronks, PA

Makes 8 servings

Prep. Time: 45 minutes
Baking Time: 45 minutes

Filling:
    3 Tbsp. butter
    3 Tbsp. flour
    1 tsp. salt
    ⅛ tsp. pepper
    1 chicken bouillon cube
    2 cups milk
    12-oz. pkg. frozen
        vegetables
    1 cup chopped cooked
        chicken

Biscuit Topping:
    2 cups flour
    3 tsp. baking powder
    1 tsp. salt
    1 tsp. paprika
    ⅓ cup shortening
    ⅔ cup milk

1. Melt butter in saucepan. Stir in flour, salt, pepper, and bouillon cube.
2. Remove from heat and gradually stir in milk.
3. Return to heat. Cook, stirring constantly until smooth and slightly thickened.
4. Add vegetables and chicken to sauce.
5. Grease 7×11 baking dish.
6. In good-sized mixing bowl, stir together flour, baking powder, salt, and paprika.

7. Cut in shortening with pastry cutter, or 2 knives, until mixture resembles small peas.
8. Stir in milk until mixture forms ball.
9. Roll out dough on lightly floured surface into 8×12 rectangle.
10. Fold dough lightly into quarters. Lift onto top of chicken mixture.
11. Unfold dough and center over dish. Pinch dough around edges of baking dish. Cut slits in dough to allow steam to escape.
12. Bake at 350° for 45 minutes, or until pie is bubbly and crust is browned.

Chicken Noodle Casserole

Leesa DeMartyn
Enola, PA

Makes 4-6 servings

Prep. Time: 15-20 minutes
Baking Time: 30 minutes

1 Tbsp. butter
¼ cup chopped onions
¼ cup chopped green bell
    pepper

8-oz. pkg. egg noodles,
    cooked and drained
2 cups cooked and cubed
    chicken
1 medium tomato, peeled
    and chopped
1 Tbsp. lemon juice
¼ tsp. salt
¼ tsp. pepper
½ cup mayonnaise
⅓ cup milk
½ cup shredded cheddar
    cheese
bread crumbs, *optional*

1. Melt butter in small skillet over medium heat.
2. Sauté onions and peppers about 5 minutes.
3. In large mixing bowl, combine sautéed vegetables with cooked noodles, chicken, tomato, lemon juice, salt, pepper, mayonnaise, and milk.
4. Turn into greased 2-quart casserole.
5. Top with cheese and bread crumbs if you wish.
6. Cover with foil. Bake at 400° for 20-25 minutes, until heated through.
7. Let stand 10 minutes before serving to allow sauce to thicken.

Try adding your favorite herbs and spices to your "tried and true" recipes, and you might come up with something even better.

Jeanne Heyerly, Shipshewana, IN

Chicken & Dumplings

Barbara Nolan
Pleasant Valley, NY

Makes 4 servings

Prep. Time: 15 minutes
Cooking Time: 30 minutes

4 carrots, cut into ½"-thick slices
2 medium onions, cut into eighths
1 clove garlic, sliced thin
3 celery ribs, cut into ½"-thick slices
2 Tbsp. butter
3 Tbsp. flour
2 14-oz. cans chicken broth
1 lb. uncooked chicken cutlets, cut into 1" cubes
2 Tbsp. grated carrots
½ tsp. poultry seasoning
¼ tsp. garlic powder
⅛ tsp. black pepper
¼ cup half-and-half
fresh parsley

Dumplings:
1½ cups flour
2 tsp. baking powder
¾ tsp. salt
1 cup milk
1 egg
2 Tbsp. vegetable oil

1. Sauté carrot pieces, onions, garlic, and celery in butter in medium saucepan-pan for 3 minutes, or until vegetables soften
2. Sprinkle with flour.
3. Stir to combine. Cook 1-2 minutes.
4. Stir in chicken broth, chicken, grated carrots, poultry seasoning, garlic powder, and pepper until smooth.
5. Bring to boil. Simmer 5 minutes, or until thickened, stirring constantly.
6. To prepare dumplings, mix together flour, baking powder, and salt in mixing bowl.
7. In a separate bowl, combine milk, egg, and oil.
8. Add egg-milk mixture to dry ingredients, barely mixing.
9. Drop dumpling batter by tablespoonfuls onto simmering chicken.
10. Cook 10 minutes uncovered.
11. Then cover and cook an additional 10 minutes.
12. Pour half-and-half between dumplings into broth.
13. Scatter fresh parsley over top. Serve immediately.

Tip:
   Chop all veggies and chicken beforehand and refrigerate until you're ready to make the dish. Doing so makes it very fast to prepare this dish.

When my nephew was in college, he used to come to our place and enjoy this dish. He often brought a few hungry roommates along. Now that he's married, this is one of his family's favorite dishes.

Lattice-Top Chicken

Stacie Skelly
Millersville, PA

Makes 6 servings

Prep. Time: 20 minutes
Cooking Time: 1 hour

10¾-oz. can cream of potato soup
1 cup milk
½ tsp. seasoned salt
2 cups cooked, cubed chicken
16-oz. bag frozen broccoli, carrots, cauliflower
1 cup shredded cheddar cheese, *divided*
2.8-oz. can French Fried Onions, *divided*
8-oz. pkg. refrigerated crescent rolls

1. In large mixing bowl, combine soup, milk, salt, chicken, vegetables, ½ cup cheese, and half can fried onions.
2. Grease 9×13 baking dish.
3. Spoon mixture into baking dish.
4. Bake, covered, at 375° for 30 minutes.
5. Unwrap crescent rolls. Separate into 2 rectangles.
6. Press together perforated cuts. Cut each rectangle lengthwise into 3 strips each.
7. Place strips on casserole to form lattice top.
8. Bake, uncovered, 15 minutes longer.
9. Top lattice with remaining cheese and onions.
10. Bake, uncovered, 3-5 minutes longer.

Overnight Scalloped Chicken Casserole

Elena Yoder
Albuquerque, NM
Carole Bolatto
Marseilles, IL

Makes 6-8 servings

Prep. Time: 30 minute
Chilling Time: 8 hours or
overnight
Baking Time: 60-65 minutes

2 10¾-oz. cans cream of
mushroom soup
2½ cups milk
½ lb. cheese of your choice,
cubed
4 cups chopped cooked
chicken, *or* turkey
2 cups macaroni, uncooked
3 hardboiled eggs, chopped
½ tsp. salt
¼ tsp. pepper
1½ cups soft bread crumbs
2 Tbsp. butter, melted

1. In large bowl, combine soup and milk until smooth.
2. Add cheese, meat, macaroni, chopped eggs, salt, and pepper.
3. Transfer to a large greased casserole dish.
4. Cover. Refrigerate 8 hours or overnight.
5. In a small bowl, combine bread crumbs and melted butter.
6. When ready to bake, sprinkle casserole with buttered bread crumbs.
7. Bake uncovered at 350° for 60-65 minutes, or until bubbly and golden brown.

Messy Crescent Roll Chicken

Janie Steele
Moore, OK

Makes 6-8 servings

Prep. Time: 1½ hours
Cooking Time: 40-45 minutes

4 boneless chicken breast
halves, about 6 oz. each
¾ cup water
2 10¾-oz. cans cream of
chicken soup, *divided*
8 oz. sour cream
½ tsp. salt
¼ tsp. pepper
2 tubes refrigerated
crescent rolls

1. Place chicken in good-sized stockpot.
2. Add ¾ cup water.
3. Cover. Simmer gently over medium heat until chicken is tender but not dry, about 15-20 minutes.
4. Remove chicken from pot to mixing bowl. Reserve chicken broth.
5. Using 2 forks, shred chicken.
6. In mixing bowl, mix shredded chicken, 1 can soup, sour cream, salt, and pepper.
7. Open tubes of rolls. Separate each roll from the others.
8. Grease 9 × 13 baking pan.
9. Place large spoonful of chicken mixture onto each crescent roll. Roll and tuck sides under. This is the messy part of the operation!

10. One by one, place filled rolls in baking pan.
11. When finished filling rolls, mix remaining can of soup and ¾ cup chicken broth in mixing bowl until smooth.
12. Pour over top of roll-ups.
13. Bake uncovered at 350° for 40-45 minutes, or until rolls have browned.

Main Dishes Turkey

FINGER FOOD

Turkey Barbecue Wonder

Erma Martin
East Earl, PA
Janet Derstine
Telford, PA

Makes 8 servings

Prep. Time: 10 minutes
Cooking Time: 15 minutes

1 celery rib, chopped
1 medium onion, chopped
¼ cup green bell pepper, chopped
1 Tbsp. oil
¼ cup brown sugar
¼ cup ketchup
¼ cup picante sauce
2 Tbsp. Worcestershire sauce
1½ tsp. chili powder
1 tsp. salt
⅓ tsp. pepper
dash of cayenne pepper
4 cups shredded, *or* cubed, cooked turkey

1. In a large skillet, sauté celery, onion, and green pepper in oil until tender.
2. Stir in brown sugar, ketchup, picante sauce, Worcestershire sauce, chili powder, salt, pepper, and cayenne pepper.
3. Bring to a boil. Reduce heat and simmer uncovered 3-4 minutes.
4. Add turkey. Simmer 10 minutes longer, or until heated through.
5. Serve on buns.

Variations:

1. Increase ketchup to ¾ cup.
2. Add 1⅓ Tbsp. prepared mustard to Step 2.

Joanne Warfel
Lancaster, PA

Tips:

Sometimes I buy turkeys when the price is right, and I end up with several in the freezer. I'll roast one and use most of it in this recipe. Turkey Barbecue freezes well, too.

I take the Barbecue to our cabin and to scrapbooking weekends.

Janet Derstine
Telford, PA

We love this for summer picnics.

Erma Martin
East Earl, PA

Turkey and Green Bean Casserole

Melva Baumer
Mifflintown, PA

Makes 6 servings

Prep. Time: 35-40 minutes
Baking Time: 30-40 minutes

2 lbs. frozen French-style green beans
3 Tbsp. butter
3 Tbsp. flour
¼ tsp. salt
dash of pepper
½ tsp. prepared mustard
1½ cups milk
½ cup mayonnaise
1½-2 Tbsp. lemon juice
4 cups cooked, cubed turkey
½ cup grated Parmesan cheese

1. Cook beans according to package directions. Drain.
2. Melt butter in saucepan. Blend in flour, salt, pepper, and mustard.
3. Over low heat, add milk, stirring constantly until mixture is smooth and thickened.
4. Remove from heat. Fold in mayonnaise and lemon juice.
5. Stir in turkey.
6. Spread beans in greased shallow baking dish.
7. Spoon turkey sauce over top of beans.
8. Sprinkle with Parmesan cheese.
9. Bake at 350° for 30-40 minutes, or until bubbly and heated through.

A fail-proof way to get the best recipes is to go to lots of potlucks. You get to try new recipes and ask for the ones you especially love.
Kathy Bless, Fayetteville, PA

Italian Sausage and White Beans

Lucille Amos
Greensboro, NC

Makes 6-8 servings

Prep. Time: 15 minutes
Cooking/Baking Time: 3 hours

1 Tbsp. olive oil
1 cup chopped onions
2 12-oz. pkgs. turkey
   kielbasa sausage
3 15½-oz. cans great
   northern beans, drained
14½-oz. can diced
   tomatoes
1 cup red wine *or* beef
   broth
1 tsp. Italian seasoning
1 tsp. chopped garlic
½ tsp. black pepper
⅓ cup cooked, crumbled
   bacon

1. Sauté onions in olive oil in skillet until softened. Set aside.

2. Cut sausages in ½-inch slices.

3. Put onions and sausages in casserole dish or Dutch oven.

4. Add beans, tomatoes, wine or broth, Italian seasoning, garlic, and black pepper. Mix gently.

5. Bake covered at 325° for 2 hours.

6. Remove lid. Stir. Return to oven, uncovered, for 20-40 minutes until liquid is reduced to your preference.

7. Sprinkle top with bacon. Check seasonings and add more salt or Italian seasoning to your taste. Serve.

Tip:
You can make this in a slow cooker. Combine everything except bacon in a slow cooker on high for 4-6 hours.

Good Go-Alongs
Cornbread

Spinach Meat Loaf

Ellie Oberholtzer
Ronks, PA

Makes 4-6 servings

Prep. Time: 25 minutes
Baking Time: 60 minutes
Standing Time: 10 minutes

1 lb. ground turkey
10-oz. box frozen chopped
   spinach, thawed and
   squeezed dry
¼ cup chopped fresh
   cilantro, *or* fresh parsley
2 oz. crumbled feta cheese
2 Tbsp. molasses
1 egg
3 pieces millet, or other
   whole-grain, bread,
   toasted and crumbled
1-2 tsp. poultry seasoning
½ tsp. salt
¼ tsp. pepper

1. In a large bowl, mix together turkey, spinach, cilantro, cheese, molasses, egg, bread crumbs, poultry seasoning, salt, and pepper.

2. Form mixture into a loaf.

3. Place in greased loaf pan.

4. Bake at 350° for 60 minutes.

5. Allow to stand 10 minutes before slicing and serving.

Tips:
Instead of mixing the spinach into the loaf, sometimes I pat the meat mixture into a rectangular shape, about ½" thick, onto a piece of waxed paper. I spread the spinach on top, in about ½" from all the edges. I press the spinach down to make it adhere. Then, using the waxed paper to lift the meat, I roll it into a loaf, taking care to keep the spinach from falling out. Then I bake as directed above.

Seafood
Main Dishes

Nutty Salmon

Mary Seielstad
Sparks, NV

Makes 4 servings

Prep. Time: 5-10 minutes
Baking Time: 20 minutes

2 Tbsp. Dijon mustard
2 Tbsp. olive oil
½ cup ground pecans
1½ lbs. salmon filets (4
   6-oz. pieces)

1. In a mixing bowl, mix together mustard, oil, and pecans.
2. Spread on salmon fillets.
3. Place on an oiled baking pan.
4. Bake at 375° for 15-18 minutes, or until fish flakes easily.

Tips:
1. You can cook this recipe on the grill. Watch closely to see that the topping doesn't burn and that you don't over-cook the fish.
2. You can easily double this recipe.

Salmon Loaf

Clara Yoder Byler
Hartville, OH

Makes 3-4 servings

Prep. Time: 15 minutes
Cooking Time: 1 hour
Standing Time: 10 minutes

14¾-oz. can salmon,
   drained and flaked
½ cup mayonnaise
10¾-oz. can cream of
   celery soup
1 egg, beaten
1 cup dry bread crumbs
½ cup chopped onion
1 Tbsp. lemon juice

1. Combine salmon, mayonnaise, soup, egg, bread crumbs, onion, and lemon juice in a bowl.
2. Shape into loaf. Place in greased 8½ x 4½ loaf pan.
3. Bake at 350° for 1 hour.
4. Allow to stand 10 minutes before slicing.

To make your own cream of mushroom or celery soup, please turn to pages 258-259.

143

Holiday Salmon Bake

Rhoda Atzeff
Lancaster, PA

Makes 6 servings

Prep. Time: 15-20 minutes
Baking Time: 35-40 minutes

1 cup shredded cheddar cheese, *divided*
1 cup shredded Swiss cheese, *divided*
3 cups cubed day old sourdough bread, *or* bagels
10-oz. bag frozen chopped broccoli, thawed and drained
8-oz. bag frozen cut asparagus, thawed and drained
4½-oz. can sliced mushrooms, drained
½ cup sliced green onions, *or* red onions
6 eggs, beaten
1 cup milk
2 tsp. garlic salt

1 tsp. pepper
½ lb. salmon filet, *or* 7.1-oz. pouch boneless, skinless pink salmon

1. In large bowl, combine ⅔ cup cheddar cheese, ⅔ cup Swiss cheese, bread, broccoli, asparagus, mushrooms, and onions.
2. In another bowl, whisk together eggs, milk, garlic salt, and pepper.
3. Add egg mixture to vegetable mixture. Blend well.
4. If using fresh salmon, remove skin. Flake salmon and fold into mixture.
5. Spoon into well-greased 9 × 13 baking dish.
6. Bake uncovered at 375° for 35-40 minutes, or until firm.
7. During last 7 minutes of baking time, sprinkle on remaining cheeses.
8. Bake uncovered until cheeses melt. Serve immediately.

Tip:
You can make this up to 24 hours before baking and serving. Prepare through Step 5, cover, and then refrigerate.

Flounder Zucchini Bundles

Betty L. Moore
Plano, IL

Makes 4 servings

Prep. Time: 15 minutes
Baking Time: 20 minutes

4 6-oz. flounder fillets
¼ tsp. lemon pepper, *divided*
1 medium lemon, thinly sliced, *divided*
1 medium zucchini, cut into ¼"-thick slices, *divided*
12 cherry tomatoes, sliced, *divided*
¼ tsp. dill weed, *divided*
¼ tsp. dried basil, *divided*

1. Place 1 fillet on double thickness of 15 × 18 piece of heavy duty foil.
2. Sprinkle with ¼ of lemon pepper.
3. Top with ¼ of lemon slices, zucchini, and tomatoes.
4. Sprinkle with ¼ of dill and basil.
5. Fold foil around fish and seal tightly. Place on baking sheet.
6. Repeat with other fillets.
7. Bake at 425° for 15-20 minutes, or until fish flakes easily.

Easy Dill Sauce for Fish Fillets

Mary Seielstad
Sparks, NV

Makes 1¼ cups sauce

Prep. Time: 10 minutes
Baking Time: 18-20 minutes

1 stick (½ cup) butter
¼ tsp. thyme
1 large bay leaf
1 Tbsp. minced onion
¾ tsp. dill weed
¼ tsp. salt
⅛ tsp. pepper
1 tsp. sugar
1 cup sour cream
fish fillets

1. Melt butter in small saucepan or in microwave in a glass bowl.
2. Remove from heat. Add thyme, bay leaf, onion, dill weed, salt, pepper, sugar, and sour cream.
3. Mix well.
4. Lay fish fillets on greased baking pan.
5. Spread sauce over top of fish fillets to cover.
6. Bake until sauce is bubbly, about 18-20 minutes at 375°.
7. Offer remaining sauce when serving fish.

Tip:
We like this on white fillets, as well as on salmon.

Scalloped Scallops

Flossie Sultzaberger
Mechanicsburg, PA

Makes 4-6 servings

Prep. Time: 15 minutes
Baking Time: 25 minutes

1 stick (½ cup) butter
1 cup snack-cracker crumbs
½ cup soft bread crumbs
1 lb. scallops (if large, cut in half)
dash of salt
dash of pepper

1. Melt butter in saucepan.
2. Stir in cracker crumbs and bread crumbs.
3. Butter a 1½-2-quart casserole.
4. Place half the scallops in bottom of baking dish.
5. Sprinkle with salt and pepper.
6. Cover with half buttered crumbs.
7. Repeat layers.
8. Bake at 400° for 25 minutes.

Tip:
Add a few shrimp to the scallops for a very special dish.

Seafood Quiche

Anne Jones
Ballston Lake, NY

Makes 6 servings

Prep. Time: 10-15 minutes
Baking Time: 30-40 minutes
Standing Time: 10 minutes

8" unbaked pie crust
1 Tbsp. chopped onion
7-oz. pkg. crab and shrimp
4 eggs
½ cup milk
½ tsp. salt
¼ tsp. pepper
8 oz. shredded Swiss cheese
dash of nutmeg, *optional*

1. Sprinkle chopped onion in crust.
2. Spread crab and shrimp over top.
3. In mixing bowl, beat eggs, milk, salt, and pepper together.
4. Add shredded cheese.
5. Pour over crab meat mixture in pie crust.
6. Sprinkle with nutmeg if you wish.
7. Bake at 375° for 30-40 minutes, or until knife inserted in center of quiche comes out clean.
8. Allow to stand 10 minutes before cutting into wedges.

Tuna Bake with Cheese Swirls

Mary Ann Lefever
Lancaster, PA

Makes 4-6 servings

Prep. Time: 30 minutes
Baking Time: 25 minutes

½ cup diced green bell
  peppers
½ cup chopped onions
3 Tbsp. butter
6 Tbsp. flour
2 cups milk
6½- *or* 7-oz. can tuna

Cheese Swirls:
  1½ cups buttermilk
    biscuit mix, *or*
    refrigerated biscuits
  ¾ cup grated cheddar
    cheese
  ½ cup milk, if using
    biscuit mix
  2 Tbsp. chopped
    pimentos

1. In saucepan, sauté green pepper and onions in butter until soft but not brown.
2. Blend in flour and cook over low heat a few minutes to get rid of raw flour taste.
3. Gradually stir in milk. Cook over low heat, stirring continually until smooth.
4. Add tuna.
5. Spoon into greased 9 × 13 baking pan. Set aside.
6. To make cheese swirls, prepare biscuits with milk according to package directions. Or open refrigerated biscuits.
7. On lightly floured board, roll out to 8 × 13 rectangle.
8. Sprinkle with cheese and chopped pimento. Press into dough to help adhere.
9. Roll up jelly-roll fashion.
10. Cut roll into 8 slices.
11. Flatten slightly and place on top of tuna mixture.
12. Bake at 450° for 25 minutes, or until tuna mix is bubbly and biscuits are browned.

Tuna Tempties

Lois Ostrander
Lebanon, PA

Makes 6 servings

Prep. Time: 15 minutes
Baking Time: 15 minutes

¼ lb. cheese of your choice,
  cubed
7-oz. can tuna, flaked
2 Tbsp. chopped green bell
  pepper
2 Tbsp. minced onion
2 Tbsp. sweet pickle
¼ cup mayonnaise
shake of salt
dash of pepper
6 sandwich rolls

1. Combine cheese, tuna, green pepper, minced onion, sweet pickle, mayonnaise, salt, and pepper in mixing bowl.
2. Split buns and fill with tuna mixture.
3. Wrap each bun in foil.
4. Bake in oven at 350° for 15 minutes until filling is heated and cheese melts.

Pasta and Vegetable Main Dishes

Creamy Crunchy Mac & Cheese

Kathy Hertzler
Lancaster, PA

Makes 6 servings
Prep. Time: 20 minutes
Baking Time: 10-12 minutes

---

1 lb. uncooked macaroni
2 cups 2% milk
half stick (4 Tbsp.) butter
3 Tbsp. flour
5 cups shredded cheddar
 cheese, *divided*
½ tsp. seasoned salt
½ tsp. ground black pepper
1 tsp. dry mustard
1 tsp. garlic powder, *or*
 2 cloves garlic, minced
1 tsp. onion powder, *or*
 ¼ cup onions, chopped
¾ cup crushed cornflakes

1. Cook macaroni until al dente, according to package directions, about 7 minutes. Drain well.

2. While pasta is cooking, warm milk until steamy but not boiling.

3. In another medium-sized saucepan, melt butter. Add flour, and whisk until smooth.

4. Add warm milk to butter/flour mixture. Whisk until smooth.

5. Cook, stirring constantly, on low heat for 2 minutes.

6. Add 4 cups shredded cheddar. Stir well, and then remove from heat. Set aside.

7. Stir salt, pepper, mustard, minced garlic or garlic powder, and chopped onions or onion powder into creamy sauce.

8. Place cooked macaroni in large mixing bowl.

9. Stir in cheese sauce.

10. Transfer mixture to greased 9 × 13 baking dish.

11. Sprinkle with cornflakes, and then remaining shredded cheddar.

12. Bake at 400° 10-12 minutes, or until hot and bubbly.

Tip:
 Don't boil the sauce after the cheese has been added. It's best to add the cheese to the sauce, stir, and remove from heat. Boiled cheese sauces usually curdle a bit or separate and don't look appetizing.

Homemade Mac and Cheese

Sherry L. Lapp
Lancaster, PA

Karissa Newswanger
Denver, PA

Karen Burkholder
Narvon, PA

Jen Hoover
Akron, PA

Makes 4-5 servings

Prep. Time: 20 minutes
Baking Time: 25 minutes

½ lb. (2 cups) uncooked
   small shell macaroni
¼ cup water
3 Tbsp. butter
3 Tbsp. flour
3 cups milk, 2% *or* whole
12 oz. extra-sharp cheddar
   cheese, grated
1 tsp. salt
2 tsp. Dijon mustard

1. Cook macaroni according to package directions until al dente. Drain.
2. Transfer to greased 3-quart baking dish.
3. Stir ¼ cup water into cooked macaroni.
4. Melt butter in medium-sized saucepan. Sprinkle in flour and stir constantly over medium heat, about 2 minutes.
5. Increase heat a bit. Add milk ½ cup at a time.
6. When milk is fully mixed in, reduce heat and stir continually until mixture bubbles and begins to thicken.
7. Add cheese 1 cup at a time, stirring continually.
8. Add salt and mustard. Mix well.
9. Transfer to casserole dish. Blend with macaroni.
10. Bake at 375° for 25 minutes, or until bubbly and heated through.

Variations:
1. Top filled casserole dish with buttered bread crumbs before baking. To prepare crumbs, melt 1½ Tbsp. butter. Stir in 1 cup dried bread crumbs.
Karissa Newswanger
Denver, PA

2. Instead of extra-sharp cheddar cheese use 2 cups grated Velveeta and 2 cups grated sharp cheese.
3. Stir in ½ tsp. pepper to Step 8.
Karen Burkholder
Narvon, PA

4. Instead of 3 cups milk, substitute with 1½ cups milk and 8 oz. sour cream.
5. Add ¼ cup grated Parmesan cheese to Step 7.
Jen Hoover
Akron, PA

Baked Macaroni

Ann Good
Perry, NY

Makes 12 servings

Prep. Time: 5 minutes
Baking Time: 3 hours

¾ stick (6 Tbsp.) butter,
   melted
3 cups uncooked macaroni
2 quarts milk
4 cups shredded cheese of
   your choice
2 tsp. salt
½ tsp. pepper

1. In large bowl, mix together butter, macaroni, milk, cheese, salt, and pepper.
2. Pour into greased 9 × 13 casserole dish.
3. Cover. Bake at 225° for 2¾ hours.
4. Remove cover. Bake 15 minutes longer to brown dish.

This was the first recipe I got as a newlywed from my mother-in-law. My husband loves when I make it. It has been a long-time favorite Sunday dinner side dish for his family.

Sesame Noodles

Sheila Ann Plock
Boalsburg, PA

Makes 10-12 servings

Prep. Time: 15 minutes
Chilling Time: 8 hours or
*   overnight*
Cooking Time: 11 minutes

¼ cup soy sauce
3 Tbsp. sesame oil, *divided*
2 Tbsp. red wine vinegar
2 Tbsp. olive oil
1½ Tbsp. sugar
1 Tbsp. prepared chili
    sauce with garlic
12-oz. box linguine noodles
4 green onions
1 red bell pepper, cut into
    thin match-stick strips

1. One day before serving
noodles, combine 2 Tbsp. soy
sauce, sesame oil, vinegar,
olive oil, sugar, and chili
sauce in food processor or
blender. Blend until well
combined.
2. Cover. Chill in fridge for
8 hours or overnight to allow
flavors to blend.
3. Cook noodles according
to package directions. Rinse,
drain, and cool.
4. In large bowl, toss
cooked noodles with 1 Tbsp.
sesame oil.
5. Stir in green onions and
pepper strips.
6. Toss with enough
dressing to coat.
7. Serve chilled or at room
temperature.

Spinach Cheese Manicotti

Kimberly Richard
Mars, PA

Makes 6 servings

Prep. Time: 35 minutes
Baking Time: 45-60 minutes

15-oz. container ricotta
    cheese
10-oz. pkg. frozen chopped
    spinach, thawed and
    squeezed dry
½ cup minced onion
1 egg
2 tsp. parsley
2 tsp. basil
½ tsp. black pepper
½ tsp. garlic powder
1½ cups shredded
    mozzarella, *divided*
½ cup grated Parmesan,
    divided
26-oz. jar spaghetti sauce
1½ cups water
1 cup diced fresh tomatoes
8-oz. pkg. uncooked
    manicotti shells

1. In large bowl combine
ricotta, spinach, onion, and
egg.
2. Stir in parsley, basil,
black pepper, and garlic.
3. Mix in 1 cup mozzarella
and ¼ cup Parmesan cheese.
4. In separate bowl, mix
together sauce, water, and
tomatoes.
5. Grease 9 × 13 baking
pan. Spread 1 cup spaghetti
sauce in bottom of pan.
6. Stuff uncooked mani-
cotti with ricotta mixture.
Arrange in single layer in
baking pan.
7. Cover stuffed manicotti
with remaining sauce.
8. Sprinkle with remaining
cheeses.
9. Cover. Bake 45-60
minutes, or until noodles are
soft.

Creamy Baked Ziti

Judi Manos
West Islip, NY

Makes 8 servings

Prep. Time: 20 minutes
Baking Time: 20 minutes

4 cups uncooked ziti pasta
26-oz. jar marinara sauce
14½-oz. can diced
  tomatoes, undrained
2 3-oz. pkgs. cream cheese,
  cubed
¾ cup sour cream
8 oz. shredded mozzarella
  cheese, *divided*
⅓ cup grated Parmesan
  cheese

1. Cook pasta as directed on package, but omit salt. Drain cooked pasta well.
2. While pasta drains, add marinara sauce, tomatoes, and cream cheese to cooking pot.
3. Cook on medium heat 5 minutes, or until cream cheese is melted and mixture is well blended. Stir frequently.
4. Return pasta to pan. Mix well.
5. Layer half the pasta mixture in greased 9 × 13 baking dish.
6. Cover with layer of sour cream.
7. Top with 1 cup mozzarella.
8. Spoon over remaining pasta mixture.
9. Top with remaining mozzarella.
10. Sprinkle with Parmesan cheese.
11. Bake 20 minutes, or until bubbly and heated through.

Tips:
1. You can use penne pasta instead of ziti.
2. You can make this dish ahead of the day you want to serve it. Prepare through Step 10. Cover and refrigerate before baking. If you put the casserole in the oven cold, increase baking time to 30-35 minutes, or until heated through.

Baked Ziti with Vegetables

Sandra Haverstraw
Hummelstown, PA

Makes 12 servings

Prep. Time: 15-20 minutes
Baking Time: 30 minutes
Standing Time: 10 minutes

12-oz. pkg. ziti, uncooked
10-oz. pkg. frozen broccoli
10-oz. pkg. frozen
  cauliflower
15-oz. container ricotta
  cheese
¾ tsp. dried oregano
1 cup part-skim shredded
  mozzarella
2 tsp. red pepper sauce,
  more or less to taste
26-oz. jar spaghetti sauce,
  divided
¾ cup grated Parmesan
  cheese

1. Cook ziti in boiling water for 6 minutes.
2. Add broccoli and cauliflower to ziti and boiling water. Cook for 2 additional minutes. Drain.
3. Blend ricotta, oregano, mozzarella, and red pepper sauce in bowl.
4. Toss ziti and veggies with 1 cup spaghetti sauce.
5. Spoon half of ziti-veggie-sauce mix into bottom of well-greased 9 × 13 baking dish.
6. Spoon ⅔ of cheese mixture over ziti.
7. Cover with remaining ziti.
8. Spoon remaining spaghetti sauce over ziti.
9. Cover with foil. Bake at 450° for 25 minutes.
10. Uncover. Sprinkle with Parmesan cheese.
11. Bake 5 minutes longer.
12. Allow to stand 10 minutes before cutting and serving to allow cheeses to firm up.

Party Spaghetti

Sheila Plock
Boalsburg, PA

Makes 12 servings

Prep. Time: 30-45 minutes
Baking Time: 30-40 minutes

1 lb. uncooked linguine,
   divided
3 Tbsp. oil
2 lbs. lean ground beef
½ lb. fresh mushrooms,
   sliced thin, *or* 2 4-oz.
   cans, undrained
2 medium onions, chopped
¼ cup chopped parsley
2 8-oz. cans tomato sauce
6-oz. can tomato paste
1 tsp. oregano
1 tsp. garlic powder
dash of salt
¼ tsp. pepper
8-oz. pkg. cream cheese,
   softened
2 cups cottage cheese
½ cup sour cream
½ cup chives
2 Tbsp. butter
½ cup dried bread crumbs

1. Prepare linguini according to package directions. Drain well.
2. Heat oil in large skillet. Add meat and cook until browned, stirring frequently to break up clumps.
3. Stir in mushrooms (and juice if canned), onions, parsley, tomato sauce, tomato paste, oregano, and garlic powder.
4. Season to taste with salt and pepper.
5. Simmer, uncovered, 15 minutes.
6. Combine cream cheese, cottage cheese, sour cream, and chives in mixing bowl. Blend well.
7. Pour half of linguine into 3½-4-quart buttered casserole.
8. Cover with all of cheese mixture.
9. Spoon in rest of linguine.
10. Top with meat mixture.
11. Melt butter in small saucepan.
12. Stir in bread crumbs.
13. Sprinkle over top of casserole.
14. Bake at 350° for 30-40 minutes, or until browned and bubbly.

So many times we end up with little bits of noodles, veggies, etc. I put them in a container and freeze them. When the container is full, I make a veggie soup by adding browned hamburger and broth. Great way to use leftovers!

Jane Geigley, Lancaster, PA

Mazetti

Sally Holzem
Schofield, WI

Makes 8 servings

Prep. Time: 30 minutes
Baking Time: 25-30 minutes

1 lb. ground beef
8-oz. pkg. uncooked wide
  noodles
1 cup chopped onion
1½ cups chopped celery
¼ stick (2 Tbsp.) butter
10¾-oz. can corn,
  undrained
10¾-oz. can tomato soup
4-oz. can mushrooms,
  undrained
½ cup milk
1½ tsp. salt
½ tsp. pepper
¼ tsp. garlic powder
½ lb. American, *or*
  cheddar, cheese,
  shredded

1. Brown beef in large skillet. Stir frequently to break up clumps. When pink no longer remains, remove from heat and drain off drippings.
2. Prepare noodles according to package directions. Drain well.
3. Add beef to drained noodles.
4. In same skillet as you cooked beef, sauté onion and celery in butter. Add to beef-noodle mixture.
5. Stir corn, soup, mushrooms, milk, salt, pepper, and garlic powder into beef-noodle mixture.

6. Turn into greased 3-quart casserole.
7. Sprinkle with cheese.
8. Bake uncovered at 400° for 25-30 minutes, or until bubbly and heated through.

Pizza Noodle Casserole

Arianne Hochstetler
Goshen, IN

Makes 15 servings

Prep. Time: 30 minutes
Baking Time: 45 minutes

12-oz. pkg. kluski noodles
1 lb. ground beef
1 small onion, chopped
26-oz. jar spaghetti sauce
1½ cups pizza sauce
4-oz. can sliced
  mushrooms, drained
½ cup chopped green bell
  pepper, *optional*
⅓ cup chopped green, *or*
  black, olives, *optional*
8 oz. shredded cheddar
  cheese
8 oz. shredded mozzarella
  cheese
¼ lb. sliced pepperoni

1. Cook noodles according to package directions. Drain.

2. Brown ground beef and onion in large saucepan. Stir frequently to break up clumps. Drain off drippings.
3. Add spaghetti and pizza sauces to meat.
4. Cover. Simmer over low heat for 10 minutes.
5. Stir mushrooms, and chopped peppers and olives into meat sauce if you wish.
6. Grease 9 × 13 baking pan. Layer in half of noodles.
7. Follow with half of meat sauce.
8. Top with half of cheeses.
9. Scatter half of pepperoni over top.
10. Repeat layers.
11. Bake in 9 × 13 baking pan at 350° for 45 minutes.

Tips:
1. You can use 1 pound of spaghetti instead of the kluski noodles.
2. You can make this casserole through Step 10 the day before serving. Cover and refrigerate. Bake chilled casserole up to 1¼ hours, or until bubbly and heated through.

If plastic wrap doesn't want to cling to a container, wipe along the sides of the container with a damp cloth and try again.
Suzanne Yoder, Gap, PA

Italian-Style Stuffed Seashells

Makes 12 servings

Prep. Time: 30 minutes
Baking Time: 35 minutes

20 uncooked jumbo
   macaroni shells
1 medium onion, chopped
½ lb. ground beef
2 tsp. garlic powder
1½ cups cottage cheese
8 oz. sharp cheddar cheese,
   shredded
1 tsp. salt
½ cup mayonnaise
2 cups spaghetti sauce,
   divided
2 tsp. oregano

1. Cook shells according to package directions. Drain well.

2. Meanwhile, brown onion and ground beef in skillet, stirring until crumbly. Drain off drippings. Allow to cool.

3. Combine garlic powder, cottage cheese, shredded cheese, salt, and mayonnaise in bowl, mixing well.

4. Stir in beef mixture.

5. Pour 1 cup spaghetti sauce over bottom of greased 9×13 baking dish.

6. Spoon ground beef-cheese mixture into shells.

7. Place filled shells on top of sauce in baking dish.

8. Pour remaining spaghetti sauce over stuffed shells.

9. Sprinkle with oregano.

10. Cover and bake at 350° for 25 minutes.

11. Uncover. Bake 10 minutes longer.

Ravioli Casserole

Kathy Bless
Fayetteville, PA

Makes 6-9 servings

Prep. Time: 15 minutes
Baking Time: 45-60 minutes
Standing Time: 10 minutes

1 lb. ground chuck, *or*
   sirloin
28-oz. jar spaghetti sauce
half a 25-oz. pkg. frozen
   cheese ravioli, *divided*
2 cups (16-oz.) small-curd
   cottage cheese, *divided*
2 cups shredded mozzarella
   cheese, *divided*

1. Cook ground chuck in large skillet, stirring often to break up clumps, until no pink remains. Drain off drippings.

2. While meat is cooking, cook cheese ravioli according to package directions.

(Use half the pkg. and save the rest for another time.) Drain well.

3. Stir spaghetti sauce into meat.

4. Grease a 10×10 baking pan. Spread in 1 cup spaghetti-meat sauce.

5. Layer in half the ravioli.

6. Top with half the remaining meat sauce.

7. Spread with 1 cup cottage cheese.

8. Top with 1 cup mozzarella cheese.

9. Repeat layering.

10. Bake at 350° for 45-60 minutes, or until bubbly.

11. Let stand 10 minutes before serving.

Tip:
   You can make this recipe ahead of serving through Step 9. Then cover and refrigerate. Take out 30 minutes before baking to warm up a bit. Then bake and serve.

Ziti Bake— BIG, Big Batch

Joy Reiff
Mount Joy, PA

Makes 25-30 servings
Prep. Time: 45-50 minutes
Baking Time: 1½-2 hours

5 lbs. uncooked ziti, *or* rigatoni
6 lbs. ground beef
5 lbs. ricotta cheese, *or* cottage cheese
2½ cups grated Parmesan cheese
1 cup chopped parsley
5 eggs, beaten
1 Tbsp. salt
1 tsp. pepper
6 quarts spaghetti sauce, *divided*
2½ lbs. mozzarella cheese, shredded

1. Prepare ziti according to package directions. (Do in several batches if you don't have large enough stockpot to do all at once.) Drain and set aside.
2. Brown ground beef in large stockpot. Stir frequently to break up clumps. Cook until pink no longer remains. Drain off drippings.
3. Stir in ricotta cheese, Parmesan cheese, parsley, eggs, and seasonings.
4. Add 5 quarts spaghetti sauce. Stir until well mixed.
5. Add ziti. Toss gently to coat well.
6. Pour mixture into 6 3-quart baking pans or roasters. Or spoon into 18-quart electric roaster.
7. Pour remaining spaghetti sauce over ziti mixture. Sprinkle with cheese.
8. Bake at 350° for 1-1½ hours, if using smaller roasters or baking pans, until bubbly and hot through. If using large electric roaster, bake up to 2 hours, or until hot through.

Tips:
Stir occasionally, to prevent a thick layer of cheese from forming on top and making it hard to scoop out.

Ziti Bake— Household Size!

Joy Reiff
Mount Joy, PA

Makes 6-8 servings
Prep Time: 30 minutes
Baking Time: 45 minutes

1 lb. ziti, *or* rigatoni
1¼ lbs. ground beef
1 lb. ricotta cheese, *or* cottage cheese
½ cup grated Parmesan cheese
3 Tbsp. chopped fresh parsley
1 egg, beaten
½ tsp. salt
¼-½ tsp. pepper, according to your taste preference
6 cups spaghetti sauce
½ lb. mozzarella sauce, shredded

1. Follow instructions above through Step 5.
2. Spoon into greased 9×13 baking pan.
3. Pour remaining spaghetti sauce over ziti mixture. Sprinkle with cheese.
4. Bake at 350° for 45-60 minutes, or until bubbly and heated through.

I like to brown hamburger when I buy it, usually adding onions because we like them mixed in. Then I freeze it in 2-cup (1-lb.) packs.

Carolyn Snader, Ephrata, PA

Rigatoni Royal

Gloria Julien
Gladstone, MI

Makes 15 servings

Prep. Time: 50 minutes
Baking Time: 45 minutes

2 lbs. hamburger
1 large onion, chopped
2 cloves garlic, diced
8 cups spaghetti sauce
1 lb. uncooked rigatoni
  noodles, *divided*
½ lb. provolone cheese,
  grated
1½ cups sour cream
½ lb. mozzarella cheese,
  grated
Italian seasoning
grated Parmesan cheese

1. Brown hamburger with onion and garlic in large stockpot. Stir frequently to break up clumps of meat, cooking until no pink remains.

2. Drain off drippings.

3. Stir in spaghetti sauce. Simmer slowly for 30 minutes.

4. Meanwhile, cook noodles until slightly under-done. Drain.

5. Grease deep 9 × 13 baking dish or lasagna pan. Layer in half the noodles.

6. Top with provolone cheese.

7. Spoon sour cream over provolone, spreading as well as possible.

8. Top with half of meat sauce.

9. Add another layer of noodles, using all that remain.

10. Top with mozzarella cheese.

11. Spoon over remainder of sauce.

12. Sprinkle generously with Italian seasoning and Parmesan cheese.

13. Bake at 350° for 45 minutes, or until bubbly and heated through.

Tips:
  You can prepare this dish through Step 12 the night before you want to serve it. Bake it just before serving. If you're going to serve this at a church potluck, bake it at a low heat (300°) during church, and it will be ready to eat at noon.

Hamburger, Corn & Noodle Casserole

Anne Jones
Ballston Lake, NY

Makes 6 servings

Prep. Time: 20-25 minutes
Baking Time: 30 minutes

1 lb. ground beef
1 small to medium-sized
  onion, diced
1 pint fresh, *or* frozen,
  corn, *or* 1-lb. can corn
  nuggets, drained
½ lb. fresh mushroom,
sliced thin, *or* 8-oz.
  can sliced mushrooms,
  drained
10¾-oz. cream of
  mushroom soup
12 oz. noodles, uncooked
16 oz. sour cream
½ cup bread crumbs

1. In large nonstick skillet, brown ground beef with chopped onion. Stir frequently, breaking up clumps of meat until no pink remains. Drain off drippings.

2. Stir in corn, mushrooms, and soup.

3. Meanwhile, cook noodles according to package directions. Drain well.

4. Stir noodles into ground-beef mixture.

5. Add sour cream and stir.

6. Place mixture in a well-greased 2-quart baking dish.

7. Top with bread crumbs.

8. Bake at 350° for 30 minutes, or until bubbly and heated through.

Creamy Beef and Pasta Casserole

Virginia Graybill
Hershey, PA

Makes 6 servings

Prep. Time: 25 minutes
Baking Time: 30 minutes

1 lb. hamburger
8-oz. pkg. noodles, *or* macaroni
8-oz. pkg. cream cheese, softened and cut in chunks
10¾-oz. can cream of mushroom soup
1 cup milk
½ cup ketchup
salt, *optional*

1. Cook hamburger in non-stick skillet until no longer pink, stirring frequently to break up clumps. Drain off any drippings.
2. Cook noodles or macaroni al dente as directed on package. Drain.
3. Mix pasta and hamburger in large mixing bowl.
4. In another mixing bowl, blend together cream cheese, soup, milk, ketchup, and salt if you wish.
5. Stir sauce into pasta and hamburger.
6. Pour into greased 9 × 13 baking pan.
7. Bake at 350° for 30 minutes, or until bubbly and heated through.

Variations:
1. I added 1 tsp. crushed garlic to Step 1.

2. When I made the dish again, I added ½ cup salsa to Step 4.

Jean Turner
Williams Lake, BC

Lasagna

Colleen Heatwole
Burton, MI

Makes 8-12 servings

Prep. Time: 45 minutes
Baking Time: 30 minutes at 375°; 2 hours at 200°

1 lb. ground beef
1 clove garlic, minced
1 scant Tbsp. basil
¾ tsp. salt
28- to 32-oz. can stewed tomatoes, *or* 28-oz. jar pasta sauce
6-oz. can tomato paste
½ tsp. oregano
10 oz. lasagna noodles, *divided*
3 cups cottage cheese
½ cup grated Parmesan cheese
1 lb. mozzarella cheese, grated
2 Tbsp. parsley flakes
2 eggs, beaten
½ tsp. pepper

1. Brown beef slowly in stockpot. Stir frequently to break up clumps. Pour off drippings.
2. Stir in garlic, basil, salt, tomatoes or pasta sauce, tomato paste, and oregano. Mix well.

3. Simmer, uncovered, 30 minutes.
4. Meanwhile, cook pasta al dente, according to package directions. Drain well.
5. In large bowl, combine cottage cheese, Parmesan cheese, mozzarella cheese, parsley flakes, eggs, and pepper.
6. Place half the noodles in greased 9 × 13 baking dish.
7. Cover with half the meat sauce.
8. Top with half the cheese mixture.
9. Repeat layers, ending with cheese mixture.
10. Bake at 375° for 30 minutes, or until bubbly and heated through.

Tips:
You can assemble this lasagna ahead of time through Step 9. Cover and refrigerate. When ready to bake, allow 15 minutes longer in oven, for bake at 200° for 2 hours if baking during church for a noon potluck. Cover during baking if baking 2 hours.

Variation:
Instead of ground beef, use ½ lb. bulk hot Italian sausage. Brown it as instructed for ground beef and drain off drippings.

Monica Leaman Kehr
Portland, MI

Weekday Lasagna

Karen Burkholder
Narvon, PA

Makes 9 servings

Prep. Time: 25-35 minutes
Baking Time: 60-65 minutes
Standing Time: 15 minutes

1 lb. ground beef
1 small onion, chopped
28-oz. can crushed
    tomatoes
1¾ cups water
6-oz. can tomato paste
1 pkg. Italian-style
    spaghetti sauce mix
1 egg, slightly beaten
2 cups cottage cheese
2 Tbsp. grated Parmesan
    cheese
6 uncooked lasagna
    noodles, *divided*
1 cup shredded mozzarella
    cheese

1. In a large saucepan, cook beef and onion over medium heat until meat is no longer pink, stirring frequently to break up clumps. Drain off any drippings.
2. Stir tomatoes, water, tomato paste, and spaghetti sauce mix into skillet.
3. Bring mixture to a boil. Reduce heat. Cover and simmer 15-20 minutes, stirring occasionally.
4. In a small bowl, combine egg, cottage cheese, and Parmesan cheese.
5. Spread 2 cups meat sauce in greased 9 × 13 baking dish.
6. Top with three uncooked noodles.
7. Layer on half of cottage cheese mixture.
8. Top with half remaining meat sauce.
9. Repeat layers.
10. Cover and bake at 350° for 50 minutes.
11. Uncover. Sprinkle with mozzarella cheese.
12. Bake uncovered 10-15 minutes longer, or until bubbly and cheese is melted.
13. Let stand 15 minutes before cutting.

Lazy Lasagna

Elaine Rineer
Lancaster, PA

Makes 10 servings

Prep. Time: 45 minutes
Baking Time: 30-45 minutes

1½ lbs. ground beef
1-lb. pkg. malfada noodles,
    divided
1-lb. container ricotta
    cheese, *or* cottage cheese
2 cups shredded
    mozzarella cheese,
    divided
32-oz. jar spaghetti sauce,
    divided
¼ lb. sliced pepperoni

1. Brown ground beef in skillet. Stir frequently to break up clumps. Cook until no pink remains. Drain off drippings.
2. Cook noodles according to package instructions. Drain well.
3. In large bowl, toss cooked noodles with all of cottage cheese and 1 cup mozzarella cheese.
4. In a greased 4-quart, or 9 × 13 baking pan, spoon in enough spaghetti sauce to just cover bottom.
5. Stir rest of spaghetti sauce into browned beef.
6. Add half of noodles to baking dish.
7. Top with half of beef-spaghetti sauce.
8. Place sliced pepperoni over sauce.
9. Repeat layers, using all of remaining noodles and beef-spaghetti sauce.
10. Sprinkle with remaining mozzarella cheese.
11. Bake at 375° for 30-45 minutes, or until bubbly and heated through.

Revamp your mom's recipes to suit your family's taste.
Lucy Stpierre, Peru, NY

Mexican Lasagna

Jeanne Heyerly
Shipshewana, IN

Makes 12-15 servings

Prep. Time: 20 minutes
Baking Time: 30-45 minutes
Standing Time: 10 minutes

1 lb. ground beef
half large onion, chopped
1 large clove garlic, minced
2½ cups salsa, *divided*
4-6 (6") wheat, *or* corn,
 tortillas, halved, *divided*
1½ cups cottage cheese
1 cup sour cream
8-oz. can chopped green
 chilies
½ cup fresh cilantro,
 chopped
2 tsp. cumin
⅛ tsp. salt
4-oz. can sliced ripe olives,
 drained, *optional*
1¼ cups (5 oz.) shredded
 Monterey Jack cheese

1. Brown ground beef in skillet, stirring frequently to break up clumps. Remove meat to platter. Reserve drippings.
2. Cook onion and garlic in drippings for 2 minutes.

3. Spread 1 cup salsa on bottom of greased 9 × 13 baking dish.
4. Layer half of tortillas over salsa.
5. In bowl, stir together cottage cheese, sour cream, green chilies, cilantro, cumin, salt, and black olives if you wish.
6. Spread half of cottage cheese mixture over tortillas.
7. Spread half of beef mixture over cheese mixture.
8. Repeat layers using rest of salsa, tortillas, cottage cheese mixture, and beef mixture.
9. Top with Monterey Jack cheese.
10. Bake at 350° for 30-45 minutes, until dish is bubbly and heated through. Cover loosely with foil if getting too brown or beginning to dry out.
11. Remove from oven and let stand 10 minutes before serving.

Vegetarian Lasagna Roll-Ups

Judy Buller
Bluffton, OH

Makes 12 servings

Prep. Time: 30 minutes
Baking Time: 25-30 minutes

12 uncooked whole-grain
 lasagna noodles
2 eggs, slightly beaten
2½ cups ricotta cheese
2½ cups (10 oz.) shredded
 mozzarella cheese,
 divided
½ cup Parmesan cheese
1 pkg. frozen, chopped
 spinach, thawed
 and squeezed dry, *or*
4 cups chopped fresh
 spinach that has
 been microwaved on
 High 1-2 minutes and
 squeezed dry
¼ tsp. salt
¼ tsp. pepper
1-2 cups black beans,
 rinsed
23½-oz. jar spaghetti
 sauce, your favorite
 variety, *divided*

1. Cook lasagna noodles according to box directions. Drain and rinse well. Lay flat.
2. In a good-sized mixing bowl, mix together eggs, ricotta cheese, 1½ cups mozzarella cheese, Parmesan cheese, spinach, salt, and pepper.
3. Spread about ⅓ cup mixture on each noodle.

For potluck items that need to be kept warm, I fold a large terrycloth tablecloth in half. I put a hot pad in the middle of the tablecloth, and set my dish squarely on it. Then I wrap it tightly to hold the heat.
Jane Geigley, Lancaster, PA

4. Sprinkle each noodle with black beans. Press down to make beans adhere.

5. Spread 1 cup spaghetti sauce in bottom of well-greased 9 × 13 baking pan.

6. Roll up noodles and place seam-side down in baking pan.

7. Top rolls with remaining sauce. Sprinkle with 1 cup mozzarella cheese.

8. Bake uncovered at 350° for 25-30 minutes, or until heated through.

Tip:

You can assemble this dish ahead of time through Step 7, and then freeze or refrigerate it until you're ready to use it. Allow more time to bake if the dish is cold, probably 45-50 minutes total. But check while baking so as not to have it dry out or be over-baked.

Florentine Roll-Ups

Elaine Rineer
Lancaster, PA

Makes 12 servings

Prep. Time: 35-45 minutes
Baking Time: 45 minutes

16-oz. pkg. lasagna noodles
4 cups (2 lbs.) ricotta, *or*
**   cottage cheese**
2 cups (8 oz.) grated
**   cheddar cheese**
1 cup cleaned, well
**   drained, and chopped**
**   fresh spinach**
½ cup chopped green
**   onion**
1 egg, beaten
¼ tsp. black pepper
¼ tsp. salt
3 cups (26-oz. jar) spaghetti
**   sauce, your favorite**
**   flavor,** *divided*
Parmesan cheese

1. Cook pasta according to package directions. Drain. Lay flat on waxed paper to cool.

2. In large mixing bowl, stir together ricotta or cottage cheese, cheddar cheese, spinach, onion, egg, pepper, and salt.

3. Spread ⅓ cup mixture on each lasagna noodle. Roll up. Secure with toothpick if needed to keep from unrolling.

4. Spread ⅔ cup spaghetti sauce on bottom of well-greased 9 × 13 baking pan.

5. Place rolls seam-side down in pan.

6. Top with remaining sauce. Sprinkle with Parmesan cheese.

7. Cover. Bake at 350° for 45 minutes.

Garden Lasagna

Deb Martin
Gap, PA

Makes 8-10 servings

Prep. Time: 2 hours (includes cooking and deboning chicken)
Baking Time: 70-75 minutes

8 oz. lasagna noodles, *divided*
1 lb. bag frozen broccoli, cauliflower, and carrots, *divided*
2 10¾-oz. cans cream of chicken soup
1 cup sour cream
¾ cup chicken broth
2 eggs
3 cups cooked, chopped chicken, *divided*
1 cup grated Parmesan cheese, *divided*
3 cups mozzarella cheese, shredded

1. Cook noodles according to package directions. Drain well.
2. Steam vegetables until lightly cooked. Drain well.
3. In large bowl, mix soup, sour cream, broth, and eggs.
4. Place small amount of sauce on bottom of greased 9 × 13 baking pan. Swirl to cover bottom.
5. Layer 3 lasagna noodles on top of sauce.
6. Add half of sauce.
7. Top with half of chicken.
8. Top with half of vegetables.
9. Sprinkle with half of Parmesan cheese.

10. Repeat layers, using all remaining amounts of ingredients.
11. Top with mozzarella cheese.
12. Bake, covered, at 350° for 1 hour.
13. Uncover. Bake another 10-15 minutes.

Pesto Lasagna Rolls

Joy Uhler
Richardson, TX

Makes 12 servings

Prep. Time: 25 minutes
Baking Time: 30-40 minutes

12 uncooked lasagna noodles
26-oz. jar pasta sauce, *divided*
2 cloves garlic, minced
24 oz. ricotta cheese
10-oz. pkg. frozen chopped spinach, thawed and squeezed dry
3½-oz. jar prepared pesto
1 egg
½ cup grated Parmesan cheese
½ tsp. salt
¼ tsp. pepper
1 cup shredded mozzarella cheese

1. Cook noodles according to package directions. Drain.
2. Spread 2 cups pasta sauce in bottom of greased 9 × 13 baking pan.

3. Combine garlic, ricotta, spinach, pesto, egg, Parmesan, salt, and pepper in bowl.
4. Place cooked noodle on clean kitchen towel or clean cutting board. Spread ¼ cup ricotta mixture on noodle.
5. Roll noodle up. Place seam-side down in baking pan.
6. Repeat with remaining noodles. Place 4 in a row the length of the pan. Make 3 such rows.
7. Pour remaining pasta sauce over noodles.
8. Sprinkle with mozzarella.
9. Cover pan with foil. Bake 20 minutes at 350°.
10. Uncover. Bake until cheese is golden brown, about 10-15 minutes longer.

Tip:
Divide the ricotta mixture into 12 parts (with hand or knife) before using it on the noodles.

I recently served this for my granddaughter's birthday; it was her pick for a main dish. She and everyone present loved the dish, eating 2 rolls a piece.

Creamy Chicken Lasagna

Joanne E. Martin
Stevens, PA

Makes 10-12 servings

Prep. Time: 30 minutes
Baking Time: 40-45 minutes

8 oz. uncooked lasagna
noodles, *divided*
10¾-oz. can cream of
mushroom soup
10¾-oz. can cream of
chicken soup
½ cup grated Parmesan
cheese
1 cup sour cream
3 cups diced, cooked
chicken
2 cups grated mozzarella
cheese, *divided*

1. Cook noodles according
to package directions. Drain.
2. In mixing bowl, blend
together soups, Parmesan
cheese, and sour cream.
3. Stir in chicken.
4. Put ¼ of chicken mix-
ture in greased 9×13 baking
pan.
5. Top with half the cooked
noodles.
6. Spoon in half the
chicken mixture.
7. Sprinkle with half the
mozzarella cheese.
8. Repeat layers, using all
remaining ingredients.
9. Bake at 350° for 40-45
minutes, or until heated
through.

Three-Cheese Chicken Bake

Dorothy VanDeest
Memphis, TN

Makes 8-10 servings

Prep. Time: 25 minutes
Baking Time: 45 minutes

½ lb. lasagna noodles,
divided
12 oz. (1½ cups) creamed
cottage cheese, *divided*
3 cups diced cooked
chicken, *divided*
2 cups shredded cheddar
cheese, *divided*
½ cup grated Parmesan
cheese, *divided*

Mushroom Sauce:
½ cup chopped onion
½ cup chopped green
bell pepper
3 Tbsp. butter
10¾-oz. can cream of
chicken soup
⅓ cup milk
¼ lb. fresh mushrooms,
sliced, *or* 4-oz. can
mushroom pieces,
drained
¼ cup chopped pimento
½ tsp. dried basil

1. Cook noodles until just
tender in large amount of
boiling water. Drain and rinse
in cold water.
2. Prepare mushroom sauce
by cooking onion and green
pepper in butter in medium-
sized saucepan.
3. Stir soup, milk, mush-
rooms, pimento, and basil

into sautéed vegetables.
4. Grease 9×13 baking dish.
5. Place half of noodles
over bottom of baking dish.
6. Cover with half the
mushroom sauce.
7. Top with half the cottage
cheese.
8. Top with half the chicken.
9. Top with half the cheddar
and Parmesan cheeses.
10. Repeat layers, using all
remaining ingredients.
11. Bake at 350° for 45
minutes.

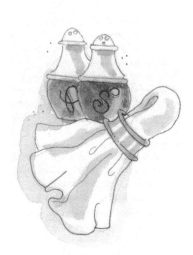

Our Favorite Tetrazzini

Carolyn Spohn
Shawnee, KS

Makes 6-8 servings

Prep. Time: 30 minutes
Baking Time: 40 minutes

5 oz. spaghetti, broken
1 medium onion, chopped
medium-sized green bell
   pepper, chopped
10¾-oz. can cream of
   chicken soup
⅓ cup milk
1 cup fat-free plain yogurt
3-4 cups diced cooked
   chicken, *or* turkey
8-oz. can sliced ripe olives,
   drained
8-oz. can mushroom stems/
   pieces, drained
4-oz. jar chopped pimento,
   drained
Parmesan cheese, grated,
   optional
1 cup grated cheddar
   cheese

1. Cook spaghetti according to package directions. Drain well.
2. Sauté onion and green pepper in non-stick skillet until soft.
3. Mix soup, milk, and yogurt together in large mixing bowl until smooth.
4. Stir into soup mixture the onion and green pepper, spaghetti, meat, olives, mushrooms, and pimento. Fold together until well mixed.
5. Pour into greased 9 × 13 baking dish.
6. Bake at 350° for 30 minutes, or until bubbly.
7. If you wish, sprinkle with Parmesan cheese. Then sprinkle with shredded cheddar cheese. Bake 10 more minutes.

Tips:
1. You can extend the number of servings easily by using more pasta.
2. This is a great way to use leftover Thanksgiving turkey.

Chicken and Bows

Arianne Hochstetler
Goshen, IN

Makes 12 servings

Prep. Time: 15-20 minutes
Cooking Time: 10-20 minutes

16-oz. pkg. bowtie pasta
2 lbs. uncooked boneless,
   skinless chicken breasts,
   cut into strips
1 cup chopped red bell
   pepper
half stick (4 Tbsp.) butter
2 10¾-oz. cans cream of
   chicken soup
2 cups frozen peas
1½ cups milk
1 tsp. garlic powder
¼-½ tsp. salt
¼ tsp. pepper
⅔ cup grated Parmesan
   cheese

1. Cook pasta according to package directions. Drain.
2. In large saucepan, cook chicken and red pepper in butter for 5-6 minutes until juices run clear.
3. Stir in soup, peas, milk, garlic powder, salt, and pepper.
4. Bring to boil. Simmer, uncovered, 1-2 minutes.
5. Stir in Parmesan cheese.
6. Add pasta and toss to coat.
7. Serve immediately, or refrigerate or freeze.
8. To heat, thaw frozen casserole in refrigerator overnight. Place in microwave-safe dish. Cover, and microwave 8-10 minutes or until heated through, stirring once. Or warm thawed dish in oven—350° for 1 hour, or until bubbly and heated through.

Overnight Chicken Hot Dish

Esther Porter
Minneapolis, MN
Ruth E. Miller
Wooster, OH

Makes 12 servings

Prep. Time: 20-30 minutes
Chilling Time: 8 hours, or
* overnight*
Baking Time: 60 minutes

10¾-oz. can cream of
  mushroom soup
10¾-oz. can cream of
  chicken soup
2½ cups milk
½ lb. Velveeta cheese,
  cubed
4 cups cooked chicken *or*
  turkey, diced
8 oz. uncooked macaroni
4-oz. can sliced
  mushrooms, sliced and
  drained, *optional*
1 stick (½ cup) melted
  butter, *divided*
1 cup finely diced celery
1 onion, chopped fine
1½ cups dry bread crumbs

1. Mix soups, milk, and
cheese in large mixing bowl.
2. Add chicken, uncooked
macaroni, and mushrooms if
you wish.
3. Stir in half the melted
butter.
4. Pour mixture into
greased 9 × 13 baking dish.
5. Cover. Refrigerate 8
hours or overnight.
6. Toss bread crumbs with
remaining melted butter.

Sprinkle over casserole.
7. Bake, uncovered, at
350° for 60 minutes, or until
bubbly and heated through.

Variation:
Instead of 2½ cups milk,
use 1½ cups milk and 1 cup
sour cream.

Ruth E. Miller
Wooster, OH

Baked Pasta with Chicken Sausage

Kim Rapp
Longmont, CO

Makes 8 servings

Prep. Time: 40 minutes
Baking Time: 20-30 minutes

1 lb. uncooked rigatoni
10-oz. pkg. fresh baby
  spinach
1 Tbsp. olive oil
1 medium red onion,
  chopped
4 cloves garlic, minced
¼ cup vodka, *optional*
28-oz. can whole tomatoes
  with juice, lightly
  crushed with hands
½ tsp. oregano
½ cup heavy cream
12-oz. smoked chicken
  sausage, halved
  lengthwise then cut into
  ¼"-thick slices
6 oz. fontina cheese: 4 oz.
  cubed; 2 oz. shredded
¼ cup grated Parmesan
  cheese

1. Cook rigatoni according
to package directions for 4
minutes.
2. Stir in baby spinach.
Continue cooking 3 minutes.
Drain pasta and spinach well.
Return to cooking pot and
keep warm.
3. Heat oil in large skillet
over medium heat. Add
onion. Cook about 3 minutes.
4. Stir in garlic. Remove
from heat.
5. Add vodka if you wish.
Return to fairly high heat and
cook until liquid is almost
evaporated, about 1 minute.
6. Stir in tomatoes and
oregano. Cook 10-15 minutes.
7. Add cream and warm,
cooking gently about 5
minutes.
8. Add sausage and cubed
fontina to pot. Toss to coat.
9. Season with several
grinds of salt and pepper.
10. Divide evenly between
2 greased 1½-quart baking
dishes, or spoon into 1
greased 9 × 13 baking dish.
11. Top with grated fontina
and Parmesan cheeses.
12. Bake at 400° until
browned, about 20-30 minutes.

Tip:
Add ¼ cup water or broth
if mixture seems dry before
baking.

Pasta Turkey Bake

Joy Sutter
Perkasie, PA

Makes 6-8 servings

Prep. Time: 20 minutes
Baking Time: 25 minutes

3 cups uncooked penne
 pasta
1½ lbs. ground turkey
½ cup chopped onion
½ cup chopped green bell
 pepper
2 15-oz. cans tomato sauce
1 Tbsp. sugar
1 tsp. salt
1 tsp. pepper
1 tsp. basil
1 tsp. oregano
12 oz. pepperoni, sliced
½ cup shredded cheddar
 cheese
½ cup shredded mozzarella
 cheese

1. Cook macaroni accord-
ing to package directions.
Drain. Set aside.

2. Meanwhile, brown
turkey in large skillet, stirring
frequently to break up clumps
until no pink remains.

3. Add onion and green
pepper to skillet. Simmer 10
minutes.

4. Add tomato sauce, sugar,
salt, pepper, basil, oregano,
and pepperoni.

5. Mix together with
macaroni.

6. Pour into greased 9 × 13
baking pan.

7. Top with shredded
cheeses.

8. Bake at 350° for 25
minutes, or until bubbly and
heated through.

Italian Pork Spaghetti Pie

Char Hagner
Montague, MI

Makes 8 servings

Prep. Time: 30 minutes
Baking Time: 10-15 minutes
Standing Time: 5 minutes

8 oz. dried spaghetti
½ cup milk
1 egg
1 lb. ground Italian pork
½ cup chopped onions
½ cup chopped green bell
 pepper
1 clove garlic, minced
½-1 Tbsp. chili powder,
 depending upon how
 much heat you like
1 tsp. Italian seasoning
15-oz. can tomato sauce
1 cup shredded Monterey
 Jack with jalapeños
 cheese
1 cup shredded cheddar
 cheese

1. Cook spaghetti according
to package directions. Drain
well. Return to pan.

2. Combine milk and egg
in small bowl. Stir into hot
pasta.

3. Butter 3-quart baking
dish. Spoon in prepared
spaghetti.

4. In a large skillet, cook

pork with onions, green
peppers, garlic, chili powder,
and Italian seasoning. Stir
frequently to break up clumps
of meat.

5. Stir in tomato sauce.
Simmer, uncovered, 5
minutes.

6. Spoon over pasta in
baking dish.

7. Sprinkle with cheeses.

8. Bake uncovered at 425°
for 10-15 minutes, or until
bubbly around edges.

9. Let stand 5 minutes
before serving.

*This is a favorite because it's
easier for small children to eat
than spaghetti with sauce.*

Mostaccioli

Sally Holzem
Schofield, WI

Makes 8 servings

Prep. Time: 45 minutes
Baking Time: 30-45 minutes

½ lb. bulk Italian sausage
½ cup chopped onion
16-oz. can tomato paste
½ cup water
½ tsp. oregano
¼ tsp. pepper
4-oz. can sliced
   mushrooms, drained
14½-oz. can diced
   tomatoes, undrained
¾ cup tomato juice
8-oz. pkg. mostaccioli
   noodles, *divided*
12 oz. shredded mozzarella
   cheese, *divided*
1½ cups cottage cheese
½ tsp. marjoram
¼ cup grated Parmesan
   cheese

1. Brown sausage and onions in saucepan, stirring often to break up clumps. When pink no longer remains, drain off drippings.
2. Stir in tomato paste, water, oregano, pepper, mushrooms, tomatoes, and tomato juice.
3. Cover. Simmer 30 minutes over medium heat.
4. Meanwhile, prepare noodles according to package directions. Drain well.
5. In mixing bowl, combine cottage cheese and marjoram.
6. In greased 7 × 13 baking pan, layer in half of noodles.
7. Top with half of meat sauce.
8. Sprinkle with half of mozzarella.
9. Spoon cottage-cheese mixture over top and spread as well as you can.
10. Layer on remaining noodles.
11. Top with remaining meat sauce.
12. Sprinkle with remaining mozzarella cheese.
13. Sprinkle with Parmesan cheese.
14. Bake at 350° for 30-45 minutes, or until bubbly, heated through, and lightly browned.

Pepperoni and Macaroni

Karen Ceneviva
Seymour, CT

Makes 6 servings

Prep. Time: 10 minutes
Cooking Time: 30 minutes

1 lb. uncooked macaroni
2 Tbsp. olive oil
8 oz. sliced pepperoni
1-2 tsp. chopped garlic
16-oz. can tomato sauce
½ cup water
dash thyme
1-lb. can garbanzo beans, *or*
   cannellini beans, drained
grated Parmesan cheese

1. Cook macaroni according to package directions. Drain well.
2. Meanwhile, sauté meat with garlic in olive oil in large stockpot.
3. Add tomato sauce and water to meat.
4. Add thyme and beans.
5. Stir in cooked noodles Mix all together.
6. Warm over low heat until heated through.
7. Sprinkle with cheese before serving.

Be sure to always ask for family recipes whenever you get the chance. Don't wait until your loved ones are gone — and their recipes with them.

Nancy Keatley, Salem, OR

Ham Noodle Casserole

Edna E. Miller
Shipshewana, IN

Makes 6 servings

Prep. Time: 45 minutes
Baking Time: 30-45 minutes

¾ stick (6 Tbsp.) butter,
  divided
4 Tbsp. flour
2 cups milk
2 cups grated cheese of
  your choice
2 tsp. salt
¼ cup ketchup
2 Tbsp. horseradish
4 cups chopped ham
2 cups peas, *or* green beans
  (if using frozen beans,
  cook lightly first)
8 cups noodles, cooked and
  well drained
2 cups dry bread crumbs

1. Melt 4 Tbsp. butter in
large saucepan. Blend in
flour, stirring well.
2. Add milk slowly. Over
low to medium heat, stir
continually until sauce
thickens.
3. Add cheese. Continue
over low heat, stirring until
cheese melts.
4. Stir in salt, ketchup,
horseradish, ham, and
vegetables.
5. Stir in noodles, mixing
together well.
6. Spoon into greased 9 × 13
baking dish.
7. Melt remaining 2 Tbsp.
butter in small saucepan. Add

bread crumbs, stirring until
browned. Sprinkle over top of
casserole.
8. Bake at 350° 30-45
minutes, or until bubbly and
heated through.

Ham and Macaroni Casserole

Jena Hammond
Traverse City, MI

Makes 8-10 servings

Prep. Time: 20 minutes
*Chilling Time: 8 hours, or
  overnight*
Baking Time: 1-1¼ hours

¼ cup chopped onions
2 Tbsp. butter
2½ cups cooked, cubed
  ham
2 10¾-oz. cans cream of
  mushroom soup
2 cups milk
2½ cups uncooked macaroni
1½ cups shredded cheddar
  cheese

1. Sauté onion in butter in
large saucepan.
2. Add ham, soup, milk,
macaroni, and cheese. Stir
until well blended.
3. Pour into greased 9 × 13
baking pan or 2-quart baking
dish.
4. Cover. Refrigerate at
least 8 hours or overnight.
5. Bake, covered, at 325°
for 45-60 minutes, or until
beginning to bubble around
edges.

6. Remove cover. Bake an
additional 15 minutes, or until
lightly browned.

Verenike Casserole

Jenelle Miller
Marion, SD

Makes 8-10 servings

Prep. Time: 30 minutes
Baking Time: 45 minutes

9 uncooked lasagna
  noodles, *divided*
3 cups cottage cheese
3 eggs
1 tsp. salt
½ tsp. pepper
1 cup sour cream
2 Tbsp. flour
1 cup half-and-half
2 cups cooked ham chunks,
  divided

1. Cook noodles according
to package directions until al
dente. Rinse and drain.
2. In a mixing bowl, stir
together cottage cheese, eggs,
salt, and pepper.
3. In a greased 9 × 13 baking
pan, layer in half the noodles.
4. Follow with layer of half
the cottage cheese mixture.
5. Scatter half the ham
chunks over all.
6. Repeat layers, using
remaining noodles, cheese,
and ham.
7. Mix flour with sour
cream in saucepan until
smooth.
8. Whisk in half-and-half.

9. Cook over medium heat until slightly thickened, stirring constantly.

10. Pour white sauce over baking pan contents.

11. Bake at 300° for 45 minutes, or until bubbly and heated through.

Tip:

You can make this the night before you want to serve it, through Step 10. Cover and refrigerate. When ready to bake, allow about 10 minutes more than stated in instructions.

We eat verenike (cheese pockets) a lot in our area of South Dakota. This is an easier version, but you get the same great taste!

Crustless Spinach Quiche

Elaine Vigoda
Rochester, NY

Makes 16-20 servings

Prep. Time: 10 minutes
Baking Time: 30-35 minutes
Standing Time: 10 minutes

1 cup flour
1 tsp. salt
1 tsp. baking powder
3 eggs, beaten
1 cup milk
half stick (4 Tbsp.) butter, melted
½ medium onion, chopped
10-oz. pkg. frozen spinach, thawed and squeezed dry*
12 oz. grated cheddar cheese
¼ tsp. nutmeg

1. Grease a 9 × 13 baking pan or 2 round pie plates.

2. In a large mixing bowl, blend together flour, salt, baking powder, eggs, milk, and butter.

3. Stir in onion, spinach, and cheese.

4. Pour into prepared pans. Sprinkle with nutmeg.

5. Bake at 350° until set and light golden brown, about 30-35 minutes. To test if the quiche is done, put the blade of a knife into the center of the baking dish. If the knife comes out clean, the quiche is finished. If it doesn't, continue baking for another 5 minutes. Test again.

Repeat if necessary.

6. Allow quiche to stand 10 minutes before cutting and serving. The standing time will allow the filling to firm up.

*You'll need to defrost the package of spinach before making this recipe. If you have time (8 hours or so), you can let it thaw in a bowl in the fridge. If you decided to make this quiche on short notice, and the spinach is frozen solid, lay the spinach in a shallow, microwave-safe dish, and defrost it in the microwave until thawed. (You can remove the box either before or after thawing the spinach.) When thawed, place the spinach in a strainer and press a spoon against it to remove as much of the water as possible. Or squeeze the spinach in your hand to remove the water. Then mix the spinach in with the rest of the ingredients and proceed with Step 3.

Tip:

You can freeze the quiche after you've baked it. When ready to serve, allow to thaw. Then bake for 10 minutes, or until heated through.

Crustless Veggie Quiche

Susan Kasting
Jenks, OK

Makes 12-15 servings

Prep. Time: 30 minutes
Baking Time: 45-50 minutes
Standing Time: 10 minutes

9 large eggs, beaten
1½ cups shredded sharp
 cheddar cheese, *divided*
1½ cups shredded
 Monterey Jack cheese,
 divided
½ cup milk
½ cup flour
1 tsp. baking powder
16 oz. cottage cheese
½ tsp. salt, *optional*
2 cups potatoes, diced
½ onion, chopped
½ cup water
4 cups sliced zucchini
1 cup chopped green bell
 pepper
½ cup chopped parsley
2 tomatoes, thinly sliced

1. In a large mixer bowl,
beat eggs until fluffy.
Add 1 cup cheddar, 1 cup
Monterey Jack cheese, milk,
flour, baking powder, cottage
cheese, and salt if you wish.
Stir together well.

2. Place potatoes in a
medium-sized saucepan,
along with onions and ½ cup
water. Cover and cook gently
until potatoes and onions are
nearly tender.

3. Add zucchini and green
pepper. Continue cooking

until just-tender. Drain off
water.

4. Add vegetable mixture
and parsley to egg-cheese
mixture.

5. Pour into greased
3-quart baking dish.

6. Top with remaining
cheese and tomato slices.

7. Bake at 400° for 15
minutes. Then reduce
temperature to 350° and bake
for an additional 35 minutes,
or until set.

8. To test if quiche is done,
insert blade of knife into
center. If knife comes out
clean, quiche is fully baked.
If it doesn't, continue baking
for another 5 minutes. Test
again. Repeat if not fully
cooked.

9. Allow quiche to stand
10 minutes before slicing to
allow it to firm up.

Tips:

1. You can serve this hot or
at room temperature.

2. You can use low-fat
cheeses and milk, as well as
an egg substitute.

3. You can use leftover
potatoes and vegetables.

4. If you're serving meat-
eaters, you can add cooked
bacon, broken up; smoked
sausage, cut into chunks; or
cooked ham, cut into pieces,
in Step 4.

Zucchini Supper

Susan Kastings
Jenks, OK

Makes 8 servings

Prep. Time: 15 minutes
Baking Time: 25-30 minutes

4 cups thinly sliced
 zucchini
1 cup buttermilk baking
 mix
½ cup chopped green onions
½ cup grated Parmesan
 cheese
2 Tbsp. chopped parsley,
 fresh *or* dried
½ tsp. oregano
½ tsp. pepper
½ tsp. garlic powder
½ tsp. seasoned salt
½ cup oil
½ cup milk
4 eggs beaten

1. In a large mixing bowl,
mix together zucchini, baking
mix, green onions, cheese,
parsley, oregano, pepper,
garlic powder, seasoned salt,
oil, milk, and eggs.

2. Pour into well-greased
9 × 13 baking pan.

3. Bake at 350° for 25-30
minutes, or until firm.

4. Serve warm or at room
temperature.

*When I come home from grocery-shopping, I
like to clean and cut up the fresh veggies and store
them in air-tight containers. Meal prep is faster
later.*
Edwina Stoltzfus, Narvon, PA

Easy Garden Vegetable Pie

Mary Keener
Mount Joy, PA

Makes 4-6 servings

Prep. Time: 20 minutes
Baking Time: 35-40 minutes
Standing Time: 10 minutes

scant ½ cup chopped onion
2 cups chopped broccoli,
  or cauliflower
1 cup shredded cheddar
  cheese
1½ cups milk
¾ cup buttermilk baking
  mix
3 eggs
1 tsp. salt
¼ tsp. pepper

1. Sauté onion in a nonstick pan until just tender.
2. Add broccoli or cauliflower and sauté until just tender. Or microwave vegetables for 2-3 minutes, again until just tender. Drain off any liquid.
3. Grease 9" pie plate.
4. Mix broccoli or cauliflower, onion, and cheese in pie plate.
5. In a separate bowl beat together milk, baking mix, eggs, salt, and pepper.
6. When smooth, pour over vegetables in pie plate.
7. Bake at 350° for 35-40 minutes, or until pie is set in the center. To test if pie is set, insert knife in center of pie. If knife comes out clean, the pie is fully baked. If it doesn't, continue baking for another 5 minutes. Test again. If clean, the pie is finished. If it isn't, repeat these steps.
8. Allow to stand 10 minutes before cutting and serving to allow pie to firm up.

Carrot Pie

Jean Harris Robinson
Pemberton, NJ

Makes 6-8 servings

Prep. Time: 20 minutes
Baking Time: 40 minutes

4 eggs, beaten
½ cup grated Parmesan
  cheese
½ cup oil
1 cup buttermilk baking
  mix
1 medium onion, chopped
3 cups raw shredded
  carrots

1. In a large mixing bowl, mix eggs, cheese, oil, baking mix, onion, and carrots together.
2. Pour into buttered 9" pie plate.
3. Bake on the middle shelf at 350° for 40 minutes, or until set in center. To test, insert blade of knife in center of pie. If it comes out clean, the pie is finished baking. If it doesn't, continue baking 5 more minutes. Test again. Continue baking in 5-minute intervals, and testing, until done.

Corn and Green Chili Casserole

Marilyn Mowry
Irving, TX

Makes 4-6 servings

Prep. Time: 10 minutes
Baking Time: 45-55 minutes
Standing Time: 10 minutes

15-oz. can creamed corn
4-oz. can chopped green
  chilies
2 eggs, beaten
¾ tsp. garlic salt
½ cup cornmeal
½ cup oil
½ lb. cheddar cheese, grated

1. In a mixing bowl, mix corn, green chilies, eggs, garlic salt, cornmeal, and oil together.
2. Spread half the corn mixture in a well-greased 9 × 13 baking pan.
3. Top with all of the cheese.
4. Top with the rest of the corn mixture.
5. Bake uncovered at 350° for 45-55 minutes, or until mixture is set. Insert knife blade in center of casserole to determine if set. If knife comes out clean, the casserole is finished baking. If not, continue baking for 5 more minutes. Test again with knife. If needed, bake another 5 minutes. Repeat test and baking if necessary.
6. Allow to stand 10 minutes after baking to allow casserole to firm up before serving.

Corn Casserole

Beth Nafziger
Lowville, NY

Makes 10 servings

Prep. Time: 25-30 minutes
Baking Time: 45 minutes

1 large onion, chopped
2 medium green peppers,
  chopped
1 stick (½ cup) butter
¼ cup flour
2 cups frozen, *or* canned,
  corn
2 cups cooked long-grain
  rice
14½-oz. can diced tomatoes
4 hardboiled eggs
2½ cups shredded sharp
  cheddar cheese, *divided*
2 Tbsp. Worcestershire
  sauce
2-3 tsp. hot pepper sauce
2 tsp. salt
1 tsp. pepper

1. In a large skillet, sauté chopped onion and green peppers in butter until tender.
2. Stir in flour.
3. Remove from heat. Add remaining ingredients except ½ cup cheese.
4. Pour into greased 2½-quart baking dish.
5. Bake uncovered at 350° for 45 minutes. Top with remaining cheese.

Calico Corn

Linda Yoder
Fresno, OH

Makes 6-8 servings

Prep. Time: 10 minutes
Cooking Time: 10 minutes

¾ cup minced onion
⅓ cup finely chopped
  green bell pepper
⅓ cup finely chopped red
  bell pepper
1 medium garlic clove,
  minced
2 Tbsp. vegetable oil
2 pints frozen sweet corn,
  thawed
½ cup quick grits, uncooked
1½ cups water
1 tsp. salt
¼ tsp. white pepper

1. In 3-quart pan, sauté onion, peppers, and garlic in oil just until tender.
2. Stir in corn, grits, water, salt and pepper.
3. Bring mixture to a boil.
4. Reduce heat, cover, and cook, stirring occasionally for about 7 minutes until grits are soft and water is absorbed.

Tip:
  If you're trying to reduce your stress by reducing the amount of last-minute preparation you do before serving a meal, you can prepare this dish in advance through Step 2. Refrigerate until it's nearly mealtime. Then begin with Step 3.

Potato Corn Bake

Donna Treloar
Muncie, IN

Makes 6 servings

Prep. Time: 15 minutes
Baking Time: 20-25 minutes

½ lb. bacon, cut in pieces
½ cup diced green bell
    pepper
⅓ cup diced onion
2½ cups milk
3 Tbsp. butter, *optional*
15-oz. can creamed corn
¾ tsp. salt
⅛ tsp. pepper
2 cups real, *or* instant,
    mashed potatoes
¾ cup sour cream
¼ cup grated Parmesan
    cheese
2 Tbsp. chopped green
    onion

1. In a sauté pan, cook
bacon until crisp. Remove
from pan and allow to drain
on a paper towel. Reserve 1
Tbsp. dripping in sauté pan.
2. Add green pepper and
onion to pan. Cook until
tender.
3. Add milk, butter if you
wish, corn, salt, and pepper
to pan. Cook over medium
heat until hot and bubbly.
4. Remove from heat. Stir
in potatoes and sour cream
until well blended.
5. Spoon into greased 7 × 11
baking dish.
6. Top with bacon, Parme-
san cheese, and green onion.
7. Cover and bake at 375°

for 20-25 minutes, or until
heated through.

Stuffed Zucchini

Janet Batdorf
Harrisburg, PA

Makes 6-8 servings

Prep. Time: 25 minutes
Baking Time: 25 minutes

1 large, *or* 2 medium,
    zucchini
3 Tbsp. butter, at room
    temperature
1 cup dry bread crumbs
2 Tbsp. chopped onion
½ cup spaghetti sauce,
    your favorite kind
1-2 good shakes of salt
1-2 full grinds of pepper
1-2 pinches dried oregano
¾ cup Italian cheese, *or*
    your favorite variety,
    grated

1. Parboil zucchini by
submerging it/them in boiling
salted water in large stockpot
for 15 minutes (10 minutes
for smaller size). Or cut in
half lengthwise and cook
in microwave until soft in
center.
2. When cool enough to
handle, scoop out pulp in the
center, leaving ½" "shell" all
around.
3. In a good-sized mixing
bowl, mix pulp with butter,
bread crumbs, onion, sauce,
salt, pepper, and oregano.
4. Fill zucchini shells
with mixture. Sprinkle with
cheese.
5. Place zucchini "boats,"
stuffed side up, next to each
other in a lightly greased
baking dish. Bake at 350°
until heated through, about
25 minutes.

Tip:
    I always use this recipe
when I have oversized zucchini, especially at the end
of summer.

Pea Casserole

Janet Batdorf
Harrisburg, PA

Makes 4 servings
Prep. Time: 20 minutes
Baking Time: 25 minutes

1-lb. pkg. frozen peas
10¾-oz. can cream of
  mushroom soup
¼ cup milk
half stick (4 Tbsp.) butter
⅓ cup diced celery
⅓ cup chopped onion
⅓ cup chopped green bell
  pepper
1 can sliced water
  chestnuts, drained
¼ cup chopped pimento
¾ cup crushed cheese
  crackers, *or* other flavor
  of your choice

1. Cook peas as directed on
package. Drain.
2. In a medium-sized bowl,
mix milk and soup together.
Stir in peas.
3. Sauté celery, onions and
green pepper in butter in a
small saucepan. Add to pea
mixture.
4. Stir in water chestnuts
and pimento. Mix well.
5. Place mixture in
1½-quart greased baking
dish.
6. Sprinkle with cheese
crackers.
7. Bake at 350° for 25 minutes, or until heated through.

Stuffed Eggplant

Jean Harris Robinson
Pemberton, NJ

Makes 4 servings
Prep. Time: 30 minutes
Baking Time: 30-45 minutes

2 large eggplants
1 medium onion, chopped
4 tomatoes, chopped
3 medium green bell
  peppers, chopped
1 rib celery, chopped
¼ cup olive oil
2 eggs, beaten
1 tsp. salt
1 tsp. pepper
1 cup grated Parmesan
  cheese
¼ tsp. cayenne pepper,
  optional
½ tsp. grated garlic,
  optional

1. Cut eggplants in half and
scrape out seeds. Parboil *
15 minutes.
2. After eggplant halves
have drained, remove pulp
within ½" of outer "shell."
Chop pulp. Set aside.
3. Place eggplant shells,
cut side up, in 12 × 24 baking
dish.
4. Empty stockpot of
water. Place onion, tomatoes,
peppers, celery, and olive oil

in stockpot. Cook until soft
and almost a pureé. Remove
from heat.
5. Stir in eggplant pulp,
beaten eggs, salt, and pepper.
6. Fill eggplant halves with
the mixture. Sprinkle with
cheese, and cayenne pepper
and garlic if you wish.
7. Distribute any leftover
stuffing in baking dish
around eggplant halves.
8. Bake at 350° for 30
minutes, or until eggplant is
tender and cheese is brown.

* To parboil eggplants,
submerge unpeeled halves in
a stockpot of boiling water
with a shake of salt added.
Cook in boiling water for 15
minutes. Remove and drain.

Tips:
  I have used 4-5 whole
canned tomatoes when I
haven't been able to find fresh
tomatoes. Before adding them
to the mixture (Step 4), I've
chopped them, and drained
off as much of their liquid as
I could.

I served this to my vegan
granddaughter, without the
cheese, and she went happily
home with the leftovers.

Shop at local markets and "invent" with what's in
season and usually less expensive.
  Barbara Forrester Landis, Lititz, PA

Mushroom Casserole

Maryann Markano
Wilmington, DE

Makes 10-12 servings
Prep. Time: 40 minutes
Baking Time: 30 minutes

3 lbs. fresh mushrooms
1 stick (½ cup) butter
1 large onion, chopped
16 oz. cheddar cheese, shredded, *divided*
3 6-oz. boxes stuffing mix—regular, herb, *or* turkey flavor, *divided*
1 pint half-and-half, regular *or* low-fat

1. Be sure mushrooms are clean. If small, leave them whole. If large, cut in half. Place in 5-quart stockpot with butter and chopped onion.
2. Cover and cook over low heat for about 30 minutes, until mushrooms are tender and have made their own juice.
3. Grease a 5-quart baking dish, or two 2½-3-quart baking dishes. Put in half the mushrooms, half the cheese, and half the stuffing mix.
4. Repeat layers, topping with remaining mushrooms and cheese. *When spooning mushrooms into baking dish(es), use some of their juices, but not all, because half-and-half must go in.*
5. Pour half-and-half on top.
6. Bake at 350° for 30 minutes, or until set and cheese

is melted. To test if mixture is done, insert blade of knife in center of dish. If knife comes out clean, the food is finished. If it doesn't, continue baking another 5 minutes. Test again. Continue baking and testing if needed.

Tips:
1. The dish may be done ahead of time, through Step 4. Pour half-and-half on just before baking. If baking dish was in refrigerator overnight, bring to room temperature and bake about 40 minutes.
2. This is a great alternative to traditional stuffing at holiday-time.

Chili Rellenos Casserole

Elena Yoder
Albuquerque, NM

Makes 12 servings
Prep. Time: 30 minutes
Baking Time: 35-40 minutes

1 can of 18-20 whole green chilies
1 lb. Monterey Jack cheese
garlic salt
4 eggs
1 Tbsp. flour
1 cup milk
¾ tsp. salt
¼-½ tsp. pepper
½ lb. cheddar, *or* longhorn, cheese, grated

1. Spray 9×13 baking pan with non-stick cooking spray.
2. Wearing gloves, cut chilies in half and remove seeds and membranes.
3. Cut Monterey Jack cheese into strips. Place strips in chili halves. Place stuffed chilies in pan side by side, cut side up.
4. Sprinkle with garlic salt.
5. In a mixing bowl, beat eggs. Stir in flour, milk, salt, and pepper.
6. Pour over chilies.
7. Sprinkle with grated cheese.
8. Bake at 350° for 35-40 minutes, or until set and beginning to brown.

Tip:
You can put this together the day before you want to serve it. Or stuff the chilies and freeze them until you need a quick meal. Then proceed with Step 5.

Good Go-Alongs:
Rice and beans and a green salad are our family's favorite go-alongs with this dish. Or as the tester's husband suggested, "I'd like this for breakfast!"

Grits New-Mexico Style

Karen Bryant
Corrales, NM

Makes 24 servings

Prep. Time: 20 minutes
Baking Time: 1 hour and 20 minutes

6 cups boiling water
1½ cups uncooked grits
1 stick (½ cup) butter, at room temperature
4-oz. can chopped green chilies
1 lb. cheddar cheese, grated
3 eggs, separated
2 tsp. salt
dash of Tabasco sauce
¼ tsp. garlic powder

1. Cook grits and water in large pan according to package directions until thick.
2. Stir in butter cut into chunks, chilies, cheese, beaten egg yolks, salt, Tabasco sauce, and garlic powder. Continue stirring until butter is completely melted.
3. Beat egg whites until soft peaks form. Fold into hot ingredients.
4. Pour into well-greased 4-quart baking dish.
5. Bake at 350° for 1 hour and 20 minutes.

Tip:
This dish is like a soufflé and makes a great brunch or light supper dish.

Eggs for Supper

Jeanette Oberholtzer
Lititz, PA

Makes 4 servings

Prep. Time: 10 minutes
Cooking Time: 20 minutes

6 hardboiled eggs, peeled
1 stick (½ cup) butter
salt and pepper to taste
cooked peas, *optional*
fried bacon, broken, *optional*
fresh parsley, *optional*
chopped fresh tomatoes, *optional*

1. Slice eggs and lay on platter.
2. Melt butter. Then allow to cook a bit longer, just until browned. Keep watch since it can quickly burn. Pour browned butter over eggs.
3. Sprinkle with salt and pepper to taste.
4. Top eggs with a sprinkling of any of the optional items that you wish.

This is an easy Sunday-night supper. Fruit salad makes a great partner.

Mercy Home Medley

Esther H. Becker
Gordonville, PA

Makes 6-8 servings

Prep. Time: 25-30 minutes
Cooking Time: 20-30 minutes

1 medium onion, chopped
2 garlic cloves, minced, *optional*
2 Tbsp. oil
3 tomatoes, chopped
2 cups finely shredded cabbage
2 cups diced potatoes, peeled, *or* unpeeled
5 cups finely shredded kale
sprinkle of salt and sprinkle of pepper
hot pepper flakes, *optional*

1. In a large pan, sauté onions and garlic in oil until translucent.
2. Add tomatoes. Cover and cook 5 minutes.
3. Add cabbage and potatoes. Simmer gently, covered, for 10 minutes, or until vegetables are nearly tender.
4. Stir in kale. Continue cooking, covered, for about 10 minutes, or just until kale is tender but not mushy.
5. Season with several grinds of salt and of pepper. Taste. Add a bit more seasoning if you wish.
6. Stir in hot pepper flakes if you like.

Good Go-Along:
Chapati

This dish was served every day when we visited Mercy Home in Maseno, Kenya, a girl's orphanage. The cooks there used only salt for seasoning, but I like the zip that pepper, pepper flakes, and minced garlic add.

Baked Rice with Spinach and Nuts

Carolyn Spohn
Shawnee, KS

Makes 4 servings

Prep. Time: 20 minutes
Baking Time: 25-30 minutes

1-2 tsp. olive oil
2 garlic cloves, minced
1 medium onion, diced
14-oz. can diced tomatoes, drained, reserving ⅓ cup juice
1½ cups cooked rice
½ tsp. salt
⅓ cup pine nuts, *or* chopped walnuts, *or* chopped pecans
half of 9-oz. pkg. fresh spinach, chopped
1 cup grated cheese—your choice of Colby Jack, Muenster, *or* mozzarella), *divided*
1-2 cups turkey *or* chicken, cooked and cubed, *optional*

1. Heat olive oil in large skillet over medium heat. Being careful not to splash yourself with hot oil, sauté garlic and onion until tender.
2. Add drained tomatoes and cook about 10 minutes, stirring frequently.
3. Stir cooked rice, salt, ⅓ cup reserved tomato juice, nuts, raw spinach, and meat if you wish into tomato mixture.
4. Spread half of mixture in greased 7×12 baking dish.
5. Sprinkle with half the cheese.
6. Repeat layers with cheese on top.
7. Cover and bake at 375° for about 25 minutes, or until bubbly.
8. Uncover for last few minutes of baking so cheese browns slightly.

Fruity Rice

Rose Hankins
Stevensville, MD

Makes 4-5 servings

Prep. Time: 20 minutes
Cooking Time: 45-55 minutes

2 tsp. olive oil
½ cup chopped onion
½ cup chopped apple
½ cup chopped dried cranberries
2 Tbsp. chopped garlic
2 cups water
1 cup uncooked brown rice

1. Place oil, onion, apple, cranberries, and garlic in good-sized saucepan.
2. Cook 5-7 minutes, or until tender.
3. Stir in water and rice. Cover. Bring to a boil.
4. Reduce heat. Simmer, covered, 35-50 minutes, or until all water is gone and rice is tender.

Tips:
   If water evaporates before rice is cooked, add 2-3 Tbsp. water. Continue cooking until rice is done. Check occasionally to make sure it isn't cooking dry before becoming tender.

Esther's Brown Rice

Esther Yoder
Hartville, OH

Makes 6 servings

Prep. Time: 10 minutes
Cooking Time: 1 hour

2 cups water
1 cup uncooked brown rice
1 cup salsa
¼ cup chopped green pepper
½ cup chopped celery
½ cup chopped onion
1 tsp. chicken bouillon
1 tsp. garlic salt
1 tsp. oil
½ tsp. sugar

1. Mix ingredients in a 4-quart saucepan.
2. Bring to boil. Turn heat to low; cover and cook 45-60 minutes. Check after 45 minutes to make sure rice isn't cooking dry. Add 3-4 Tbsp. water if needed.

Tip:
Serve with more salsa at the table.

Almond Rice

Dorothy VanDeest
Memphis, TN

Makes 6-8 servings

Prep. Time: 20 minutes
Cooking Time: 20 minutes

2 cups long-grain rice, uncooked
1 Tbsp. butter
3½ cups water
4 beef bouillon cubes
½ cup slivered toasted almonds
6 green onions, chopped
4-5 Tbsp. soy sauce

1. Mix rice and butter in skillet. Sauté until rice begins to brown, stirring frequently to prevent burning.
2. In a small saucepan, bring water to a boil. Dissolve bouillon cubes in boiling water.
3. Add water to rice. Mix together. Cover and simmer until liquid disappears, 15-20 minutes.
4. Stir in almonds, chopped green onions, and soy sauce. Heat 1 minute longer.

Lentil, Rice, and Veggie Bake

Andrea Zuercher
Lawrence, KS

Makes 12 servings

Prep. Time: 20 minutes
Cooking/Baking Time: 65-70 minutes

1 cup uncooked long-grain rice
5 cups water, *divided*
2 cups uncooked red lentils
2 tsp. vegetable oil
2 small onions, chopped
6 cloves garlic, minced
2 fresh tomatoes, chopped
⅔ cup chopped celery
⅔ cup chopped carrots
⅔ cup chopped summer squash
16-oz. can tomato sauce, *divided*
2 tsp. dried, *or* 2 Tbsp. fresh basil, *divided*
2 tsp. dried, *or* 2 Tbsp. fresh oregano, *divided*
2 tsp. ground cumin, *divided*
¾ tsp. salt, *divided*
½ tsp. pepper, *divided*

1. Cook rice according to package directions, using 2 cups water and cooking about 20 minutes. Set aside.
2. Cook lentils with remaining 3 cups water until tender, about 15 minutes. Set aside.
3. Heat oil in good-sized skillet over medium heat. Being careful not to splash yourself with hot oil, stir

in onion and garlic. Sauté 5 minutes, or until just tender.

4. Stir in tomatoes, celery, carrots, squash, and half the tomato sauce.

5. Season with half the herbs and seasonings.

6. Cook until vegetables are tender. Add water if too dry.

7. Place cooked rice, lentils, and vegetables in well-greased 9 × 13 baking pan, or equivalent-size casserole dish. Layer, or mix together, whichever you prefer.

8. Top with remaining tomato sauce and herbs.

9. Bake at 350° for 30 minutes, or until bubbly.

Tips:

1. As the vegetables cook in Step 6, keep checking that they are not getting too dry. Add water or tomato juice to vegetables if needed.

2. If you are not cooking for vegetarians or vegans, you can use broth or stock in place of water.

3. Substitute with other herbs if you wish.

4. If you don't have fresh tomatoes available, substitute canned tomatoes.

This is a favorite at the Lawrence (Kansas) Interdenominational Nutrition Kitchen (LINK), to which our church contributes and serves casseroles one Sunday each month.

Middle Eastern Lentils

Judith Houser
Hershey, PA

Makes 8 servings

Prep. Time: 20 minutes
Cooking Time: 50-60 minutes

Lentils:
  2 large onions, chopped
  1 Tbsp. olive oil
  ¾ cup uncooked brown rice
  1½ tsp. salt
  1½ cups uncooked lentils, rinsed
  4 cups water

Salad:
  1 bunch leaf lettuce
  2 medium tomatoes, diced
  1 medium cucumber, peeled and sliced
  2 green onions, chopped
  1 red bell pepper, diced

Dressing:
  2 Tbsp. olive oil
  2 Tbsp. lemon juice
  ½ tsp. paprika
  ¼ tsp. dry mustard
  1 garlic clove, finely minced
  ¼ tsp. salt
  ½ tsp. sugar

1. In a large kettle, prepare lentils by sautéing onions in olive oil until soft and golden.

2. Add rice and salt. Continue cooking over medium heat for 3 minutes.

3. Stir in lentils and water. Bring to a simmer.

4. Cover and cook until rice and lentils are tender, 50-60 minutes.

5. While the lentil mixture cooks, prepare salad by tossing together lettuce, tomatoes, cucumber, onions, and pepper in a good-sized mixing bowl.

6. Place all dressing ingredients in a jar with a tight-fitting lid. Shake vigorously until well mixed.

7. Just before serving, shake dressing again to make sure it's thoroughly mixed. Then toss salad with dressing.

8. To serve each individual, place serving of lentil mixture on dinner plate and top with a generous serving of salad.

Tip:

This is a traditional, Middle Eastern dish. As strange as it may sound, the combination of the salad on top of the hot lentil mixture is marvelous!

Check your local library for cookbooks with unusual recipes. Make copies of something new that sounds good, and try it ... but not for company, just in case it doesn't work.

John and Carol Ambrose, McMinnville, OR

Corn Balls

Rhoda Nissley
Parkesburg, PA
Jeanette Oberholtzer
Lititz, PA

Makes 8-10 servings

Prep. Time: 10-15 minutes
Baking Time: 35 minutes

11-oz. pkg. soft bread cubes
1-lb. can crushed corn, *or*
  2 cups fresh corn
3 eggs, beaten
½-1 chopped onion
½ tsp. salt
¼ tsp. pepper
1 stick (½ cup) melted
  butter

1. Combine bread cubes, corn, eggs, onion, salt, and pepper in a large mixing bowl.
2. Form into balls, each about ⅓ cup in size. If balls are too dry to hold together, add 2 Tbsp. hot water to full mixture.
3. Place in greased 9 × 13 baking pan.
4. Pour melted butter over balls.
5. Bake uncovered at 325° for 35 minutes.

Tips:
1. I use about 3 cups of my home-frozen sweet corn for these. I like to put the corn in the blender with the eggs and onions before mixing with the bread and seasonings.
Rhoda Nissley
Parkesburg, PA

2. After forming balls, you can cover and refrigerate them until you're ready to bake them. Add about 10 minutes to the baking time.

Stuffing Balls

Joan Brown
Warriors Mark, PA

Makes 6-8 servings

Prep. Time: 15 minutes
Baking Time: 20-25 minutes

1 loaf stale bread
3 ribs celery, diced
1 medium, *or* small, onion,
  diced
2 eggs, beaten
10¾-oz. can cream of
  mushroom, *or* cream of
  chicken soup, *divided*

1. Tear bread in small pieces and place in large mixing bowl.
2. Add celery, onion, eggs, and half of soup. Mix together well.
3. Form into balls, each ⅓ cup in size. If too dry to hold together, add boiling water, 1-2 Tbsp. at a time to all of bread mixture.
4. Place balls in greased 9 × 13 baking pan.
5. Pour remaining soup over top.
6. Bake at 350° for 20-25 minutes.

Tips:
1. Use an ice cream scoop to make evenly sized balls.
2. After forming the balls, you can cover and refrigerate them until you're ready to bake them. Add about 10 minutes to the baking time. You can make them on Saturday to bake for Sunday noon dinner.

To make your own cream of mushroom or celery soup, please turn to pages 258-259.

Grilling

Grilled Chicken Breasts

Gloria Mumbauer
Singers Glen, VA
Thelma F. Good
Harrisonburg, VA

*Makes 2½-2¾ cups marinade;
10-12 chicken breast halves*

Prep. Time: 5 minutes
**Marinating Time: 6-8 hours or
overnight**
Grilling Time: 15-18 minutes

**10-12 boneless skinless
chicken breast halves,
½-¾"-thick**
¾ cup vegetable oil
¾ cup soy sauce
½ cup apple cider vinegar
**¼ cup Worcestershire
sauce**
⅓ cup lemon juice
2 tsp. prepared mustard
1 tsp. black pepper
2 garlic cloves, minced, *or*
1½ tsp. garlic powder

1. Place chicken breasts in
a single layer in a nonmetallic
dish.
2. In a bowl, mix together
rest of ingredients.
3. When well blended, pour
over chicken.
4. Cover. Marinate 6-8
hours or overnight. Turn
chicken over about half-way
through, if it's not the middle
of the night and you're able
to, to coat both sides.
5. Remove from marinade.
Grill over medium heat until
cooked through, about 15-18
minutes. Do not overcook or
meat will dry out!

Tips:
To serve at a potluck,
slice grilled chicken into
strips about ¾" wide so lots
of people get a taste. Do not
expect to bring any of this
chicken home from a potluck!
Thelma Good
Harrisonburg, VA

*Our children are delighted
when this recipe is on our menu
at home. They love to slice it
over a big salad for a delicious
meal that is both healthy and
tasty!*

Thelma Good
Harrisonburg, VA

179

Subtly Wonderful Grilled Chicken

Joyce Zuercher
Hesston, KS

Makes 6-8 servings

Prep. Time: 5 minutes
Marinating Time: 2 hours
Grilling Time: 10-15 minutes,
depending on type and size of
chicken pieces

chicken breasts, *or* legs
    and/or thighs, to serve
    6-8 people
½ cup oil
½ cup lemon juice, *or*
    vinegar of your choice
¼ cup water
2 tsp. salt
¼ tsp. pepper
1 Tbsp. sugar
1 tsp. paprika
1 Tbsp. minced onion

1. Measure ingredients into
bowl except for chicken, and
mix well.
2. Let sauce stand 1 hour to
allow flavors to blend.
3. Place chicken in single
layer in nonmetallic bowl.
4. Pour sauce over chicken.
Cover. Marinate chicken
1 hour in fridge.
5. Turn pieces over during
grilling, allowing about 5-10
minutes total for breasts and
10-15 minutes total for legs
and/or thighs. Brush on more
sauce while grilling.

This was my first grilling
sauce recipe. I have tried many
fancier recipes since, but always
return to this one.

Barbecued Chicken Thighs

Ida H. Goering
Dayton, VA

Makes 8-10 servings

Prep. Time: 10 minutes
Chilling Time: 3-6 hours
Grilling Time: 15-20 minutes

16-20 boneless, skinless
    chicken thighs
½ cup oil
1 cup vinegar
¼ cup ketchup
4 tsp. salt
½ tsp. poultry seasoning
½ tsp. black pepper

1. Place chicken in a single
layer, if possible, in a nonmetallic dish.
2. Combine oil, vinegar,
ketchup, salt, poultry seasoning, and pepper. Mix well.
3. Pour sauce over chicken
pieces.
4. Marinate 3-6 hours in
the fridge.
5. Grill chicken over
medium heat until done,
about 15-20 minutes.

Tips:
    I like this recipe because
I can make it ahead of time
and keep it hot until ready to
serve at the potluck. Or I can
easily heat it up by placing
it in a microwave-safe dish,
covering it tightly, and mic-
ing it over medium heat until
heated through, but without
cooking it again.

Tender Flank Steak

Kayla Snyder
North East, PA

Makes 6 servings

Prep. Time: 15 minutes
Marinating Time: 6-8 hours, or
overnight
Grilling Time: 20 minutes

1 cup soy sauce
¼ cup lemon juice
¼ cup honey
6 garlic cloves, minced, *or*
    less if you prefer
1-1½ lbs. beef flank steak

1. In a large re-sealable
plastic bag, combine soy
sauce, lemon juice, honey,
and garlic.
2. Add steak. Seal bag and
turn to coat. Place in shallow
dish with sides to catch any
leaks.
3. Refrigerate 6-8 hours,
or overnight to marinate in
sauce.
4. When ready to grill,
drain meat and discard
marinade.
5. Grill over medium heat
8-10 minutes, on each side or
until meat reaches desired
doneness (for medium-rare,
a meat thermometer should
read 145°; medium 160°;
well-done 170°).
6. Allow to stand off heat
10 minutes before slicing.
7. Slice steak into thin
slices across the grain.

Peppered Rib-Eye Steaks

Meredith Miller
Dover, DE

Makes 4 servings

Prep. Time: 10 minutes
Marinating Time: 1 hour or more
Grilling Time: 8-10 minutes

1 Tbsp. olive oil
1 Tbsp. garlic powder
1 Tbsp. paprika
2 tsp. dried thyme
2 tsp. dried oregano
1½ tsp. black pepper
1 tsp. salt
1 tsp. lemon pepper seasoning
1 tsp. cayenne pepper
4 beef rib-eye steaks, 1½" thick

1. In a bowl, mix together oil, garlic powder, paprika, thyme, oregano, pepper, salt, lemon pepper, and cayenne pepper.

2. Brush each steak well on both sides with mixture.

3. Lay steaks in single layer in nonmetallic baking dish. Pour remaining marinade over top.

4. Cover. Refrigerate at least 1 hour.

5. Grill, uncovered, over medium-high heat, 4-5 minutes on first side.

6. Turn and grill 4-5 minutes on other side.

Tips:

1. For medium-rare, steaks should register 145° in the center (medium 160°, and well-done 170°).

2. We like to take our steaks off the grill while still pink in the middle, wrap them in foil, and let them set in an ice chest until ready to serve. With a large quantity, you can keep them up to 2 hours in that way. The steaks remain soft and juicy.

3. For a potluck, we cut the meat in strips so more people can enjoy them.

Pork Tenderloin with Teriyaki Apricot Sauce

Jennifer Kuh
Bay Village, OH

Makes 8-12 servings

Prep. Time: 10 minutes
Marinating Time: 6-8 hours or overnight
Grilling Time: 20-25 minutes
Standing Time: 10 minutes

3-4-lb. pork tenderloin
8-12-oz. bottle teriyaki sauce, *divided*
12-oz. jar apricot preserves

1. Place meat in nonmetallic pan.

2. Pour half bottle of teriyaki sauce over meat.

3. Cover. Marinate in fridge for 6-8 hours, or overnight.

4. Grill pork over medium heat, 10-12 minutes per side.

5. Meanwhile, mix preserves and 3 Tbsp. teriyaki sauce together in microwave-safe bowl.

6. Cover. Microwave until bubbly.

7. Place pork on serving platter after grilling. Pour bubbling sauce on top.

8. Allow to stand 10 minutes before cutting and serving.

Venison Backstrap Deluxe

Tammy Smith
Dorchester, WI

Makes 9-12 servings

Prep. Time: 20 minutes
Grilling Time: 30-40 minutes
Standing Time: 10 minutes

3-4-lb. venison backstrap
1 tsp. salt
½ tsp. pepper
2 tsp. Whisky, *or*
 McCormick's, steak
 seasoning
1 lb. bacon

1. Season tenderloin well with salt, pepper, and steak seasoning.
2. Wrap bacon pieces around meat, overlapping slices of bacon if necessary.
3. Wrap in heavy duty aluminum foil. Be sure it is sealed tightly.
4. Grill on medium heat 15-20 minutes.
5. Turn over and do other side for 15-20 minutes, or until done to your liking.
6. Allow to stand 10 minutes before unwrapping and slicing.

Grilled Pizza Crusts

Tammy Smith
Dorchester, WI

Makes 2 large pizza crusts

Prep. Time: 10-15 minutes
Rising Time: 1 hour, or so
Grilling Time: 2-3 minutes

1¼ cups warm water
3½ cups flour, plus more if
 necessary
1 envelope (1 Tbsp.) active
 dry yeast
1 tsp. sugar
1½ tsp. coarse salt
1¼ cups warm water
¼ cup olive oil

1. Put water in bowl of mixer with a dough hook.
2. Add flour, yeast, sugar, and salt.
3. Add oil. Mix well.
4. If too sticky, add more flour, a tablespoon at a time, until dough pulls away from sides of bowl.
5. Place ball of dough on lightly floured surface. Knead by hand a few minutes.
6. Cover with plastic wrap. Set in warm place.
7. Let rise until double in bulk, an hour or so.
8. Generously oil 2 baking sheets. Divide dough in half, and place one half on each pan.
9. Stretch each ball of dough to form a 9 × 13 rectangle, about ⅛-¼" thick.
10. Slide crust off baking sheet and right onto grill grate after grill is hot.

11. Grill 1-2 minutes until first side is lightly browned.
12. Flip over. Grill 1-2 minutes on that side until lightly browned.
13. When crust is done, cover with your favorite toppings. Put back on grill on low heat until heated through.
14. Cut into wedges and serve.

Grilled Onions

Loretta Weisz
Auburn, WA

Makes 2 servings

Prep. Time: 5 minutes
Grilling Time: 35-45 minutes

2 medium white, *or* yellow,
 sweet onions
dab of butter
dash of pepper
sprinkling of salt

1. Slice each onion into 4 wedges, but without slicing through the bottom, so that each onion stays whole.
2. Add a dab of butter and sprinklings of pepper and salt between each wedge.
3. Wrap stuffed onions tightly in foil.
4. Grill until soft and tender, 35-45 minutes.

Good Go-Alongs:
 These onions are delicious with grilled steaks and chicken.

Vegetables

Donna's Baked Beans

Kathy Bless
Fayetteville, PA

Makes 6-8 servings

Prep. Time: 15 minutes
Cooking/Baking Time: 1¼ hour

½ lb. bacon, diced
1 onion, diced
2 16-oz. cans pork and
   beans
2 16-oz. cans French-style
   green beans, drained,
   ⅓ cup liquid reserved
6-oz. can tomato paste
1 cup brown sugar, packed

1. In a frying pan, fry bacon until crisp and set aside.
2. In the bacon grease, fry the onion until soft.
3. Combine bacon, onion, beans, tomato paste, and brown sugar in a large bowl. Mix well.

4. If you want the mixture juicier, add extra green bean liquid now.
5. Pour into a 2½-quart baking dish. Bake at 375° for 1 hour.

Tip:
Use 2 Tbsp. dried minced onion in place of the fresh. Just add it to step 1.

I got this recipe from my friend, Donna, at a church seniors' get-together. We had a camp-site cookout near another friend's mountain cabin—great fun and I'm not a camp-out person.

Plan ahead when preparing food for home-entertaining or potlucks. Do as much preparation ahead of time as possible to avoid a last-minute rush. I like to sit down and relax just prior to the event.
Naomi Ressler, Harrisonburg, VA

183

Doctoring 15½-oz. Cans of Baked Beans

Baked beans are a potluck staple, but the flavors can really vary according to the cook's taste. If you have two 15½-oz. cans of baked beans (that's almost 4 cups) that you want to spruce up, look at this list of add-ins for ideas.

You can choose sweet and savory ingredients to get the flavor your family and guests love. My mom always started with ketchup, brown sugar, and prepared mustard.

Add just a little bit of something if you're unsure, and then taste-test. Baked beans are a matter of opinion!

Also, you don't have to actually bake the beans if you don't have time. Just heat them on the stove with the flavorings you chose.

½ cup ketchup
Annabelle Unternahrer
Shipshewana, IN

4 Tbsp. brown sugar
Judi Robb
Manhattan, KS

1 tsp. prepared mustard
½ onion, chopped
Deb Martin
Gap, PA

2 tsp. dry onion flakes
½ cup light molasses
Louise Stackhouse
Benton, PA

⅔ cup apple butter
Lois Ostrander
Lebanon, PA

1 Tbsp. cider vinegar
Carla Elliot
Phoenix, AZ

2 tsp. Worcestershire sauce
Jennie Martin
Richfield, PA

½ lb. pork sausage links
Sally Holzem
Schofield, WI

1 tsp. paprika
Esther Shisler
Lansdale, PA

few drops liquid smoke
Joette Droz
Kalona, IA

garlic salt or seasoning salt
Sally Esh
Gordonville, PA

4-oz. can crushed pineapple
Shelia Heil
Lancaster, PA

4 Tbsp. barbeque sauce
Jena Hammond
Traverse City, MI

1 tsp. dry mustard
Karen Ceneviva
Seymour, CT

chili sauce instead of ketchup
½ green pepper, chopped
Frances & Cathy Kruba
Dundalk, MD

½ tsp. chili powder
½ lb. ground beef, cooked, and drained
Joy Martin
Myerstown, PA

4 slices bacon, browned and crumbled
Nadine Martinitz
Salina, KS

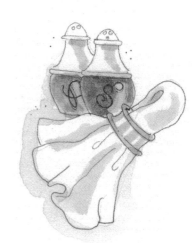

Try adding your favorite herbs and spices to your "tried and true" recipes, and you might come up with something even better. Jeanne Heyerly, Shipshewana, IN

Baked Beans

Barbara Hershey
Lititz, PA

Makes 8-10 servings

*Prep. Time: 30 minutes +
overnight soaking time
Cooking/Baking Time: 2½ hours*

1 lb. dry northern beans
1 tsp. salt
½ tsp. baking soda
2 cups V-8 juice
1 small onion, minced
2 Tbsp. molasses
1 tsp. dry mustard
7-8 pieces bacon, fried
 (reserve grease)
½ cup ketchup
½ cup brown sugar

1. Cover beans with about 3 inches water and allow to soak overnight.
2. In morning, add salt and baking soda.
3. Bring to boil. Cook about 20-25 minutes until beans are soft. Drain.
4. Pour beans into large baking dish.
5. Add juice, onion, molasses, mustard, bacon, ketchup, brown sugar and most of bacon grease. Mix.
6. Bake at 325° for 2 hours or on Low in slow cooker for 5-6 hours.

Tip:
 If you don't have time to soak dry beans, you could purchase 6 16-oz. cans of northern beans and drain before adding other ingredients.

Good Go-Alongs:
 Hamburgers, hot dogs, coleslaw.

Lima Bean Supreme

Lizzie Ann Yoder
Hartville, OH

Jean Butzer
Batavia, NY

Makes 6 servings

*Prep. Time: 20 minutes
Soaking Time: 8 hours or
 overnight
Cooking/Baking Time: 3 hours*

1 lb. dry lima beans
1 stick (½ cup) butter
1 cup sour cream
½ cup brown sugar
1 Tbsp. dry mustard
1 tsp. molasses *or* 1 Tbsp.
 light corn syrup

1. Soak the dried beans overnight covered in water. Drain.
2. Cook until almost tender in salted water. Drain, rinse, and place in a deep casserole.
3. Mix well the butter, sour cream, sugar, mustard, and molasses. Pour over beans and mix well.
4. Bake at 300° for 2 hours, stirring several times. Mixture will be thin when you take it from the oven, but thickens as it cools.

Variation:
 Using the same procedures

and baking times, dress the beans with 1 cup light brown sugar, 1 cup ketchup, 1 Tbsp. prepared mustard, 2 tsp. Worcestershire sauce, 2 tsp. vinegar. Fry together ½ lb. bacon and 1 onion; drain; mix in.

Joanne Warfel
Lancaster, PA

Tips:
 1. I usually use low-fat sour cream.
 2. To speed up this preparation, bring the beans to a boil in the salted water. Let stand a couple of hours vs. overnight. Then proceed to boil until almost tender.
 3. May be served warm or cold.

Green Beans Caesar

Carol Shirk
Leola, PA

Makes 6-8 servings

Prep. Time: 10 minutes
Cooking/Baking Time: 30 minutes

1½ lbs. green beans, trimmed
2 Tbsp. oil
1 Tbsp. vinegar
1 Tbsp. minced onion
salt
pepper
2 Tbsp. bread crumbs
2 Tbsp. Parmesan cheese
1 Tbsp. butter, melted

1. Cook the green beans until barely tender. Drain.
2. Toss with oil, vinegar, onion, salt, and pepper.
3. Pour into an ungreased 2-quart casserole.
4. Mix bread crumbs, Parmesan cheese, and butter. Sprinkle over beans.
5. Bake at 350° for 20 minutes.

Sweet & Sour Green Beans

Meredith Miller
Dover, DE

Makes 8 servings

Prep. Time: 15 minutes
Cooking Time: 30 minutes

9 strips bacon
1 medium onion, diced
4 cups green beans, trimmed
1 Tbsp. flour
½ cup sugar
2 Tbsp. vinegar
¼ cup water
1 tsp. mustard
½ tsp. salt

1. Fry the bacon, keeping the grease in the pan. Cool and crumble.
2. Sauté the onion in the bacon drippings. Set aside.
3. Meanwhile put the beans in a pot with a little water. Cover and cook until beans are tender, 10-15 minutes.
4. Combine flour, sugar, vinegar, water, mustard and salt.
5. In a small saucepan, stir and cook until thickened, then add the sautéed onions.
6. Put the drained, cooked beans in a serving dish. Pour the sauce over the beans and sprinkle with crumbled bacon.

Tips:
1. To evenly distribute the bacon, stir it into the sauce along with the onions then pour over beans and toss gently.
2. The sauce can be made ahead of time, then added to beans when ready.

Tasty Beans

Linda Yoder
Fresno, OH

Makes 6 servings

Prep. Time: 5 minutes
Cooking Time: 10 minutes

1 cup thinly sliced onion
1 clove garlic, minced
4-oz. fresh *or* canned
   mushrooms, sliced
1 Tbsp. olive oil
2 pints (4 cups) frozen
   green beans, partially
   thawed
1 tsp. salt
1 Tbsp. dill seeds
dash of cayenne pepper
¾ cup water

1. Sauté onions and garlic, plus fresh mushrooms if using, in olive oil just until tender but not brown.
2. Add green beans, salt, dill seeds, cayenne pepper and water and bring to boil.
3. Reduce heat; cover. Simmer until beans are crisp-tender.

Tips:
1. This recipe may be doubled. It's best if it can be cooked just before the meal.
2. Garnish with sliced almonds for more color and crunch.

Barbecued Green Beans

Naomi Ressler
Harrisonburg, VA

Makes 6-8 servings

Prep. Time: 15 minutes
*Cooking/Baking Time: 20
   minutes*

4 slices bacon, chopped
   into small pieces
½ cup sliced *or* chopped
   onions
½ cup ketchup
¼ cup brown sugar
1 Tbsp. Worcestershire
   sauce
1½ quarts (3 lb. 2-oz. can)
   green beans, drained

1. Fry bacon and onion together until bacon is crisp.
2. Add ketchup, brown sugar and Worcestershire sauce. Simmer several minutes.
3. Add to drained beans in a 1½-quart casserole dish.
4. Bake at 350° for 20 minutes or until heated throughout.

Tips:
1. I save part of the bacon dripping in the pan with the rest of ingredients for added flavor, but discard part for health reasons.
2. I often double the recipe and put in my slow cooker on Low for 3 hours. This is a favorite at our church potlucks.

Variation:
   Double the bacon and brown sugar. Increase the ketchup to ¾ cup. And you can use bacon bits instead of frying your own bacon.
   Esther A. Hershbeger
Murphysboro, IL

Ranch Potato Cubes

Charlotte Shaffer
East Earl, PA

Makes 8 servings

Prep. Time: 20 minutes
Cooking/Baking Time: 1 hour

6 medium potatoes, cut into ½" cubes
half stick (4 Tbsp.) butter, cubed
1 cup sour cream
1 packet Ranch salad dressing mix
1 cup (4-oz.) shredded cheddar cheese

1. Place potatoes in a greased 7×11 baking dish. Dot with butter.
2. Cover. Bake at 350° for 1 hour.
3. Combine sour cream and salad dressing mix.
4. Spoon over potatoes. Sprinkle with cheese.
5. Bake uncovered 10 minutes until cheese is melted.

Cottage Potatoes

Janice Yoskovich
Carmichaels, PA

Makes 6 servings

Prep. Time: 15 minutes
Baking Time: 45 minutes

6 boiled potatoes, diced
½ onion, diced
½ green pepper, diced
3 slices bread, broken in pieces
½ lb. cheddar cheese, cubed
1 stick (½ cup) butter

1. Melt butter in the microwave in a medium glass bowl.
2. Mix melted butter with potatoes, onion, green pepper, bread, and cheese.
3. Put mixture in greased 2-quart casserole dish.
4. Bake at 350° for 45 minutes.

Tips:
You can add 4 Tbsp. more butter. I use Italian bread.

This is a great old recipe from one of my mother's best friends.

Sour Cream Potatoes

Renee Baum
Chambersburg, PA

Makes 6-8 servings

Prep. Time: 30 minutes
Cooking/Baking Time: 60 minutes

10 medium red potatoes
8-oz. pkg. cream cheese
8-oz. sour cream
¼ cup 2% milk
2 Tbsp. butter, *divided*
1 Tbsp. dried parsley flakes, *or* 2 Tbsp. chopped fresh parsley
1¼ tsp. garlic salt
¼ tsp. paprika

1. Peel and quarter potatoes. Place in a large saucepan and cover with water. Bring to a boil.
2. Reduce heat and cover and cook 15-20 minutes or until tender. Drain.
3. Mash the potatoes.
4. Add cream cheese, sour cream, milk, 1 Tbsp. butter, parsley, and garlic salt; beat until smooth.
5. Spoon into a greased 2-quart baking dish.
6. Dot with remaining butter. Sprinkle with paprika.
7. Bake, uncovered, at 350° for 30-40 minutes or until heated through.

Add a little sliver of butter to cooking potatoes. It keeps them from boiling over.

Esther Hersberger, Murphysboro, IL

Rosemary Roasted Potatoes

Pamela Pierce
Annville, PA

Makes 8 servings

Prep. Time: 10 minutes
Baking Time: 45-60 minutes

---

8 medium red potatoes,
  scrubbed, dried, and cut
  into wedges
3 Tbsp. olive oil
1 tsp. crushed dried
  rosemary
1 tsp. crushed dried thyme
½ tsp. salt
⅛ tsp. pepper

1. Toss potato wedges in oil.
2. Place in shallow roasting pan and sprinkle evenly with seasonings. Stir.

3. Roast in 375° oven for 45-60 minutes, stirring every 10-15 minutes, until golden and fork tender.

Good Go-Alongs
Great with roast pork.

Aunt Jean's Potatoes

Jen Hoover
Akron, PA

Makes 8 servings

Prep. Time: 30 minutes
Cooking/Baking Time: 1 hour
Cooling Time: 1 hour

---

6 medium potatoes
half stick (4 Tbsp.) butter
⅓ cup onions, chopped
  fine
2 cups shredded cheddar
1½ cups sour cream

1 tsp. salt
¼ tsp. pepper
2 Tbsp. butter
4 slices bacon, fried and
  crumbled
paprika

1. Microwave, cook, or bake potatoes in skins; cool at least an hour.
2. Peel and shred coarsely.
3. In saucepan over low heat, sauté onion in butter, about 8 minutes. Do not brown!
4. Add cheese and stir until almost melted.
5. Remove from heat. Blend in sour cream, salt, and pepper.
6. Fold in shredded potatoes.
7. Put in greased casserole.
8. Dot with 2 Tbsp. butter, and sprinkle with paprika and bacon.
9. Bake at 350° for 30 minutes or until heated through.

Tips:
1. Can be made the day before baking or frozen for later use.
2. Use frozen shredded potatoes instead—this is more costly but quicker to prepare.

Mom brings these potatoes to our Diener family gatherings. She is not allowed to not bring them!

Yummy Cheese Potatoes

Julie Burkholder
Robesonia, PA

Makes 4-6 servings

Prep. Time: 20 minutes
Cooking/Baking Time: 1 hour

2 Tbsp. butter *or* margarine
4 Tbsp. mustard
¼ tsp. pepper
½ tsp. salt
2 cups milk
½ lb. cheese—Velveeta *or* American, sliced
30-oz. bag frozen shredded potatoes (hash browns)

1. Melt butter in a saucepan.
2. Add mustard, pepper, salt, and milk. Stir and heat until steaming.
3. Add slices of cheese one at a time while stirring. Stir until melted. Remove from heat.
4. Pour frozen potatoes in 3-quart casserole dish.
5. Pour cheese sauce over them and stir gently.
6. Cover. Bake at 350° for 45-50 minutes.

Tips:
1. Don't go light on the mustard; that's what makes them good.
2. Add cubed ham and peas and you have a complete meal.
3. Sauté a little onion in the butter first.
4. Sprinkle top with paprika for added color.

Shredded Baked Potatoes

Alice Miller
Stuarts Draft, VA

Makes 6 servings

Prep. Time: 35 minutes
Cooking/Baking Time: 1 hour

6 medium potatoes
1 cup sour cream
6-8 green onions, chopped
1 cup shredded cheddar cheese
1 stick (½ cup) butter
1½ tsp. salt

1. Cook, cool, peel, and shred potatoes.
2. Combine potatoes, sour cream, onions, cheese, and salt.
3. Spoon into 2-quart casserole dish.
4. Melt butter and pour over top of casserole.
5. Bake at 400° for 45 minutes, until light brown.

To make your own frozen hash browns, please turn to page 259.

Night Before Potatoes

Susan Tjon
Austin, TX
Jennie Martin
Richfield, PA
Leona Miller
Millersburg, OH
Leona M. Slabaugh
Apple Creek, OH

Makes 6-8 servings

Prep. Time: 45 minutes
Cooking/Baking Time: 35 minutes
Chilling Time: 8 hours or overnight

8-10 potatoes, peeled
8-oz. cream cheese
1 cup sour cream
1 tsp. salt
¼ tsp. pepper
2 Tbsp. butter
1 tsp. seasoned salt *or* garlic salt *or* onion salt

1. Cook potatoes until soft. Mash.
2. Add cream cheese and sour cream. Beat until fluffy and smooth. Add salt and pepper.
3. Place in buttered 9 × 13 dish or 2-quart casserole.
4. Dot with butter and sprinkle with seasoned salt.
5. Refrigerate 8 hours or overnight. May also be frozen at this point (just thaw before baking).
6. Preheat oven to 325°. Cover and bake 15 minutes.
7. Uncover and bake another 20 minutes or until peaks are light brown.

Tips:

1. Low fat cream cheese and sour cream may be used.

2. These potatoes can be rewarmed in a slow cooker before serving.

3. For convenience sake, you can bake the mashed potatoes at 350° for up to an hour. This is handy when you are serving a holiday dinner, juggling oven space and temperatures.

Variations:

To the mashed potatoes, add one package of frozen spinach which has been cooked and well-drained. After putting the potato mixture in a greased pan, sprinkle top with 1 cup cheddar cheese.

Arianne Hochstetler
Goshen, IN

Double the sour cream. Top with grated cheese. These potatoes can keep up to two weeks in the refrigerator before baking.

Brittany Zimmerman
Wrightsville, PA

Sweet Potato Balls

Dorothy Schrock
Arthur, IL

Makes 8 servings

Prep. Time: 35 minutes
Cooking/Baking Time (including potatoes): 45 minutes

6 medium sweet potatoes, cooked, peeled, and mashed (approx. 4 cups mashed)
1 stick (½ cup) butter *or* margarine
1 cup chopped pecans *or* walnuts
1 cup brown sugar
12 large marshmallows
2 cups crushed cornflakes

1. Mix sweet potatoes with margarine, sugar, and nuts.

2. Form a ball around 1 marshmallow; roll in crushed cornflakes. Repeat with remaining marshmallows.

3. Place balls in greased 9 × 13 baking dish.

4. Bake at 400° for 15 minutes.

Tips:

1. Balls may be made ahead of time and refrigerated or frozen.

2. You can cut the marshmallows in half and make twice as many. At potlucks, people often like smaller portions so they can sample more!

Honey Maple Sweet Potatoes

Lorraine Kratz
Sinking Spring, PA

Makes 6-8 servings

Prep. Time: 30 minutes
Cooking/Baking Time: 50 minutes

6-8 medium sweet potatoes
½ cup honey
½ cup maple syrup
½ cup milk
4 Tbsp. butter

1. Cook sweet potatoes in a pot with water to cover. Test with a fork and remove from heat when they are becoming soft. Do not overcook.

2. Run cold water over the sweet potatoes. Peel them.

3. Place the honey, maple syrup, milk, and butter in a pan and bring to a boil for about 30 seconds.

4. Place sweet potatoes in a 9" square pan. Pour the sauce over them.

5. Bake at 350° for 30 minutes.

Sweet Onion Corn Bake

Rebecca B. Stoltzfus
Lititz, PA

Sherry Mayer
Menomonee Falls, WI

Makes 12 servings

Prep. Time: 30 minutes
Baking Time: 45-50 minutes

2 large sweet onions,
    thinly sliced
1 stick (½ cup) butter
1 cup (8-oz.) sour cream
½ cup milk
½ tsp. dill weed
¼ tsp. salt
2 cups (8-oz.) shredded
    cheddar cheese, *divided*
1 egg, lightly beaten
14¾-oz. can cream style
    corn
8½-oz. pkg. corn bread
    muffin mix
4 drops hot pepper sauce,
    or to taste

1. In a large skillet, sauté onions in butter until tender.
2. In a small bowl, combine sour cream, milk, dill, and salt until blended.
3. Stir in 1 cup cheese.
4. Stir cheese mixture into onion mixture; remove from heat and set aside.
5. In a bowl, combine egg, corn, corn bread mix, and hot pepper sauce.
6. Pour into a greased 9 × 13 baking dish.
7. Spoon onion mixture over top. Sprinkle with remaining cheese.
8. Bake at 350° for 45-50 minutes or until top is set and lightly browned.
9. Let stand 10 minutes before cutting and serving.

Scalloped Corn

Rhonda Freed
Croghan, NY

Makes 4-6 servings

Prep. Time: 15 minutes
Baking Time: 30-50 minutes

2 eggs
1 cup milk
⅔ cup cracker crumbs
    (Ritz *or* Club crackers)
2 cups frozen *or* canned
    creamed or crushed corn
    (not whole kernel)
⅓ cup shredded cheddar
    cheese
3 Tbsp. butter, melted
1 tsp. dried minced onion
1 Tbsp. sugar
½ tsp. salt
⅛ tsp. pepper

1. In a medium bowl, beat eggs with a whisk.
2. Add milk and cracker crumbs. Whisk again.
3. Add rest of ingredients. Stir together well.
4. Pour into greased 7 × 11 casserole dish.
5. Bake at 350° for 30-50 minutes, checking at 30 minutes. If center is still jiggly, allow to bake 5-10 more minutes and check again. Repeat until the center is firm.

Grandma's Baked Corn

Jen Hoover
Akron, PA

Makes 4-6 servings

Prep. Time: 15 minutes
Baking Time: 45 minutes

3 cups corn
½ tsp. salt
1½ Tbsp. flour
2½ Tbsp. melted butter
3 eggs
1 cup milk
1 tsp. sugar

1. Place all ingredients in blender and blend.
2. Pour into 1½-quart greased baking dish.
3. Bake at 350° for 45 minutes, until center is set and not jiggly.

Tip:
    This is extra-yummy when made with frozen sweet corn from the summer.

I got this from my mother-in-law and it is a favorite of my husband and 3 boys, especially when served with a Mexican dish such as tacos, taco salad, or bean and cheese tortillas.

Asparagus Bake

Leona M. Slabaugh
Apple Creek, OH

Makes 4-6 servings

Prep. Time: 20 minutes
Baking Time: 45-60 minutes

5 medium potatoes, sliced
2 medium onions, diced
2 cups asparagus, canned
***or* fresh, chopped *or* left**
whole
4 slices orange cheese
half stick (4 Tbsp.) butter
salt and pepper

1. Lay potatoes in greased 2-quart casserole. Sprinkle with salt and pepper.
2. Sprinkle diced onions over potatoes.
3. Add asparagus. (Chopped is better for potlucks to dish single servings.)
4. Add salt and pepper to taste.
5. Slice butter and lay butter pieces over top.
6. Cover tightly.
7. Bake at 325° for 45-60 minutes, or until potatoes are tender when poked with a fork.
8. Remove from over and lay sliced cheese over hot vegetables to melt.

Tip:
Experiment with adding garlic salt, fresh parsley or other herbs, or even a dash of cayenne.

Good Go-Alongs:
Meat loaf, corn, apple crisp – a meal made entirely in the oven.

Baked Asparagus Roll-Ups

Peggy C. Forsythe
Memphis, TN

Makes 12 roll-ups

Prep. Time: 20 minutes
Baking Time: 15 minutes

12 slices white bread, with
crusts removed
½ cup crumbled blue
cheese *or* feta cheese
1-2 Tbsp. mayonnaise
12 asparagus spears,
canned and patted dry,
or fresh and lightly
steamed, dried, and
cooled
2 Tbsp. butter, melted
paprika
grated Parmesan cheese

1. Flatten bread with a rolling pin. Set aside.
2. In a small bowl, mix blue cheese and mayonnaise to a spreading consistency, starting with 1 Tbsp. mayonnaise and adding by teaspoons as needed. Set aside.
3. Divide cheese mixture among bread slices and spread evenly.
4. Place an asparagus spear on one end of a bread slice. Starting with the spear end, roll up the bread with the spear inside. Pinch seam a little bit to hold in place.
5. Place roll-up seam side down on greased cookie sheet. Roll up remaining bread and asparagus.
6. Brush each roll-up with melted butter. Sprinkle with Parmesan cheese and paprika.
7. Bake for 15 minutes at 375° or until golden brown.

Have everyone bring a dish of food, plus its printed recipe to share.

Nancy Wagner Graves, Manhattan, KS

Glazed Carrot Coins

Dorothy Lingerfelt
Stonyford, CA

Makes 4-6 servings
Prep. Time: 20 minutes
Cooking Time: 30 minutes

12 medium carrots, cut
   into 1" pieces
½ cup brown sugar, packed
3 Tbsp. butter *or* margarine
1 Tbsp. grated lemon peel
¼ tsp. vanilla

1. In saucepan, cook carrots
in a small amount of water
until crisp-tender. Do not
overcook.
2. Drain. Remove and keep
warm.
3. In the same pan, heat
brown sugar and butter until
bubbly. Stir in lemon peel.
4. Return carrots to pan;
cook and stir over low heat
for 10 minutes or until glazed.
5. Remove from heat; stir
in vanilla.

Variations:
For horseradish carrots,
melt together half stick
(4 Tbsp.) butter, ⅓ cup honey,
and 2 Tbsp. horseradish. Add
to cooked carrots.
Janet Batdorf
Harrisburg, PA

Add 1 cup raisins to the
cooking carrots in Step 4.
Add ½ cup brown sugar,
half stick (4 Tbsp.) butter,
2 Tbsp. lemon juice, and
1 tsp salt also.
Jeanette Oberholtzer
Lititz, PA

Substitute 2 Tbsp. Dijon
mustard for the lemon peel
and vanilla.

Joette Droz
Kalona, IA

Crisp Carrot Casserole

Jan McDowell
New Holland, PA

Makes 6-8 servings
Prep. Time: 30 minutes
Cooking/Baking Time: 50 minutes

6 cups sliced carrots
half stick (4 Tbsp.) butter
1 large onion, chopped
1½ cups shredded cheese
   of your choice
potato chips, lightly
   crumbled

1. In a covered saucepan,
cook carrots in small amount
of water until barely crisp
tender. Drain.
2. Place carrots in a
buttered 9 × 13 baking dish.
3. Slice butter into pieces.
Lay over top of carrots in
dish.
4. Sprinkle with cheese.
5. Top with a few or as
many potato chips as you
wish.
6. Bake at 350° for 30-40
minutes, until casserole is
hot through and bubbling at
edges.

*I always have an empty dish
to take home from potlucks!*

German Red Cabbage

Annie C. Boshart
Lebanon, PA

Makes 12 servings

Prep. Time: 30-40 minutes
Cooking Time: 3-4 hours

1 large red cabbage,
  shredded
3 apples, peeled and cored,
  sliced thin
1 medium onion, chopped
  or sliced
4 tsp. sugar
salt to taste
2 bay leaves
10 whole cloves
½ lb. bacon, chopped
2 Tbsp. white vinegar (or
  more to taste)

1. Place water in bottom of Dutch oven or 4 quart pot. Put in half the apples, half the onions, half the sugar, and some salt to taste.

2. Put in all the cabbage.

3. Top with the rest of the apples, onions, sugar, and any more salt desired. Add bay leaves and cloves.

4. Cover and cook on low heat.

5. Meanwhile, fry bacon until brown.

6. Add bacon and its grease on top of the cabbage.

7. Add vinegar. Simmer 3-4 hours on low. Add more vinegar or salt to your taste.

Tip:

1. This could be cooked to completion in a slow cooker to serve at a buffet meal.

2. To shred the cabbage efficiently and with less mess, use a food processor with a slicer blade. You can run the apples and onions through as well.

3. This dish improves with age and reheating!

Good Go-Alongs:
  Sausage and hot German potato salad

Originally a German immigrant cooked and served us this delicious dish.

Cabbage Casserole

Cova Rexroad
Baltimore, MD

Makes 6-8 servings

Prep. Time: 20 minutes
*Cooking/Baking Time: 45
  minutes*

1½ cups crushed corn
  flakes, *divided*
1 stick (½ cup) butter *or*
  margarine
10¾-oz. can cream of
  celery soup
¼ cup mayonnaise
6-7 cups shredded cabbage
1½ cups grated yellow
  cheese, *divided*

1. Put 1 cup corn flakes in bottom of 9 × 13 baking dish.

2. Heat together butter, soup, mayonnaise and ¾ cup cheese until the cheese is melted.

3. Add to cabbage and mix.

4. Pour and spread the cabbage mixture over the cornflakes in the baking dish. Pat it down to fill the baking dish.

5. Sprinkle ½ cup corn flakes on top.

6. Cover with foil and bake at 350° for 30 minutes.

7. Remove cover, sprinkle on remaining ¾ cup cheese. Bake 15 minutes longer to finish.

Tips:

Chopped red sweet pepper added to the cabbage gives a festive look. I use frozen peppers from my freezer.

My campers' group often has covered dish parties. This is the recipe they ask me to bring. I've taken it to church potlucks, too.

Oven Roasted Vegetables

Martha G. Zimmerman
Lititz, PA

Makes 4 servings

Prep. Time: 20 minutes
Baking Time: 30 minutes

1 medium zucchini
1 medium summer squash
  or another zucchini
1 medium red bell pepper
1 medium yellow bell
  pepper
1 lb. fresh asparagus
1 sweet potato, *optional*
1 red onion
1-3 garlic cloves, minced
3 Tbsp. olive oil
salt & pepper, to taste
Italian seasoning, to taste

1. Cut vegetables into bite-size pieces.
2. Place on two large rimmed baking sheets.
3. Drizzle olive oil evenly over vegetables. Sprinkle evenly with garlic, salt, pepper, and Italian seasoning.
4. Mix well. (Hands work well for this!)
5. Bake at 400° for 25-35 minutes, stirring and flipping every 5-10 minutes. Test a few vegetables at 25 minutes to see if they are done to your preference. Keep roasting and stirring as needed.

Aunt Judy's Veggies

Judy Wantland
Menomonee Falls, WI

Makes 6 servings

Prep. Time: 5 minutes
Baking Time: 35-40 minutes

16-oz. bag California
  Medley frozen vegetables
  (broccoli, cauliflower,
  carrots), thawed
10¾-oz. can cream of
  mushroom soup
⅓ cup sour cream
1½-2 cups mozzarella
  cheese, shredded
6-oz. can Durkee fried
  onions, *divided*

1. Mix together vegetables, soup, sour cream, cheese, and half the fried onions.
2. Pour into greased casserole dish.
3. Cover and bake at 350° for 30 minutes or until bubbly.
4. Sprinkle remaining fried onions on top and bake, uncovered, for 5 additional minutes.

This is a favorite of my youngest brother and his family. I finally gave the recipe to my sister-in-law, after making her wait years! She now makes it for my brother and their 4 boys.

Cheesy Vegetable Casserole

Judy Newman
St. Mary's, ON

Makes 10 servings

Prep. Time: 10 minutes
Cooking/Baking Time: 1¼ hours

5 lbs. carrot *or* 1 large head
  broccoli *or* 1 large head
  cauliflower
2 cups grated cheese
2 10¾-oz. cans cream of
  celery soup
2 cups bread crumbs

1. Prepare vegetables by cutting into bite-sized chunks.
2. In a covered saucepan, cook in a small amount of water until barely crisp-tender. Do not overcook or the finished casserole will be mushy.
3. In a large greased casserole dish, layer vegetable, then cheese, then soup.
4. Sprinkle top evenly with bread crumbs.
5. Cover with lid or tinfoil.
6. Bake at 350° for 40 minutes. Remove lid or tin foil and bake 10-20 minutes longer, until crumbs are golden and sauce is bubbling around the edges.

To make your own cream of mushroom or celery soup, please turn to pages 258-259.

Onion Casserole

Jan McDowell
New Holland, PA

Makes 8-10 servings

Prep. Time: 30 minutes
Baking Time: 30 minutes

8-10 medium-large cooking
  onions (not sweet), sliced
1¼ sticks (¾ cup) butter,
  melted
1½ tubes Ritz crackers,
  crushed (approx. 2 cups)
10-oz. (approx. 2¼ cups)
  shredded Parmesan
  cheese

1. Stir together melted
butter and crackers in a bowl.
2. Put half the crackers in
a 9 × 13 baking pan, layer half
the cracker mixture, then
onions, then crackers.
3. Top with Parmesan
cheese.
4. Bake at 350° for 30
minutes.

Tip:
   You can use a food processor and coarsely chop the
onions, but the slices make a
better visual presentation.

*I remember tasting this at a
family meal and knew I wanted
the recipe. It's so simple and
tasty.*

Cheesy Zucchini

Louise Stackhouse
Benton, PA

Makes 4-6 servings

Prep. Time: 10 minutes
*Cooking/Baking Time: 20
  minutes*

2 small to medium size
  zucchini, peeled, sliced
1 large onion, sliced
1 stick (½ cup) butter,
  sliced
salt and pepper to taste
4-6 slices of American
  cheese
 basil, fresh *or* dry

1. Spray microwavable
casserole bowl with non-stick
cooking spray.
2. Layer zucchini and
onion in bowl, adding slices
of butter, salt and pepper as
you go.
3. Lay cheese on top.
Sprinkle with basil.
4. Cover and microwave
approximately 20 minutes
until zucchini is tender when
tested with a fork.

Variation:
   Sauté onion and zucchini
in butter in a large skillet.
Add cheese and basil on top.
Cover and cook on low until
tender.

Cheese covers a multitude of cooking sins!
Marla Folkerts, Holland, OH

Oven Brussels Sprouts

Gail Martin
Elkhart, IN

Makes 6-8 servings

Prep. Time: 15 minutes
Baking Time: 15 minutes

1½ lbs. Brussels sprouts, halved
¼ cup plus 2 Tbsp. olive oil
juice of 1 lemon
½ tsp. salt
½ tsp. pepper
½ tsp. crushed red pepper flakes

1. In a large bowl, toss halved sprouts with 2 Tbsp. olive oil.
2. Place them in a single layer on a rimmed cookie sheet.
3. Roast sprouts in the oven at 470°, stirring twice, until crisp and lightly browned, 10-15 minutes.
4. Whisk together in a large bowl ¼ cup oil, lemon juice, salt, pepper, and red pepper flakes.
5. Toss sprouts with dressing and serve.

Good Go-Alongs:
This is a lovely dish for any meal, but especially nice at Easter with ham and new potatoes.

Garlic Mushrooms

Lizzie Ann Yoder
Hartville, OH

Makes 4 servings

Prep. Time: 20 minutes
Cooking Time: 15-20 minutes

half stick (4 Tbsp.) butter
2 cloves garlic, minced
1 lb. mushrooms, sliced
4 scallions, chopped
1 tsp. lemon juice

1. In a skillet, melt the butter and sauté the garlic briefly.
2. Add mushrooms, scallions, and lemon juice and cook, stirring, about 10 minutes.

Good Go-Alongs:
A nice side dish for meat.

When I come home from grocery-shopping, I like to clean and cut up the fresh veggies and store them in air-tight containers. Meal prep is faster later.
Edwina Stoltzfus, Narvon, PA

Salads

Orange-Spinach Salad

Esther Shisler
Lansdale, PA

Makes 6-8 servings
Prep. Time: 25 minutes

10-oz. bag spinach *or* romaine
1 medium head iceberg lettuce, shredded
2 Tbsp. diced onion
2 Tbsp. diced canned pimento, *or* red bell pepper
2 large oranges, peeled and chopped
1 small cucumber, sliced

Honey-Caraway Dressing:
   ¾ cup mayonnaise
   2 Tbsp. honey
   1 Tbsp. lemon juice
   1 Tbsp. caraway seeds

1. In small bowl, whisk mayonnaise, honey, lemon juice, and caraway seeds until blended. Cover and refrigerate. Stir before using.
2. Into large salad bowl, tear spinach into bite-size pieces.
3. Add lettuce, onion, pimento, oranges, and cucumber. Toss gently with dressing.

Tips:
   A 15-oz. can mandarin oranges, drained, can be used instead of the 2 oranges. I use romaine and spinach instead of the iceberg lettuce sometimes.

Good Go-Alongs:
   Lasagna, calico bean bake, and pasta dishes go well with this salad.

Festive Apple Salad

Susan Kasting
Jenks, OK

Makes 8 servings
Prep. Time: 15 minutes

Dressing:
2 Tbsp. olive oil
2 Tbsp. vinegar, *or* lemon juice
2 Tbsp. Dijon mustard
1½-3 Tbsp. sugar
salt and pepper

4-6 Tbsp. chopped walnuts, *or* cashews
1 Granny Smith apple, chopped
1 large head romaine lettuce, chopped
4 Tbsp. crumbled blue cheese, *or* shredded baby Swiss, *optional*

1. In the bottom of a large salad bowl, make dressing by mixing together the oil, vinegar, mustard, sugar, salt, and pepper.
2. Add the nuts and apple and stir to coat. Put lettuce and blue cheese on top without stirring.

3. Mix it all together when ready to serve.

Tips:
1. This is so nice to take places because it has the dressing in the bottom so the salad doesn't wilt. You can also serve the dressing on the side.
2. You can add a little chopped onion and 1 Tbsp. poppy seeds to the dressing. Add ¼ cup craisins and one diced pear to the salad.
Mary Ann Bowman
Ephrata, PA

BLT Salad

Alica Denlinger
Lancaster, PA

Makes 10-12 servings
Prep. Time: 30 minutes

2 heads romaine lettuce, torn
2 cups chopped tomatoes
8 bacon strips, cooked and crumbled
1 cup shredded Parmesan cheese
1 cup croutons

Dressing:
¾ cup oil
½ tsp. salt
½ tsp. pepper
¼ cup fresh lemon juice
2 cloves garlic, crushed

1. Toss together salad ingredients in a large bowl.
2. Shake together dressing ingredients.
3. Pour dressing over salad immediately before serving.

Set your table early. Have ready any soup, salad or dessert plates. Clear well after each entrée. Do dishes the next day—enjoy your guests.
Karen Ceneviva, Seymour, CT

Olive Garden Salad

Erma Martin
East Earl, PA

Makes 8-10 servings
Prep. Time: 15-20 minutes

1 head iceberg lettuce, torn
1 head romaine lettuce,
  torn

Add to taste:
  black olives
  diced red onion
  grape tomatoes, halved
  croutons
  sliced banana peppers
  Parmesan cheese

Dressing:
  ½ cup white vinegar
  ½ cup mayonnaise
  1 tsp. olive oil
  4 Tbsp. corn syrup
  2 Tbsp. Parmesan cheese
  2 Tbsp. Romano cheese
  ½ tsp. garlic salt
  ½ tsp. parsley
  ½ tsp. Italian seasoning
  1 Tbsp. lemon juice

1. Combine lettuces and desired amount of olives, onion, tomatoes, croutons, peppers, and Parmesan cheese. Toss lightly.
2. Mix dressing ingredients.
3. Just before serving, pour dressing over salad and toss lightly.

Italian Green Salad

Jane Geigley
Lancaster, PA

Makes 4 servings
Prep. Time: 10 minutes

16-oz. pkg. green salad mix
2½-oz. pkg. pastrami,
  chopped in ½" pieces, *or*
  pepperoni
1 cup shredded mozzarella
  cheese
4 plum tomatoes, chopped
1 tsp. Italian seasoning
⅓ cup Italian salad
  dressing
6-oz. can ripe olives, *divided*
1 cup seasoned croutons

1. Combine salad mix, pastrami or pepperoni, mozzarella, tomatoes, and seasoning.
2. Drizzle with salad dressing; toss to coat.
3. Before serving, top with olives and croutons. Serve immediately.

Good Go-Alongs:
  Great with a pizza party!

It's a great dish on a hot day. People just love this salad when I take it to gatherings.

Lettuce Salad with Hot Bacon Dressing

Mary B. Sensenig
New Holland, PA

Makes 1½ cups dressing
Prep. Time: 5 minutes
Cooking Time: 15 minutes

5 pieces bacon
½ cup sugar
1 Tbsp. cornstarch
½ tsp. salt
1 beaten egg
1 cup milk
¼ cup vinegar
1-2 heads lettuce, torn

1. Sauté bacon in skillet until crisp.
2. Remove bacon from heat and drain. Reserve drippings in skillet.
3. Add sugar, cornstarch, and salt to drippings in skillet. Blend together well.
4. Add egg, milk, and vinegar, stirring until smooth.
5. Cook over low heat, stirring continually until thickened and smooth.
6. When dressing is no longer hot, but still warm, toss with torn lettuce leaves. (Depending upon how much dressing you like on your salad greens, this will dress 1-2 heads lettuce, torn.)
7. Serve immediately.

Tortellini Caesar Salad

Rebecca Meyerkorth
Wamego, KS

Makes 10 servings

Prep. Time: 30-35 minutes
Cooking Time: 15 minutes

9-oz. pkg. frozen cheese
  tortellini
½ cup mayonnaise
¼ cup milk
¾ cup shredded Parmesan
  cheese, *divided*
2 Tbsp. lemon juice
2 garlic cloves, minced
8 cups torn romaine lettuce
1 cup seasoned croutons,
  optional
halved cherry tomatoes,
  optional

1. Cook tortellini according to package directions. Drain and rinse with cold water.
2. Meanwhile in a small bowl, combine mayonnaise, milk, ½ cup Parmesan cheese, lemon juice, and garlic. Mix well.
3. Put cooled tortellini in large bowl.
4. Add romaine and remaining ¼ cup Parmesan.
5. Just before serving, drizzle with dressing and toss to coat. Top with croutons and tomatoes, if desired.

Tips:
  Tomatoes add great color. Also, I don't always have seasoned croutons on hand. They are optional.

Just plain delicious! This salad is especially good in hot summer weather. Our family loves it.

Two Cheese Tossed Salad

Elaine Hoover
Leola, PA

Makes 6-8 servings

Prep. Time: 20 minutes

10 cups spinach and
  romaine lettuce,
  chopped, *divided*
½ lb. mushrooms, sliced,
  divided
8-oz. cottage cheese, *divided*
10 strips bacon, fried and
  crumbled, *divided*

Dressing:
  ½ cup vegetable oil
  ½ cup minced red onion
  ¼ cup sugar
  ¼ cup vinegar
  1 tsp. poppy seed
  ¼-½ tsp. prepared
    mustard
  ¼-½ tsp. salt

4-oz. shredded Swiss cheese

1. Layer in a large serving bowl: half of the spinach/lettuce, half mushrooms, half cottage cheese, and half bacon. Repeat layers.
2. Combine dressing ingredients together in a shaker or lidded jar and shake well.
3. Add dressing and Swiss cheese just before serving.

My mentor served this to my husband and me in her home when we were going through a time of discerning the call of God in our lives.

Lettuce and Egg Salad

Frances & Cathy Kruba
Dundalk, MD

Makes 6 servings

Prep. Time: 25 minutes

Dressing:
  2 cups mayonnaise
  ¼ cup vinegar
  2 Tbsp. sugar

1 head lettuce, washed and
  dried, torn
2-3 hardboiled eggs,
  chopped
1-4 green onions, chopped

1. In a jar, mix mayonnaise, vinegar, and sugar and shake well.
2. Just before serving, mix lettuce, eggs, and onion. Add dressing, a little at a time, to your taste preference.

Corn Chip Salad

Rosie Glick
Perry, NY

Joyce Nolt
Richland, PA

Kinita Martin
East Earl, PA

Lorna Rodes
Port Republic, VA

Makes 6 servings
Prep. Time: 10 minutes

1 large head iceberg
  lettuce, torn
6 hardboiled eggs, chopped
½ lb. bacon, fried and
  crumbled
¾ lb. grated cheese
4-6 cups corn chips,
  crushed

Dressing:
  ¼ cup brown sugar
  1 cup mayonnaise
  2 Tbsp. vinegar
  ¼ cup milk

1. Mix lettuce, eggs, bacon, cheese, and corn chips together.
2. Mix brown sugar, mayonnaise, vinegar, and milk. Pour over salad just before serving.

Crunchy Romaine Toss

Jolene Schrock
Millersburg, OH

Jamie Mowry
Arlington, TX

Lucille Hollinger
Richland, PA

Makes 4-6 servings
Prep. Time: 20-30 minutes
Cooking Time: 10 minutes

Dressing:
  ½ cup sugar
  ½ cup vegetable oil
  ¼ cup cider vinegar
  2 tsp. soy sauce
  salt and pepper to taste

3-oz. pkg. Ramen noodles,
  broken up, seasoning
  packets discarded
2 Tbsp. butter
1½ cups chopped broccoli
1 small head romaine
  lettuce, torn up
4 green onions, chopped
½ cup chopped walnuts

1. In the blender, combine sugar, oil, vinegar, soy sauce, salt, and pepper. Blend until sugar is dissolved.
2. In a skillet, sauté Ramen noodles in butter until golden brown.

3. In a large bowl, combine broccoli, lettuce, onions, and noodles.
4. Just before serving toss with nuts and dressing.

Tips:
  Sometimes I serve the dressing on the side and let everybody put their own dressing on. Plus, if you have any leftover salad, it won't get soggy.

Variations:
  Use 2 cups sliced fresh strawberries in place of broccoli. Increase walnuts to 1 cup.

Janice Nolt
Ephrata, PA

Add 1 small can mandarin oranges, drained.

Janet Derstine
Telford, PA

Wash and dry whole lettuce leaves. Put a scoop of tuna or egg salad in each one. Enjoy your lettuce boats! You can also slip these into wraps or pitas.

Donna Conta, Saylorsburg, PA

Simple Salad Dressing

Cynthia Morris
Grottoes, VA

Makes 1½ cups
Prep. Time: 5-10 minutes

½ cup packed brown sugar
½ cup oil
⅓ cup vinegar
⅓ cup ketchup
1 Tbsp. Worcestershire
   sauce

In a bottle or jar, combine ingredients. Cover and shake well to mix.

Tips:
   Keep the salad dressing in an empty ketchup bottle. Shake well before each use.

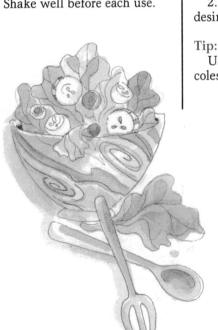

Very Good Salad Dressing

Lydia K. Stoltzfus
Gordonville, PA

Makes 3¼ cups
Prep. Time: 10 minutes

2 cups mayonnaise
½ cup sugar
1 Tbsp. prepared mustard
1 Tbsp. vinegar
¼ tsp. salt
¼ tsp. celery seed
¼ tsp. dried parsley
dash pepper
¼-½ cup pickle juice

1. Mix together mayonnaise, sugar, mustard, vinegar, salt, celery seed, parsley, and pepper to taste.
2. Add pickle juice last to desired consistency.

Tip:
   Use on tossed salads or coleslaw.

Our Favorite Dressing

Carol Eberly
Harrisonburg, VA

Makes 3½ cups
Prep. Time: 10 minutes

1 cup sugar
1 cup ketchup
1½ tsp. paprika
1½ tsp. salt
1½ tsp. celery seed
1½ tsp. grated onion,
   optional
1½ cups vegetable oil
½ cup vinegar

Shake ingredients together well in a quart jar. Keep in refrigerator.

Good Go-Alongs:
   This dressing is great on tossed salads or used as a dip for veggies.

This is our family's favorite salad dressing. I always have a jar in the refrigerator.

Greek Pasta Salad

Edie Moran
West Babylon, NY
Judi Manos
West Islip, NY

Makes 8 servings

Prep. Time: 15 minutes
Cooking Time for pasta: 15 minutes

2 cups cooked pasta, rinsed and cooled (1 cup dry)
4 medium plum tomatoes, chopped
15-oz. can garbanzo beans, rinsed and drained
1 medium onion, chopped
6-oz. can pitted black olives, drained
4-oz. pkg. crumbled feta cheese
1 garlic clove, minced
½ cup olive oil
¼ cup lemon juice
1 tsp. salt
½ tsp. pepper

1. In a large bowl, combine macaroni, tomatoes, garbanzo beans, onion, olives, feta cheese, and garlic.
2. In a small bowl, whisk together oil, lemon juice, salt and pepper. Pour over salad and toss to coat.
3. Cover and chill in refrigerator. Stir before serving.

Tips:
1. I like to serve this salad in a clear glass salad bowl.
2. Add some baby spinach leaves. Combine vegetables with hot pasta right after draining it.

3. Kraft Greek Vinaigrette is a good dressing, too.
Judi Manos
West Islip, NY

When we visited my husband's family on the island of Samos, Greece, they made this with all fresh ingredients grown in their garden.

Judi Manos
West Islip, NY

Macaroni Salad

Frances & Cathy Kruba
Dundalk, MD
Marcia S. Myer
Manheim, PA

Makes 8-10 servings

Prep. Time: 30 minutes
Cooking Time for pasta: 15 minutes

1 lb. macaroni, cooked and cooled
1 cup diced celery
1 cup diced onions
1 cup diced carrots
12 hardboiled eggs, diced
2 cups sugar
½ cup vinegar, *or* lemon juice
2 cups mayonnaise

Dressing:
  5 eggs
  1 Tbsp. mustard
  1 Tbsp. butter
  ½-1 tsp. salt

1. Mix together macaroni, celery, onions, carrots, hardboiled eggs, sugar, and vinegar or lemon juice. Add mayonnaise.
2. In a saucepan, mix eggs, mustard, and butter. Cook on medium heat until thickened and steaming, stirring constantly. Do not boil.
3. Remove from heat and cool 5 minutes. Add to macaroni mixture.

Tips:
1. Grate the carrots instead of dicing them.
2. Reduce the sugar by a half-cup if desired.

Chicken Pasta Salad

Esther Gingerich
Kalona, IA

Makes 12 servings

Prep. Time: 15 minutes
Cooking Time for pasta: 15 minutes

2¼ cups diced, cooked chicken
2 cups cooked small pasta, *or* macaroni (1 cup dry)
2 cups diced celery
2 cups seedless grape halves
4 hardboiled eggs, diced
15-oz. can pineapple tidbits, drained

Dressing:
1 cup mayonnaise
½ cup sour cream
½ cup frozen whipped topping, thawed
1 Tbsp. lemon juice
1 Tbsp. sugar
½ tsp. salt

½ cup cashew pieces

1. In a large bowl, combine chicken, macaroni, celery, grapes, eggs, and pineapple.
2. Whisk dressing ingredients until smooth. Pour dressing over salad; toss to coat.
3. Chill at least one hour. Just before serving, fold in cashews.

Tip:
It's simple to put this together if chicken is cooked and diced, macaroni is cooked, and eggs are boiled ahead of time.

I often take this to summer potlucks for a "cooler" dish. This could be a one-dish meal.

Creamy Pasta Salad

Irma Wengerd
Dundee, OH

Makes 8-10 servings

Prep. Time: 30 minutes
Cooking Time for pasta: 15 minutes

1½ lbs. spiral pasta, cooked
½ cup chopped celery
2 tomatoes, chopped
1 small onion, chopped
1 green bell pepper, chopped
3-oz. can black olives, drained, sliced
12-oz. ham, diced
1 lb. cheddar cheese, diced

Dressing:
3 cups Miracle Whip
¼ cup spicy brown mustard
¾ cup oil
¼ cup vinegar
1¼ cups sugar
½ tsp. salt
1 Tbsp. onion salt
½ Tbsp. celery seed

1. In large bowl, toss together pasta, celery, tomatoes, onion, green pepper, olives, ham, and cheese.
2. In a separate bowl, blend the dressing ingredients together.
3. Pour dressing over pasta in the amount that you like and toss.

Good Go-Alongs:
This salad is delicious with grilled chicken. Reserve any leftover dressing for green salads.

½ cup heavy whipping cream = 1-1½ cups whipped

Spaghetti Salad

Lois Stoltzfus
Honey Brook, PA

Makes 6-8 servings

Prep. Time: 15 minutes
Cooking Time: 15 minutes
Cooling Time: 30 minutes

16-oz. angel-hair pasta
½ cup vegetable, *or* olive, oil
½ cup lemon juice
1 Tbsp. seasoned salt
½ cup mayonnaise
1 green bell pepper,
  chopped
1 cup grape tomatoes
1 red onion, chopped
1 cup grated cheddar
  cheese
½ cup black olives, sliced
pepperoni, *optional*

1. Cook pasta according to directions.
2. Mix oil, lemon juice, seasoned salt, and mayonnaise together. Add to drained pasta while it is still warm.
3. When pasta mixture has cooled at least 30 minutes, stir in pepper, tomatoes, onion, cheese, olives, and optional pepperoni. Chill.

Apple Chicken Salad

Marlene Fonken
Upland, CA

Makes 6 servings

Prep. Time: 30-40 minutes
Chilling Time: 2-12 hours

Dressing:
  ½ cup mayonnaise, *or*
    salad dressing
  2 Tbsp. cider vinegar
  2 Tbsp. lemon juice
  2-3 Tbsp. Dijon mustard

2 cups chopped, cooked
  chicken breast
2 ribs celery, chopped
¼ cup diced onion
1 green apple, chopped
1 red apple, chopped
⅓ cup dried cranberries
salt and pepper to taste

1. Whisk together mayonnaise, vinegar, lemon juice, and mustard. Set aside.
2. Mix together chicken, celery, onion, apples, cranberries, salt, and pepper.
3. Pour on dressing and toss to mix. Refrigerate until serving. Flavor develops with longer chilling.

Tips:
1. Break up and soften a handful of rice sticks; drain and add to the finished salad. This salad is gluten-free!
2. If you're starting with raw chicken, chop it into bite-sized pieces. In a saucepan, cover the chicken pieces with water or chicken broth. Cover and cook on medium heat until the chicken pieces are white through, 10-20 minutes. Drain. This can be done ahead of time.
3. You can substitute 12½-oz. can chicken, drained and broken up, for this salad.

At a church dinner, a man asked who had made my dish, found me, and asked for the recipe.

Chicken Salad with Blue Cheese

Susan Smith
Monument, CO

Makes 4-6 servings
Prep. Time: 15 minutes

3 cups cooked chicken, diced, *or* julienned
6 cups shredded lettuce
1-2 cups mayonnaise
2 Tbsp. tarragon vinegar
4 Tbsp. chili sauce, *or* cocktail sauce
2 Tbsp. chopped green pepper
4-oz. blue cheese, crumbled
whole lettuce leaves

1. Mix chicken with shredded lettuce.
2. Mix mayonnaise, vinegar, chili sauce, and green pepper. Add crumbled blue cheese.
3. Gently combine chicken and mayonnaise mixtures.
4. Place salad in a bowl lined with lettuce or in individual lettuce cups.

Tips:
1. White meat chicken is ideal for this salad.
2. The salad is best made and eaten on the same day.

Almond-Apricot Chicken Salad

Tracey Hanson Schramel
Windom, MN

Makes 6-8 servings
Prep. Time: 15 minutes
Cooking Time for pasta: 20 minutes

½ lb. bowtie pasta, cooked, rinsed, and drained
3 cups chopped broccoli
2½ cups chopped, cooked chicken
1 cup chopped celery
1 cup dried apricots, cut into ¼" strips
¾ cup toasted whole almonds
½ cup finely chopped green onions

Dressing:
¾ cup mayonnaise
¾ cup sour cream
2 tsp. grated lemon peel
1 Tbsp. lemon juice
1 Tbsp. Dijon-style mustard
1 tsp. salt
¼ tsp. pepper

1. In a large bowl, combine salad ingredients.
2. In another bowl, combine dressing ingredients.
3. Pour dressing over pasta mixture and toss.

Tips:
1. Instead of stirring the almonds into the salad, sprinkle them on top if you like that look better.
2. Pass the dressing in a small pitcher so each person can put on the amount they like. The leftovers don't get soggy then either!

Tomato Basil Couscous

Amber Martin
Mount Joy, PA

Makes 6 servings

Prep. Time: 25 minutes
Cooking Time for couscous: 10 minutes
Chilling Time: 2 hours

2 cups cooked couscous, cooled
1 cup chopped tomato
2 Tbsp. chopped fresh basil
2-oz. feta cheese, crumbled fine
¼ cup olive oil
2 Tbsp. lemon juice
1 tsp. Dijon mustard
1 clove garlic, crushed
fresh black pepper to taste

1. Mix together couscous, tomato, basil, and feta cheese.
2. In separate bowl, mix together olive oil, lemon juice, mustard, garlic, and black pepper. Pour over couscous mixture and toss.
3. Chill at least 2 hours before serving.

Tips:
To cook couscous, boil 1½ cups water and ½ tsp. salt. Remove from heat. Add 1 cup couscous, stir, and cover. Let stand 5 minutes. Fluff couscous lightly with fork. Cool before using in salad.

Tortellini and Kidney Bean Salad

Mary C. Wirth
Lancaster, PA

Makes 4-6 servings

Prep. Time: 10-15 minutes
Cooking Time for pasta: 9 minutes
Chilling Time: 2 hours

9-oz. pkg. cheese tortellini
15½-oz. can kidney beans, rinsed and drained
1 cup sliced cucumber
¼ cup chopped red onion

Dressing:
3 Tbsp. balsamic vinegar
3 Tbsp. olive oil
½ tsp. sugar
½ tsp. Italian seasoning
2 Tbsp. chopped fresh parsley

1. Cook tortellini according to package directions. Do not overcook. Rinse with cold water; drain.
2. Mix dressing ingredients in a small jar or bottle. Shake well.
3. In a large bowl, stir together tortellini, kidney beans, cucumber, and onion.
4. Add dressing and stir to coat.
5. Cover and refrigerate at least 2 hours.

Variation:
Dress warm tortellini with ¼ cup olive oil, 2 Tbsp. sugar, 2 Tbsp. white vinegar, ¼ tsp. dill weed, and ½ tsp. wine vinegar mustard. Omit vegetables. Serve warm or cold.
Janice Muller
Derwood, MD

Good Go-Alongs:
This makes a good side dish at cook-outs, especially with grilled chicken.

Grape Broccoli Salad

Arianne Hochstetler
Goshen, IN

Makes 6-8 servings
Prep. Time: 15-20 minutes
Chilling Time: 1 hour

4 cups broccoli florets
3 cups halved seedless red
   grapes
1⅓ cups chopped celery
1 cup chopped green onions
1 cup sliced water chestnuts,
   optional
1 cup raisins
4 tsp. honey
½ cup reduced-fat
   mayonnaise
2 cups fat-free, *or* light,
   plain yogurt

1. In a large bowl, combine broccoli, grapes, celery, onions, water chestnuts if you wish, and raisins.
2. In a small bowl, combine honey, mayonnaise, and yogurt.
3. Pour over broccoli mixture and toss to coat.
4. Cover and refrigerate for at least 1 hour or until chilled.

Tip:
   The broccoli, celery, and green onions can be prepared the night before. Putting the salad together then is quick.

Good Go-Alongs:
   This salad goes well with cheese and crackers.

I'm always looking for good healthy foods and I think this is a winner.

The Best Broccoli Salad

Sandra Haverstraw
Hummelstown, PA

Makes 10-12 servings
Prep. Time: 20-25 minutes
Chilling Time: 8-12 hours

2 bunches fresh broccoli,
   cut or broken into florets
   (save stems for another
   use)
1 cup golden raisins
1 small onion, chopped
10 slices bacon, fried and
   chopped
1 cup chopped cashews

Dressing:
   ½ cup sugar
   2 Tbsp. vinegar
   1 cup Miracle Whip
      dressing
   2 Tbsp. horseradish
   ¼ tsp. salt
   ½ tsp. prepared mustard

1. Mix broccoli florets, raisins, chopped onion, and bacon.
2. Prepare dressing by blending sugar, vinegar, Miracle Whip, horseradish, salt, and mustard until smooth.
3. Pour dressing over broccoli mix and toss gently until evenly coated.
4. Cover and refrigerate 8-12 hours. Add cashews just before serving.

Tip:
   Precooked bacon works well.

A dear lady named Betty Beaver brought this salad to our quilting group's Christmas lunch. Betty is no longer with us, but we still enjoy her salad when someone else makes it for our lunches, and we always think of her.

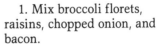

Cauliflower Salad

Janice Deel
Paducah, KY

Makes 6 servings

Prep. Time: 20 minutes
Chilling Time: 1-2 hours

1 medium cauliflower, cut
  into florets
15-oz. can English, *or*
  regular peas, drained
3 ribs celery, chopped
3 eggs, hardboiled and
  chopped
1 cup mayonnaise
3 Tbsp. chopped onion
¾ tsp. seasoned salt
½ tsp. ground pepper
3 Tbsp. milk

1. In a large bowl, combine
cauliflower, peas, celery and
eggs.
2. Blend together mayon-
naise, onion, seasoned salt,
pepper and milk.
3. Pour over cauliflower
mixture and mix well. Chill
1-2 hours before serving.

Unique Tuna Salad

Brenda J. Hochstedler
East Earl, PA

Makes 6-8 servings

Prep. Time: 10 minutes
Cooking Time (for potatoes and
  eggs): 20-30 minutes
Cooling Time: 30 minutes

10 medium potatoes

Dressing:
  ¼ cup mayonnaise
  1½ tsp. salt
  ¼ tsp. pepper
  ¼ tsp. paprika
  1-3 Tbsp. sweet pickle
    relish

4-5 eggs, hardboiled,
  chopped
6-oz. can tuna, drained
  and flaked
½ cup chopped celery
½ head lettuce, torn
2 tomatoes, cut into wedges
Parmesan cheese, grated

1. Chop potatoes (peeled if
you wish). Boil over medium
heat until fork-tender but not
mushy. Drain and cool.
2. Mix dressing ingredi-
ents. Stir gently into potatoes.
3. Add eggs, tuna, celery,
and lettuce. Toss lightly.
4. Garnish with tomato
wedges and Parmesan cheese.

Tips:
  1. This is an enriched
potato salad, or a simplified
Salade Nicoise.
  2. If you already have
potato salad in the refrigerator, stir the additional
ingredients into it and garnish
as directed. This transforms a
leftover completely!

*When you plan menus, look at your calendar
and plan for the busy days. I try to use leftovers on
especially busy days.*
Jen Hoover, Akron, PA

Pink Potato Salad

Dawn Landowski
Eau Claire, WI

Makes 8-10 servings

Prep. Time: 30 minutes
Cooking Time: 20 minutes
Cooling Time: 1 hour

3 lbs. baby red potatoes
1 medium onion, diced
7 hardboiled eggs, sliced, *divided*
½ green bell pepper, diced
6 sliced radishes
1 cucumber, peeled and diced
½ cup frozen peas, thawed
3 Tbsp. fresh, chopped parsley

Dressing:
  ½ cup chili sauce
  2 cups mayonnaise
  ½ cup French dressing
  2 tsp. salt
  3 tsp. onion powder
  ½ tsp. pepper
  ¼ tsp. garlic powder

paprika for garnish

1. Boil potatoes until tender but firm. Allow to cool. Peel and dice potatoes.
2. Mix dressing ingredients together and add to potatoes.
3. Fold in 6 eggs, green pepper, radishes, cucumber, peas, and parsley.
4. Refrigerate. Garnish with remaining sliced egg and paprika.

My granny always made this for me.

Grandpa Steve's Potato Salad

Nanci Keatley
Salem, OR

Makes 6-8 servings

Prep. Time: 20 minutes
Cooking Time for potatoes: 20 minutes

6 russet potatoes, peeled, cooked, and cubed
1 cup finely chopped onion
1 cup thinly sliced celery
1 cup sliced black olives (reserve 1 Tbsp. for top of salad)
1 large carrot, grated
6 hardboiled eggs (4 chopped, 2 sliced for top of salad)
1 pint Best Foods, *or your* choice of, mayonnaise
salt and pepper to taste
Tabasco, *optional*

1. Gently mix potatoes, onion, celery, olives, carrots, and chopped eggs together.
2. Add the mayonnaise and blend.
3. Season with salt and pepper to taste. Add Tabasco sauce to taste. Garnish with egg slices and olives.

My Grandpa Steve was an amazing cook! A butcher for most of his life, he retired when I was young. My sister and I spent many days at Grandpa and Grandma's house. It was there I developed my love for cooking and the joy of hospitality!

Good Go-Alongs:
  I helped Grandpa cater a few weddings with this recipe, along with ham, beans, rolls, and green salad.

If you're making potato salad that also calls for hardboiled eggs, you can boil the eggs along with the potatoes in the same pot. Just take the eggs out after 12 minutes!
Susan Smith, Monument, CO

German Potato Salad

Rhonda Burgoon
Collingswood, NJ

Makes 4 servings

Prep. Time: 15 minutes
Cooking Time: 20 minutes

3 cups diced, peeled
  potatoes
4 slices bacon
1 small onion, diced
¼ cup white vinegar
2 Tbsp. water
3 Tbsp. sugar
1 tsp. salt
⅛ tsp. ground black pepper
1 rib celery, chopped

1. Place potatoes in pot
and just cover with water.
Bring to boil and cook about
11 minutes or until tender.
Drain and set aside to cool.
2. Fry bacon in a large
skillet until browned and
crisp. Remove from pan and
set aside.

3. Add onion and celery to
bacon drippings and sauté for
5 minutes.
4. Mix together vinegar,
water, sugar, salt, and pepper.
5. Over low heat, add
vinegar mixture to onion and
celery in skillet. Bring to a
boil; pour over potatoes and
stir gently to combine.

Tip:
  My family prefers this cold;
however, you can serve it
warm.

*This has been part of our
family Easter tradition for over
50 years. My grandmother
taught me how to make this
when I was a teen.*

Red Bliss Potato Salad

Tim Smith
Wynnewood, PA

Makes 6 servings

Prep. Time: 15 minutes
Cooking Time: 20-25 minutes
Chilling Time: 2½ hours

12 medium red bliss
  potatoes
3 ribs celery, diced
2 hardboiled eggs, diced
¼ cup mayonnaise
2 Tbsp. white vinegar
1 Tbsp. Old English, *or*
  your choice of, dry
  mustard
1 tsp. celery seed
1 tsp. white pepper
1 tsp. black pepper
salt to taste

1. Cook whole potatoes
until medium soft, but still
firm. Drain. Allow to cool,
then dice.
2. Put diced potatoes
in large bowl. Add rest of
ingredients and stir gently.
3. Chill in refrigerator for 2
hours before serving.

Tip:
  Do not overcook the
potatoes! You want them
soft but not soft like you're
making mashed potatoes.

*Everybody in my family loves
this potato salad. My nieces
and nephews always ask if I'm
bringing it.*

Summer Salad

June S. Groff
Denver, PA

Makes 8 servings

Prep. Time: 20 minutes
Cooking Time for couscous: 10 minutes

1½ cups cooked garbanzo beans, drained
½ cup chopped onion
½ cup chopped celery
½ cup chopped cucumber
½ cup chopped red grapes
2 medium tomatoes, chopped
2¼-oz. can sliced black olives, drained
¾ cup dry couscous, cooked and cooled

Dressing:
   ½ cup olive oil
   ½ cup lemon juice, *or* vinegar
   ⅛ tsp. minced garlic
   1 Tbsp. Dijon mustard
   ¼ tsp. dried oregano
   ¼ tsp. dried basil
   1 Tbsp. sugar
   ⅛ tsp. coriander
   ⅛ tsp. onion powder
   1 tsp. dried parsley

2 Tbsp. shredded Parmesan cheese

1. Toss salad ingredients together.
2. Mix dressing ingredients together. Pour dressing over salad mixture and toss.
3. Top with Parmesan cheese.

Tips:
1. Using flavored couscous adds interesting flavor.
2. I enjoy this recipe because I can adjust vegetables as I wish or according to what I have on hand. Seasonings can also be adjusted to your preferred taste.

Marinated Italian Salad

Tammy Smith
Dorchester, WI

Makes 6-8 servings

Prep. Time: 30 minutes
Chilling Time: 1 hour

1 cup baby carrots, sliced lengthwise
1 cup chopped sweet red pepper
1 cup chopped celery
1 cup diced, peeled jicama
1 cup diced zucchini
1 cup small cauliflower florets
½ cup chopped red onion
½ cup sliced green onion tops (use whites for another purpose)
15-oz. can black beans, rinsed and drained
6-oz. pkg. pepperoni slices, cut in half

Dressing:
   0.7-oz. packet Italian salad dressing mix, dry
   ¼ cup apple cider vinegar
   3 Tbsp. water
   ½ cup oil

8-oz. pkg. sharp cheddar cheese, diced or cubed

Shop at local markets and "invent" with what's in season and usually less expensive.
Barbara Forrester Landis, Lititz, PA

1. Place salad ingredients (except cheese) in large bowl.
2. Whisk together dressing mix, vinegar, water, and oil. Drizzle over salad. Toss to coat.
3. Chill at least 1 hour. Add cheese just before serving.

Tips:
1. You may use any vegetables you wish. Try to use 7-8 cups of vegetables for 1 recipe of dressing.
2. Bacon bits, nuts and seeds also work well if added just before serving.
3. Cubed pepperoni sticks or turkey ham can replace pepperoni slices.
4. For a change, serve this salad as a sauce over pasta.
5. Jicama is a Mexican vegetable with a mild sweet taste and a nice crunch. Look for it in the produce section of a big grocery store.

Southwestern Bean Salad

Ellie Oberholtzer
Ronks, PA

Makes 7 cups

Prep. Time: 20 minutes
Chilling Time: 2 hours

15-oz. can kidney beans, rinsed and drained
15-oz. can black beans, rinsed and drained
15-oz. can garbanzo beans, rinsed and drained
2 celery ribs, sliced
1 medium red onion, diced
1 medium tomato, diced
1 cup frozen corn, thawed

Dressing:
  ¾ cup thick and chunky salsa
  ¼ cup vegetable oil *or* olive oil
  ¼ cup lime juice
  1-2 tsp. chili powder
  ½ tsp. ground cumin

1. In a bowl, combine beans, celery, onion, tomato, and corn.
2. Mix together salsa, oil, lime juice, chili powder, and cumin.
3. Pour over bean mixture and toss. Cover and chill 2 hours.

Tips:
1. I like to serve this salad with kale leaves lining the bowl.
2. It's also good with a dollop of sour cream on individual servings.

Corn and Black Bean Salad

Jamie Mowry
Arlington, TX

Makes 5 cups

Prep. Time: 15 minutes
Chilling Time: 30 minutes

4 medium ears uncooked sweet corn, kernels cut off (2 cups)
1 large red bell pepper, diced
½ cup thinly sliced green onions
½ cup chopped fresh cilantro
15½-oz. can black beans, rinsed and drained
¼ cup red wine vinegar
2 tsp. canola oil
1 tsp. sugar
½ tsp. garlic powder
½ tsp. ground cumin
½ tsp. freshly ground black pepper
salt to taste

1. Combine corn, bell pepper, onions, cilantro, and beans in a medium bowl.
2. Whisk together vinegar, oil, sugar, garlic powder, cumin, black pepper, and salt.
3. Stir dressing gently into corn mixture.
4. Cover and chill for 30 minutes.

Good Go-Alongs:
  This is wonderful alone or good served with fish. We enjoyed it with chips outside at the lake one Memorial Day in Texas.

Chili Cornbread Salad

Marie Davis
Mineral Ridge, OH

Makes 10-12 servings

Prep. Time: 30 minutes
Baking Time: 20-25 minutes
Chilling Time: 2 hours

Cornbread:
8½-oz. pkg. cornbread
 mix
4-oz. can chopped green
 chilies, undrained
⅛ tsp. ground cumin
⅛ tsp. dried oregano
pinch of sage

Dressing:
1 cup mayonnaise
1 cup sour cream
1 envelope Ranch
 dressing mix

2 cans (15-oz. ea.) pinto *or*
 black beans, drained
2 15¼-oz. cans whole
 kernel corn, drained
3 medium tomatoes,
 chopped
1 cup chopped green bell
 pepper
1 cup chopped green
 onions *or* red onion
10 bacon strips, cooked
 and crumbled
2 cups shredded cheddar
 cheese

1. Prepare cornbread batter according to package directions. Stir in chilies, cumin, oregano, and sage. Spread into greased 8" square baking dish.

2. Bake at 400° for 20-25 minutes or until knife comes out clean in center. Cool.

3. In a small bowl, combine mayonnaise, sour cream, and dressing mix; set aside.

4. Crumble half of cornbread into glass 9 × 13 baking dish.

5. Layer with half of the beans, mayonnaise mixture, corn, tomatoes, green pepper, onions, bacon, and cheese.

6. Repeat layers (dish will be very full).

7. Cover and refrigerate for 2 hours.

Tips:
1. If you want a less-full serving dish, make it in a 9 × 13 plus an 8 × 8 pan.
2. The cornbread seasonings are optional. Just use regular cornbread if you wish. The cheese is optional as well. This really is a meal in itself!

Karen Waggoner
Joplin, MO

To make your own cornbread mix, please turn to page 259.

Swedish Salad

Anne Townsend
Albuquerque, NM

Makes 7 cups

Prep. Time: 20 minutes

14½-oz. can French style
 green beans
11-oz. can white shoepeg
 corn
1 cup frozen peas, thawed
2-oz. jar chopped pimento
 or half red bell pepper,
 chopped
1 cup chopped celery
1 cup chopped onion
salt and pepper

Dressing:
½ cup sugar
½ cup oil
½ cup cider vinegar

1. In medium non-metallic bowl, combine green beans, corn, peas, pimento, celery, onion, salt, and pepper.
2. Combine dressing ingredients and mix well. Pour on top of salad and stir.

Tip:
Use a slotted spoon for serving.

Good Go-Alongs:
Hamburgers and potato salad go well with this favorite salad.

Fresh Corn and Tomato Salad

Dawn Landowski
Eau Claire, WI

Makes 12 servings

Prep. Time: 20 minutes
Standing Time: 15 minutes–
2 hours

6 ears corn, husked and
  corn cut off of cob
2 cups halved grape
  tomatoes
½ lb. fresh mozzarella, cut
  into small cubes
4-6 scallions, thinly sliced

Vinaigrette:
  3 Tbsp. white vinegar
  2 tsp. salt
  Fresh ground pepper
  ¼ cup extra virgin olive
    oil

1½ cups fresh basil leaves,
  torn

1. Stir together corn,
tomatoes, mozzarella, and
scallions in a large bowl.
2. Whisk vinegar, salt, and
pepper together in a small
bowl. Gradually whisk in oil
to make a smooth dressing.
3. Pour vinaigrette over
salad and toss to coat.
4. Cover and let set for 15
minutes to 2 hours.
5. Right before serving,
tear the basil over the salad
and stir.

Tip:
  For cutting corn off the
cob, put the end of the cob in
a Bundt pan and cut down.
Kernels fall into the pan.

*People can't believe the
corn is raw—there are always
discussions!*

Cable Car Salad

Nanci Keatley
Salem, OR

Makes 6½ cups

Prep. Time: 20 minutes
Cooking Time for Rice-A-Roni:
* 20 minutes*
Chilling Time: 2 hours

14½-oz. can artichoke
  hearts, chopped
1 cup sliced fresh
  mushrooms
½ cup chopped green onions
½ cup sliced olives (green
  or black)
½ cup water chestnuts,
  sliced and drained
1 box Rice-A-Roni, chicken
  flavor, prepared as
  directed
½-¾ cup mayonnaise, to
  taste
salt and pepper

1. Mix artichoke hearts,
mushrooms, onion, olives, water
chestnuts, and rice together.
2. Add mayonnaise and salt
and pepper to taste. Chill at
least 2 hours.

Tip:
  This is good with leftover
chicken or turkey added.

Picnic Pea Salad

Mary Kathryn Yoder
Harrisonville, MO

Makes 4-6 servings

Prep. Time: 30 minutes
Chilling Time: 1 hour

10-oz. pkg. frozen peas,
  thawed
¼ cup chopped onion *or*
  green onions
½ cup chopped celery
½ cup sour cream
2 Tbsp. mayonnaise
1 tsp. salt
1 tsp. dill weed
¼ tsp. pepper

1 cup Spanish peanuts
¼-½ cup fried and
  crumbled bacon
1 cup cherry tomatoes for
  garnish, *optional*

1. Mix peas, onion, celery,
sour cream, mayonnaise, salt,
dill weed, and pepper. Chill.
2. Just before serving, stir
in peanuts. Garnish with
bacon and tomatoes.

Variation:
  Omit celery, peanuts, and
dill weed. Add a chopped
hardboiled egg and a dash of
garlic powder.

Dorothy VanDeest
Memphis, TN

Asian Rice Salad

Lois Mae E. Kuh
Penfield, NY

Makes 6-8 servings

Prep. Time: 15 minutes
Cooking Time (for rice): 35
  minutes
Chilling Time: 12 hours

3 cups cooked rice (1½
  cups dry)
1 cup fresh bean sprouts
8-oz. fresh spinach,
  chopped
1 red bell pepper, sliced
  thin
1 cup thinly sliced
  mushrooms
½ cup diced shallots
1 cup cashews

Dressing:
  ¼ cup soy sauce
  ½ cup vegetable oil
  1 clove garlic, minced

1. Cook rice. Allow to cool
to room temperature.
2. Toss together rice,
sprouts, spinach, pepper,
mushrooms, and shallots.
3. Mix soy sauce, vegetable
oil, and garlic. Pour over
salad ingredients and mix.
4. Make a day ahead of
serving. Add cashews just
before serving.

*This is a nice change from
potato and macaroni salads.*

Cherry Wild Rice Salad

Edie Moran
West Babylon, NY

Makes 8 servings

Prep. Time: 20 minutes
Cooking Time (for rice): 35
  minutes
Chilling Time: 30 minutes

2 cups snow peas, chopped
  in half
2 cups cooked wild rice,
  cooled
1 cup cooked long grain
  rice, cooled
8-oz. can sliced water
  chestnuts, drained
1 cup dried cherries
½ cup thinly sliced celery
¼ cup chopped green
  onions
¾ cup cashews, halved and
  toasted

Dressing:
  6 Tbsp. sugar
  3 Tbsp. cider vinegar
  4½ tsp. soy sauce
  1 garlic clove, peeled
  ¾ tsp. minced fresh
    ginger root

1. Toast the
cashews in a
medium oven or
toaster oven for 5
minutes or until
fragrant. Cool.
2. In a large
bowl, combine peas,
cooled rice, water
chestnuts, cherries,
celery, onions, and cashews.

3. Combine dressing
ingredients in the blender and
process until well blended.
4. Pour dressing over rice
mixture and toss to coat.
Cover and refrigerate no more
than an hour until serving.

*We always serve it at our
annual cousins' reunion.
I double the recipe for that.*

Carrot Raisin Salad

Shelia Heil
Lancaster, PA

Makes 6 servings

Prep. Time: 10 minutes
Chilling Time: 4-12 hours

5 large carrots, shredded
1 cup raisins
⅔ cup plain yogurt
4 Tbsp. mayonnaise
2 tsp. honey

1. Combine ingredients in a medium non-metallic bowl.
2. Chill for several hours or overnight. Serve cold.

My mother often made a recipe like this for guests in our home. It adds color to a meat and potato meal.

Pickled Beets, Sugar-Free

Sue Hamilton
Benson, AZ

Makes 4 cups

Prep. Time: 5 minutes
Cooking Time: 2 minutes
Chilling Time: 24 hours

2 15-oz. cans sliced beets
⅔ cup vinegar
1 cup Splenda
½ tsp. pumpkin pie spice
1 tsp. vanilla
¼ tsp. butter powder
1 small onion, thinly sliced

1. Drain beets and save the liquid.
2. Combine the beet liquid with vinegar, Splenda, pumpkin pie spice, vanilla, and butter powder in a microwaveable bowl. Heat on High for 2 minutes.
3. In a large jar or glass dish, layer the beets and onions. Pour hot liquid mixture over top.
4. Refrigerate 24 hours or longer. Drain and serve.

Tips:
1. Save the liquid when you serve your beets. You can bring it to a boil and then pour it over *new* beets and onions.
2. 1 cup sugar can be substituted for the Splenda.

Marinated Asparagus

Rebecca Meyerkorth
Wamego, KS

Makes 8-10 servings

Prep. Time: 20 minutes
Cooking Time: 5-10 minutes
Chilling Time: 2-12 hours

½ cup brown sugar
½ cup cider vinegar
½ cup soy sauce
½ cup vegetable oil
4 tsp. lemon juice
1 tsp. garlic powder
2 lbs. asparagus
¼ cup sliced almonds,
optional

1. In saucepan, stir together brown sugar, vinegar, soy sauce, oil, juice, and garlic powder.
2. Bring to a boil and simmer 5 minutes. Cool.
3. Meanwhile, microwave or cook asparagus until just crisp tender. Plunge it in cold water to stop the cooking. Drain well.
4. In large resealable plastic bag, put asparagus and marinade. Zip bag and turn to coat asparagus.
5. Refrigerate at least 2 hours or overnight, turning occasionally.
6. Drain and discard marinade.
7. Place asparagus on plate to serve. Sprinkle with sliced almonds, if desired.

Tangy Tomatoes Slices

Mary H. Nolt
East Earl, PA

Makes 10-12 servings

Prep. Time: 20 minutes
Chilling Time: 2-4 hours

Marinade:
  1 cup vegetable oil
  ⅓ cup vinegar
  ¼ cup minced fresh
    parsley
  3 Tbsp. minced fresh
    basil *or* 1 Tbsp. dried
    basil
  1 Tbsp. sugar
  ½ tsp. pepper
  1 tsp. salt
  ½ tsp. dry mustard
  ½ tsp. garlic powder

1 medium sweet onion,
  thinly sliced
6 large tomatoes, thinly
  sliced

1. Mix marinade in a lidded jar and shake well. Or whisk marinade ingredients together in a small bowl.
2. Layer onions and tomatoes in a shallow non-metallic dish.
3. Pour the marinade over onions and tomatoes.
4. Cover and refrigerate for several hours.

Our daughter has a big greenhouse with tomatoes. At picnics or gatherings when tomatoes are in season, she always brings this dish.

Salad Tomatoes

Lois Ostrander
Lebanon, PA

Makes 4-6 servings

Prep. Time: 15 minutes
Cooking Time: 10 minutes

3 medium tomatoes
1 Tbsp. dried minced
  onion
¼ cup chopped fresh
  parsley
½ cup water
1 tsp. salt
½ cup cider vinegar
2 Tbsp. sugar
⅛ tsp. pepper

1. Peel tomatoes and slice. Overlap slices in a shallow glass serving bowl or pie plate.
2. Sprinkle with parsley and onion.
3. Combine vinegar, water, sugar, salt and pepper in a small saucepan. Heat to boiling, stirring constantly.
4. Drizzle hot dressing over tomatoes. Chill until serving time.

Marinated Carrots

Sarah Fisher
Christiana, PA

Makes 10-12 servings

Prep. Time: 15 minutes
Cooking Time: 15 minutes
Chilling Time: 12 hours

2 lbs. carrots, sliced
1 large onion, diced
1 large green pepper,
  chopped
8-oz. can tomato sauce
1 cup sugar
½ cup salad oil
¾ cup apple cider vinegar
1 tsp. salt
1 tsp. black pepper

1. Cook carrots in a covered saucepan in a little water until crisp-tender. Drain. Cool.
2. Combine cooled carrots, peppers, and onions in a medium non-metallic bowl.
3. In a medium saucepan, mix tomato sauce, sugar, oil, vinegar, salt, and pepper. Bring to a boil, stirring constantly.
4. Pour hot mixture over vegetables and stir. Cool and refrigerate overnight before serving.

Tip:
  Using baby carrots for this recipe saves chopping time.

Try a recipe first the way it is written. After that, experiment with changes to suit your taste.

Jenny R. Unternahrer, Wayland, IA

Southwestern Copper Pennies

Sue Hamilton
Benson, AZ

Makes 8 servings

Prep. Time: 10 minutes
Cooking Time: 3 minutes
Chilling Time: 12 hours

1 lb. carrots, peeled and sliced
1 small onion, diced
1 green pepper, diced
1 cup peach *or* pineapple salsa
½ cup Splenda
⅓ cup vinegar

1. In a glass bowl, combine the carrots, onion, and green pepper.
2. Heat the salsa, Splenda, and vinegar on stovetop or microwave until hot and steaming. Stir to prevent scorching.
3. Pour marinade over carrots. Stir.
4. Allow to marinate 12 hours or more before serving.

Variation:
Replace the Splenda with ¾ cup sugar.

I took these carrots to a gathering and I only told the diabetic that they were sugar-free. When they were all gone and people asked for the recipe, I had to tell them!

Mixed Vegetable Salad

Sharon Miller
Holmesville, OH

Makes 6-8 servings

Prep. Time: 15 minutes
Cooking Time: 10 minutes
Standing Time: 15 minutes
Chilling Time: 8-12 hours

16-oz. frozen mixed vegetables, thawed
15-oz. can kidney beans, rinsed and drained
½ cup chopped celery
½ cup chopped onion
½ cup chopped green *or* red bell pepper
¾ cup sugar
1 Tbsp. cornstarch
½ cup vinegar

1. In a covered saucepan cook mixed vegetables in a little water until crisp-tender. Drain.
2. Put mixed vegetables in non-metallic bowl. Add kidney beans, celery, onion, and pepper.
3. In saucepan, combine sugar and cornstarch. Add vinegar.
4. Cook over low heat until thick, stirring constantly. Or microwave uncovered until thickened, stirring once or twice.
5. Cool for 15 minutes. Pour over vegetables stir gently. Refrigerate overnight for best flavor.

Tip:
The cornstarch-vinegar mix eliminates the oil usually used in a salad of this type. I use this same sauce in 3-bean salad recipes or other similar recipes.

Sour Cream Cucumber Salad

Mary Jones
Marengo, OH

Makes 6 servings

Prep. Time: 20-30 minutes

3 medium cucumbers, sliced thinly
½ tsp. salt
½ cup finely chopped green onions
1 Tbsp. white vinegar
dash pepper, *optional*
¼ cup sour cream

1. Place cucumbers in glass bowl. Sprinkle cucumber with salt. Let stand 15 minutes. Drain liquid.
2. Add onions, vinegar and pepper.
3. Just before serving, stir in sour cream.

Variation:
Use lemon juice instead of vinegar and make a dressing with sour cream, salt, lemon juice, and 2 tsp. sugar. Simply add the dressing to the cucumbers and onions, chilling 2 hours before serving.
Joyce Shackelford
Green Bay, WI

Green Bean and Walnut Salad

Mary Wheatley
Mashpee, MA

Makes 4 servings

Prep. Time: 20 minutes
Cooking Time: 5-7 minutes

¾ lb. fresh green beans, trimmed
¼ cup walnut pieces
3 Tbsp. finely chopped fresh parsley
3 Tbsp. finely chopped onion
1 Tbsp. walnut *or* olive oil
1½ tsp. red wine vinegar
1 tsp. Dijon mustard
salt to taste
freshly ground pepper to taste

1. Steam beans in basket over boiling water for 4 minutes. Transfer to a medium serving bowl.
2. Toast walnuts in a small dry skillet, stirring frequently until fragrant, 3-5 minutes. Chop the toasted walnuts fine.
3. Stir parsley and onion into walnuts.
4. Whisk together oil, vinegar, and mustard. Add to green beans.
5. Season with salt and pepper and top with walnut mixture.
6. Serve warm or at room temperature.

Tips:
1. You'll want to double or triple the recipe, since people come back for more.
2. Pecans or almonds can be substituted for the walnuts.

This is a good alternative to the green bean casseroles so often used for holidays.

Five Bean Salad

Jeanne Heyerly
Shipshewana, IN

Makes 8-10 servings

Prep. Time: 20 minutes
Chilling Time: 12 hours

15-oz. can green beans
15-oz. can wax beans
15-oz. can lima beans
15-oz. can kidney beans
15-oz. can garbanzo beans
1 green *or* red bell pepper, chopped
1 medium onion, chopped
1 large clove garlic, minced
½ cup canola *or* light olive oil
½ cup apple cider vinegar
¾ cup sugar
1 tsp. salt
1 tsp. pepper
1 tsp. dry mustard
1½ tsp. celery seed

1. Drain all beans and combine in a large non-metallic bowl.
2. Heat (but do not boil) the oil, vinegar, sugar, salt, pepper, mustard, and celery seed in microwave or on stovetop.
3. Mix with bean mixture and let stand overnight.
4. Add onion, green pepper, and garlic about 1 hour before serving.

Tips:
1. Omit dry mustard, celery seed, and garlic.
2. If there is another type of bean you like, add it; or you could double up on the kinds you do like. There is enough dressing to cover it.
Jean Halloran
Green Bay, WI

3. Add ½ cup chopped celery and 2-oz jar pimento.
Joyce Kaut
Rochester, NY

Going Away Salad

Judith Govotsos
Frederick, MD

Makes 12-15 servings

Prep. Time: 30-45 minutes
Chilling Time: 8-12 hours

15 oz.-can kidney beans,
  drained
15 oz.-can wax beans,
  drained
15 oz.-can green beans,
  drained
15 oz.-can garbanzo beans,
  drained
1 English cucumber, thinly
  sliced
2 carrots, thinly sliced
2-3 ribs celery, thinly
  sliced
1 medium to large onion,
  thinly sliced
1 medium cabbage
  shredded *or* 2 1 lb.
  packages coleslaw mix

Marinade:
  2 tsp. salt
  2 tsp. black pepper
  ⅔ cup white vinegar
  ½ cup canola oil
  ½ cup sugar

1. Combine vegetables in a large non-metallic bowl.
2. In saucepan, combine salt, black pepper, vinegar, oil, and sugar. Bring to boil. Allow to cool.
3. Pour cooled marinade over vegetables. Cover.
4. Let vegetables marinate in the refrigerator at least overnight before serving.

Good Go-Alongs:
  Fried chicken or ham.

Sauerkraut Salad

Wilma Haberkamp
Fairbank, IA

Makes 6 cups

Prep. Time: 10-15 minutes

Dressing:
  ⅓ cup vinegar
  1 cup sugar
  ⅓ cup vegetable oil

1 quart jar sauerkraut,
  drained
1 cup minced green bell
  pepper
1 cup minced celery
½ cup minced onion

1. In a saucepan, heat vinegar, sugar, and oil to lukewarm so they dissolve and mix better. Cool.
2. Combine sauerkraut, green pepper, celery, and onion. Pour vinegar mixture over top and mix.

Tips:
  1. This is better after it sets for a couple days, and it keeps almost indefinitely in the refrigerator.
  2. Serve it as salad, but it's also great on hot dogs or brats.

We enjoy gathering for a simple meal with friends. We roast hot dogs in the fireplace and everyone brings something they have on hand. The meal usually ends up well balanced even though unplanned.
Karen Sauder, Adamstown, PA

Chinese Cabbage Salad

Kim McEuen
Lincoln University, PA

Makes 6-8 servings

Prep. Time: 15-20 minutes
Cooking Time: 10 minutes

1 head bok choy, chopped
6 green onions, sliced
half stick (4 Tbsp.) butter
2 pkgs. Ramen noodles,
   crunched up, seasoning
   packs discarded
4-oz. slivered almonds
4-oz. sunflower seeds

Dressing:
   ½ cup tarragon vinegar
   2 Tbsp. soy sauce
   1 cup vegetable oil
   1 cup sugar

1. Mix bok choy and onions in a large bowl. Set aside.
2. In a frying pan, melt butter. Sauté noodles, almonds and sunflower seeds until lightly browned. Cool.
3. Mix dressing ingredients together.
4. Just before serving, mix together the bok choy mixture and noodle mixture.
5. Add half the dressing, tossing to coat. Add more dressing to your taste.

Creamy Coleslaw

Jane Geigley
Lancaster, PA

Makes 8-10 servings

Prep. Time: 15 minutes

1 head cabbage, shredded
1 medium carrot, shredded
1½ cups mayonnaise
2 Tbsp. milk
1 tsp. prepared mustard
1-2 Tbsp. vinegar
½ cup sugar
½-1 tsp. salt

1. In a bowl, mix together cabbage and carrot. Set aside.
2. To make dressing, mix together mayonnaise, milk, mustard, vinegar, sugar and salt. Taste and add more vinegar or salt as desired.
3. Pour dressing over cabbage and carrot. Stir.

Variation:
   Make a dressing with ½ cup milk, 3 Tbsp. mayonnaise or salad dressing, ½ cup sugar, ¼ cup vinegar, pinch of salt.

Orpha M. Herr
Andover, NY

Good Go-Alongs:
   Barbecued chicken and baked beans.

Apple Coleslaw

Joy Uhler
Richardson, TX

Makes 4-6 servings

Prep. Time: 20 minutes

2 cups *or* 1 pkg. coleslaw
   mix
1 unpeeled apple, cored
   and chopped
½ cup chopped celery
½ cup chopped green bell
   pepper
½ cup chopped broccoli,
   optional
¼ cup vegetable oil
2 Tbsp. lemon juice
2 Tbsp. honey

1. In a large bowl, combine coleslaw mix, apple, celery, green pepper, and broccoli.
2. In a small bowl, whisk together oil, lemon juice and honey.
3. Pour over coleslaw and toss to coat evenly.

Tips:
   1. This is a great recipe for potlucks, as it doesn't contain mayonnaise, so there's no need to worry about it sitting out.
   2. Use red or yellow peppers for even more color.

Cranberry Relish

Winifred Erb Paul
Scottdale, PA

Makes 7 cups

Prep. Time: 20 minutes
Chilling Time: at least a week

4 cups cranberries
2 apples, cored but not
  peeled, quartered
2 oranges, including rind,
  quartered
1 lemon, including rind,
  quartered
2½ cups sugar

1. Grind the whole fruit together using meat grinder. Alternatively, use a food processor and pulse just until most fruits are diced, but not mushy. (See Tips for more details.)

2. Be sure to keep the juice after fruits are ground. Add sugar. Mix. Let it set a week in the refrigerator before serving.

Tips:
  To get a good grind from a food processor, put in only a few pieces of fruit—do not fill up the processor bowl. Push the pulse button once and allow everything to come to a stop before pushing the button again. Look at the size of the fruit carefully after each pulse. Stop when most of the pieces are ½" cubes.

The Tillman Erb family emigrated to Hesston, Kansas, in 1885. The brought this recipe with them from Lancaster County, PA. It was always served at the Erb Christmas get-together. My husband makes it every year, and we like it with turkey, chicken or ham on Christmas Day.

Hawaiian Delight

Esther H. Becker
Gordonville, PA

Makes 4-6 servings

Prep. Time: 20 minutes
Chilling Time: 2 hours

2 cups sour cream
2 Tbsp. sugar
3 Tbsp. lemon juice
2 cups pineapple chunks
2 cups thinly sliced celery
1 cup coarsely chopped
  walnuts
2 cups diced papaya

1. Mix sour cream, sugar, and lemon juice.
2. Gently mix in pineapple chunks, celery, walnuts, and papaya. Chill 2 hours.

Tip:
  Add some sliced bananas to Step 2.

Poppy Seed–Lime Fruit Salad

Diann Dunham
State College, PA

Makes 4½ cups

Prep. Time: 20 minutes

2 cups pineapple chunks, fresh or canned, juice reserved
1 orange, peeled and chopped
1 kiwi fruit, peeled and sliced
1 cup red *or* green grapes
1 cup quartered strawberries

Dressing:
¼ cup reserved pineapple juice
¼ tsp. grated lime peel
2 Tbsp. fresh lime juice
1 Tbsp. honey
1 tsp. poppy seeds

whole strawberries, *optional*

1. Mix pineapple chunks, orange, kiwi, grapes, and strawberries in a non-metallic bowl.
2. In a separate bowl, mix dressing ingredients. Add dressing to salad.
3. If desired, garnish with a few whole strawberries before serving.

Tips:
1. It looks very pretty in a clear bowl.
2. The salad is best made and eaten the same day.

Strawberries get mushy if stored too long.

Good Go-Alongs:
It's lovely for a simple dessert with shortbread cookies or coconut macaroons.

Five Minute Salad

Jane Geigley
Lancaster, PA
Becky Frey
Lebanon, PA
Heidi Hunsberger
Harrisonburg, VA

Makes 4-6 servings

Prep. Time: 5-10 minutes
Chilling Time: 5-60 minutes

1 pint cottage cheese
3-oz. pkg. orange gelatin
2 cups frozen whipped topping, thawed
11-oz. can mandarin oranges, drained

1. Mix cottage cheese and gelatin powder.
2. Add orange slices and whipped topping.
3. Allow to stand at least 5 minutes or can be refrigerated to chill completely.

Tips:
1. This can be either a salad or a light dessert.
2. You can use other flavors of gelatin. Strawberry or lime is also delicious.
3. My husband enjoys having this in his lunch box.

Variations:
Use lemon gelatin and crushed pineapple.
Carla Koslowsky
Hillsboro, KS

Substitute 20-oz. can crushed pineapple or pineapple tidbits for mandarin oranges.
Christine Lucke
Aumsville, OR

I got this recipe from a lady I was with on a bus tour. Thelma brought this to a potluck reunion we had. It brings back fond memories of that trip to Ottawa and the 1,000 Islands.
Becky Frey
Lebanon, PA

Strawberry Velvet Salad

Colleen Heatwole
Burton, MI

Makes 6-8 servings

Prep. Time: 30 minutes
Chilling Time: 6 hours

6-oz. pkg. strawberry
    gelatin
2 cups boiling water
2 cups frozen strawberries,
    drained and thawed
    (syrup reserved)
8-oz. cream cheese,
    softened
¼ cup mayonnaise
¼ cup orange juice

1. Dissolve gelatin in boiling water. Set aside.
2. Add syrup drained from strawberries.
3. Meanwhile in a small bowl beat cream cheese until creamy.
4. Add mayonnaise and orange juice and whisk or beat to combine well.
5. Whip thickened, but not set, gelatin.
6. Add cream cheese mixture and combine again.
7. Stir in strawberries.
8. Pour into 6-8 cup mold or pretty dish. Chill until firm.

I first ate this salad when I worked at McLaren Hospital as an RN, so this recipe is about 40 years old. I got it from a dietician there. It is not "health food," however!

I have taken this recipe to many potlucks and it is one of the first salads to disappear! It looks pretty.

Cranberry Salad

Eileen M. Landis
Lebanon, PA

Makes 8-10 servings

Prep. Time: 15 minutes
Chilling Time: 2-4 hours

6-oz. cherry *or* raspberry
    gelatin
1½ cups boiling water
20-oz. can crushed
    pineapple, undrained
16-oz. can whole cranberry
    sauce
1½ cups halved red
    seedless grapes
½ cup chopped pecans *or*
    walnuts, *optional*

1. Dissolve gelatin in hot water in a medium glass bowl.
2. Add pineapple, cranberry sauce and grapes. Add nuts, if desired.
3. Cover. Chill until set.

Apricot Salad

Gladys Shank
Harrisonburg, VA

Makes 15 servings

Prep. Time: 50 minutes
Cooking Time: 10 minutes
Chilling Time: 3-4 hours

2 3-oz. packages orange
   gelatin
2 cups boiling water
20-oz. can crushed
   pineapple, drained
   (reserve juice, *divided*)
2 15-oz. cans apricots,
   diced and drained
   (reserve juice, *divided*)
½ cup reserved pineapple
   juice
½ cup reserved apricot
   juice

Topping:
   1 egg, slightly beaten
   1 cup reserved pineapple
      and apricot juice
   2 Tbsp. butter
   3 Tbsp. flour
   ½ cup sugar
   3-oz. pkg. cream cheese
   1 pkg. Dream Whip,
      prepared
   grated cheese, *optional*

1. Dissolve gelatin in boiling
water in a medium bowl.
2. Add ½ cup pineapple
juice and ½ cup apricot juice.
Mix.

3. Add pineapple and
apricots. Mix.
4. Pour into 9 × 13 glass
pan. Refrigerate to set gelatin,
2-3 hours.
5. After gelatin is set,
make topping. Melt butter in
saucepan.
6. Add flour, sugar, juice,
and egg.
7. Stir and cook 3-5 min-
utes until thickened. Remove
from heat.
8. Whisk in cream cheese
until smooth. Cool at least 1
hour in the refrigerator.
9. Add prepared whipped
topping to cooled mixture.
10. Spread on gelatin.
Return to refrigerator.
11. Garnish with grated
cheese, if desired, before
serving.

Tip:
   This can also be used for
dessert.

White Pineapple Salad

Arlene Yoder
Hartville, OH

Makes 7 cups

Prep. Time: 15 minutes
Cooling Time: 20-40 minutes
Chilling Time: 2-4 hours

20-oz. can crushed
   pineapple, drained
   (reserve juice)
1 Tbsp. (1 envelope) Knox
   unflavored gelatin
¾ cup sugar
½ cup mayonnaise
8-oz. cream cheese,
   softened
1 large carrot, shredded
1 rib celery, diced
⅓ cup chopped nuts
8-oz. frozen whipped
   topping, thawed

1. Stir gelatin into pineapple juice until dissolved.
Add sugar.
2. Heat mixture just to
boiling. Pour over pineapple
in heat-safe bowl.
3. Cool until syrupy, 20-40
minutes.
4. Add mayonnaise, cream
cheese, carrot, celery, nuts,
and whipped topping. Mix
gently.
5. Pour into nice serving
dish. Cover. Chill until set,
2-3 hours.

1 Dream Whip packet + ½ cup milk = 2 cups whipped topping

Desserts

Jumbleberry Crumble

Joanna Harrison
Lafayette, CO

Makes 6-8 servings

Prep. Time: 20 minutes
Baking Time: 50 minutes

3 cups strawberries
1½ cups blueberries
1½ cups raspberries
⅔ cup sugar
3 Tbsp. minute tapioca
½ cup flour
½ cup quick oats
½ cup brown sugar,
  packed
1 tsp. cinnamon
⅓ cup (5 Tbsp.) butter,
  melted

1. In large bowl, combine berries, tapioca, and sugar.
2. Pour into a greased 11 × 7 baking dish. Let stand 15 minutes.
3. Combine flour, oats, brown sugar, and cinnamon in small bowl.
4. Stir in melted butter.
5. Sprinkle over berry mixture.
6. Bake at 350° for 45-50 minutes or until filling is bubbly and topping is golden brown. Serve warm.

Tip:
  I've used fresh or frozen berries depending on the season. Yummy with vanilla ice cream.

It's smart to always keep a can of fruit pie filling on hand — for a quick cobbler or dessert topping.
Lena Mae Jones, Lane, KS

Apple Gingerbread Cobbler

Esther H. Becker
Gordonville, PA

Makes 12-15 servings

Prep. Time: 15 minutes
Cooking/Baking Time: 35 minutes

half stick (4 Tbsp.) butter, melted
2 21-oz. cans apple pie filling
15-oz. box gingerbread mix

1. Melt butter in large saucepan.
2. Stir in 2 cans apple pie filling. Remove from heat.
3. Spread into 9 × 13 cake pan.
4. Make gingerbread batter according to directions on box.
5. Pour on top of apple pie filling.
6. Bake at 350° for 35 minutes, or until a toothpick inserted in the middle of the cake comes out clean.

Quick Fruit Cobbler

Lena Mae Janes
Lane, KS

Makes 6 servings

Prep. Time: 15 minutes
Baking Time: 30 minutes

⅔ cup sugar
1 cup flour
⅛ tsp. salt
2 tsp. baking powder
¼ cup milk
1 stick (½ cup) margarine *or* butter, melted
21-oz. can fruit pie filling, any kind

1. In a medium-sized mixing bowl, mix sugar, flour, salt, baking powder, and milk.
2. Add melted butter and mix well.
3. Put pie filling in bottom of greased 8 × 8 baking dish.
4. Pour the batter evenly over the pie filling.
5. Bake at 350° for 30 minutes.

Tips:
1. Serve warm or cold. Top it with ice cream or whipped topping.
2. This is a good last-minute dessert when unexpected company comes and you want to serve a dessert.

Cherry Crisp

Veronica Marshall-Varela
Chandler, AZ

Makes 8 servings

Prep. Time: 15 minutes
Baking Time: 30 minutes

21-oz. can cherry pie filling
16-oz. bag frozen pitted cherries, thawed

Topping:
  1 cup rolled oats
  1 cup brown sugar, packed
  1 stick (½ cup) butter
  ½ tsp. cinnamon
  ¾ cup coarsely chopped walnuts *or* pecans
  ½ cup coconut

vanilla ice cream *or* whipped cream

1. Mix pie filling and cherries together and place in greased 8 × 8 baking dish.
2. To make topping, place the butter in a medium-sized microwaveable bowl. Microwave in 20-second increments, checking until butter is completely melted.
3. Add oats, brown sugar, cinnamon, nuts, and coconut. Stir.
4. Sprinkle topping over cherry filling.
5. Bake for 30 minutes at 375° or until bubbly around the edges. Serve warm with ice cream or whipped cream.

Peach Crumble

Nathan LeBeau
Rapid City, SD

Makes 6-8 servings
Prep. Time: 10 minutes
Baking Time: 20-30 minutes

4 cups peeled, sliced fresh peaches
¾ cup brown sugar
⅓ cup (5⅓ Tbsp.) butter, softened
¾ tsp. nutmeg
¾ tsp. cinnamon
1 cup graham cracker crumbs

1. Mix brown sugar and peaches together.
2. Place in a greased 8" baking pan.
3. Combine butter, nutmeg, cinnamon and graham crackers. Mix well.
4. Sprinkle mixture over top of peaches.
5. Bake at 375° for 20-30 minutes until bubbling.

Variation:
Use apples instead of peaches.

Pecan Pie Squares

Mary Ann Bowman
Ephrata, PA
Arianne Hochstetler
Goshen, IN

Makes 24 bars
Prep. Time: 15 minutes
Baking Time: 35-40 minutes

Crust:
   1½ cups flour
   3 Tbsp. brown sugar
   ¼ tsp. salt
   1 stick (½ cup) butter

2 eggs
½ cup light corn syrup
½ cup brown sugar
1 cup chopped pecans
2 Tbsp. butter, melted
½ tsp. vanilla

1. Mix together flour, 3 Tbsp. brown sugar and salt.
2. Cut butter into mixture with a pastry cutter or two knives until crumbly.
3. Press mixture into a greased 11 × 7 pan to form a crust.
4. Bake at 350° for 15 minutes. Set aside, but do not turn off oven.
5. In a medium mixing bowl, beat eggs slightly.
6. Stir in corn syrup, ½ cup brown sugar, pecans, butter, and vanilla.
7. Pour over baked crust.
8. Put the pan back in the oven. Bake at 350° for 20-25 minutes. Cool slightly. Cut into bars.

Tips:
Try cutting back some of the sugar. I also use half whole wheat flour for the crust.

Arianne Hochstetler
Goshen, IN

Peanut Butter Bars

Kinita Martin
East Earl, PA

Makes 24 bars

Prep. Time: 20 minutes
Baking Time: 20-25 minutes
Cooling Time: 10 minutes

1 stick (½ cup) **butter** *or*
  margarine, softened
½ cup **sugar**
½ cup **brown sugar, packed**
½ cup **peanut butter**
1 **egg, beaten**
1 tsp. **vanilla**
1 cup **flour**
½ cup **quick oats**
1 tsp. **baking soda**
¼ tsp. **salt**
1 cup (6-oz.) **semi-sweet
  chocolate chips**

Icing:
  ½ cup **confectioners
    sugar**
  2 Tbsp. **peanut butter**
  2 Tbsp. **milk**

1. In a mixing bowl, cream butter, sugars, and peanut butter with a mixer.
2. Add egg and vanilla; mix well.
3. In another bowl, combine flour, oats, baking soda, and salt. Stir into the creamed mixture.
4. Spread dough into greased 9 × 13 baking pan.
5. Sprinkle with chocolate chips.
6. Bake at 350° for 20-25 minutes or until lightly browned.
7. Spread melted chocolate chips evenly over bars. Cool 10 minutes.
8. Combine confectioners sugar, peanut butter and milk. Stir until smooth. Drizzle over bars.

Candy Bar Cookies

Arianne Hochstetler
Goshen, IN

Makes 36 bars

Prep. Time: 15-20 minutes
Baking Time: 15 minutes

1 cup **brown sugar**
1 stick (½ cup **butter**),
  softened
½ cup **light corn syrup**
3 tsp. **vanilla**
1 tsp. **salt**
4 cups **rolled oats**
½ cup **peanut butter**
1 cup **semi-sweet
  chocolate chips**

1. Cream brown sugar and butter in a large bowl until fluffy.
2. Add corn syrup, vanilla, salt, and rolled oats. Mix well.
3. Spread mixture evenly in greased 9 × 13 pan.
4. Bake at 350° for 15 minutes. Do not overbake.
5. Meanwhile, combine peanut butter and chocolate chips in a small bowl.
6. When the bars are done baking, immediately spread peanut butter/chocolate mixture over the hot bars so heat melts chocolate chips.
7. When cool, cut into bars and remove from pan.

Good Go-Alongs:
  Milk, fresh fruit like bananas.

I found this recipe in a cookbook I checked out at the library. Our daughters loved both making and eating them. They loved having their friends ask for them.

Mocha Brownie Dessert

Beverly High
Bradford, PA

Makes 12-16 servings

Prep. Time: 20 minutes
Baking Time: 20-25 minutes

18-oz. box chocolate
  brownie mix
2 3.4-oz. pkgs. vanilla
  instant pudding
2 cups milk
¼ cup instant coffee
  granules
16-oz. frozen whipped
  topping, thawed, *divided*

1. Prepare and bake
brownie mix in 9 × 13 pan
according to instructions on
box. Cool.
2. In mixing bowl, mix
milk, pudding, and coffee. Let
this set until coffee granules
are dissolved.
3. Fold in half (8-oz.) the
whipped topping.
4. Spread mixture over
cooled brownies.
5. Top with remaining
plain whipped topping.

Tip:
  Garnish with chocolate
sprinkles.

Chocolate Cream Cheese Bars

Joyce Shackelford
Green Bay, WI

Makes 24 bars

Prep. Time: 15 minutes
Baking Time: 35-40 minutes

18.3-oz. pkg. brownie mix
8-oz. cream cheese,
  softened
½ cup sugar
1 egg
½ tsp. vanilla

1. Mix brown mix as
directed on package.
2. Spread batter in a
greased 9 × 13 pan, reserving
about ¼ of the brownie
mixture in a bowl.
3. Mix cream cheese, sugar,
egg, and vanilla until smooth.
4. Dollop cream cheese
mixture on top of first batter.
5. Add the reserved
brownie batter and cut
through with a knife for a
marble effect.
6. Bake at 350° for 35-40
minutes or until a toothpick
inserted in the center comes
out clean.

Speedy Brownies

Kitty Hilliard
Punxsutawney, PA

Makes 24 bars

Prep. Time: 10 minutes
Baking Time: 30 minutes

2 cups sugar
1¾ cups flour
½ cup baking cocoa
1 tsp. salt
5 eggs
1 cup vegetable oil
1 tsp. vanilla
1 cup (6-oz.) semi-sweet
  chocolate chips

1. In a mixing bowl,
combine sugar, flour, cocoa,
salt, eggs, oil, and vanilla.
Beat until smooth.
2. Pour into a greased 9 × 13
baking pan.
3. Sprinkle with chocolate
chips.
4. Bake at 350° for 25-30
minutes or until a toothpick
inserted near the center
comes out clean. Cool in pan
on a wire rack.

Tip:
  Use butterscotch or
peanut butter chips instead of
chocolate.

16 oz. frozen whipped topping = 6 cups whipped cream.

Marshmallow Fudge Bars

Andrea Zuercher
Lawrence, KS

Makes 24 bars

Prep. Time: 20 minutes
Cooking/Baking Time: 33 minutes
Cooling Time: 45 minutes

1½ cups flour
½ tsp. baking powder
½ tsp. salt
4 Tbsp. unsweetened cocoa powder
1 cup shortening
1½ cups white sugar
4 eggs
2 tsp. vanilla
1 cup chopped nuts
12 marshmallows, cut in half

Frosting:
½ brown sugar, packed
¼ cup water
2 squares (2-oz.) unsweetened chocolate, chopped
3 Tbsp. butter
1 Tbsp. vanilla
1½ cups confectioners sugar

1. In a medium mixing bowl, sift flour, baking powder, salt, and cocoa.
2. Using a mixer, cream shortening and white sugar in another bowl.
3. Add eggs one at a time; mix well after each one.
4. Add sifted dry ingredients and mix briefly. Stir in vanilla and nuts.
5. Spread batter into greased and floured 9 × 13 pan. Bake at 350° for 25-30 minutes or until toothpick inserted near center comes out clean.
6. Cover top of bars with halved marshmallows. Return to hot oven for 3 minutes.
7. Spread melted marshmallows evenly. Cool for at least 30 minutes.
8. To make frosting, combine brown sugar, water, and chocolate in saucepan.
9. Bring to a boil. Boil for 3 minutes, stirring constantly. Remove from heat.
10. Add butter and vanilla. Cool for 10-15 minutes.
11. Blend in confectioners sugar.
12. Spread frosting over cooled marshmallow topping on top of bars.

This is a favorite at our high school choir bake sale.

Cowboy Cookies

Karen Waggoner
Joplin, MO

Makes 4 dozen

Prep. Time: 20 minutes
Baking Time: 10-12 minutes per cookie sheet

1 cup brown sugar
1 cup sugar
1 cup oil
3 eggs
2 cups flour
1 tsp. baking soda
1 tsp. baking powder
2 cups rice cereal
1 cup quick oats
1 cup chopped nuts
1 tsp. vanilla
1 cup coconut

1. In a large mixing bowl, beat brown sugar, sugar, oil and eggs together.
2. Separately, sift flour, baking soda, and baking powder. Stir into sugar mixture.
3. Add cereal, oats, nuts, vanilla and coconut. Mix well with a spoon.
4. Drop by teaspoonsfuls on ungreased cookie sheets.
5. Bake at 350° for 10-12 minutes. Remove cookies to a wire rack to cool completely.

Don't apologize if your house is not spotless; your guests will feel more relaxed when they invite you.
Karen Sauder, Adamstown, PA

White Chip Pumpkin Cookies

Joanna Harrison
Lafayette, CO

Makes 4-5 dozen

Prep. Time: 15 minutes
Baking Time: 11-14 minutes

2 sticks (1 cup) butter
½ cup brown sugar
½ cup sugar
1 egg
2 tsp. vanilla
1 cup pumpkin
2 cups flour
1 tsp. cardamom
2 tsp. cinnamon
1 tsp. baking soda
2 cups white chocolate
   chips
⅔ cup chopped nuts,
   optional

1. Using a mixer, cream together butter, sugars, egg, and vanilla in a large mixing bowl. Beat in pumpkin.
2. Separately, stir together flour, cardamom, cinnamon, and baking soda.
3. Stir flour mixture into butter mixture. Stir in chocolate chips and optional nuts.
4. Drop by spoonfuls onto greased cookie sheet.
5. Bake at 350° for 11-14 minutes. Remove cookies to a wire rack to cool completely.

Tips:
   I've used almonds or pecans for the nuts, but macadamia nuts would also be good.

No Bake Chocolate Cookies

Penny Blosser
Beavercreek, OH

Makes 2-3 dozen

Prep. Time: 20 minutes
Cooking Time: 15 minutes
Cooling Time: 30 minutes

1 stick (½ cup) butter
½ cup milk
2 cups sugar
1 cup chocolate chips
½ cup peanut butter
3 cups quick oats
1 tsp. vanilla

1. Put butter, milk, sugar and chocolate chips in a saucepan.
2. On the stove, bring to boil, and boil 1 minute. Remove from heat.
3. Stir in peanut butter and vanilla until melted and smooth.
4. Add rolled oats. Mix.
5. Drop by heaping tablespoon onto waxed paper lined baking sheet.
6. Let cool until set.

Sour Cream Fudge

Veronica Marshall-Varela
Chandler, AZ

Makes 24 pieces

Prep. Time: 15 minutes
Cooking Time: 5 minutes
Standing Time: 2 hours

12-oz. chocolate chips
2 sticks (1 cup) butter (not
   margarine)
½ cup sour cream
4 cups confectioners sugar
1 tsp. vanilla
2 cups chopped nuts

1. In a microwaveable bowl, melt chocolate chips and butter in microwave, checking and stirring in 20-second increments.
2. Add sour cream, confectioners sugar, and vanilla.
3. Beat together with mixer, then stir in nuts.
4. Pour into buttered 9" pan.
5. Chill until firm, 2 hours or longer.

Tip:
   To make a nice gift, pour in a disposable pie tin. Chill, then wrap in plastic wrap with bow on top.

Chocolate Orange Balls

Donna Barnitz
Rio Rancho, NM

Makes 4½ dozen

Prep. Time: 25 minutes
Cooking Time: 5 minutes
Standing Time: several days

1 cup semi sweet chocolate
  morsels
½ cup sugar
¼ cup light corn syrup
¼ cup water
2½ cups finely crushed
  vanilla wafers *or*
  graham cracker crumbs
1 cup finely chopped nuts
1 tsp. orange extract

1. Melt morsels in a double boiler over hot water or in the microwave. Remove from heat.
2. Stir in sugar, corn syrup, and water.
3. Combine crushed wafers or graham crackers and nuts.
4. Stir chocolate mixture and nut mixtures together. Mix well.
5. Form into 1" balls. Roll in confectioners sugar.
6. Let ripen in covered containers for at least several days.

Peanut Butter Balls

Janice Muller
Derwood, MD

Makes 30-36 balls

Prep. Time: 20 minutes
Cooking Time: 5 minutes
Standing Time: 45 minutes

4-6 cups confectioners
  sugar
1 cup creamy peanut
  butter
2 sticks (1 cup) margarine,
  or butter, softened
2 tsp. vanilla
2-oz. parwax, *optional*
12-oz. semisweet chocolate
  pieces, *optional*

1. Mix together sugar, peanut butter, margarine, and vanilla. Add more sugar as needed to get a dough like consistency that is not crumbly.
2. Form into small balls.
3. Melt parwax and chocolate in a double boiler. To make your own double boiler, set a heat proof bowl over a saucepan of boiling water. The bowl should act as a lid without touching the water.
4. Using a toothpick, poke a ball and dip it into chocolate to cover. Dip balls into chocolate one at a time.
5. Set on waxed paper covered trays to harden.

Tips:
Instead of balls, pat peanut butter mixture into 9 × 13 pan. Chill before cutting into bars.

The truth is … I have never made these into balls because everyone has always loved them as fudge. When I first started working, I would be one of the last people in the building to get lunch. The cafeteria women would always save me a treat when they made up the fudge. Before leaving that job, I asked if they had a scaled-down version for home use, and so this is what I've been making for over 30 years.

This recipe is so easy to make that sometimes I feel guilty taking it to parties!

Beside each dish of food on the buffet, place a stack of cards with its recipe written on them. Then guests can take the recipe if they wish.

Anita Troyer, Fairview, MI

Peanut Brittle

Lois Niebauer
Pedricktown, NJ

Makes 3 cups

Prep. Time: 5 minutes
Cooking Time: 9 minutes
Cooling Time: 1 hour

1½ cups raw Spanish
　peanuts
1 cup sugar
½ cup light corn syrup
1 tsp. vanilla
1 tsp. butter
1 tsp. baking soda
⅛ tsp. salt

1. In an 8 cup glass bowl or measuring cup (works well because of handle), mix peanuts, sugar, corn syrup, and salt.
2. Microwave on High for 3 minutes. Stir.
3. Microwave for 3 more minutes. Add butter and vanilla and stir.
4. Microwave 3 more minutes.
5. Working quickly, add baking soda and stir rapidly.
6. Quickly pour into a buttered 9 × 13 pan.
7. Let cool and when completely cool, break into pieces and store in an airtight container.

Peanut Butter Fudge

Jamie Schwankl
Ephrata, PA

Makes 16 servings

Prep. Time: 10 minutes
Cooking Time: 5-8 minutes

1 cup peanut butter
2 sticks (1 cup) butter *or*
　margarine
1 tsp. vanilla
pinch of salt
3 cups confectioners sugar

1. Melt butter in a medium saucepan over low heat.
2. Add vanilla, salt and peanut butter. Mix with a spoon until smooth. Remove from heat.
3. Add confectioners sugar. Stir until well blended.
4. Spread mixture in an 8 × 8 pan to cool.
5. Refrigerate 1 hour. Cut into small squares.

Tips:
1. A 7 × 9 pan also works well.
2. Do not use a mixer.

This was a treat may husband's grandmother enjoyed making.

Christmas Candy Pudding

Joan Brown
Warriors Mark, PA

Makes 7 lbs.

Prep. Time: 15 minutes
Cooking Time: 20 minutes
Chilling Time: 2 weeks

3 cups sugar
1 cup light cream
1 tsp. butter
1 lb. raisins
1 lb. dates, chopped small
1 lb. figs, chopped small
1 lb. coconut
1-2 cups ground nuts
1 tsp. vanilla

1. In a saucepan, cook butter, sugar, and cream to 234° (soft ball stage), stirring frequently.
2. Remove from heat. Beat until creamy with electric mixer.
3. Beat in nuts and fruit with a spoon. Mix well.
4. When well mixed, roll into 2 logs.
5. Wrap logs in dampened cloth and then in waxed paper. Refrigerate to ripen for at least 2 weeks. Cut in slices to serve.

My grandmother always made this candy for the family carry-in meal at Christmas in the 1950s. After she passed, I could not find her recipe. I was thrilled when I found the recipe in a 1924 cookbook.

Easy Style Pralines

Janice Muller
Derwood, MD

Makes 10-12 servings

Prep. Time: 15 minutes
Cooking/Baking Time: 20
minutes
Cooling Time: 1 hour

15 graham crackers
(almost 2 packs)
¾-1 cup pecans, chopped
1¾ cups light brown sugar,
packed
2 sticks (1 cup) butter *or*
margarine
½ cup semisweet chocolate
pieces
½ cup white chocolate
pieces
2 tsp. oil, divided

1. Line a 15 × 10 jellyroll
pan with aluminum foil and
lightly grease the foil. Make
sure the foil extends over the
pan's edges so that you can
use the foil to lift the pralines
from the pan.
2. Place graham crackers
in pan so that they cover the
surface.
3. Sprinkle with chopped
pecans.
4. Bring brown sugar and
butter to a boil in a saucepan.
Boil 2 minutes.
5. Pour brown sugar
mixture evenly over graham
crackers in pan.
6. Bake at 350° for 10
minutes. Cool at least 30
minutes.
7. Microwave semisweet
chocolate and 1 tsp. oil in a

microwave-safe bowl at 30
seconds. Stir and microwave
on High 30 seconds or until
smooth.
8. Drizzle melted chocolate
evenly over cooled graham
cracker layer.
9. Repeat melting and
drizzling procedure with
white chocolate morsels.
10. Allow to completely
cool; lift bars out of pan using
the foil. Break into pieces to
serve.

Variations:
Reduce brown sugar to
1 cup; increase chocolate to
2 cups.

Amy Bauer
New Ulm, MN

Use club crackers instead
of graham grackers.

Colleen Heatwole
Burton, MI

*This is one of my most
requested recipes to bring to
office parties because it can
be broken into little irregular
pieces. People often enjoy taking
the little pieces instead of large
chunks!*

Cherry Cheese Cake Tarts

Jan Mast
Lancaster, PA

Makes 18 servings

Prep. Time: 15 minutes
Baking Time: 15-20 minutes

18 vanilla wafers
8-oz. cream cheese,
softened
3 eggs
¾ cup sugar
21-oz. can cherry pie filling

1. Fill cupcake tins with 18
paper cupcake liners.
2. Place one vanilla wafer
in each paper liner. Set aside.
3. Beat cream cheese just
until soft and smooth. Do not
overbeat.
4. Add eggs and sugar,
beating until just blended. Do
not overbeat.
5. Pour cream cheese
mixture evenly into 18
cupcake liners, covering
vanilla wafer.
6. Bake at 325° for 15-20
minutes. Cool completely.
7. Top each cooled tart
with cherry pie filling.

Tips:
1. Substitute blueberry pie
filling or eliminate pie filling
and use slices of assorted
fresh fruits like kiwi, orange,
strawberry, etc.
2. Refrigerate after preparing.
3. Do not over-beat the
cream cheese mixture—it
needs to be heavy enough

to keep the wafers at the bottom. If too much air is beaten into it, the wafers will float to the top.

These are especially popular and attractive around Valentine's Day when made with cherry pie filling, and are equally appealing in summer with assorted fresh fruits.

Cheesecake

Dot Hess
Willow Street, PA

Makes 12 servings

Prep. Time: 30 minutes
Baking Time: 1 hour 10 minutes
Chilling Time: 3 hours

Crust:
    1½ cups crushed graham crackers
    ¼ cup sugar
    half stick (4 Tbsp.) butter, softened

Filling:
    3 8-oz. pkgs. cream cheese, softened
    5 eggs
    1 cup sugar
    1½ tsp. vanilla

Topping:
    1½ pints sour cream
    ⅓ cup sugar
    1½ tsp. vanilla

1. Combine graham crackers, sugar, and butter. Press into bottom of 9" spring-form pan.
2. Beat cream cheese well with mixer. Add eggs, one at a time, mixing well after each one.
3. Add sugar and vanilla. Mix well.
4. Pour gently over prepared crust.
5. Bake at 300° for 1 hour. Cool 5 minutes. Do not turn off oven.
6. As the cake cools, mix sour cream, sugar, and vanilla.
7. Spread topping on cake and bake 5 minutes more at 300°.
8. Chill for at least 3 hours before serving.

Good Go-Alongs:
    Good with canned pie filling on top.

Variations:
    Omit crust. Bake at 350° for 35 minutes and proceed with topping.

Renée Hankins
Narvon, PA

Date Pudding
(an old-fashioned
trifle from scratch!)

Clara Byler
Hartville, OH

Makes 10-12 servings

Prep. Time: 30 minutes
Cooking/Baking Time: 45
*   minutes*
Cooling Time: 1 hour

1 cup dried, pitted dates
1 tsp. soda
1 Tbsp. butter
1 cup boiling water
1 cup sugar
1 egg
1½ cups flour
1 cup chopped nuts
1 tsp. vanilla

Sauce:
   2 cups water
   1 cup brown sugar
   1 Tbsp. butter
   2 Tbsp. flour
   1 tsp. vanilla
   pinch of salt

whipping cream *or*
   whipped topping

1. In a heatproof mixing bowl, pour boiling water over the dates, baking soda and butter. Let sit for 30 minutes.
2. Add sugar, flour, egg, and vanilla to the date mixture. Beat well.
3. Stir in nuts.
4. Pour batter into greased 8 × 8 pan.
5. Bake at 350° for 35 minutes or until toothpick comes out clean. Cool at least 1 hour.
6. To make sauce, bring water to boil in covered saucepan.
7. Add rest of sauce ingredients and bring to a boil again, uncovered.
8. Remove from heat. Allow to cool for at least 30 minutes.
9. Break the cooled cake (date pudding) into pieces and put in pretty glass serving dish.
10. Add a layer of sauce and whipping cream.
11. Repeat layers until the dish is filled.

One of the grandchildren said, "Grandma, you need only bring date pudding."

Chocolate Trifle

Ruth E. Martin
Loysville, PA

Makes 6-8 servings

Prep. Time: 15-20 minutes
Cooking Time: 20 minutes
Chilling Time: 1 hour

Chocolate Pudding:
   1 egg yolk, slightly
      beaten
   ⅔ cup sugar
   3 Tbsp. unsweetened
      cocoa powder
   3 Tbsp. cornstarch
   1½ cups milk
   2 tsp. instant coffee
      granules

1 Tbsp. butter
½ tsp. vanilla

3 cups chocolate cake
   crumbs
12-oz. whipped topping
½ cup Heath candy bar
   bits

1. Put egg yolk in a medium bowl.
2. In medium saucepan, stir together sugar, cocoa, cornstarch, milk and instant coffee.
3. Cook, stirring constantly until mixture boils. Boil and stir 1 minute. Remove from heat.
4. Gradually stir small amount of hot mixture into egg yolk, whisking well.
5. Return to pan, stir and heat again until boiling. Remove from heat.
6. Stir in butter and vanilla. Lay plastic wrap directly on the surface. Chill at least one hour.
7. To assemble the trifle, in a clear glass bowl, put a third of the cake crumbs, then a third of the pudding, then a third of the whipped topping. Sprinkle with Heath bits. Repeat twice more, ending with Heath bits on top.

Chocolate Éclair Dessert

Rhonda Freed
Croghan, NY

Makes 10 servings

Prep. Time: 25 minutes
Cooking/Baking Time: 50 minutes
Cooling Time: 30 minutes

1 cup water
1 stick (½ cup) butter
1 cup flour
¼ tsp. salt
4 eggs
7-oz. instant vanilla pudding mix
2½ cups milk
8-oz. cream cheese, softened
8-oz. frozen whipped topping, thawed

Topping:
  6-oz. chocolate chips
  half stick (4 Tbsp.) butter
  2 cups confectioners sugar
  7 Tbsp. milk

1. Heat water and butter just until boiling.
2. Remove from heat and add flour and salt. Beat until a ball forms.
3. Add eggs one at a time, beating after each one.
4. Spread in an ungreased 15 × 10 jelly roll pan.
5. Bake at 400° for 35 minutes.
6. Remove from oven and immediately punch down flat. Cool at least 30 minutes.
7. Mix pudding mix and 2½ cups milk for 2 minutes.
8. Add cream cheese and mix until smooth.
9. Spread over cooled crust. Top with whipped topping.
10. Make chocolate topping by melting chocolate chips and butter in microwave for 1-2 minutes.
11. Add confectioners sugar and milk and mix until smooth.
12. Drizzle on top. Refrigerate.

Chocolate Cream Dessert

Mary H. Nolt
East Earl, PA

Makes 12 servings

Prep. Time: 30 minutes
Cooking Time: 15-20 minutes
Cooling Time: 30 minutes
Chilling Time: 3 hours

1½ sticks (¾ cup) cold butter
18¼-oz. chocolate cake mix
1 egg, slightly beaten
8-oz. pkg. cream cheese, softened
1 cup confectioners sugar
12-oz. container whipped topping, thawed, *divided*
3 cups cold milk
2 3.9-oz. pkgs. instant chocolate pudding mix
chocolate curls

1. In a large bowl, cut the butter into the cake mix using a pastry cutter or two knives until the mixture resembles coarse crumbs.
2. Add the egg and mix well.
3. Press into 13 × 9 baking dish.
4. Bake at 350° for 15-18 minutes or until set. Cool at least 30 minutes.
5. In a small bowl, beat cream cheese until fluffy. Add confectioners sugar and beat until smooth.
6. Fold in 1 cup of the whipped topping.
7. Carefully spread over cooled crust. Cover and refrigerate at least 1 hour.
8. In a large bowl, combine the milk and pudding mix by whisking with a wire whisk for 2 minutes.
9. Let stand 5 minutes or until slightly thickened.
10. Spread over cold, firm cream cheese layer.
11. Top with remaining whipped topping.
12. Refrigerate for 2 hours before cutting. Garnish with chocolate curls.

8-oz. container frozen whipped topping = 3 cups

Whoopie Pie Cake

Sheila Plock
Boalsburg, PA

Makes 20-24 servings

Prep. Time: 20 minutes
Cooking/Baking Time: 20-25 minutes
Cooling Time: 1 hour

1 chocolate cake mix
1 egg

Filling:
   1 stick (½ cup) margarine, softened
   ½ cup shortening
   1 cup sugar
   pinch of salt
   1 tsp. vanilla
   ½ cup milk
   4 Tbsp. flour

1. Mix cake mix as directed on package with the addition of one extra egg.

2. Grease one 9 × 13 pan. Pour half the batter in it.

3. Line another 9 × 13 pan with waxed paper on the bottom and up the sides to use as handles after the cake is baked.

4. Pour the other half of the batter in the waxed paper pan.

5. Bake according to package directions, possibly decreasing baking time because the mix is halved per pan. Check for doneness by inserting toothpick near center of cake. If toothpick is clean, cake is done. Cool at least 1 hour.

6. Make the filling by creaming margarine, shortening, and sugar in a medium mixing bowl.

7. Slowly add vanilla and milk.

8. Add flour, 5 Tbsp. at a time. Beat on high 5 minutes until sugar dissolves.

9. Spread filling on bottom cake layer in greased pan.

10. To make the top layer, lift the other cake out of pan with waxed paper. Remove waxed paper. Place on top of filling.

Tip:
   This is an easier alternative than baking and icing the individual cakes.

Cookie Icebox Cake

Virginia Graybill
Hershey, PA

Makes 6-8 servings

Prep. Time: 15 minutes
Chilling Time: 6 hours

80 chocolate chip *or* Oreo cookies (almost 3 18-oz. pkgs.)
2 cups milk
3 12-oz. containers frozen whipped topping, thawed

1. Dip 25 of the cookies quickly in bowl of milk. Do not soak cookies.

2. Lay the dipped cookies in ungreased 9 × 13 glass pan. Spread one container of whipped topping over them.

3. Repeat dipping and layers two more times.

4. Crumble the 5 remaining dry cookies. Sprinkle over the top.

5. Cover and chill for at least 6 hours.

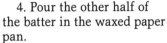

Chocolate Applesauce Cake

Krista Hershberger
Elverson, PA

Makes 20-24 servings

Prep. Time: 20 minutes
Cooking/Baking Time: 40 minutes

1½ cups sugar
½ cup oil
2 eggs
2 cups applesauce
2 cups flour
1½ tsp. baking soda
½ tsp. cinnamon
2 Tbsp. unsweetened cocoa powder

Topping:
3 Tbsp. sugar
1 cup chocolate chips
½ cup chopped nuts, *optional*

1. In a medium mixing bowl, combine 1½ cups sugar, oil, eggs, and applesauce. Mix well.
2. Add flour, baking soda, cinnamon, and cocoa. Stir to mix.
3. Pour batter into greased 9 × 13 pan.
4. Mix 3 Tbsp. sugar, chocolate chips and optional nuts. Sprinkle mixture over batter.
5. Bake at 350° for 40 minutes or until toothpick inserted into cake comes out clean.

Chocolate Cake in a Mug

Peggy Howell
Hinton, WV

Makes 1-2 servings

Prep. Time: 5 minutes
Cooking Time: 3 minutes

4 Tbsp. cake flour
4 Tbsp. sugar
2 Tbsp. cocoa
1 egg
3 Tbsp. milk
3 Tbsp. vegetable oil
dash of vanilla
3 Tbsp. chocolate chips

1. Add flour, sugar, and cocoa to a large coffee mug; mix well.
2. Add egg and mix thoroughly.
3. Pour in milk, oil, vanilla, and chocolate chips. Mix well.
4. Cook on High in microwave for about 3 minutes. Cake will rise over top of mug. Test for firmness by pressing on the top with a spoon. Microwave in 30 second increments until done.
5. Allow to cool a little before eating.

Tip:
After mixing, split cake batter into 2 mugs. Bake. This will give you space on top to add a scoop of ice cream to each mug.

Jen's Chocolate Peanut Butter Frosting

Colleen Heatwole
Burton, MI

Makes 12-16 servings

Prep. Time: 20 minutes

½ cup peanut butter
⅓ cup unsweetened cocoa powder
1½ cups confectioners sugar
1 tsp. vanilla
⅓-½ cup evaporated milk

1. Cream peanut butter and cocoa powder until smooth.
2. Add confectioners sugar, vanilla, and ⅓ cup evaporated milk; beat well. Add remainder of milk if needed to make it spread well.

My daughter adapted this from another frosting recipe. It is her father's favorite frosting.

243

Vanilla Butternut Pound Cake

Mary Puskar
Forest Hill, MI
Frances & Cathy Kruba
Dundalk, MD

Makes 12 servings

Prep. Time: 15 minutes
Baking Time: 1½ hours

½ cup vegetable oil
2 sticks (1 cup) butter, softened
3 cups sugar
¼ tsp. salt
6 eggs, room temperature
3 cups flour
1 cup milk
1 Tbsp. vanilla-butternut extract

1. Cream together oil, butter, sugar and salt. Beat in eggs, one at a time.
2. Add extract to milk.
3. Add some milk to the batter and mix well.
4. Add some flour to the batter and mix well. Continue alternating milk mixture with flour until done, ending with flour.
5. Pour batter into a buttered and floured 10" tube pan.
6. Bake 1½ hours or until toothpick comes out clean.
7. Cool in pan 20 minutes, then turn out onto a wire rack to cool.

Good Go-Alongs:
Strawberries and whipped cream.

Seven Flavor Cake

Lynn Higgins
Marion, OH

Makes 10 servings

Prep. Time: 20 minutes
Cooking/Baking Time: 1½ hours

2 sticks (1 cup) butter
½ cup shortening
2½ cups sugar
5 eggs
3 cups flour
½ tsp. baking powder
1 cup milk
1 tsp. vanilla extract
1 tsp. coconut extract
1 tsp. rum extract
1 tsp. butter extract
1 tsp. lemon extract
1 tsp. almond extract
1 tsp. mixed fruit extract

Glaze:
  ½ cup water
  1 cup sugar
  1 tsp. vanilla extract
  1 tsp. coconut extract
  1 tsp. rum extract
  1 tsp. butter extract
  1 tsp. lemon extract
  1 tsp. almond extract

1. In a large bowl, cream butter, shortening, and sugar until light and fluffy.
2. In another bowl, beat eggs very well until lemon colored, then add baking powder.
3. In a glass measuring cup, add extracts to milk.
4. Add egg mixture to creamed mixture, alternating with milk, and beating well after each addition.

5. Spoon batter into greased and floured 10" tube pan.
6. Bake at 325° for 1½ hours or until cake tests done with inserted toothpick.
7. To make glaze, combine water, sugar, and flavorings in saucepan. Bring to boil and stir until sugar is melted.
8. Pour glaze over warm cake.

Good Go-Alongs:
Tall glass of cold milk.

My grandmother made this cake. It was always made with love.

Almond Sheet Cake

Esther Gingerich
Kalona, IA

Makes 24-30 servings

Prep. Time: 20 minutes
Cooking/Baking Time: 20 minutes

2 sticks (1 cup) butter
1 cup water
2 cups flour
1½ cups sugar
2 eggs, beaten
½ cup sour cream
1 tsp. almond extract
½ tsp. salt
1 tsp. baking soda

Frosting:
  1 stick (½ cup) butter
  ¼ cup milk

4½ cups confectioners
   sugar
½ tsp. almond extract

1 cup slivered almonds

1. In a large saucepan,
bring butter and water to a
boil.
2. Remove from heat and
stir in flour, sugar, eggs, sour
cream, almond extract, salt,
and baking soda; stir until
smooth.
3. Pour into a greased
10 × 15 jelly roll pan.
4. Bake at 375° for 20-25
minutes or until cake is
golden brown. Let cool for 20
minutes.
5. For frosting, combine
butter and milk in a saucepan
and bring to a boil; remove
from heat.
6. Add confectioners sugar
and extract. Beat well.
7. Spread over warm cake,
working fast as frosting sets
quickly. Immediately sprinkle
almonds over frosting.

*A friend brought this after a
death in our family. I've often
made it for others since and
am usually asked for the recipe
when I take it to potlucks.*

Dark Apple Cake

Amy Bauer
New Ulm, MN

Makes 20-24 servings

Prep. Time: 30 minutes
Baking Time: 50 minutes

---

1 stick (½ cup) butter
½ cup shortening
4 eggs
2 cups sugar
1 cup cold coffee
3 cups flour
1½ tsp. baking soda
1½ tsp. cinnamon
½ tsp. nutmeg
½ tsp. cloves
½ tsp. salt
1 tsp. vanilla
1 cup chopped nuts
½ cup raisins
2 cups chopped apples

1. Cream sugar, shortening
and eggs. Blend in coffee.
2. Add rest of ingredients.
Mix well.
3. Pour into greased 9 × 13
pan. Bake at 350° for 50
minutes or until cake tests
done with toothpick inserted
near center.

Blue Ribbon Banana Cake

Joan Dietrich
Kutztown, PA

Makes 20-24 servings

Prep. Time: 20 minutes
Baking Time: 30-35 minutes

¾ cup shortening
1½ cups sugar
½ cup buttermilk
1 cup mashed bananas
2 eggs
¼ tsp. salt
1 tsp. vanilla
2 cups flour
1 tsp. baking soda
1 tsp. baking powder
1 cup coconut

1. Using a mixer, cream
shortening and sugar together
until fluffy.
2. Add mashed bananas,
buttermilk, vanilla and eggs.
Beat until creamy.
3. Sift flour, salt, baking
soda and baking powder
together.
4. Add sifted ingredients to
shortening mixture and beat
for 2 minutes.
5. Add coconut.
6. Pour into greased and
floured 9 × 13 pan. Bake at
350° for 25-30 minutes or
until toothpick inserted near
center comes out clean.
7. When cool, frost with a
butter cream or cream cheese
frosting.

*Prep as much as possible, so that you can enjoy
your guests or family during the meal. Sharing food
around your table is precious time, don't miss it.*

Julie Horst, Lancaster, PA

Banana Split Snack Cake

Marla Folkerts
Holland, OH

Makes 20-24 servings

Prep. Time: 15 minutes
Cooking/Baking Time: 30 minutes

5 Tbsp. (⅓ cup) butter *or* margarine, softened
¾ cup sugar
1 egg
1 medium ripe banana, mashed
½ tsp. vanilla
1¼ cups flour
1 tsp. baking powder
¼ tsp. salt
⅓ cup chopped walnuts
2 cups mini marshmallows
1 cup chocolate chips
⅓ cup quartered maraschino cherries

1. Using a mixer, cream butter and sugar.
2. Beat in egg, banana and vanilla.
3. Stir in flour, baking powder, salt, and walnuts.
4. Spread evenly into greased 9 × 13 baking pan. Bake at 350° for 20 minutes.
5. Sprinkle mini marshmallows, chocolate chips, and maraschino cherries over the hot cake. Bake 10 minutes longer or until lightly browned.

Gingerbread with Lemon Sauce

Fran Sauder
Mount Joy, PA

Makes 10 servings

Prep. Time: 20 minutes
Baking Time: 45 minutes
Cooking Time: 20 minutes

2 cups flour
1 cup sugar
1 tsp. ginger
1 tsp. cinnamon
½ cup shortening
1 egg, beaten
2 Tbsp. molasses
½ tsp. salt
1 tsp. baking soda
1 cup buttermilk
whipped cream, *optional*

1. Sift together flour, sugar, ginger, and cinnamon.
2. Cut shortening into flour mixture to make fine crumbs. Take out ½ cup crumbs and set aside.
3. To remaining, add egg, molasses, salt, baking soda, and buttermilk. Beat well.
4. Pour into 9 × 9 greased and floured cake pan. Sprinkle with reserved crumbs.
5. Bake at 350° for 45 minutes. Serve warm with lemon sauce and whipped cream.

Lemon Sauce:
2 cups water
4 Tbsp. cornstarch
1½ cups sugar
¼ tsp. salt
3 egg yolks
1½ Tbsp. butter
juice of 2 lemons
zest of 1 lemon

1. Bring water to boil in covered saucepan.
2. Combine cornstarch, sugar, and salt. Mix well.
3. Add to boiling water, stirring constantly. Cook about 5 minutes on low heat. Mixture should be thickened.
4. Stir a small amount of hot sugar mixture into beaten egg yolks, whisking continuously.
5. Return the whole mixture to pan and cook 1 more minute, stirring constantly.
6. Remove from heat; add lemon juice, zest, and butter. Stir to combine.

Over-ripe bananas can be peeled and frozen in a plastic bag until it's time to bake a bread or a cake.
Deb Kepiro, Strasburg, PA

Pumpkin Cupcakes

Shelley Burns
Elverson, PA

Makes 24 cupcakes

Prep. Time: 20 minutes
Baking Time: 20-25 minutes

2 cups sugar
2 cups cooked pumpkin
2 cups flour
1½ cups oil
4 eggs
1 tsp. salt
2 tsp. baking powder
2 tsp. baking soda
2 tsp. cinnamon
dash of nutmeg
½ cup coconut, *optional*
cinnamon and sugar

1. Mix together sugar, pumpkin, oil, and eggs.
2. Add flour, salt, baking powder, baking soda, cinnamon, and nutmeg.
3. Fold in coconut.
4. Line 24 muffin cups with cupcake papers.
5. Divide batter among them.
6. Sprinkle cinnamon and sugar on tops of cupcakes.
7. Bake at 350° for 20-25 minutes or until toothpick inserted comes out clean.

Tip:
I use frozen pumpkin. I get it out of the freezer a few hours before I am going to use it. I let it thaw and drain any excess water off before using it in the recipe.

Fruity Streusel Cake

Mamie Christopherson
Rio Rancho, NM

Makes 8-10 servings

Prep. Time: 20 minutes
Baking Time: 50-60 minutes

2 cups flour
1 cup sugar
2 tsp. baking powder
1 tsp. salt
1½ tsp. grated orange rind
1 stick (½ cup) butter *or* margarine
2 eggs
1 cup milk
1 tsp. vanilla
3½ cups fresh fruit (blueberries; pitted sweet cherries, apricot halves, plum or nectarine pieces, peeled sliced apples)

Streusel:
⅓ cup brown sugar
¼ cup flour
1 tsp. cinnamon
2 Tbsp. butter
½ cup chopped nuts

1. In a medium bowl, stir together flour, sugar, baking powder, salt, and orange rind.
2. Cut in butter with pastry cutter or two knives.
3. In a separate bowl, beat eggs; stir in milk and vanilla.
4. Add liquids to flour mixture. Stir briefly.
5. Spoon into greased 7½ × 11½ baking pan.
6. Arrange fruit on top.
7. Mix streusel ingredients. Sprinkle over top.
8. Bake at 350° for 50-60 minutes or until toothpick inserted near center comes out clean.

Tips:
For dessert, top with whipped cream or ice cream. This is also nice for a brunch with an egg casserole.

Nantucket Pie

Barbara Nolan
Pleasant Valley, NY

Makes 8 servings

Prep. Time: 10-15 minutes
Baking Time: 45 minutes

2 cups whole cranberries,
    fresh *or* frozen
1½ cups sugar, divided
½ cup chopped walnuts
1 cup flour
1 tsp. almond extract
1½ sticks (¾ cup) butter,
    melted
2 eggs
coarse sugar

1. Mix together cranberries,
½ cup sugar and walnuts.
2. Put into bottom of very
well greased 9" pie plate.
3. Beat together flour, 1 cup
sugar, almond extract, butter
and eggs. Pour evenly over
cranberry mixture.
4. Bake at 350° for 45
minutes.
5. Immediately sprinkle
top with coarse sugar.

I took one piece of this pie
for myself and left the rest of it
on the kitchen counter. I went
out for a walk only to find my
husband watching a football
game with fork in hand finish-
ing the entire pie. He never even
put it on a plate—just ate it
right out of the pie plate.

Fudge Sundae Pie

Deb Martin
Gap, PA

Makes 6 servings

Prep. Time: 30 minutes
Freezing Time: 2 hours

¼ cup + 3 Tbsp. light corn
    syrup, *divided*
2 Tbsp. brown sugar
3 Tbsp. butter *or*
    margarine
2½ cups rice krispies
    cereal
¼ cup peanut butter
¼ cup ice cream fudge
    sauce
1 quart vanilla ice cream

1. Combine ¼ cup corn
syrup, brown sugar, and
butter in medium saucepan.
2. Cook over low heat,
stirring occasionally until
mixture begins to boil.
Remove from heat.
3. Add rice krispies,
stirring until well
coated.
4. Press evenly into a
9" pie plate to form crust.
5. Stir together peanut
butter, fudge sauce, and
3 Tbsp. corn syrup.
6. Spread half the
peanut butter mixture over
crust. Freeze until firm,
1 hour.
7. Allow ice cream to
soften slightly.
8. Spoon into frozen
pie crust; spread evenly.
Freeze until firm, 1 hour.

9. Let pie stand at room
temperature 10 minutes
before cutting and serving.
10. Warm the other half
of the peanut butter mixture
and drizzle over the top.

Tip:
    Add chopped peanuts to
the top, or whipped topping
and maraschino cherries.
Use butterscotch topping as
drizzle.

Swiss Coconut Custard Pie

Elsie Schlabach
Millersburg, OH

Makes 8 servings

Prep. Time: 8 minutes
Baking Time: 50 minutes

4 eggs, beaten
2 cups milk
½ cup flour
1 tsp. vanilla
¼ cup brown sugar
2 drops maple extract
¾ cup sugar
6 Tbsp. butter *or*
    margarine, softened
1 cup coconut
½ tsp. baking powder

1. Beat eggs in a medium mixing bowl.
2. Add sugars, vanilla, milk, flour and butter. Beat 2 minutes.
3. Stir in coconut.
4. Pour into 10" greased pie pan. Bake at 350° for 50 minutes until center of pie is set.

Tip:
    After it's baked, the crust will be on the bottom, custard in the middle and coconut on top. An easy trick to get a pie!

New England Blueberry Pie

Krista Hershberger
Elverson, PA

Makes 8 servings

Prep. Time: 15 minutes
Cooking Time: 12 minutes
Chilling Time: 1 hour

4 cups fresh blueberries,
    divided
1 cup sugar
3 Tbsp. cornstarch
¼ tsp. salt
¼ cup water
1 Tbsp. butter
pre-baked 9" pie shell
whipped cream

1. Place 2 cups of blueberries in a baked pie shell.
2. In medium saucepan, cook sugar, cornstarch, salt, water, remaining 2 cups blueberries and butter. Stir continuously until thick.
3. Cool blueberry mixture for ½ hour. Pour cooled mixture over berries in pie crust. Chill.
4. Top with whipped cream before serving.

We have our own blueberry bushes, so this is the first recipe we bring out when we pick our first batch!

½ cup heavy whipping cream = 1-1½ cups whipped

Simple Egg Custard Pie

Peggy Howell
Hinton, WV

Makes 8 servings

Prep. Time: 10 minutes
Baking Time: 25-30 minutes
Cooling Time: 1 hour

4 eggs
½ cup sugar
½ tsp. salt
2 cups milk
1 tsp. vanilla
9" unbaked pie shell
nutmeg, *optional*
cinnamon and sugar,
    optional

1. Mix eggs, sugar, salt, milk, and vanilla together.
2. Pour into unbaked pie shell.
3. Sprinkle with nutmeg or cinnamon and sugar if you wish.
4. Place on lower oven rack. Bake at 425° for 25-30 minutes. Center may still be a little jiggly, but it will firm up as it cools.
5. Allow to cool 1 hour before serving.

Variation:
    Spread ½ can prepared pie filling (blueberry or cherry) evenly over bottom of pie crust. Slowly pour custard filling over it so as not to disturb the fruit. Bake as instructed. The fruit under the custard makes for a tasty treat!

Lemon Pie for Beginners

Jean M. Butzer
Batavia, NY

Makes 8 servings

Prep. Time: 10 minutes
Cooking Time: 10-12 minutes
Cooling Time: 15 minutes

9" baked pastry shell
1 cup sugar
4 Tbsp. cornstarch
¼ tsp. salt
1¾ cups water, divided
3 egg yolks, slightly beaten
2 Tbsp. butter
⅓ cup lemon juice
meringue *or* whipped
    cream, *optional*

1. Combine sugar, corn-starch, salt, and ¼ cup water in 1½ quart microwave safe bowl.
2. Microwave remaining ¼ cup water on High until boiling. Stir into sugar mixture.
3. Microwave 4 to 6 minutes until very thick, stirring every 2 minutes.
4. Mix a little hot mixture into egg yolks. Blend yolks into sugar mixture.
5. Microwave 1 minute more.
6. Stir in butter and lemon juice.
7. Cool for 15 minutes and pour into pie shell.
8. If desired, top with meringue and brown in oven for 10-15 minutes at 350° or serve with whipped cream.

Tips:
1. To make a meringue, beat 3 egg whites adding ¼ tsp. cream of tartar and 3 Tbsp. sugar slowly. Continue beating until stiff peaks form. Cover the lemon filling with meringue to edge of crust. Bake in 350° oven for 10-12 minutes or until meringue is golden.
2. Using the microwave is so much easier than cooking the filling on the top of the stove. You don't have to worry about it sticking or burning to the bottom of the pan.

Zucchini Strudel

Judith Houser
Hershey, PA

Makes 20 servings

Prep. Time: 30 minutes
Cooking/Baking Time: 50 minutes

Dough Part:
4 cups flour
1½ cups sugar
½ tsp. salt
2 sticks (1 cup) butter

Filling Part:
4 cups peeled and cubed
    zucchini
½ to ⅔ cup lemon juice
¾ cup sugar
¼ tsp. nutmeg
½ tsp. cinnamon

1. Cut together flour, sugar, salt, and butter until crumbly.
2. Press half of the mixture into a 9×13 baking pan to make a crust.
3. Bake at 375° for 10 minutes.
4. Combine zucchini and lemon juice in saucepan. Bring to a boil, covered.

Invest in a microplane grater. They are wonderful for zesting citrus. Freeze amounts of lemon or orange zest to use in any given recipe. Orange zest is great in blueberry muffins or sweet potato casserole. Anything that calls for lemon juice will be even better if you also add some lemon zest.

Becky Frey, Lebanon, PA

5. Add sugar and nutmeg. Simmer 5 minutes.

6. Add ½ cup reserved crumbs and stir over low heat until thickened.

7. Spread zucchini mixture over baked dough.

8. Cover with remaining crumbs. Sprinkle with cinnamon.

9. Bake at 375° for 30 minutes.

Tips:

Use smaller amount of lemon juice if you want a less tart dessert. A great way to use extra zucchini—people will think it's an apple strudel.

Good Go-Alongs:

This is delicious served warm with vanilla ice cream.

Mock Pecan Pie

Ruth E. Martin
Loysville, PA

Makes 8 servings

Prep. Time: 10 minutes
Cooking/Baking Time: 50 minutes

half stick (4 Tbsp.) butter, softened
½ cup sugar
1 cup light corn syrup
¼ tsp. salt
3 eggs
¾ cup coconut
¾ cup quick oats
9" unbaked pie shell

1. Cream butter in a medium mixing bowl.

2. Add sugar gradually and cream until fluffy.

3. Add syrup and salt; beat well.

4. Add eggs, one at a time, beating thoroughly after each addition.

5. Stir in coconut and oatmeal.

6. Pour into unbaked pie shell.

7. Bake at 350° for 50 minutes until center is not jiggly. Allow to cool before slicing.

FINGER FOOD

Taffy Apple Pizza

Lauren Eberhard
Seneca, IL

Makes 12 servings

Prep. Time: 15 minutes
Baking Time: 10-20 minutes
Cooling Time: 30 minutes

16½-oz. tube peanut butter cookie dough
8-oz. cream cheese, softened
¼ cup sour cream
¼ cup brown sugar
2 crisp apples, Gala or Brauburn
¼ cup chopped peanuts
¼-½ cup caramel sauce *or* ice cream topping
¼-½ cup chocolate sauce *or* ice cream topping

1. Roll out cookie dough to a 12 × 14 circle. Place on a pizza stone or baking sheet.

2. Follow package directions for baking. Cool at least 30 minutes.

3. Mix cream cheese, sour cream and brown sugar together in a small mixing bowl.

4. Spread on cooled cookie.

5. Slice unpeeled apples thinly. Layer in a decorative pattern on top of cream cheese mixture.

6. Sprinkle peanuts over apple slices.

7. Drizzle with caramel sauce and chocolate sauce.

8. Refrigerate until ready to serve.

Desserts

Creamy Peanut Butter Dessert

Kristine Martin
Newmanstown, PA

Makes 14-16 servings

Prep. Time: 15 minutes
Chilling Time: 30 minutes + 3 hours

Crust:
1¾ cups graham cracker crumbs
half stick (4 Tbsp.) butter, melted
2 Tbsp. peanut butter

Filling:
8-oz. cream cheese, softened
½ cup peanut butter
½ cup sugar
2 tsp. vanilla
16-oz. frozen whipped topping, thawed
3-4 Tbsp. chocolate syrup

1. Combine cracker crumbs, butter, and peanut butter. Mix well. Set aside ½ cup for topping.
2. Press remaining crumb mixture into greased 9×13 baking dish.
3. Cover and refrigerate 30 minutes.
4. Meanwhile, make the filling. In a mixing bowl, beat cream cheese and peanut butter until smooth.
5. Beat in sugar and vanilla. Fold in whipped topping.
6. Spoon filling over chilled crust.
7. Drizzle with chocolate syrup. Sprinkle with reserved ½ cup crumbs.
8. Cover. Freeze for at least 3 hours before serving.
9. Remove from freezer 15 minutes before serving.

Tips:
1. I take this often to hot and cold dish dinners. Everyone always thinks it has ice cream in it, but it doesn't, so it's a lot easier to keep from melting. I always get requests for the recipe.
2. This dessert can be frozen up to three months, so it's convenient to make ahead for many occasions.

Lemon Pudding Dessert

Rhonda Freed
Croghan, NY

Makes 12 servings

Prep. Time: 40 minutes
Baking Time: 15 minutes
Chilling Time: 25 hours

1 stick (½ cup) butter, softened
1 cup flour
½ cup chopped nuts
8-oz. cream cheese, softened
8-oz. container frozen whipped topping, thawed, *divided*
1 cup confectioners sugar
2 3-oz. pkgs. lemon instant pudding
3 cups milk

1. Cut together butter, flour, and nuts with a pastry cutter.
2. Press into a 11×7 baking dish to form a bottom crust.
3. Bake at 375° for 15 minutes. Cool for at least 30 minutes.
4. Cream together cream cheese, half of the container of whipped topping (1½ cups), and sugar.
5. Spread over cooled crust.
6. Beat pudding mix and milk until thick.
7. Spread over cream cheese mixture.
8. Top with rest of whipped topping.

Tip:
Substitute chocolate or pistachio pudding.

Not Yo' Mama's Banana Pudding

Barbara Shie
Colorado Springs, CO

Makes 20 servings
Prep. Time: 20-30 minutes

2 7¼-oz pkgs. Pepperidge Farm Chessmen Cookies
6-8 bananas, peeled and sliced
2 Tbsp. lemon juice
2 cups milk
5-oz. box instant French vanilla pudding
8-oz. pkg. cream cheese, softened
14-oz. can sweetened condensed milk
12-oz. frozen whipped topping, thawed

1. Line the bottom of 9 × 13 pan with 1 bag of cookies.
2. Gently mix the bananas with lemon juice to prevent browning.
3. Layer bananas on top of cookies.
4. In a small bowl, combine milk and pudding mix and blend well until thick. Set aside.
5. Using a large bowl, combine cream cheese and condensed milk together and mix until smooth.
6. Fold the whipped topping into the cream cheese mixture.
7. Add the pudding to the cream cheese mixture and stir until well blended.
8. Pour the mixture over the cookies and bananas.
9. Cover with the remaining cookies.
10. Refrigerate until ready to serve.

Strawberry Pretzel Dessert

Deb Kepiro
Strasburg, PA
Dottie Schmidt
Kansas City, MO

Makes 20 servings
Prep. Time: 35 minutes
Baking Time: 10 minutes
Chilling Time: 3 hours or overnight

2 cups crushed pretzels
1 stick (½ cup) butter, melted
1 Tbsp. sugar
8-oz. pkg. cream cheese, softened
8-oz. frozen whipped topping, thawed
1 cup confectioners sugar
2 3-oz. pkgs. strawberry gelatin
2 cups boiling water
2 10-oz. pkgs. frozen strawberries

1. Stir together crushed pretzels, melted butter, and 1 Tbsp. sugar.
2. Press mixture into bottom of 9 × 13 baking dish.
3. Bake at 350° for 10-15 minutes. Set aside to cool at least 30 minutes.
4. In a mixing bowl, cream together cream cheese and confectioners sugar.
5. Fold in whipped topping.
6. Spread mixture onto cooled crust.
7. Dissolve gelatin in boiling water.
8. Stir in frozen strawberries and allow to set 15 minutes.
9. When mixture begins to gel, spread it over cream cheese layer.
10. Refrigerate at least 3 hours or overnight until set.

Variations:
Reduce sugar to ½ cup. Use just one box of gelatin.
Janie Steele
Moore, OK

Use raspberry gelatin and raspberries.
Berenice M. Wagner
Dodge City, KS

Use cherry or blueberry pie filling instead of the gelatin and frozen berries.
Joy Uhler
Richardson, TX

8-oz. container frozen whipped topping = 3 cups

Raspberry Crème Puff Dessert

Meredith Miller
Dover, DE

Makes 8-10 servings
Prep. Time: 10 minutes
Chilling Time: 2 hours

32-oz. plain Greek-style
 yogurt
14-oz. can sweetened
 condensed milk
6-8-oz. fresh red raspberries
48 mini frozen crème puffs

1. In a large serving bowl,
stir yogurt and milk together
until blended.
2. Fold in raspberries.
3. Cover and refrigerate at
least 1 hour or longer.
4. Approximately 1 hour
before serving, stir in frozen
crème puffs.

Tips:
1. We had this at our
family Christmas gathering.
My uncle mixed it up before
we ate. By dessert-time it
was perfect, still cold but
not frozen. Nor was it soggy.
Everyone loved it, even the
less adventuresome eaters!
There wasn't enough of it!
2. We buy the mini-crème
puffs at Sam's Club in the
frozen food section.

Rhubarb Dessert

Ruth Schiefer
Vassar, MI

Makes 20 servings
Prep. Time: 20 minutes
Cooking Time: 15 minutes
Cooling Time: 30 minutes

2 cups + 2 Tbsp. sugar,
 divided
8 cups diced rhubarb
1 cup water
3 Tbsp. cornstarch
3-oz. pkg. raspberry gelatin
2 cups graham cracker
 crumbs
1 stick (½ cup) butter,
 melted
8-oz. frozen whipped
 topping, thawed
1½ cups mini
 marshmallows, melted
3-oz. pkg. instant vanilla
 pudding
1½ cups milk

1. Combine 2 cups sugar,
rhubarb, water, and corn-
starch in saucepan.
2. Bring to a boil, stirring
frequently. Cook until
thickened and clear.
3. Remove saucepan from
heat. Stir in powdered gelatin.
4. Cool at least 30 minutes.
5. Mix graham cracker
crumbs, butter, and 2 Tbsp.
sugar. Set aside ⅓ cup for
topping.
6. Press remaining crumbs
in bottom of greased 9 × 13
pan to form crust.
7. Spread cooled rhubarb
over crust.
8. In microwave safe
bowl, melt marshmallows in
microwave. Check and stir
until smooth.
9. Mix together melted
marshmallows and whipped
topping, stirring vigorously to
combine.
10. Spread mixture over
rhubarb layer.
11. Mix vanilla pudding
with milk for 2 minutes until
thickened.

254

12. Gently spread pudding over marshmallow layer.
13. Sprinkle reserved crumbs on top. Refrigerate.

Fresh Peach Delight

Jan Mast
Lancaster, PA

Makes 20 servings

Prep. Time: 20 minutes
Cooking/Baking Time: 35 minutes
Cooling Time: 1½ hours

1 stick (½ cup) butter, softened
¼ cup brown sugar
1 cup chopped pecans
1 cup + 2 Tbsp. flour
8-oz. cream cheese, softened
1 cup confectioners sugar
1 tsp. vanilla
2 cups frozen whipped topping, thawed
2 Tbsp. cornstarch
⅓ cup sugar
1½ cups water
3-oz. box peach gelatin
4 cups sliced fresh peaches

1. To make a crust, combine butter, brown sugar, pecans, and flour. Press into a 9×13 baking pan.
2. Bake at 350° for 25 minutes. Cool at least 30 minutes.
3. Beat cream cheese until soft and smooth. Beat in vanilla and sugar.

4. Fold in whipped topping.
5. Spread filling on cooled crust.
6. To make topping, combine cornstarch and sugar in a saucepan. Add water.
7. Cook until boiling. Boil and stir for 2 minutes.
8. Add gelatin and stir well. Allow to cool at least 30 minutes.
9. Combine gelatin mixture with sliced peaches and stir gently.
10. Refrigerate until cool but not gelled—between 15-30 minutes.
11. Pour cooled topping over filling.
12. Chill and cut into squares to serve.

Everyone loves this yummy dessert. It works well with fresh strawberries, fresh blueberries, etc. Just change the gelatin flavor and fruit for your own variation!

Pineapple Dessert

Joyce Nolt
Richland, PA

Makes 20 servings

Prep. Time: 20 minutes
Chilling Time: 24 hours

10-oz. shortbread cookies
12-oz. whipped topping
20-oz. crushed pineapple with juice
6-oz. vanilla instant pudding
16-oz. sour cream

1. Lightly grease the bottom of a 9×13 pan. Lay cookies in single layer on bottom.
2. Mix whipped topping, crushed pineapples with juice, powdered pudding mix and sour cream.
3. Spread mixture over cookies.
4. Cover. Refrigerate 24 hours.

Wash fruit and vegetables very well before using them.
Arianne Hochstetler, Goshen, IN

255

Orange Tapioca Fruit

Carol Eberly
Harrisonburg, VA

Makes 8-10 servings

Prep. Time: 15 minutes
Cooking Time: 10 minutes
Chilling Time: 2-4 hours

½ cup minute tapioca
1 quart water
½ cup sugar
6-oz. frozen orange juice
  concentrate
2 14-oz. cans mandarin
  oranges, drained
2 15-oz. cans sliced
  peaches, drained
1-2 bananas, sliced

1. In a saucepan, heat water, sugar, and tapioca, stirring often.
2. Cook until clear.
3. Remove from heat and stir in juice concentrate until dissolved.
4. Mix in fruit. Pour into serving dish.
5. Chill for 2-4 hours.
6. Stir in bananas just before serving.

Variations:
1. Use 20-oz. can crushed pineapple instead of fruit above. Use its juice, plus 6-oz. can pineapple juice to make 1 quart liquid.
2. Use same method above, adding 12 oz. frozen orange juice concentrate.

3. Also delicious topped with whipped cream.
Ruth Hershey
Paradise, PA

Fruit Slush

Julette Rush
Harrisonburg, VA

Makes 14-16 servings

Prep. Time: 20 minutes
Freezing Time: 5-12 hours

½ cup sugar
2 cups boiling water
6-oz. can frozen orange
  juice
12-oz. can apricot nectar
6 bananas, firmly ripe,
  mashed
1 Tbsp. lemon juice
20-oz. can crushed
  pineapple, undrained
16-oz. frozen strawberries

1. In large bowl, dissolve sugar in 2 cups boiling water.
2. Add frozen orange juice and 2 cans of water. Add apricot nectar.
3. Mash the bananas with the lemon juice to prevent browning. Add them to the bowl.
4. Add pineapple and strawberries. Stir all gently together.
5. Put bowl in freezer. Stir once an hour for 5 hours until slushy.

Tips:
For a potluck event, make this a day or more in advance. Get it out of the freezer 2-3 hours ahead of time to get to the right slushy consistency. Time to thaw may vary greatly depending on your home's temperature. The slush keeps indefinitely in the freezer.

Mom's Baked Rice Pudding

Stacie Skelly
Millersville, PA

Makes 4-6 servings

Prep. Time: 5 minutes
Baking Time: 1½ hours
Cooling Time: 30 minutes

1 quart (4 cups) whole
  milk
½ cup white rice (not
  instant)
½ cup sugar
pinch of salt
1 Tbsp. vanilla
cinnamon *or* nutmeg

1. Mix together milk, rice, sugar, salt, and vanilla.
2. Pour into buttered 1½ quart casserole.
3. Bake at 325° for 1½ hours. Stir every 20 minutes.
4. Sprinkle with cinnamon or nutmeg.
5. Cool at least 30 minutes and serve warm, or chill for several hours and serve cold.

Cracker Pudding

Anna Musser
Manheim, PA

Makes 4-6 servings

Prep. Time: 15 minutes
Cooking Time: 15 minutes
Chilling Time: 2 hours

1 quart (4 cups) milk
1 cup coarse saltine
  cracker crumbs
2 eggs
¾ cup sugar
¾ cup coconut
pinch salt
1 Tbsp. vanilla

1. Combine milk and cracker crumbs in saucepan.
2. Heat to steaming.
3. In a mixing bowl, beat eggs, sugar, coconut, and salt.
4. Add egg mixture to hot milk, stirring continuously.
5. Bring to boil, stirring.
6. Add vanilla. Boil 1 minute longer.
7. Pour into a heatproof serving dish. Cover.
8. Refrigerate until chilled, 2 hours.

Variation:
Top the cold pudding with 1½ cups whipped cream and sprinkle with one crushed 5th Avenue candy bar.

Esther S. Martin
Ephrata, PA

Butterscotch Pudding

Lindsey Spencer
Morrow, OH

Makes 8 servings

Prep. Time: 10 minutes
Cooking Time: 20 minutes
Chilling Time: 2-4 hours

2 cups packed brown sugar
½ cup corn starch
6 cups milk
1 tsp. salt
½ cup butter
2 tsp. vanilla extract
6 egg yolks, beaten

1. In small bowl, mix together brown sugar, cornstarch, and salt. Add enough milk to make thick paste.
2. In a saucepan over medium heat, bring milk to a boil.
3. Whisk in brown sugar paste, return to a boil, and cook and stir for 1 minute.
4. Place egg yolks in a small bowl.
5. Temper the yolks by quickly stirring in about ¼ of hot milk mixture.
6. Pour yolk mixture back into hot milk mixture. Cook, stirring constantly for 1 minute.
7. Remove from heat. Stir in butter and vanilla until butter is melted.
8. Refrigerate until well chilled, 2-4 hours.

Tips:
1. Great with pecans on top or mixed in.
2. Layer with whipped cream, bananas, and crushed graham crackers.

From-Scratch Replacement Recipes

When I first began making cookbooks, I was a purist. No canned cream-of-xxx soups for me, whether I was working on cookbooks or making dinner. I resolutely turned any reference to canned creamed soups into a multi-step process, which wasn't too bad if I took a magazine along to the stove or the microwave. I would do Steps 1-4 (on next page); then I'd whip out the magazine while I stirred. It made the time fly.

But when I became a mom, I began to compromise on a few things. It was a little harder to hold a wiggly child than it was to read a magazine while I stirred up a creamy soup.

Then I heard from other people who were juggling things that didn't always allow them to stand and read while stirring. So I switched and began to permit canned soups in recipes.

If you like to know exactly what you are eating, and if you have the time, I applaud your making cream soups and bases from scratch. Here is a recipe for doing this on the stove-top or in the microwave.

If you're tight time-wise, or aren't sure you want to make the extra effort to create a creamy soup or base, you'll find canned cream soups in the ingredient lists of many recipes in this cookbook. Because my first intent is to make sure you can make a meal at home and serve it to your friends and family, no matter how full or chaotic your life is.

Homemade Cream of Mushroom Soup –on the stove

Makes about 1¼ cups (10 oz.)

3 Tbsp. butter
¼ cup mushrooms, chopped
1 Tbsp. onion, chopped
3 Tbsp. flour
1 cup milk (skim, 1%, 2%, *or* whole)

1. In a small saucepan, melt butter.
2. Sauté mushrooms and onion in butter until tender. Stir frequently.
3. Add flour and stir until smooth. Cook over low heat for a minute or so to cook off the raw flour taste.
4. Continuing over low heat, gradually add milk, stirring the whole time.
5. Stir frequently to keep soup from sticking. When soup begins to bubble, stir continuously until it thickens to a creamy consistency.

Homemade Cream of Mushroom Soup
–in the microwave

Makes about 1¼ cups (10 oz.)

3 Tbsp. butter
¼ cup mushrooms, chopped
1 Tbsp. onion, chopped
3 Tbsp. flour
1 cup milk (skim, 1%, 2%, *or* whole)

1. In a 1- or 2-qt. microwave-safe container, melt 3 Tbsp. butter on high for 30 seconds.
2. Stir chopped mushrooms and onions into melted butter.
3. Microwave on high for 1 minute, or just enough to make the vegetables tender.
4. Stir in flour until well blended.
5. Microwave on high for 1 minute, just enough to overcome the raw flour taste.
6. Gradually stir in milk until as well blended as possible.
7. Microwave on Power 5 for 45 seconds.
8. Stir until well blended.
9. Microwave on Power 5 for another 45 seconds. The mixture should be starting to bubble and thicken.
10. Stir again until well blended.
11. If the mixture isn't fully bubbling and thickened, microwave on high for 20 seconds.
12. Stir. If the mixture still isn't fully bubbling and thickened, microwave on high for 20 more seconds.
13. Repeat Step 12 if needed.

Note:
If your microwave is fairly new and powerful, you will probably have a creamy soup by the end of Step 8 or 10 below. If you're working with an older, less powerful, microwave, you will likely need to go through Step 12, and maybe Step 13.

To make cream of celery soup, substitute ¼ cup finely chopped celery for the ¼ cup chopped mushrooms.

Homemade Cornbread Mix

Makes the equivalent of an 8½-oz. box of Jiffy Cornbread Mix

⅔ cup flour
½ cup cornmeal
3 Tbsp. sugar
1 Tbsp. baking powder
¼ tsp. salt
2 Tbsp. oil

Variation:
To make muffins from this mix, add:

1 egg
⅓ cup milk

1. Stir just until combined.
2. Fill muffin cups half-full.
3. Bake at 400° for 15-20 minutes, or until toothpick inserted in center of muffins comes out clean.

Homemade Frozen Hash Browns

1. Bake potatoes until tender.
2. Cool.
3. Grate coarsely.
4. Freeze.

Equivalent Measurements

dash = little less than ⅛ tsp.

3 teaspoons = 1 Tablespoon

2 Tablespoons = 1 oz.

4 Tablespoons = ¼ cup

5 Tablespoons plus 1 tsp. = ⅓ cup

8 Tablespoons = ½ cup

12 Tablespoons = ¾ cup

16 Tablespoons = 1 cup

1 cup = 8 ozs. liquid

2 cups = 1 pint

4 cups = 1 quart

4 quarts = 1 gallon

1 stick butter = ¼ lb.

1 stick butter = ½ cup

1 stick butter = 8 Tbsp.

Beans, 1 lb. dried = 2-2½ cups (depending upon the size of the beans)

Bell peppers, 1 large = 1 cup chopped

Cheese, hard (for example, cheddar, Swiss, Monterey Jack, mozzarella), 1 lb. grated = 4 cups

Cheese, cottage, 1 lb. = 2 cups

Chocolate chips, 6-oz. pkg. = 1 scant cup

Crackers (butter, saltines, snack), 20 single crackers = 1 cup crumbs

Herbs, 1 Tbsp. fresh = 1 tsp. dried

Lemon, 1 medium-sized = 2-3 Tbsp. juice

Lemon, 1 medium-sized = 2-3 tsp. grated rind

Mustard, 1 Tbsp. prepared = 1 tsp. dry or ground mustard

Oatmeal, 1 lb. dry = about 5 cups dry

Onion, 1 medium-sized = ½ cup chopped

Pasta

Macaronis, penne, and other small or tubular shapes, 1 lb. dry = 4 cups uncooked

Noodles, 1 lb. dry = 6 cups uncooked

Spaghetti, linguine, fettucine, 1 lb. dry = 4 cups uncooked

Potatoes, white, 1 lb. = 3 medium-sized potatoes = 2 cups mashed

Potatoes, sweet, 1 lb. = 3 medium-sized potatoes = 2 cups mashed

Rice, 1 lb. dry = 2 cups uncooked

Sugar, confectioners, 1 lb. = 3½ cups sifted

Whipping cream, 1 cup unwhipped = 2 cups whipped

Whipped topping, 8-oz. container = 3 cups

Yeast, dry, 1 envelope (¼ oz.) = 1 Tbsp.

Substitute Ingredients
for when you're in a pinch

For one cup **buttermilk**—use 1 cup plain yogurt; or pour 1⅓ Tbsp. lemon juice or vinegar into a 1-cup measure. Fill the cup with milk. Stir and let stand for 5 minutes. Stir again before using.

For 1 oz. **unsweetened baking chocolate**—stir together 3 Tbsp. unsweetened cocoa powder and 1 Tbsp. butter, softened.

For 1 Tbsp. **cornstarch**—use 2 Tbsp. all-purpose flour; or 4 tsp. minute tapioca.

For 1 **garlic clove**—use ¼ tsp. garlic salt (reduce salt in recipe by ⅛ tsp.); or ⅛ tsp. garlic powder.

For 1 Tbsp. **fresh herbs**—use 1 tsp. dried herbs.

For ½ lb. **fresh mushrooms**—use 1 6-oz. can mushrooms, drained.

For 1 Tbsp. **prepared mustard**—use 1 tsp. dry or ground mustard.

For 1 **medium-sized fresh onion**—use 2 Tbsp. minced dried onion; or 2 tsp. onion salt (reduce salt in recipe by 1 tsp.); or 1 tsp. onion powder. Note: These substitutions will work for meat balls and meat loaf, but not for sautéing.

For 1 cup **sour milk**—use 1 cup plain yogurt; or pour 1 Tbsp. lemon juice or vinegar into a 1-cup measure. Fill with milk. Stir and then let stand for 5 minutes. Stir again before using.

For 2 Tbsp. **tapioca**—use 3 Tbsp. all-purpose flour.

For 1 cup canned **tomatoes**—use 1⅓ cups diced fresh tomatoes, cooked gently for 10 minutes.

For 1 Tbsp. **tomato paste**—use 1 Tbsp. ketchup.

For 1 Tbsp. **vinegar**—use 1 Tbsp. lemon juice.

For 1 cup **heavy cream**—add ⅓ cup melted butter to ¾ cup milk. *Note: This will work for baking and cooking, but not for whipping.*

For 1 cup **whipping cream**—chill thoroughly ⅔ cup evaporated milk, plus the bowl and beaters, then whip; or use 2 cups bought whipped topping.

For ½ cup **wine**—pour 2 Tbsp. wine vinegar into a ½-cup measure. Fill with broth (chicken, beef, or vegetable). Stir and then let stand for 5 minutes. Stir again before using.

Assumptions about Ingredients

flour = unbleached *or* white, and all-purpose

oatmeal or oats = dry, quick *or* rolled (old-fashioned), unless specified

pepper = black, finely ground

rice = regular, long-grain (not minute or instant unless specified)

salt = table salt

shortening = solid, not liquid

sugar = granulated sugar (not brown and not confectioners)

Three Hints

1 If you'd like to cook more at home—without being in a frenzy—go off by yourself with your cookbook some evening and make a week of menus. Then make a grocery list from that. Shop from your grocery list.

2 Thaw frozen food in a bowl in the fridge (not on the counter-top). If you forget to stick the food in the fridge, put it in a microwave-safe bowl and defrost it in the microwave just before you're ready to use it.

3 Let roasted meat, as well as pasta dishes with cheese, rest for 10-20 minutes before slicing or dishing. That will allow the juices to redistribute themselves throughout the cooked food. You'll have juicier meat, and a better presentation of your pasta dish.

Index

Index

Index

Index

Index

Index

Index

Index

Index

Index